Unraveling the Crime-Place Connection represents the cutting edge of current thinking on crime and place. It brings together some of the finest minds in the business in a well-structured volume compiled by two of the most insightful thinkers I know.

—Jerry Ratcliffe, *Temple University*

Unraveling the Crime-Place Connection is a brilliant and timely book. With contributions by leading authors in the field, this volume will, no doubt, be a defining contribution to criminological thought for years to come, inspiring much research on the theoretical dimension of crime and place.

—Martin A. Andresen, *Simon Fraser University*

Unraveling the Crime-Place Connection

Unraveling the Crime-Place Connection examines in a new light how places enhance our understanding of crime and its control. While there has been much work in this area focused on policy, few have examined the underlying theories that inform this work. Theory has played a secondary role in the "criminology of place," and this volume brings it to the forefront of scholarly concerns.

Each part and its chapters illuminate cutting-edge ideas in the etiology and control of crime at place, beginning with an introductory Part I. Crime is often concentrated in very small geographies, and Part II emphasizes the importance of capturing the dynamic nature of places in order to understand crime clustering. Part III offers integrative theories on the varying contextual arrangements of places and links theories of places to other theories of individuals, neighborhoods, and other social contexts. In Part IV, theorists ask how the actions of place owners facilitate or control crime and what policies governments can institute to regulate place management.

This volume will be of interest to criminologists worldwide and useful for graduate-level or advanced undergraduate courses on environmental criminology or crime prevention.

David Weisburd is Distinguished Professor of Criminology, Law and Society at George Mason University and Walter E. Meyer Professor of Law and Criminal Justice at the Hebrew University of Jerusalem. He is also Executive Director of the Center for Evidence Based Crime Policy. Professor Weisburd is an elected Fellow of the American Society of Criminology and of the Academy of Experimental Criminology. He is a member of the Science Advisory Board of the Office of Justice Programs (USA), the Steering Committee of the Campbell Crime and Justice Group, and the Scientific Commission of the International Society of Criminology. He is also a National Associate of the National Academy of Sciences (USA) and Chair of its Committee on Proactive Policing. Professor Weisburd is author or editor of more than 25 books and more than 175 scientific articles that cover a wide range of criminal justice research topics. Professor Weisburd was the Founding Editor of the *Journal of Experimental Criminology* and is now the General Editor of the *Journal of Quantitative Criminology*. He has received many international prizes for his groundbreaking research on crime hot spots and policing, including the Stockholm Prize in Criminology (2010), the Klachky Family Prize for Advances on the Frontiers of Science (2011), the Robert Boruch Award for Contributions to Research that Informs Public Policy (2014), and the Sutherland Award from the ASC for "outstanding contributions to the field of criminology" (2014). In 2015 he received the Israel Prize, generally regarded as the State of Israel's highest honor. He received the Vollmer Award from the American Society of Criminology for his contributions to the science of crime prevention in 2017.

John E. Eck is a professor at the School of Criminal Justice of the University of Cincinnati. His research has focused on police effectiveness and crime prevention, and the theories that can guide effective police and public actions to reduce crime. Central to Dr. Eck's enquiries are how crime patterns evolve and the role of owners in facilitating prevention at their places. He has been a leader in the use of computer simulation to understand how multiple agent interactions give rise to enduring hot spots of crime. He developed the concepts of place manager and place management to explain why a few locations have far more crime than others. Dr. Eck has conducted systematic reviews of what works to control crime at places. He is the coeditor of two books, *Crime and Place* (with David Weisburd) and *Artificial Crime Analysis Systems: Using Computer Simulation and Geographic Information Systems* (with Lin Liu).

SERIES EDITORS

Advances in Criminological Theory

Francis T. Cullen
University of Cincinnati

William S. Laufer
University of Pennsylvania

Freda Adler
University of Pennsylvania

Unraveling the Crime-Place Connection

New Directions in Theory and Policy
Volume 22

Advances in Criminological Theory

David Weisburd and John E. Eck

editors

Routledge
Taylor & Francis Group

NEW YORK AND LONDON

First published 2018
by Routledge
711 Third Avenue, New York, NY 10017

and by Routledge
2 Park Square, Milton Park, Abingdon, Oxon, OX14 4RN

Routledge is an imprint of the Taylor & Francis Group, an informa business

Library of Congress Cataloging-in-Publication Data
A catalog record for this book has been requested

ISBN: 978-1-138-55239-5 (hbk)
ISBN: 978-1-315-14815-1 (ebk)

Typeset in Times New Roman
by Apex CoVantage, LLC

Contents

Part IV. The Role of Place-Based Theory in Criminal Justice

Theoretical Foundations and Frontiers for Understanding High Crime Places: An Introduction

David Weisburd and John E. Eck

More than two decades ago, we edited the first book on crime and place (Eck and Weisburd 1995). At that time, it appeared to us that places would become an important unit of analysis for studying crime, but we could not have foreseen how important it was to become 20 years later. When we edited *Crime and Place*, the first police hot spots patrol experiment (Sherman and Weisburd 1995) was completed, but its findings were not yet published. More generally at the time, there was an assumption that criminal justice (e.g. see Martinson 1974; Visher and Weisburd 1998; Weisburd, Farrington and Gill, 2017), and particularly the police, could do little to prevent crime (Bayley 1994; Gottfredson and Hirschi 1995).

Today there are more than 20 experimental and quasi-experimental hot spots trials, and overall they provide strong evidence that place-based interventions can be effective without displacing crime to nearby areas (Braga, Papachristos, and Hureau 2012). Further, there are many more studies that show the salience of place-based interventions of all types (Eck 2002; Eck and Guerette 2012). Indeed, the evidence today shows that crime cannot only be prevented at places, but that when such prevention approaches are used crime declines in nearby areas (e.g. see Weisburd et al. 2006; Guerette and Bowers 2009). Clarke and Weisburd (1994) coined the term "diffusion of crime control benefits" to capture this seemingly surprising but important outcome of place-based prevention only a year before our book was published. Today the idea of diffusion of crime control benefits is widely accepted.

When we edited *Crime and Place* (1995), the concept of place management was in its infancy and had only been applied to drug dealing locations (see Eck 1994). Today it is a key explanation for why a few proximal places (Madensen and Eck 2013) have far more crime than others do. In the 1990s few scholars imagined that place managers could play a key role in crime prevention.

Indeed, given the assumption that the police could not prevent crime, it was difficult to imagine that informal control agents such as storeowners or doormen could successfully prevent crime. Today such schemes are widely implemented and widely accepted as key elements of crime prevention.

However, the study of crime and place did not develop in a vacuum. Indeed, it can be traced to a group of ground breaking theoretical ideas that began to take root in the two decades before our book was published. In the next section, we review those theoretical perspectives, recognizing their importance for the development of both the criminology of place (Sherman, Gartin, and Buerger 1989; Weisburd, Groff, and Yang 2012) and place-based prevention. But after identifying the importance of theory to the development of this work, we return to the purpose of this volume—to reinforce the importance of theory for future development of study of crime at place. Indeed, in a broader discipline (criminology) that has been criticized for being focused too much on theory and not enough on empirical facts and crime prevention (Cullen 2011), the study of crime and place has sometimes failed to engage fully with criminological theory. We seek in this volume to bring theory to center stage, emphasizing how it can play a key role in advancing criminology and advancing crime prevention. Our volume emphasizes new theoretical ideas, while tying them to empirical work and with an eye toward utility.

Theory in the Emergence of Crime and Place

Although the traditional focus of criminology has been on individuals and communities (Nettler 1978; Sherman 1995), criminologists recognized from the outset that the situational opportunities provided by specific places, or contexts, can affect the occurrence of crime. Edwin Sutherland, for example, whose main focus was upon the learning processes that bring offenders to participate in criminal behavior, noted in his classic criminology textbook that the immediate situation influences crime in many ways. For example, "a thief may steal from a fruit stand when the owner is not in sight but refrain when the owner is in sight; a bank burglar may attack a bank which is poorly protected but refrain from attacking a bank protected by watchmen and burglar alarms" (Sutherland 1947: 5). Nonetheless, Sutherland, like other criminologists, did not see crime places as a relevant focus of criminological study. This was the case, in part, because crime opportunities provided by places were assumed so numerous as to make concentration on specific places of little utility for theory or policy. In turn, criminologists traditionally assumed that situational factors played a relatively minor role in explaining crime as compared with the "driving force of criminal dispositions" (Clarke and Felson 1993: 4; Trasler 1993). Combining an assumption of a wide array of criminal opportunities and a view of offenders that saw them as highly motivated to commit crime, it is understandable that criminologists paid little attention to crime at places.

In 1979, Cohen and Felson launched an influential critique of criminology's resistance to examining the situational influences of places. They argued that criminology's emphasis on individual motivation failed to recognize the importance of other elements of the crime equation. They noted that more than a motivated criminal is necessary for there to be a crime: there must also be a suitable target and the absence of a capable guardian. And these three components of the crime equation must come together in specific places for a crime to occur. They showed that altering the convergence of targets or of guardianship at places could drive crime rates, irrespective of the nature of criminal motivations. That Cohen and Felson suggested that crime could be affected without reference to the motivations of individual offenders was a truly radical idea in criminological circles in 1979. More than a quarter of a century later, the implications of their challenge are still being felt. The routine activities perspective they presented established the micro-context of crime as an important focus of study. Summarizing their approach, for example, they emphasized the importance of place in the commission of crime:

> Unlike many criminological inquiries, we do not examine why individuals or groups are inclined criminally, but rather we take criminal inclination as given and examine the manner in which the spatio-temporal organization of social activities helps people to translate their criminal inclinations into action. Criminal violations are treated here as routine activities which share many attributes of, and are interdependent with, other routine activities. This interdependence between the structure of illegal activities and the organization of everyday sustenance activities leads us to consider certain concepts from human ecological literature.
>
> (Cohen and Felson 1979: 589)

Drawing upon similar themes, British scholars led by Ronald V. Clarke began to explore the theoretical and practical possibilities of situational crime prevention (Clarke 1980, 1983, 1992, 1995; Cornish and Clarke 1986a; 1986b). This approach looked to develop greater understanding of crime and more effective crime prevention strategies through concern with the physical, organizational, and social environments that make crime possible. The situational approach does not ignore offenders or their motivations; it merely places them as one part of a broader crime prevention equation that is centered on the production of crime in proximal contexts. It demands a shift in the approach to crime prevention, from one that is concerned primarily with why people commit crime to one that looks primarily at why they commit crimes in specific settings. Whereas standard criminology looks for temporal and spatially distal causes of offender motivation, situational prevention looks to the temporally and spatially immediate influences on offender decisions. It moves the context of crime into central focus and shifts the traditional focus of crime—the offender—to just one of a number of factors that affect it.

Situational crime prevention is concerned with the "opportunity structures" of specific places: the context that matters for most crimes. By opportunity structures, advocates of this perspective are not referring to the broad societal structure of opportunities that underlie individual motivations for crime (e.g. see Merton 1938), but to the immediate situational components of the context of crime. In this perspective, crime prevention may involve efforts as simple and straightforward as target hardening (e.g. Poyner 1988; Webb and Laycock 1992) or access control (e.g. Matthews 1990; Poyner and Webb 1987), and often follows a straightforward and common sense notion of how to deal with crime problems that has long been accepted by citizens and practitioners who deal with crime prevention at the everyday level of protecting property or reducing victimization (Tonry and Farrington 1995). Importantly, context at a "micro" level is key to situational crime prevention theory since it focuses on the immediate opportunities for crime, which are generally structured within very small geographic areas: places.

Around the same time as routine activities theory and situational crime prevention developed, Paul and Patricia Brantingham published in their seminal book *Environmental Criminology* a theory of how offenders search for targets (Brantingham and Brantingham 1981). Crime pattern theory explores the distribution and interaction of targets, offenders, and opportunities across time and space (Brantingham and Brantingham 1993). Two of the key elements of crime pattern theory are routes offenders take and nodes, which represent destinations at the ends of routes. Nodes are places, as are the crime sites scattered around the route-node structure. Not only are places logically required (an offender must be in a place when an offense is committed), but also their characteristics are seen to influence the likelihood of a crime being committed and the likelihood that particular places will become crime hot spots. Crime pattern theory links places with desirable targets and the context within which they are found by focusing on how places come to the attention of potential offenders.

The Brantinghams' crime pattern theory identified high crime places as locations where the routines of offenders frequently brought them into contact with unprotected targets. However, these simple connections were insufficient. In the early 1990s, one of us (Eck), then a doctoral student studying under Lawrence Sherman at the University of Maryland, was examining San Diego drug dealing locations. Drawing on police data, observations of dealing places, and interviews with police he saw a need to expand theory about the routines of offenders. The lack of guardianship—which might be useful for explaining predatory crime—could not explain routine use of a few locations to sell crack cocaine: a consensual crime. In his 1994 dissertation, he suggested that crime researchers need to take into account the actions of the people who own and operate places: "place managers" (Eck 1994). Place management is one of those ubiquitous (and therefore easily overlooked) phenomena that fit Cohen and Felson's "organization of everyday sustenance" (1979: 589). How owners and their surrogates operate their properties has a strong influence on how much crime occurs at their places. Locations with strong place management would entail a much lower risk of drug dealing than those where place management was weak or absent, and the economics of real estate and commercial activities played a large role in the strength of place management.

More than a decade later, Madensen, in her dissertation on bars, written under Eck's supervision, created a model of place management (Madensen 2007). While Eck had identified place managers, he had not described what they do. In her work, Madensen answered this question. She described place management as a set of interwoven decisions, and showed that place managers' functions fall into at least one of four areas: organization of space (all actions dealing with the physical environment); regulation of conduct (all actions undertaken to encourage or discourage particular behaviors); control of access (all actions to draw in or to keep out particular types of place users); and acquisition of resources (all actions to secure the revenue necessary to keep the place operating and to undertake the first three functions). These four functions are sufficient to address all extant mechanisms for explaining the variation in crime across places, including guardianship, availability of targets, presence of offenders, shared norms, and informal social controls (Madensen and Eck 2012). As property owners have property rights over their places, they form a key, if not *the* key, locus of control over places. No situational crime prevention can be undertaken on property without the explicit consent, and usually the cooperation, of place managers. Therefore, any test of the efficacy of situational crime prevention is at least an indirect test of place management theory.

These theories have played an important role in encouraging researchers to examine crime at micro geographic units. They may be seen together as "opportunity theories" of crime (Lilly, Cullen, and Ball 2010; Wilcox, Land, and Hunt 2004), and they formed the theoretical basis for focusing on places instead of people (e.g. see Eck 1994; Sherman et al. 1989; Weisburd et al. 2004). The study of crime and place would not have emerged without this group of theoretical perspectives that provided a justification for reorienting criminology and crime prevention.

Reintroducing Traditional Criminological Theory to Crime and Place

Routine activities theory, situational prevention, crime pattern theory, and place management theory all put great emphasis on the specific opportunities available to offenders at places. In contrast, study of crime at higher geographic levels has traditionally placed emphasis on the social characteristics of areas, for example, the socioeconomic levels of people who live in certain neighborhoods (Bursik and Grasmick 1993; Morenoff and Sampson 1997), or the degree to which there is strong population heterogeneity (Shaw and McKay

1942). More recently scholars have emphasized the "collective efficacy" of communities, which focuses on the mechanisms through which informal social controls are developed (Sampson, 2014). Neighborhoods with high collective efficacy are places where people trust each other and are willing to intervene when problems emerge in their community. Such perspectives may be grouped more generally as social disorganization theories (see Bursik 1988; Kubrin and Weitzer 2003; Sampson and Groves 1989).

In introducing the idea of the criminology of place, Sherman, Gartin, and Buerger argued that "traditional collectivity theories [termed here as social disorganization theories] may be appropriate for explaining community-level variation, but they seem inappropriate for small, publicly visible places with highly transient populations" (1989: 30). More recently, place-focused criminologists have argued that such theories do have relevance for study of crime and place. This is illustrated in the work of a team of researchers working with one of us (Weisburd) who carried out the first large scale longitudinal studies of crime at micro geographic units of analysis (see Weisburd et al.2004; Weisburd et al. 2012). They decided upon a unit of analysis for crime and place— the street segment (both block faces between intersections) —that was based on the idea of micro communities that would have elements of shared routines and norms. Theoretically, they note that scholars have long recognized the relevance of street segments in organizing life in the city (Appleyard, Gerson and Lintell 1981; Brower 1980; Jacobs 1961; Taylor, Gottfredson, and Brower 1984; Unger and Wandersman 1983). Taylor (1997, 1998) made the case for why street segments (his terminology was street blocks) function as behavior settings. First, people who frequent a street segment get to know one another and become familiar with each other's routines. Second, residents develop certain roles they play in the life of the street segment (e.g. the busybody, the organizer). Third, norms about acceptable behavior develop and are generally shared. Fourth, blocks have standing patterns of behavior that are temporally specific. Fifth, a street block has boundaries that contain its setting. It is bounded by the cross streets on each end. Interaction is focused inward toward the street. Finally, street segments, like other behavior settings, are dynamic. Residents move out, and new ones move in.

Weisburd et al. (2012) show that variables that indicate social disorganization such as poverty, physical disorder, and collective efficacy are concentrated at micro geographic units of analysis and are strongly correlated with crime and place. Their work reinforces the importance of considering a broad array of theoretical perspectives in investigating the criminology of place, and not simply relying on those perspectives that led to its development.

The Importance of Theory in Advancing Crime and Place

Empirical studies are not enough if we are to advance our understanding of crime at place. Theory is key to the development of any area of study. As noted earlier, the criminology of place has its theoretical roots in opportunity theories. Many of the scholars who have pioneered opportunity theories of crime have been focused on crime prevention rather than criminological theory. Situational crime prevention (Clarke 1980, 1995, 2000; Cornish and Clarke 2003), for example, simply by its name identifies the primary interest of its originators. Routine activity theory (Cohen and Felson 1979) at first appearance seems to be of theoretical importance only, as does one of its subsidiaries, place management theory (Madensen and Eck 2008). However, its development over time has emphasized a concern with preventing crime rather than with developing criminological theory (Felson 1995). In practice, researchers operating within the environmental criminological perspective tend to view theories as mental tools useful for solving practical problems. Theory is often seen as secondary in importance to the development of practical crime prevention policy.

One of the strengths of the criminology of place is that it has sought to not only think and talk about crime, but to do something about it. One reason for the strong evidence of crime prevention effectiveness in this area is the enduring interest in crime prevention that has motivated it. In contrast, many traditional criminological theories have little connection to the reality of crime prevention, and often deal with prevention problems only as an afterthought (Gottfredson and Hirschi 1995; Hirschi, Reiss, and Roth 1993). We think the emphasis on crime prevention is one of the keys to the success of the development of crime and place research. But, we also believe that it is a mistake to undervalue the importance of theory and its role in providing the logic models for the modeling of successful crime prevention programs.

We developed this volume with the idea of creating opportunities for scholars to think more about theory in crime and place. We sought to encourage a group of key researchers in this area to focus on theory and its role in understanding crime at place and developing effective crime prevention policies. We think our effort has yielded important new insights, and has suggested important new directions for research and theorizing in this area.

Our volume begins with two papers on innovative inquiries into the concentration of crime at places. The first, by George Mohler, Martin Short, and Jeffrey Brantingham, looks at crime concentrations at different spatial scales. One of the most important scientific contributions of the study of crime at place has been its identification of strong crime concentrations at a micro geographic level. One of us has called this "the iron law of troublesome places" (Wilcox and Eck 2011) concerning specific addresses or facilities (see Eck, Clarke and Guerette 2007). The other has described a startling degree of consistency in crime concentrations at similar units of analysis using similar measures of crime, which is termed "the law of crime concentration at places" (Weisburd et al. 2012; Weisburd 2015). Mohler and colleagues explore the extent to which the spatial concentration of crime varies at different units of analysis.

They find that crime is more concentrated at micro geographic units. But, at the same time, there is greater stability in crime concentrations at higher geographic levels. They term this the concentration-dynamics tradeoff, pointing to a key problem that has so far been ignored in developing crime prevention work. While crime hot spots may offer greater efficiency in focus, over time they are likely to show more variability than higher level clustering. While this work must be replicated in other settings, it raises an important set of questions about the clustering of crime and crime prevention policies.

Wilpen Gorr and YongJei Lee also expand thinking about crime concentrations raising the issue of the mix of chronic and temporary crime hot spots. Noting Weisburd's law of crime concentration of places, they raise the question of the degree to which theory and practice must take into account not just "chronic crime hot spots" but also "temporary crime hot spots." They argue that temporary crime hot spots are not trivial but include an important part of the crime problem in cities. They describe chronic crime hot spots as those that continue for a year, or in many cases over a large number of years. Temporary crime hot spots are dynamic within a year, with an on and off behavior for weeks or months at a time. Gorr and Lee are particularly concerned with early detection and accurate predictions of such hot spots, arguing that use of criminological theory can aid in prediction. In the end the paper makes the case that a "combination chronic and temporary hot spot program is the most effective and equitable" way to allocate crime prevention resources. Their paper emphasizes that not enough attention has been paid to temporary hot spots in prior work.

The second section of the volume includes papers that seek to push the boundaries of theory in crime and place, and includes three papers that address core theoretical questions in the discipline. The first, by Gerben Bruinsma and Lieven Pauwels, seeks to develop theory for understanding the law of crime concentration and its prediction of consistently high levels of concentration of crime at place. They argue that we must go beyond traditional criminological theories if we are to arrive at a theory that explains crime at place. They call not only for use of opportunity and social disorganization theories but also the introduction of insights from other disciplines such as the philosophy of science, (the psychology of) geography, or sociology. They argue that what is needed "is to have a solid meta-theoretical framework that allows for the integration of micro places in the study of its productive, law-like causes." The chapter aims at contributing to theorizing on crime place by introducing fundamental ideas from philosophers of science and methodologists to the criminology of place that can be very fruitful to the understanding of why crimes cluster. These innovative ideas are centered on the concepts of "causal mechanisms" and "emergence."

The second contribution in this section, by David Weisburd, Maor Shay, Shai Amram, and Roie Zamir, uses unique data provided by the Israeli Census

Bureau at the level of street segments to critically examine recent theorizing regarding social disorganization at places. Weisburd et al. (2012) have argued that crime hot spots are also places of high levels of social disorganization. However, as pointed out by Braga and Clarke (2014), the measures used in that study were often drawn from proxy variables that were not directly measured at the street segment level. Such variables have not been available to researchers in the US and other countries because of privacy restrictions regarding government data provided, for example, by the US Census Bureau. Weisburd and colleagues were able to gain information from the Census Bureau in Israel at the street segment level and to merge those data with data on residential streets in Tel Aviv. They find that social disorganization variables directly measured at the street segment level are strongly correlated with levels of crime over time at street segments. This provides support for the earlier work of Weisburd et al. (2012). However, they do not find clear relationships when examining increasing crime trends. Weisburd et al. argue that the descriptive nature of the analysis may be masking such relationships, suggesting the importance of more carefully modelling trends over time. However, the basic findings of this paper reinforce the salience of social disorganization theory for understanding the micro communities of street segments.

Pamela Wilcox and Marie Skubak Tillyer author the final paper in this section, which seeks to integrate community-based and place-based theory. They argue that traditionally advocates of these different levels of geographic analysis have simply ignored each other, and that this is not productive for theory in either area. The chapter notes that the utility of place-based thinking would be enhanced if it recognized the value of considering the broader neighborhood contexts in which places are situated. Specifically, they propose a theoretical approach that emphasizes the embeddedness of places in larger neighborhoods, or a "place in neighborhood" (PIN) approach.

In the next section, we turn to theories of place-based crime control. The first two papers in this section consider opposite sides of the same coin: place managers. Troy Payne looks at crime through the eyes of the place managers and considers their motivations, much as a criminologist would examine offender motivation. As place managers have not been the subject of study by crime researchers, he builds on research in the rental-housing field. Landlords, Payne argues, are motivated by profit, but there are other important concerns as well. It may seem strange, but Payne claims, "The truth of the matter is that *ignoring crime is probably a rational business decision for most property owners most of the time*" (emphasis in original).

Co-editor John Eck looks at the opportunity structure in which place managers are embedded: the context within which Payne's place managers make their choices. Eck begins with a call for a theoretical understanding of how places become crime hot spots. He asks why streets in the same area that have similar social and economic contexts are often very different. His answer is that place managers take into consideration the larger geographic areas within which their properties are located, echoing a similar theme to one found in the paper by Wilcox and Tillyer. As Eck notes,

> I contend that the spatial clustering of high crime places is due to a combination of economic, social, and political factors that create opportunity structures for place management. In some areas, the opportunity structure provides strong incentives for good place management. In these areas, the number of high crime places will be small. In other areas, the opportunity structure provides fewer incentives for good place management and more incentives for bad place management. It is in these areas that high crime places will cluster.

He particularly notes the interplay of economics, racial prejudice and segregation, and political influence in structuring place managers' decisions as to how to address crime.

The final section of the volume contains four papers that look specifically at the issue of criminal justice and crime at place. The first, by Lacey Schaefer, Francis T. Cullen, and Sarah M. Manchak, examines how the place idea can be expanded beyond policing to other parts of the criminal justice system, in this case probation. They argue that the "overwhelming majority of community supervision agencies fail to reduce offenders' inclinations to commit crime, and even more so, ignore the role of the offender's environment in providing chances to commit crime." Accordingly, the key contribution of this paper is to apply the crime and place perspective to probation-based crime prevention. They identify two routes through which offender supervisors can reduce recidivism, organized around the role of place. First, probation and parole agencies can reduce the crime opportunities of their supervisees, developing case plan stipulations that reorganize offenders' routine activities so that criminogenic settings are avoided and replaced with prosocial influences. Second, probation and parole agents can provide cognitive skills training to their supervisees to get them thinking about places differently, such that remaining crime opportunities are avoided and resisted. This paper presents an innovative and promising approach to probation.

The second paper in this section, by Breanne Cave, examines how the context of micro places influences police decision-making. Drawing upon a unique data base collected in Baltimore, Maryland, Cave is able to examine how contextual factors at the street segment level influence the decisions of police to issue citations in response to citizen calls. A key finding of her paper is that the racial composition of streets has an important impact on whether police write reports. She notes that "a 1% increase in the percentage of African Americans on a street increased the odds of a report being written during a narcotics call by 223%, and the odds of a report being written were 74% greater on streets with any Hispanic or Latino respondents as compared to streets with no Hispanic or Latino respondents. However, African American composition was not a significant predictor of car stop report writing." This implies that segment racial composition may have differing effects for police actions during different types of calls for service. Her findings are intriguing and suggest that we need to understand not just the community context of policing but also the micro geographic context of police decision-making.

The third paper in this section, by Cody Telep, digs deep into the theoretical mechanisms underlying crime and place, in this case focusing on those that encourage the crime prevention salience of place-based policing. Telep argues that there is less known about why place-based policing works than about the actual crime prevention value of these approaches. We know that hot spots policing, for example, leads to crime prevention gains. But, what exactly is the mechanism that leads to these outcomes? To date such theorizing has not been informed by empirical data. Telep sets out to illustrate how we can advance our understanding of such mechanisms. He argues that studies need to invest in the "why" of what works, and not simply in the outcomes. This is the case in exploring whether deterrence is the primary mechanism of success, or whether new mechanisms being explored, such as collective efficacy, are the factors leading to reductions in crime. He calls for using body cameras and qualitative data collection, for example, to dig deeper into the why of what works, and for multi-site studies to observe variation in program impacts that relate to contextual factors.

The final paper in this section and in the volume is by Anthony Braga and Cory Schnell, and seeks to employ theoretical analysis to develop more effective crime prevention at micro geographic places. They illustrate how the complexity of problems at crime places requires more nuanced police responses than traditional police tactics provide. It is simply not enough to crack down on high crime streets; we need to understand the dynamics of those streets and the problems found there, and develop tailor made responses. They emphasize moreover that the community impact of crime prevention at hot spots is an important consideration, and propose that community policing activities can be important complements to problem-oriented and situational crime prevention responses implemented to control crime hot spots. They conclude, "hot spots policing programs that seek to change crime conditions in crime places and engage community members seem well positioned to generate stronger crime prevention gains and improve police-community relationships in these vulnerable places."

Conclusion

The discerning reader will discover that behind the authors' consensus over the importance of micro places, they have a number of healthy and productive disagreements. There is disagreement over what is the most relevant micro place: the address, the street segment, or other micro-spatial units. There is disagreement over which institutions can best control crime at places: the public, property owners, police, or even correctional officials. There is disagreement over whether one should focus on chronically crime-ridden places, or those that have acute crime spurts. There is disagreement over which social mechanism will have greatest impact at high crime locations: informal social order, or property owners and their minions. These disagreements could not have been envisioned in 1995. Today, they highlight the vibrancy of the criminology of place, and why theory is critical for driving valid empirical description and useful policy.

This volume seeks to showcase the importance of theory in advancing not only our understanding of crime at place, but also in enhancing our abilities to prevent crime at place. Theory has sometimes been on the sidelines, as crime and place researchers have focused on practical crime prevention. It is time in our view to bring theoretical questions to center stage in the study of crime and place. This will help advance not only our basic understanding of crime at place, but also practical crime prevention. Theory cannot be left behind. That is the message we hope that this volume will give in encouraging crime and place researchers to make the scene of theorizing in this area.

References

Appleyard, Donald, M. Sue Gerson, and Mark Lintell. 1981. *Livable Streets, Protected Neighborhoods*. Berkeley, CA: University of California Press.

Bayley, David H. 1994. *Police for the Future*. Oxford: Oxford University Press.

Braga, Anthony A., and Ronald V. Clarke. 2014. "Explaining High-Risk Concentrations of Crime in the City: Social Disorganization, Crime Opportunities, and Important Next Steps." *Journal of Research in Crime and Delinquency* 51: 480–498.

Braga, Anthony, Andrew Papachristos, and David Hureau. 2012. "Hot Spots Policing Effects on Crime." *Campbell Systematic Reviews* 8: 1–96.

Brantingham, Patricia L., and Paul J. Brantingham. 1981. "Notes on the Geometry of Crime." Pp. 27–54 in Paul J. Brantingham, and Patricia L. Brantingham (eds.), *Environmental Criminology*. Prospect Heights, CA: Waveland.

Brantingham, Patricia L., and Paul J. Brantingham. 1990. "Situational Crime Prevention in Practice." *Canadian Journal of Criminology* 32: 17.

Brantingham, Patricia L., and Paul J. Brantingham. 1993. "Environment, Routine, and Situation: Toward a Pattern Theory of Crime." Pp. 259–294 in Marcus Felson and Ronald V. Clarke (eds.), *Routine Activity and Rational Choice*. Piscataway NJ: Transaction Publishers.

Brower, Sidney N. 1980. "Territory in Urban Settings." Pp. 179–207 in Irwin Altman, Joachim F. Wohlwill (eds.), *Environment and Culture*. New York, NY: Springer Verlaag.

Bursik, Robert J. 1988. "Social Disorganization and Theories of Crime and Delinquency: Problems and Prospects." *Criminology* 26: 519–552.

Bursik, Robert J., Jr., and Harold G. Grasmick. 1993. "Economic Deprivation and Neighborhood Crime Rates, 1960–1980." *Law & Society Review* 27: 263.

Clarke, Ronald V. 1980. "'Situational' Crime Prevention: Theory and Practice." *The British Journal of Criminology* 20: 136–147.

Clarke, Ronald V. 1983. "Situational Crime Prevention: Its Theoretical Basis and Practical Scope." *Crime and Justice* 4: 225–256.

Clarke, Ronald V. 1992. "Introduction." Pp. 1–43 in Ronald V. Clarke (ed.), *Situational Crime Prevention: Successful Case Studies*. Albany, NY: Harrow and Heston.

Clarke, Ronald V. 1995. "Situational Crime Prevention." *Crime and Justice* 19: 91–150.

Clarke, Ronald V. 2000. "Situational Prevention, Criminology, and Social Values." Pp. 97–112 in Ronald V. Clarke (ed.), *Ethical and Social Perspectives on Situational Crime Prevention*. Oxford: Hart.

Clarke, Ronald, Victor Gemuseus, and Marcus Felson. 1993. *Routine Activity and Rational Choice*. New Brunswick, NJ: Transaction Publishers.

Clarke, Ronald V., and David Weisburd. 1994. "Diffusion of Crime Control Benefits: Observations on the Reverse of Displacement." Pp. 165–183 in Ronald V. Clarke (ed.), *Crime Prevention Studies*. New York, NY: Criminal Justice Press.

Cohen, Lawrence E., and Marcus Felson. 1979. "Social Change and Crime Rate Trends: A Routine Activity Approach." *American Sociological Review* 43: 588–608.

Cornish, Derek, and Ronald V. Clarke. 1986a. "Situational Prevention, Displacement of Crime and Rational Choice Theory." Pp. 1–16 in Kevin Heal and Gloria Laycock (eds.), *Situational Crime Prevention: From Theory Into Practice*. London: Her Majesty's Stationery Office.

Cornish, Derek B., and Ronald V. Clarke, 1986b. *The Reasoning Criminal*. New York, NY: Springer.

Cornish, Derek, and Ronald V. Clarke. 2003. "Opportunities, Precipitators and Criminal Decisions: A Reply to Wortley's Critique of Situational Crime Prevention." *Crime Prevention Studies* 16: 41–96.

Cullen, Francis T. 2011. "Beyond Adolescence-Limited Criminology: Choosing Our Future: The American Society of Criminology 2010 Sutherland Address." *Criminology* 49: 287–330.

Eck, John E. 1994. *Drug Markets and Drug Places: A Case-Control Study of the Spatial Structure of Illicit Drug Dealing*. Ph.D. Dissertation. College Park, MD: University of Maryland.

Eck, John E. 2002. "Preventing Crime at Places." Pp. 241–294 in Lawrence W. Sherman, David Farrington, Brandon Welsh, and Doris L. MacKenzie (eds.), *Evidence-Based Crime Prevention*. New York, NY: Routledge.

Eck, John E., Ronald V. Clarke, and Rob T. Guerette. 2007. "Risky Facilities: Crime Concentration in Homogeneous Sets of Establishments and Facilities." *Crime Prevention Studies* 21: 225.

Eck, John E., and Rob T. Guerette. 2012. "Place-Based Crime Prevention: Theory, Evidence, and Policy." Pp. 354–383 in Brandon Welsh and David Farrington (eds.), *The Oxford Handbook of Crime Prevention*. New York, NY: Oxford University Press.

Eck, John E., and David Weisburd. 1995. *Crime and Place, Crime Prevention Studies*. Monsey, NY: Criminal Justice Press.

Felson, Marcus. 1995. "Those Who Discourage Crime." *Crime and Place* 4: 53–66.

Gottfredson, Michael R., and Travis Hirschi. 1995. "National Crime Control Policies." *Society* 32: 30–36.

Guerette, Rob T., and Kate J. Bowers. 2009. "Assessing the Extent of Crime Displacement and Diffusion of Benefits: A Review of Situational Crime Prevention Evaluations." *Criminology* 47: 1331–1368.

Hirschi, Travis, Albert J. Reiss, and Jeffrey A. Roth. 1993. "Administrative Criminology." *Contemporary Sociology* 22: 348–350.

Jacobs, Jane. 1961. "The Uses of Sidewalks: Safety." Pp. 114–118 in Richard LeGates and Frederic Stout (eds.), *The City Reader*. New York, NY: Routledge.

Kubrin, Charis E., and Ronald Weitzer. 2003. "New Directions in Social Disorganization Theory." *Journal of Research in Crime and Delinquency* 40: 374–402.

Lilly, J. Robert, Francis T. Cullen, and Richard A. Ball. 2010. *Criminological Theory: Context and Consequences*. Los Angeles, CA: Sage.

Madensen, Tamara D. 2007. *Bar Management and Crime: Toward a Dynamic Theory of Place Management and Crime Hotspots*. Ph.D. Dissertation. Division of Criminal Justice, University of Cincinnati.

Madensen, Tamara D., and John E. Eck. 2008. "Violence in Bars: Exploring the Impact of Place Manager Decision-Making." *Crime Prevention & Community Safety* 10: 111–125.

Madensen, Tamara D., and John E. Eck. 2013. "Crime Places and Place Management." Pp. 554–578 in Francis Cullen and Pamela Wilcox (eds.), *Oxford Handbook of Criminological Theory*. New York, NY: Oxford University Press.

Martinson, Robert. 1974. "What Works? Questions and Answers about Prison Reform." *The Public Interest* 35: 22.

Matthews, Roger. 1990. "Developing More Effective Strategies for Curbing Prostitution." *Security Journal* 1: 182–187.

Merton, Robert K. 1938. "Social Structure and Anomie." *American Sociological Review* 3: 672–682.

Morenoff, Jeffrey D., and Robert J. Sampson. 1997. "Violent Crime and the Spatial Dynamics of Neighborhood Transition: Chicago, 1970–1990." *Social Forces* 76: 31–64.

Nettler, Gwynn. 1978. *Explaining Crime*. New York, NY: McGraw.

Poyner, Barry. 1988. "Video Cameras and Bus Vandalism." *Security Administration* 11: 44–51.

Poyner, Barry, and Barry Webb. 1987. *Successful Crime Prevention: Case Studies*. London: Tavistock Institute.

Sampson, Robert J. 2014. Collective efficacy theory. In (Tammy L. Anderson, ed.), Understanding Deviance: Connecting Classical and Contemporary Perspectives. New York, NY: Routledge.

Sampson, Robert J., and W. Byron Groves. 1989. "Community Structure and Crime: Testing Social-Disorganization Theory." *American Journal of Sociology* 94: 774–802.

Shaw, Clifford Robe, and Henry Donald McKay. 1942. *Juvenile Delinquency and Urban Areas*. Chicago, IL: University of Chicago Press.

Sherman, Lawrence W. 1995. "Hot Spots of Crime and Criminal Careers of Places." *Crime and Place* 4: 35–52.

Sherman, Lawrence W., Patrick R. Gartin, and Michael E. Buerger. 1989. "Hot Spots of Predatory Crime: Routine Activities and the Criminology of Place." *Criminology* 27: 27–56.

Sherman, Lawrence W., and David Weisburd. 1995. "General Deterrent Effects of Police Patrol in Crime 'Hot Spots': A Randomized, Controlled Trial." *Justice Quarterly* 12: 625–648.

Sutherland, Edwin H. 1947. *Principles of Criminology*. Chicago, IL: J.B. Lippincott Company.

Taylor, Ralph B. 1997. "Social Order and Disorder of Street Blocks and Neighborhoods: Ecology, Microecology, and the Systemic Model of Social Disorganization." *Journal of Research in Crime and Delinquency* 34: 113–155.

Taylor, Ralph B. 1998. "Crime and Small-Scale Places: What We Know, What We Can Prevent, and What else We Need to Know." Pp. 1–22 in Jeremy Travis and John Thomas (eds.), *Crime and Place: Plenary Papers of the 1997 Conference on Criminal Justice Research and Evaluation*. Washington, DC: National Institute of Justice.

Taylor, Ralph B., Stephen D. Gottfredson, and Sidney Brower. 1984. "Block Crime and Fear: Defensible Space, Local Social Ties, and Territorial Functioning." *Journal of Research in Crime and Delinquency* 21: 303–331.

Tonry, Michael, and David Farrington. 1995. "Building a Safer Society." *Crime and Justice* 19.

Trasler, Gordon. 1993. "Conscience, Opportunity, Rational Choice, and Crime." *Cohen & Felson* 1: 305–322.

Unger, Donald G., and Abraham Wandersman. 1983. "Neighboring and Its Role in Block Organizations: An Exploratory Report." *American Journal of Community Psychology* 11: 291–300.

Visher, Christy, and David Weisburd. 1998. "Identifying What Works: Recent Trends in Crime." *Crime, Law and Social Change* 28: 223–242.

Webb, Barry, and Gloria Laycock. 1992. "Reducing Crime on the London Underground." *Crime Prevention Unit Paper*: 30.

Weisburd, David. 2015. "The Law of Crime Concentration and the Criminology of Place." *Criminology* 53: 133–157.

Weisburd, David, Shawn Bushway, Cynthia Lum, and Sue-Ming Yang. 2004. "Trajectories of Crime at Places: A Longitudinal Study of Street Segments in the City of Seattle." *Criminology* 42: 283–322.

Weisburd, D., Farrington, D., and Gill, C. (2017). What works in crime prevention and rehabilitation: An assessment of systematic reviews. *Criminology and Public Policy* 16 (2): 415-449.

Weisburd, David, Elizabeth R. Groff, and Sue-Ming Yang. 2012. *The Criminology of Place: Street Segments and Our Understanding of the Crime Problem*. Oxford: Oxford University Press.

Weisburd, David, Laura A. Wyckoff, Justin Ready, John E. Eck, Joshua C. Hinkle, and Frank Gajewski. 2006. "Does Crime Just Move around the Corner? A Controlled Study of Spatial Displacement and Diffusion of Crime Control Benefits." *Criminology* 44: 549–592.

Wilcox, Pamela, and John E. Eck. 2011. "Criminology of the Unpopular: Implications for Policy Aimed at Payday Lending Facilities." *Criminology & Public Policy* 10: 473–482.

Wilcox, Pamela, Kenneth Land, and Scott A. Hunt. 2004. "Criminal Circumstance: A Multicontextual Criminal Opportunity Theory." *Symbolic Interaction* 27: 123–125.

Part I

Crime Concentration and the Dynamic Nature of Places

1

The Concentration-Dynamics Tradeoff in Crime Hot Spotting

George O. Mohler, Martin B. Short,
and P. Jeffrey Brantingham

Introduction

Current thinking in crime pattern theory relies on two somewhat contradictory observations. On the one hand, it is well-known that a small fraction of locations in any one environment accounts for a large fraction of the crime (Sherman, Gartin, and Buerger 1989; Weisburd 2015). On the other, there is good evidence that crime events themselves occur with a high degree of spatial-temporal variability (Bowers, Johnson, and Pease 2004; Mohler et al. 2015; Short, D'Orsogna, Brantingham, and Tita 2009; Wang, Rudin, Wagner, and Sevieri 2013; Wang and Brown 2012; Wang, Gerber, and Brown 2012).

Both observations hold important implications for not only understanding the causes of crime, but also designing crime prevention strategies. The former observation tends to encourage the view that crime patterns are predominantly static, persisting from one time period to the next in a roughly constant spatial configuration. The implication is that there is a tight coupling between crime and place that remains reasonably stable over time (Weisburd, Groff, and Yang 2012). If true, then it is clearly advantageous for police to repeatedly target the same places to achieve crime reduction (Sherman and Weisburd 1995).

The latter observation, by contrast, encourages the view that crime patterns are predominantly dynamic, with hotspots emerging, spreading, and dissipating only to reemerge in new locations (Johnson, Lab, and Bowers 2008; Short, Brantingham, Bertozzi, and Tita 2010). The implication is that crime is coupled to place quite loosely via a probabilistic decision making process (Brantingham and Brantingham 1978, 1981; Maltz, Gordon, and Friedman 1990: 1).

If true, then police may find advantage in anticipating how that probabilistic process is evolving in space and time and target a shifting series of locations on the landscape (Bowers et al. 2004; Mohler et al. 2011; Wang et al. 2013; Wang and Brown 2012; Wang et al. 2012). Recent work has looked at whether dynamic targeting of places by police has an impact on crime (Gorr and Lee 2015; Mohler et al. 2015; Telep, Mitchell, and Weisburd 2014). The present work seeks to show how both of these perspectives can simultaneously be true.

Our presentation gets straight to the point. We forego a review of the theoretical and empirical literature on crime and place, as there are several recent works that cover such information in great detail (see Eck and Weisburd 1995; Weisburd et al. 2016; Weisburd et al. 2012). We therefore focus singularly on the analysis of crime concentration and the dynamics of crime hotspots. The paper is structured as follows. In the first section, we introduce our analytical approach, which is motivated by recent studies on the micro-geographic patterning of crime and place (Weisburd 2015; Weisburd, Bushway, Lum, and Yang 2004; Weisburd et al. 2012; Wyant, Taylor, Ratcliffe, and Wood 2012). As in Weisburd (2015), we are interested in the concentration of crime in a small number of geographic locations. However, we focus on how measured crime concentration changes as both the temporal and spatial windows for counting crime change (Brantingham, Dyreson, and Brantingham 1976; Chainey, Thompson, and Uhlig 2008; Steenbeek and Weisburd 2016; Townsley 2008). We are also interested in measuring the stability of crime patterns in the context of changing spatial and temporal scales. We introduce a very simple measure that counts the percentage overlap in hotspot locations from one time period to the next when measured at different temporal and spatial scales (see Mohler et al. 2015). The approach is far simpler than other recent assessments of crime pattern stability (Johnson et al. 2008; Weisburd et al. 2004; Weisburd et al. 2012), but offers practical advantages in terms of ease of interpretation.

The second section turns to empirical assessments. We analyze crime patterns in Los Angeles during the years 2009–2015, and Chicago during 2008–2015. In both settings, we analyze assault, burglary, motor vehicle theft, and robbery, independently for each crime type. We offer theoretical motivation for choosing these crimes based on fundamental differences in the potential mobility of offenders and victims involved in each of these crime types (Tita and Griffiths 2005).

The third section presents our two principal findings. First, hotspots defined at smaller temporal and spatial scales capture the same amount of crime, while covering less total land area. In other words, crime appears to be much more concentrated when using smaller, short-term counting units compared with larger, long-term counting units. Second, hotspots defined at smaller temporal and spatial scales are much more dynamic than those defined at larger temporal and spatial scales. In other words, small, short-term hotspots spatially overlap much less from one time period to the next compared with larger, long-term hotspots. There is thus an apparent tradeoff with crime hotspot characterization. Smaller, short-term hotspots are better at identifying the highest crime concentrations in an environment, but those locations change substantially in placement at that short time scale. Alternatively, more stable crime patterns can be identified by adopting larger spatial and temporal scales, but at the cost of reduced crime concentration.

The final section discusses implications of the work. We discuss how the concentration-dynamics tradeoff impacts our understanding of crime causation. We then draw some general observations about the scale of analysis and policing and crime prevention. The punchline is that crime patterns do not exist only at one scale (Brantingham, Brantingham, Vajihollahi, and Wuschke 2009; Steenbeek and Weisburd 2016). This is not necessarily an indication of aggregation bias. Rather, it is indicative of behavioral processes operating at different scales. Policing and crime prevention efforts can benefit from calibrating to these scales.

Methods

Our methodological approach is divided into four principal parts. The first involves defining the spatial and temporal counting units for hotspot quantification. The second concerns measuring the global concentration of crime given those spatial and temporal units. The third concerns assessing the spatial stability (or lack thereof) of hotspots from one time period to the next. Our measure of spatial stability of hotspots is likely dependent upon macroscopic patterns of how smaller spatial units are organized into larger clusters (see Steenbeek and Weisburd 2016; Weisburd et al. 2012). The fourth part is therefore tabulating cluster sizes for each spatial and temporal scale.

We adopt a straightforward method for defining spatial and temporal counting units. Our spatial units are constructed as a regular square lattice or grid laid out over the entire jurisdiction. Specifically, we examine grids where each cell is 200 × 200, 400 × 400, or 800 × 800 m in size. Fixed grid counting units may be contrasted with categorical spatial units such as street segments (Davies and Bishop 2013; Weisburd et al. 2012), reporting districts, census tracts, or formally recognized neighborhoods (Wooldredge 2002). Our temporal units are similarly defined in discrete terms as fixed time windows measured in days, months, or years. These discrete spatial-temporal units lead naturally to a histogram method for counting crime. We count all of the crimes of a specified type occurring in each grid cell during each defined time period. For example, we will count all of the robberies occurring in each 200 × 200 m grid cell per day, or all burglaries in each 400 × 400 m grid cell per month. Note that common hot spotting methods such as kernel density estimation (KDE) are closely related to the histogram counting procedure suggested here, as both are nonparametric estimators for the probability density function of a point process.

After the number of crimes within grid cells have been counted, the resulting counts are ranked in decreasing order by crime count. For example, the Rank 1 cell will contain the greatest number of crimes among all cells, the Rank 2 cell will contain the second greatest number of crimes, and so on. It follows that the Rank 1 cell will capture the greatest percentage of crime compared to all other individual cells for that specific time period, the Rank 2 cell will capture the next greatest percentage, and so on. Starting at the top of the ranked list, we flag each cell in order until the collection of flagged cells in total represents a predefined cumulative percentage of the total crime over that time window. For example, we might flag cells until 5%, 10%, 25%, or 50% of all crime within that time period is captured by those cells.

For simplicity, we will use the term hotspot to refer to an individual grid cell flagged in this way. All of the cells not flagged in this way are not considered crime hotspots for that particular cell size and time period. Collections of flagged grid cells are referred to as clusters, when they form contiguous spatial blocks, or simply by the plural hotspots, when their spatial arrangement is not relevant. Note that our procedure is very closely related to that of Weisburd (2015), who counts the percentage of all street segments needed to capture a fixed percentage of crime (see also Weisburd et al. 2004; Weisburd et al. 2012). To facilitate comparison with Weisburd's results we report results for hotspots capturing 25% and 50% of crime, respectively. We caution, however, that crime counts aggregated by street segments and areal units such as grid cells may not be strictly equivalent (see Steenbeek and Weisburd 2016).

It is a simple matter to convert the number of crime hotspots into a measure of crime concentration. First, the number of flagged hotspots is converted into an area by multiplying by the known area of each cell (e.g., 200 × 200m). Dividing this total hotspot area by the total land area of the jurisdiction yields the percentage of land area needed to capture a fixed percentage of crime. The smaller the percentage of land area sufficient to capture a target crime percentage, the more concentrated crime is in space. For example, crime is two times more concentrated if 0.1% of a jurisdiction's land area captures 25% of crime, compared with 0.2% of the total land area capturing 25% of crime.

We measure hotspots stability in a similarly direct manner. For any given collection of crime hotspots, we measure the percentage overlap in hotspot locations from one time period to the next. For example, imagine a collection of one hundred hotspots each 400 × 400 m in size sufficient to capture 25% of recorded crime over the course of one month. Now imagine that we perform the same analysis for the following month, again yielding one hundred hotspots of the same size. We then compare the hotspot locations from month 2 with those present in month 1 and find that 50% of the locations are the same. Thus half of the pattern is stationary at this temporal and spatial scale, and the other half is dynamic. Our approach is similar to that of Andresen and Malleson (2011) wherein spatial units are compared across two time periods for the volume of crime present. Units are scored as stationary if the volume of crime is statistically equivalent across time periods. Our approach is considerably different from that of Weisburd et al. (2004) and Weisburd et al. (2012) who use group-based trajectory analysis to identify latent hotspot groups given the entire history of crime on street segments over a 16 year time period. They find that some latent groups display very stable crime patterns at an annual time scale over the study period, while others display secular variation in crime volume over time.

We also examine hotspot cluster sizes. To find the size of a hotspot cluster, we simply count the number of contiguous flagged hotspots present in a given time window. The counting procedure is as follows. Given a starting grid cell flagged as a hotspot, each immediately adjacent cell is joined to the same cluster if it is also flagged as a hotspot. These first-order neighbors are then used to look for unique adjacent cells that are also flagged as hotspots. These comprise second-order neighbors. The process is repeated until no unique hotspots can be joined to the component. We are primarily interested in how cluster size changes as a function of the spatial and temporal scale of measurement. To assess whether observed cluster sizes are different from what would be expected given random occurrence of crime, we simulate random hotspot placement for equivalent hotspot densities and then compute cluster sizes using the aforementioned method for these randomly placed hotspots.

Crime Patterns in Los Angeles and Chicago

Our analyses focus on crime patterns in Los Angeles, California, and Chicago, Illinois. Los Angeles is a city of nearly four million people and encompasses a land area of approximately 1,301 square km (509 square miles). Address-geocoded data on aggravated assault, burglary, motor vehicle theft, and robbery were provided by the Los Angeles Police Department for the years 2009–2015. Chicago is a city of approximately 2.7 million people and covers an area of 606 square km (234 square miles). We obtained block-geocoded open source data from the City of Chicago Open Data Portal (https://data. cityofchicago.org), which we examine for the years 2008–2015.

Our focal crime types are chosen because each encompasses different fundamental potentials for dynamic behavior given the mobility of offenders and victims or targets. At one extreme, we might expect burglary hotspots to inherently have lower dynamic potential. By definition, the offender in a burglary is mobile, but the target is stationary. Assuming that houses change in their baseline attractiveness only very slowly, then any temporal and spatial dynamics in burglary hotspots must be tied only to how burglars move and mix in the broader environment. At the other extreme, we might expect assault and robbery to inherently have higher dynamic capacity. Both crime types can involve mobile offenders and mobile victims (see Tita and Griffiths 2005). Hence, robbery and assault hotspots may be less tied to place because offenders and victims can move and mix independent of place. Between these extremes we might expect to find motor vehicle theft. In this case, the offender is mobile, but targets experience short-term turnover in the composition of the car assemblage (Brantingham 2013). The nature of the opportunity for motor vehicle theft shifts through space and time as car assemblages change. At an abstract level, we might expect motor vehicle theft hotspots to have intermediate dynamic capacity.

For both Los Angeles and Chicago, we count crimes in grid cells of size 200 × 200, 400 × 400, and 800 × 800m. While ultimately each of these is an arbitrary length scale, the finer spatial unit is consistent with the linear dimensions of street blocks in many American cities. Thus a short-hand way to think about the length scales is as one, four, and 16 square block areas. The largest length scale we consider is at the small end (~0.064 square km) of what would be perceived as a neighborhood in inner-city contexts (Pebley and Sastry 2009).

The availability of years' worth of crime data means that we can examine multiple time windows for scoring hotspots. We use one week, one month, three month, six month, and one year time windows for both Los Angeles and Chicago. In Chicago, we also examine crime patterns at two year intervals. In both Los Angeles and Chicago, we also look at each sample as a whole, representing seven years in Los Angeles and eight years in Chicago.

Results

We first examine patterns in Los Angeles. Figure 1.1 presents crime concentration as a function of the time window at which hotspots are quantified. Shown is the percentage of land area necessary to capture 25% and 50% of crime, respectively, with time windows ranging from one week (seven days) to seven years (2555 days). The length scale for hot spotting in Figure 1.1 is 200 × 200 m. Figure 1.1A shows the results for robbery, while Figure 1.1B shows the

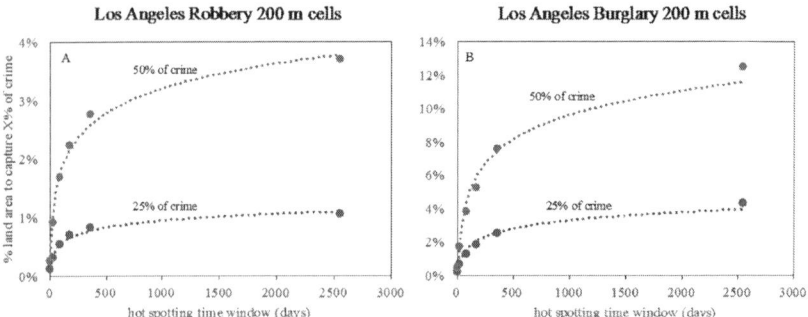

Figure 1.1 Percentage of land area needed to capture a fixed percentage of crime increases as the time window for hot spotting increases. A. Robberies. B. Burglaries. Results are shown for micro-geographic hotspots 200 × 200 m in size.

Table 1.1
Los Angeles 2009–2015 average area fraction of 200 × 200 m hotspots
required to capture 25% and 50% of total crime along with the average
area fraction of hotspots that overlap from period to period

Crime Type	Time Window	Days	Area Fraction (25%)	Overlap (25%)	Area Fraction (50%)	Overlap (50%)
Assault	7 year	2555	0.017	NA	0.052	NA
Assault	year	365	0.011 ± 0.001	0.281 ± 0.038	0.032 ± 0.003	0.344 ± 0.031
Assault	6 month	182.5	0.008 ± 0.001	0.176 ± 0.032	0.023 ± 0.003	0.250 ± 0.024
Assault	3 month	91.3	0.005 ± 0.001	0.094 ± 0.029	0.015 ± 0.002	0.146 ± 0.032
Assault	month	30.4	0.002 ± 0.000	0.044 ± 0.028	0.007 ± 0.002	0.071 ± 0.022
Assault	week	7.0	0.001 ± 0.000	0.008 ± 0.021	0.002 ± 0.001	0.023 ± 0.021
Burglary	7 year	2555	0.043	NA	0.125	NA
Burglary	year	365	0.025 ± 0.001	0.230 ± 0.015	0.076 ± 0.003	0.317 ± 0.008
Burglary	6 month	182.5	0.018 ± 0.001	0.149 ± 0.018	0.052 ± 0.003	0.217 ± 0.014
Burglary	3 month	91.3	0.012 ± 0.001	0.116 ± 0.016	0.038 ± 0.003	0.182 ± 0.018
Burglary	month	30.4	0.006 ± 0.001	0.072 ± 0.020	0.017 ± 0.002	0.105 ± 0.016
Burglary	week	7.0	0.002 ± 0.000	0.025 ± 0.020	0.004 ± 0.001	0.032 ± 0.016
MVT	7 year	2555	0.035	NA	0.097	NA
MVT	year	365	0.023 ± 0.001	0.258 ± 0.027	0.066 ± 0.002	0.352 ± 0.017
MVT	6 month	182.5	0.017 ± 0.001	0.176 ± 0.022	0.047 ± 0.003	0.257 ± 0.026
MVT	3 month	91.3	0.012 ± 0.001	0.117 ± 0.02	0.036 ± 0.003	0.192 ± 0.016
MVT	month	30.4	0.006 ± 0.001	0.068 ± 0.017	0.016 ± 0.002	0.099 ± 0.016
MVT	week	7.0	0.002 ± 0.000	0.027 ± 0.021	0.004 ± 0.001	0.031 ± 0.016
Robbery	7 year	2555	0.011	NA	0.037	NA
Robbery	year	365	0.008 ± 0.001	0.472 ± 0.031	0.028 ± 0.004	0.490 ± 0.019
Robbery	6 month	182.5	0.007 ± 0.001	0.357 ± 0.027	0.022 ± 0.003	0.385 ± 0.022
Robbery	3 month	91.3	0.005 ± 0.001	0.250 ± 0.030	0.017 ± 0.002	0.250 ± 0.028
Robbery	month	30.4	0.003 ± 0.000	0.119 ± 0.033	0.009 ± 0.002	0.137 ± 0.022
Robbery	week	7.0	0.001 ± 0.000	0.029 ± 0.029	0.003 ± 0.001	0.047 ± 0.023

results for burglary. Numerical results for all four crime types are presented in Table 1.1.

Crime is clearly more concentrated when the time window used for hotspot quantification is shorter. For example, when hotspots are computed with seven day time windows, approximately 0.1% of the total land area must be flagged as hotspots to capture 25% of robberies (Table 1.1). The percentage of land area needed increases to 0.3% when the time window is one month. In other words, robberies are three times more concentrated with hotspots measured on the scale of seven days compared with one month. When the time window is further increased to three months, six months, and one year, the percentage of land area needed climbs to 0.5%, 0.7%, and 0.8%, respectively. At seven years, the full temporal extent of our data, 1.1% of the total land area needs to be flagged to capture 25% of crime. In other words, robberies are 11 times more concentrated when measured at the seven day scale compared with the seven year scale. This pattern is replicated for each of the crime types considered here and when the target crime fraction for hotspots changes to 50% (Table 1.1). For example, the percentage of land area necessary to explain 50% of burglaries increases from 0.4% of land area to 12.5% of land area when the time window for hot spotting increases from seven days to seven years. Burglaries are 31 times more concentrated at the shortest versus the longest time scale considered. The empirical pattern is well-fit by a logarithmic function of the form $y = a * LN[x] + b$.

Figure 1.2 examines the dynamics of crime hotspots as a function of hot spotting time window. The percentage overlap in the location of crime hotspots from one time period to the next increases as the time window increases (Table 1.1). This indicates that hotspots measured at shorter time scales are much more dynamic than those measured at longer time scales. For example, only 2.9% of robbery hotspots flagged in one week are in the same locations in the following week, when those hotspots are set to capture 25% of crime (Figure 1.2A). The vast majority of flagged robbery hotspots are in different places from week to week. When the time window is increased to one month, 11.9% of robbery hotspots on average are flagged in the same location from one month to the next. This represents a greater degree of stability in crime patterns, but the majority of flagged locations still differ from month to month. For hotspots quantified on a yearly time scale, 47.2% of hotspots are the same location from year to year. The quantitative pattern is the same when the criterion for

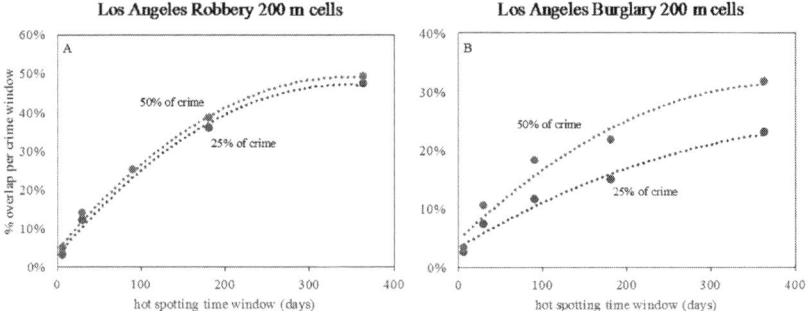

Figure 1.2 The percentage overlap in hotspot locations from one time period to the next increases as the hot spotting time window increases. A. Robbery. B. Burglary. Results are shown for micro-geographic hotspots 200 × 200 m in size.

designating robbery hotspots shifts to capturing 50% of crime (Figure 1.2A). Burglary crime patterns similarly increase in stability with an increasing hot spotting time window, but here the stability is more pronounced when seeking to capture 50% of crime compared with 25% of crime (Figure 1.2B). The relationship is well-fit by an exponential function of the form $y = a - ae^{-bx}$.

Given the data on hand, we can examine the interaction between crime concentration and hotspot dynamics. Figure 1.3 shows the percentage overlap in hotspot locations from one time period to the next against the percentage of land area sufficient to capture 25% and 50% of crime (Table 1.1). Hotspots flagged using shorter time windows are more concentrated in space, but also more dynamic. Those flagged using longer time windows are less concentrated, but also more stable. The relationship between these two measures of crime patterns is non-linear. The non-linear trend is very pronounced for robbery patterns (Figure 1.3A). It is also visible for burglary patterns where hotspots are flagged for 25% of crimes. It is less obvious that the trend is non-linear where hotspots are flagged for 50% of burglaries. Assault and motor vehicle theft follow the burglary pattern (Table 1.1). Nevertheless, the relationship is well-fit by a polynomial equation of the form $y = ax^2 + bx$.

All of the results presented in Figures 1.1–1.3 were computed for a spatial grid with 200 × 200 m cells. A larger spatial length scale produces equivalent results (Table 1.2). Figure 1.4 is a direct extension of Figure 1.3 across three different spatial length scales for hotspots capturing 25% of crime. Note that the 200 m curves in Figures 1.4A and 1.4B match exactly the 25% curves in Figures 1.3A and 1.3B, respectively. At each spatial length scale it is clear that shorter time windows produce greater crime concentration, but also yield more dynamic hotspots. Longer time windows produce lower crime concentration, but hotspots are more stable. With the 200 m curve from Figure 1.3 for

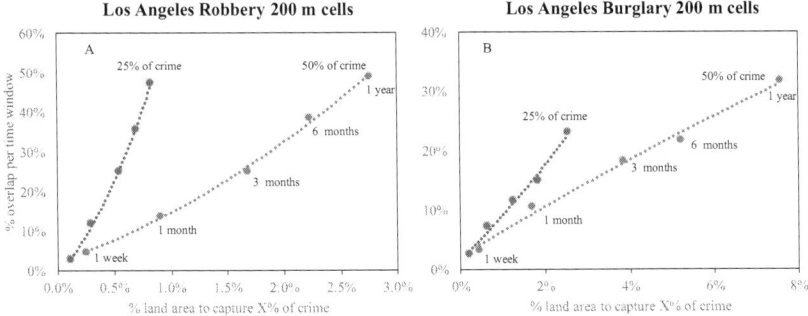

Figure 1.3 The percentage overlap in hotspot locations from one time period to the next increases in tandem with the percentage of land area needed to capture a fixed percentage of crime. A. Robbery. B. Burglary. Results are shown for micro-geographic hotspots 200 × 200 m in size.

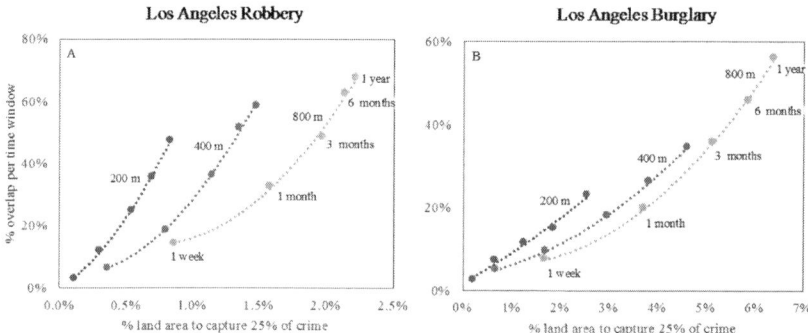

Figure 1.4 Larger hot spotting spatial scales require greater total land area to capture the same amount of crime, but also produce greater overlap in hotspot locations from one time period to the next. A. Robbery. B. Burglary. Results are shown for 200 m, 400 m, and 800 m cells at one week, one month, three month, six month, and one year time windows.

reference, it is clear that increasing the spatial length scale shifts the relationship between concentration and dynamics up and to the right. A larger grid size requires a greater percentage of land area to capture the same amount of crime, but also produces greater stability in hotspots across time periods. Table 1.2 illustrates the relationship for hotspots defined for one year time windows. For example, for assaults the mean percentage of land area sufficient to capture 25% of crime increases from 1.1% to 2.8% as the spatial length scale increases from 200 × 200 m to 800 × 800 m. The percentage overlap in assault hotspots also increases from 28.1% to 63.3% over the same range of spatial scales.

To illustrate that the observed patterns are not unique to the Los Angeles setting we computed the same metrics for Chicago. Tables 1.3 and 1.4 present the primary results. Figure 1.5A shows the percentage overlap in hotspot locations against the percentage of land area required to capture 25% of robberies and burglaries for a 200 × 200 m length scale. The functional form for the relationship is equivalent to that seen in Los Angeles, though the quantitative parameters for the fitted models differ depending upon crime type. In Chicago, for example, hotspots sufficient to capture 25% of robberies over a one year time scale cover 2.3% of the total land area (Figure 1.5A; Table 1.3). The overlap in hotspot locations is 46.5% from year to year. By contrast, in Los Angeles, hotspots sufficient to capture 25% of robberies cover only 0.8% of the total land area, while 47.2% of locations overlap from year to year. The numerical comparisons for burglary are more similar (see Tables 1.1 and 1.2).

Shifting to a larger spatial length scale of 800 × 800 m replicates many of the same patterns (Figure 1.5B; Table 1.3). For example, at a yearly time scale hotspots needed to capture 25% of robberies in Chicago cover 5.7% of land

Table 1.2

Yearly hotspots of variable sizes in Los Angeles 2009–2015. Average fraction of hotspots each year required to capture 25% and 50% of total crime along with the average fraction of hotspots that overlap year over year

Crime Type	Area Fraction (25%)	Overlap (25%)	Area Fraction (50%)	Overlap (50%)	Cell Size (km)
Assault	0.011 ± 0.001	0.281 ± 0.038	0.032 ± 0.003	0.344 ± 0.031	0.2
Assault	0.019 ± 0.001	0.438 ± 0.066	0.058 ± 0.003	0.547 ± 0.026	0.4
Assault	0.028 ± 0.001	0.633 ± 0.061	0.081 ± 0.003	0.750 ± 0.036	0.8
Burglary	0.025 ± 0.001	0.230 ± 0.015	0.076 ± 0.003	0.317 ± 0.008	0.2
Burglary	0.046 ± 0.001	0.345 ± 0.043	0.129 ± 0.003	0.480 ± 0.019	0.4
Burglary	0.064 ± 0.002	0.560 ± 0.070	0.174 ± 0.004	0.665 ± 0.027	0.8
MVT	0.023 ± 0.001	0.258 ± 0.027	0.066 ± 0.002	0.352 ± 0.017	0.2
MVT	0.039 ± 0.002	0.411 ± 0.025	0.105 ± 0.004	0.558 ± 0.014	0.4
MVT	0.053 ± 0.002	0.631 ± 0.032	0.139 ± 0.004	0.715 ± 0.026	0.8
Robbery	0.008 ± 0.001	0.472 ± 0.031	0.028 ± 0.004	0.490 ± 0.019	0.2
Robbery	0.015 ± 0.002	0.586 ± 0.035	0.048 ± 0.005	0.629 ± 0.026	0.4
Robbery	0.022 ± 0.003	0.676 ± 0.041	0.067 ± 0.006	0.804 ± 0.029	0.8

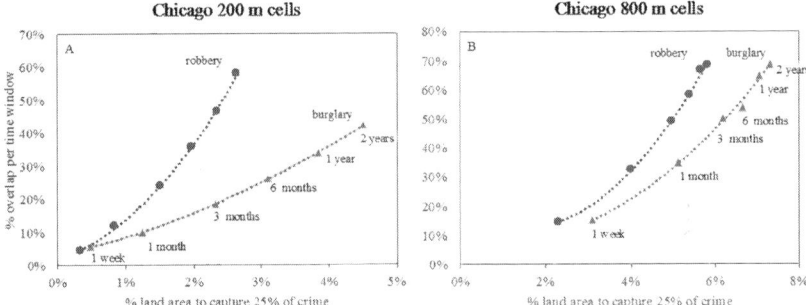

Figure 1.5 The percentage overlap in hotspot locations from one time period to the next increases in tandem with the percentage of land area needed to capture 25% of crime. A. Robbery and burglary hotspots at a 200 × 200 m spatial scale. B. Robbery and burglary hotspots at an 800 × 800 m spatial scale. Results are shown for one week, one month, three month, six month, one year, and two year time windows.

area, while 66.4% of those hotspots remain in the same place from year to year. In Los Angeles, the comparable figures are 2.2% of land area and 67.6% overlap. Overall, the relationship between crime concentration and the dynamics of hotspots displays considerable regularity across regions.

Table 1.3

Chicago 2008–2015 average area fraction of 200 × 200 m hotspots required to capture 25% and 50% of total crime along with the average fraction of hotspots that overlap from period to period

Crime Type	Time Window	Days	Area Fraction (25%)	Overlap (25%)	Area Fraction (50%)	Overlap (50%)
Assault	8 year	2920	0.037	NA	0.11	NA
Assault	2 year	730	0.033 ± 0.001	0.559 ± 0.022	0.098 ± 0.003	0.63 ± 0.02
Assault	year	365	0.030 ± 0.001	0.478 ± 0.02	0.089 ± 0.003	0.55 ± 0.017
Assault	6 month	182.5	0.025 ± 0.001	0.349 ± 0.024	0.074 ± 0.004	0.436 ± 0.021
Assault	3 month	91.3	0.020 ± 0.002	0.259 ± 0.048	0.057 ± 0.007	0.325 ± 0.038
Assault	month	30.4	0.012 ± 0.002	0.137 ± 0.038	0.035 ± 0.005	0.206 ± 0.03
Assault	week	7.0	0.005 ± 0.001	0.057 ± 0.031	0.011 ± 0.002	0.077 ± 0.026
Burglary	8 year	2920	0.054	NA	0.152	NA
Burglary	2 year	730	0.045 ± 0.003	0.421 ± 0.027	0.128 ± 0.007	0.519 ± 0.051
Burglary	year	365	0.038 ± 0.004	0.338 ± 0.040	0.110 ± 0.009	0.437 ± 0.048
Burglary	6 month	182.5	0.031 ± 0.004	0.260 ± 0.039	0.088 ± 0.010	0.340 ± 0.037
Burglary	3 month	91.3	0.023 ± 0.003	0.184 ± 0.035	0.065 ± 0.010	0.262 ± 0.048
Burglary	month	30.4	0.012 ± 0.003	0.098 ± 0.033	0.037 ± 0.008	0.184 ± 0.037
Burglary	week	7.0	0.005 ± 0.001	0.056 ± 0.032	0.012 ± 0.003	0.072 ± 0.029
MVT	8 year	2920	0.064	NA	0.165	NA
MVT	2 year	730	0.051 ± 0.003	0.337 ± 0.055	0.136 ± 0.007	0.473 ± 0.050
MVT	year	365	0.042 ± 0.003	0.246 ± 0.035	0.114 ± 0.008	0.370 ± 0.043
MVT	6 month	182.5	0.033 ± 0.003	0.179 ± 0.035	0.088 ± 0.012	0.275 ± 0.048
MVT	3 month	91.3	0.023 ± 0.004	0.122 ± 0.036	0.063 ± 0.007	0.220 ± 0.021
MVT	month	30.4	0.012 ± 0.002	0.075 ± 0.022	0.033 ± 0.007	0.130 ± 0.032
MVT	week	7.0	0.004 ± 0.001	0.034 ± 0.026	0.009 ± 0.002	0.040 ± 0.022
Robbery	8 year	2920	0.03	NA	0.098	NA
Robbery	2 year	730	0.026 ± 0.000	0.577 ± 0.018	0.085 ± 0.002	0.601 ± 0.033
Robbery	year	365	0.023 ± 0.001	0.465 ± 0.046	0.074 ± 0.003	0.488 ± 0.032
Robbery	6 month	182.5	0.002 ± 0.001	0.355 ± 0.050	0.060 ± 0.005	0.380 ± 0.037
Robbery	3 month	91.3	0.015 ± 0.001	0.240 ± 0.048	0.044 ± 0.004	0.279 ± 0.037
Robbery	month	30.4	0.008 ± 0.001	0.117 ± 0.042	0.025 ± 0.004	0.171 ± 0.039
Robbery	week	7.0	0.003 ± 0.001	0.043 ± 0.032	0.007 ± 0.002	0.063 ± 0.028

All of the analysis to this point has focused on discrete hotspot locations. For example, we have examined the concentration of crime within and the dynamics of discrete 200 × 200 m cells defined with fixed time windows. Here we consider whether these discrete locations cluster to form larger components and how cluster size is dependent upon the spatial and temporal length scales used. This was an issue first addressed by Brantingham et al. (1976).

Table 1.4

Yearly hotspots of variable sizes in Chicago 2008–2015. Average fraction of hotspots each year required to capture 25% and 50% of total crime along with the average fraction of hotspots that overlap year over year

Crime Type	Area Fraction (25%)	Overlap (25%)	Area Fraction (50%)	Overlap (50%)	Location Scale (km)
Assault	0.030 ± 0.001	0.478 ± 0.020	0.089 ± 0.003	0.55 0± 0.017	0.2
Assault	0.048 ± 0.001	0.578 ± 0.024	0.132 ± 0.001	0.709 ± 0.016	0.4
Assault	0.065 ± 0.001	0.768 ± 0.035	0.171 ± 0.002	0.838 ± 0.017	0.8
Burglary	0.038 ± 0.004	0.338 ± 0.040	0.110 ± 0.009	0.437 ± 0.048	0.2
Burglary	0.056 ± 0.003	0.510 ± 0.032	0.157 ± 0.005	0.598 ± 0.046	0.4
Burglary	0.071 ± 0.002	0.648 ± 0.030	0.193 ± 0.002	0.738 ± 0.034	0.8
MVT	0.042 ± 0.003	0.246 ± 0.035	0.114 ± 0.008	0.370 ± 0.043	0.2
MVT	0.066 ± 0.002	0.407 ± 0.040	0.170 ± 0.004	0.576 ± 0.047	0.4
MVT	0.085 ± 0.002	0.549 ± 0.053	0.212 ± 0.003	0.722 ± 0.037	0.8
Robbery	0.023 ± 0.001	0.465 ± 0.046	0.074 ± 0.003	0.488 ± 0.032	0.2
Robbery	0.039 ± 0.001	0.572 ± 0.041	0.113 ± 0.002	0.667 ± 0.027	0.4
Robbery	0.057 ± 0.001	0.664 ± 0.054	0.150 ± 0.002	0.783 ± 0.021	0.8

Table 1.5

Observed and expected average size of the largest cluster for 200 × 200 m hotspots given different time windows in Los Angeles

Days	Assault		Burglary		MVT		Robbery	
	Observed	Expected	Observed	Expected	Observed	Expected	Observed	Expected
7	1.3	2.9	2.3	3.4	2.4	3.6	2.0	3.9
30.4	2.9	5.0	4.8	6.1	5.3	6.5	4.9	6.5
91.25	6.7	7.1	8.3	8.2	8.0	8.9	10.6	8.4
182.5	11.5	8.5	11.1	9.9	11.9	10.9	15.7	7.7
365	19.6	8.4	18.0	12.0	24.4	12.7	21.1	8.1
2555	34	13	74	12	53	12	32	7

Tables 1.5 and 1.6 show the observed and expected average size of the largest hotspot cluster for any given hot spotting time window. Results are presented for 200 × 200 m hotspots sufficient to capture 25% of crime. The results are consistent for larger spatial length scales and for higher crime percentage targets. Table 1.5 presents data from Los Angeles. Table 1.6 presents data from Chicago.

Table 1.6
Observed and expected average size of the largest cluster for 200 × 200 m
hotspots given different time windows in Chicago

	Assault		Burglary		MVT		Robbery	
Days	Observed	Expected	Observed	Expected	Observed	Expected	Observed	Expected
7	3.3	4.4	3.7	4.7	2.9	3.9	2.9	4.1
30.4	5.1	7.1	6.9	7.6	6.6	6.8	4.7	6.3
91.25	9.0	9.1	15.7	10.2	10.6	9.7	8.9	9.1
182.5	11.3	9.6	29.2	11.1	16.5	11.6	11.4	9.6
365	16.8	10.4	41.3	11.9	22.3	13.3	14.5	10.1
2920	28	10	121	11	76	17	19	9

For any given spatial and temporal length scale, individual hotspots cluster to form larger components. For example, the largest assault hotspot clusters in Los Angeles for a seven day time window contain on average 1.3 cells each 200 × 200 m in size (Table 1.5). At one month, the largest assault hotspot clusters are typically 2.9 cells. This rises to 6.7, 11.5, 19.6, and 34 grid cells for three months, six months, one year, and seven years, respectively. Whether these clusters are larger or smaller than those expected by chance varies with the time window for hot spotting. The expected hotspot cluster size is computed by taking the observed number of hotspots for any given time window and generating 10^3 repeated random spatial placements of that same number of hotspots. We restrict random cell placement to only those locations that recorded at least one crime over the given time period. The largest observed clusters are typically smaller than that expected by chance for hot spotting time windows of one month or less. For example, the largest observed 30 day robbery cluster in Los Angeles is typically 4.9 cells in size, while that generated by random placement is typically 6.5 cells in size (Table 1.5). For hot spotting time windows of three months, however, the typical maximum cluster size is very similar to that occurring by chance. Beyond three month hot spotting windows, the observed maximum cluster sizes are larger than that expected by chance. For example, six month burglary hotspots in Los Angeles are typically 11.1 cells in size compared with 9.9 cells by chance. The size difference is much larger at one year with observed burglary hotspot clusters of 18 cells compared with 12 expected by chance. At the maximum time window, the gap becomes 74 cells observed compared with 12 expected by chance for burglary hotspot clusters. Equivalent patterns are observed in Chicago (Table 1.6). Importantly, crime appears to be more concentrated into spatially contiguous counting units when measured at larger temporal scales than at smaller temporal scales.

Discussion and Conclusion

There is a clear tradeoff between crime concentration and the dynamics of the corresponding crime patterns. The tradeoff is driven by the spatial and temporal scale of measurement. Crime appears to be more concentrated when measured using smaller spatial units and shorter time windows. The same percentage of crime is captured in a smaller percentage of land area when the flagged hotspots are small in spatial extent and brief in temporal duration. However, crime measured at finer scales is also more dynamic. A larger fraction of hotspots shift locations from one time period to the next when those locations are small in spatial extent and brief in temporal duration.

The tradeoff between concentration and dynamics is more than just an artifact of the scale of measurement. There is good reason to link the tradeoff to fundamental causal processes occurring at different scales. Short-term crime pattern dynamics reflect local stochastic fluctuations in situational conditions and criminal opportunities. This is where we expect random effects in offender decision making and crime opportunities to dominate measured patterns. For example, a collection of street segments may differ in the total number of parking spaces from one segment to the next, which may lead to differences in the average density of motor vehicle theft (Brantingham 2013). However, that one of these street segments *today* happens to have more late 1990s model Honda Civics parked there, and therefore more thefts *today*, may be entirely random. Tomorrow it may be another of the street segments in the set that has a higher density of such cars, or perhaps none of them does. Such random fluctuations in opportunity will be very visible if hotspots are measured at short spatial and temporal scales. Such variation is averaged out when measured at larger spatial and temporal scales. It is at these larger scales that mesoscopic routine activity processes take hold. The density of parking spaces regulates not only the relative volume of offenders and targets, but also how they move and mix. We expect these routine activity patterns to be more stable precisely because the density of parking spaces across street segments does not change on short time scales. Such processes will generate a clear signal when measuring motor vehicle theft hotspots over months or years.

Close inspection of Tables 1.1 and 1.3 suggests that our assumptions about the dynamic capacities of different crime types are inconsistent with observed patterns. We relied on general principles from routine activities theory to suggest that burglary would be the least spatially and temporally dynamic of crimes, robbery and assault the most dynamic, and motor vehicle theft somewhere in between. If we compare robbery and burglary in Los Angeles, robbery hotspots overlap to a much greater degree from one time period to the next compared with burglary hotspots (Table 1.1). For example, with 200 × 200 m cells sufficient to capture 25% of crime on a yearly basis, 47.2% of robbery hotspots remain stationary from one year to the next. Only 23% of the burglary hotspots remain in the same place from year to year. This general observation holds true for robbery and burglary across all time scales of observation. The pattern also holds true for robbery and burglary in Chicago for all time scales save the shortest time window (Table 1.3). It would seem that robbery hotspots are less dynamic than burglary hotspots in spite of the potential mobility of both offenders and victims in the case of robbery. The patterns are somewhat more complex for assault and motor vehicle theft (Table 1.1). Assault and motor vehicle theft hotspots are more dynamic than burglary hotspots in Los Angeles for longer time scales of a year or more, contrary to our initial assumptions, but more dynamic at shorter time scales, consistent with our assumptions. In Chicago, assault hotspots are less dynamic and motor vehicle thefts more dynamic compared to burglary hotspots across all time scales. These results also show that there are potential regional differences in relative hotspot dynamics among different crime types.

Nevertheless, the concentration-dynamics tradeoff observed in both Los Angeles and Chicago is very regular, or law-like, in its behavior. A candidate law-like statement is $PAI*O = K$. Here PAI is the predictive accuracy index and O is the percentage overlap in hotspot locations for crime patterns measured at a given spatial and temporal scale. Recall that PAI is the percentage of predicted crime C divided by the percentage of area covered by predictions A. Here we equate the area covered by predictions with the area covered by flagged hotspots, making PAI retrospective rather than prospective. PAI is thus an index of crime concentration. For the aforementioned equation to be law-like in its behavior we want K to be a constant for all temporal and spatial scales. For the target levels of crime considered previously, the equation becomes $C*O/A = K$, with $C = 25\%$ or 50%. This form of the equation clearly shows that the percentage overlap in hotspots between two adjacent time windows O must increase proportionally with A for K to be a constant. The constant of proportionality linking hotspot overlap to area flagged as hotspots is K/C.

Figure 1.6 shows values of K plotted against the time window for crime hot spotting for all four crime types considered here. For K to be a constant for a given crime type, we would expect the slope of the curve relating K to the time window for crime hot spotting in Figure 1.6 to be zero. In both Los Angeles and Chicago, computed slopes for these curves are not significantly different from zero for burglary (Los Angeles: $p = 0.158$; Chicago: $p = 0.158$) and motor vehicle theft (Los Angeles: $p = 0.576$; Chicago: $p = 0.809$). In other words, K is a constant estimated by the intercept of the regression equation (Figure 1.6). In Los Angeles, the computed slope is also not significantly different from zero for assault ($p = 0.186$), but is marginally different from zero for robberies ($p = 0.053$). This indicates law-like behavior for assaults in Los Angeles, but not necessarily for robberies. In Chicago, the computed slope is significantly different from zero for both assaults ($p = 0.005$) and robberies ($p = 0.002$). Thus, for five out of eight examined crime types, the tradeoff between

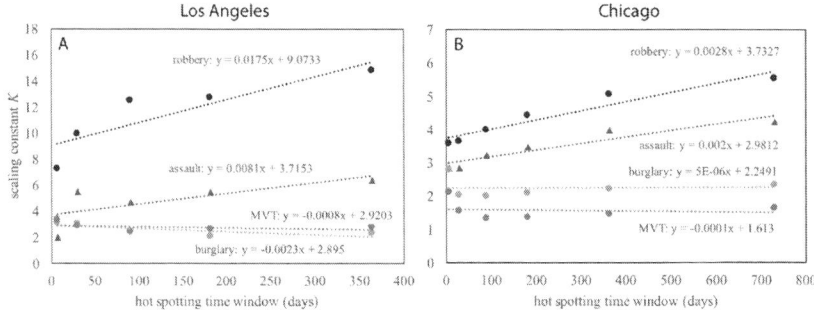

Figure 1.6 Law-like behavior in the concentration-dynamics tradeoff. Shown is the value of the scaling constant K against the hot spotting time window. A. Los Angeles crime types. B. Chicago crime types.

concentration and dynamics appears to be constant over a range of temporal scales. Whether this is truly law-like behavior will require more theoretical and empirical investigation, focusing not only on more geographic settings, but also on the full combinatorial range of spatial and temporal scales.

The concentration-dynamics tradeoff presents some practical challenges beyond the theoretical ones mentioned earlier. The tradeoff is an inherent challenge for policing and crime prevention at a given focal scale. It seems reasonable to suggest that the more concentrated crime is in an environment the greater the potential impact of directed police patrol on crime given limited policing resources (Sherman and Weisburd 1995; Weisburd 2015). Since crime is demonstrably more concentrated when measured at finer spatial and temporal scales, a clear recommendation is that place-based policing should be focused at such micro-geographic *and* micro-temporal scales. For example, 25% of assaults in Los Angeles are successfully captured by flagging just 0.1% of the total land area on a weekly basis with 200 × 200 m grid cells (Table 1.1). Policing such a small fraction of the city may have an outsized impact on the problem. However, focusing at such small scales also necessitates that place-based policing be dynamic. To consistently capture 25% of assaults each week, 99.2% of those locations must also change each week. If, however, we determine hotspot cells every month rather than every seven days, then we must double the number of cells to 0.2% of the city to capture the same 25% of crime. In other words, failing to adjust micro-geographic hotspots in sufficiently dynamic fashion would either necessitate a doubling of police resources to cover the increased number of hotspots, or reduce the amount of crime targeted by place-based policing as crime concentration is necessarily lower if we hold constant a fixed number of flagged hotspots. Assuming that the same policing tactic has equal effects across different places, the simple difference in exposure arising from insufficiently dynamic hot spotting would be expected to produce less crime prevention.

The assumption of equal effects of policing and crime prevention efforts across space is of course dangerous (Cousineau 1973; Groff et al. 2015). Efforts to build community trust, for example, may find great success in some places and fail in others (Tyler 2005). Moreover, there is still considerable uncertainty about the comparative effects of different tactics in and of themselves (see Groff et al. 2015). It seems plausible that different policing and crime prevention tactics also have effects that operate at different spatial and temporal scales. We expect that policing and crime prevention strategies targeting places and times proximal to the criminal event will mainly have local, short-term effects. Strategies targeting places and times distal to the criminal event may primarily drive broader, long-term changes.

Consider, for example, a city in which bars and nightclubs are widely dispersed across the urban landscape. Knowing that a range of criminal and nuisance behavior often follows last call, police might choose to have a physical presence at some of those bars at closing time, especially on Friday nights. The presence of police exactly at closing time may go a long way toward disrupting the opportunity for robberies, assaults, drug deals, vandalism, and public disorder (Berkley and Thayer 2000). Offenders and victims are already in contact with one another in a setting ripe for problems. Police simply prevent some types of interactions from occurring in spite of the existing conditions. However, the impact of such proximate interventions is limited to the bars targeted and likely dissipates soon after the police leave (Cohen et al. 2003; Koper 1995). By contrast, better training of place managers such as bartenders for all of the city's bars may also reduce crime and disorder rates (Sampson et al. 2010). Here small nudges to the routine activities of bar patrons by well-trained bartenders tweak the probabilities that victims and offenders will mix as well as the conditions under which that mixing occurs. In the same way that you can only identify a subtly biased coin after a large number of coin flips, small probabilistic shifts in routine activities will only amount to real crime reduction over larger areas and over longer time horizons. Strategies that aim to change the physical environment or core features of culture and social organization may operate at even longer temporal horizons. Changing tax incentives to encourage the development of balanced-use entertainment districts may take years to effect change (Berkley and Thayer 2000), with a correspondingly long time horizon for effects on crime and disorder. Programs designed to alter risk preferences among youth, for example, smoking or alcohol consumption, may only yield results over decades and then only at the spatial scale of whole populations (Ng et al. 2014).

A reasonable implication is that policing and crime prevention activities may benefit from adopting an analytical scale and dynamic capability appropriate to the behavioral processes targeted by deterrence or prevention programs

(Greenberg et al. 1981). In general, policing and crime prevention tactics with known or expected hyper-local and short-term effects are best supported by analytics focused on very small-scale geographic targets. This is what is advocated by Weisburd (2015) and others (e.g., Groff et al. 2015; Wyant et al. 2012). But the evidence here suggests that such a small-scale focus should also be dynamic to approach optimal effectiveness. Indeed, fighting crime on short time scales may require dynamic prediction (Mohler et al. 2015; Mohler et al. 2011). By contrast, those policing strategies known or expected to have effects that operate over larger geographic areas and longer time horizons may benefit most from analytics that encompass larger geographic spaces and are static over time. In other words, fighting crime on long time scales requires stationary pattern characterization. Aggregating in larger units averages over spatial and temporal heterogeneity in the system (Cousineau 1973). Policing and crime prevention tactics paired with analytics that are suboptimal with respect to the scale and dynamics of the underlying behavior may therefore also perform suboptimally. Though recent research seems to argue that micro-geographic units are superior to other scales, the present work suggests that this is only true for policing tactics and crime processes operating at such a micro-geographic scale. Further research is required to assess how scale matching might be put to best effect in understanding not only the dynamics of crime, but also how best to attack such problems.

References

Andresen, Martin A., and Nicolas Malleson. 2011. "Testing the Stability of Crime Patterns: Implications for Theory and Policy." *Journal of Research in Crime and Delinquency* 48(1): 58–82.

Berkley, Blair J., and John R. Thayer. 2000. "Policing Entertainment Districts." *Policing: An International Journal of Police Strategies & Management* 23(4): 466–491.

Bowers, Kate J., Shane D. Johnson, and Ken Pease. 2004. "Prospective Hot-Spotting the Future of Crime Mapping?" *British Journal of Criminology* 44(5): 641–658.

Brantingham, Patricia L., Paul Jeffrey Brantingham, Mona Vajihollahi, and Kathryn Wuschke. 2009. "Crime Analysis at Multiple Scales of Aggregation: A Topological Approach." Pp. 87–107 in David Weisburd, Wim Bernasco, and Gerben J. N. Bruinsma (eds.), *Putting Crime in Its Place: Units of Analysis in Geographic Criminology*. New York, NY: Springer New York.

Brantingham, Paul Jeffrey. 2013. "Prey Selection among Los Angeles Car Thieves." *Crime Science* 2(1): 1–11.

Brantingham, Paul Jeffrey, and Patricia L. Brantingham. 1978. "A Theoretical Model of Crime Site Selection." Pp. 105–118 in Marvin Krohn and Ronald L. Akers (eds.), *Theoretical Perspectives on Crime and Criminal Justice*. Beverly Hills, CA: Sage.

Brantingham, Paul Jeffrey, and Patricia L. Brantingham. 1981. *Environmental Criminology*. Beverly Hills, CA: Sage.

Brantingham, Paul Jeffrey, Delmar A. Dyreson, and Patricia L. Brantingham. 1976. "Crime Seen Through a Cone of Resolution." *American Behavioral Scientist* 20(2): 261–273.

Chainey, Spencer, Lisa Thompson, and Sebastian Uhlig. 2008. "The Utility of Hotspot Mapping for Predicting Spatial Patterns of Crime." *Security Journal* 21(1–2): 4–28.

Cohen, Jacqueline, Wilpen Gorr, and Piyusha Singh. 2003. "Estimating Intervention Effects in Varying Risk Settings: Do Police Raids Reduce Illegal Drug Dealing at Nuisance Bars." *Criminology* 41: 257.

Cousineau, Douglas F. 1973. "A Critique of the Ecological Approach to the Study of Deterrence." *Social Science Quarterly* 54(1): 152–158.

Davies, Toby P., and Steven R. Bishop. 2013. "Modelling Patterns of Burglary on Street Networks." *Crime Science* 2(1): 1–14.

Eck, John E., and David L. Weisburd. 1995. "Crime Places in Crime Theory." Pp. 1–34 in John E. Eck and David L. Weisburd (eds.), *Crime and Place: Crime Prevention Studies Volume 4*. Monsey, NY: Criminal Justice Press.

Gorr, Wilpen L., and Yong Jei Lee. 2015. "Early Warning System for Temporary Crime Hot Spots." *Journal of Quantitative Criminology* 31(1): 25–47.

Greenberg, David F., Ronald C. Kessler, and Charles H. Logan. 1981. "Aggregation Bias in Deterrence Research: An Empirical Analysis." *Journal of Research in Crime and Delinquency* 18(1): 128–137.

Groff, Elizabeth R., Jerry H. Ratcliffe, Cory P. Haberman, Evan T. Sorg, Nola M. Joyce, and Ralph B. Taylor. 2015. "Does What Police Do at Hot Spots Matter? The Philadelphia Policing Tactics Experiment." *Criminology* 53(1): 23–53.

Johnson, Shane D., Steven P. Lab, and Kate J. Bowers. 2008. "Stable and Fluid Hotspots of Crime: Differentiation and Identification." *Built Environment (1978–)* 34(1): 32–45.

Koper, Christopher S. 1995. "Just Enough Police Presence: Reducing Crime and Disorderly Behavior by Optimizing Patrol Time in Crime Hot Spots." *Justice Quarterly* 12(4): 649–672.

Maltz, Michael, Andrew C. Gordon, and Warren Friedman. 1990. *Mapping Crime in Its Community Setting: Event Geography Analysis*. New York, NY: Springer New York.

Mohler, George, Martin B. Short, Paul Jeffrey Brantingham, Frederic Paik Schoenberg, and George E. Tita. 2011. "Self-Exciting Point Process Modeling of Crime." *Journal of the American Statistical Association* 106: 100–108.

Mohler, George, Martin B. Short, Sean Malinowski, Mark Johnson, George E. Tita, Andrea L. Bertozzi, and P. Jeffrey Brantingham. 2015. "Randomized Controlled Field Trials of Predictive Policing." *Journal of the American Statistical Association* 110(512): 1399–1411.

Ng, Marie, Michael K. Freeman, Thomas D. Fleming, Margaret Robinson, Laura Dwyer-Lindgren, Blake Thomson, Alexander Wollum, Ella Sanman, Sarah Wulf, Alan D. Lopez, Christopher J. L. Murray, and Gakidou Emmanuela. 2014. "Smoking Prevalence and Cigarette Consumption in 187 Countries, 1980–2012." *JAMA* 311(2): 183–192.

Pebley, Anne R., and Narayan Sastry. 2009. "Our Place: Perceived Neighborhood Size and Names in Los Angeles." Los Angeles, CA: California Center for Population Research, University of California.

Sampson, Rana, John E. Eck, and Jessica Dunham. 2010. "Super Controllers and Crime Prevention: A Routine Activity Explanation of Crime Prevention Success and Failure." *Security Journal* 23(1): 37–51.

Sherman, Lawrence W., Patrick R. Gartin, and Michael E. Buerger. 1989. "Hot Spots of Predatory Crime: Routine Activities and the Criminology of Place." *Criminology* 27: 27–56.

Sherman, Lawrence W., and David Weisburd. 1995. "General Deterrent Effects of Police Patrol in Crime 'Hot Spots': A Randomized, Controlled Trial." *Justice Quarterly* 12(4): 625–648.

Short, Martin B., Paul Jeffrey Brantingham, Andrea L. Bertozzi, and George E. Tita. 2010. "Dissipation and Displacement of Hotspots in Reaction-Diffusion Models of Crime." *Proceedings of the National Academy of Sciences* 107(9): 3961.

Short, Martin B., Maria R. D'Orsogna, Paul Jeffrey Brantingham, and George E. Tita. 2009. "Measuring and Modeling Repeat and Near-Repeat Burglary Effects." *Journal of Quantitative Criminology* 25: 325–339.

Steenbeek, Wouter, and David Weisburd. 2016. "Where the Action Is in Crime? An Examination of Variability of Crime Across Different Spatial Units in The Hague, 2001–2009." *Journal of Quantitative Criminology* 32(3): 449–469.

Telep, Cody W., Renée J. Mitchell, and David Weisburd. 2014. "How Much Time Should the Police Spend at Crime Hot Spots? Answers from a Police Agency Directed Randomized Field Trial in Sacramento, California." *Justice Quarterly* 31: 905–933.

Tita, George, and Elizabeth Griffiths. 2005. "Traveling to Violence: The Case for a Mobility-Based Spatial Typology of Homicide." *Journal of Research in Crime and Delinquency* 42(3): 275–308.

Townsley, Michael. 2008. "Visualising Space Time Patterns in Crime: The Hotspot Plot." *Crime Patterns and Analysis* 1(1): 61–74.

Tyler, Tom R. 2005. "Policing in Black and White: Ethnic Group Differences in Trust and Confidence in the Police." *Police Quarterly* 8(3): 322–342.

Wang, Tong, Cynthia Rudin, Daniel Wagner, and Rich Sevieri. 2013. "Learning to Detect Patterns of Crime." Pp. 515–530 in Hendrik Blockeel, Kristian Kersting, Siegfried Nijssen, and Filip Železný (eds.), *Machine Learning and Knowledge Discovery in Databases*. Berlin: Springer, Berlin, Heidelberg.

Wang, Xiaofeng, and Donald E. Brown. 2012. "The Spatio-Temporal Modeling for Criminal Incidents." *Security Informatics* 1(1): 1–17.

Wang, Xiaofeng, Matthew S. Gerber, and Donald E. Brown. 2012. "Automatic Crime Prediction Using Events Extracted from Twitter Posts." Pp. 231–238 in Shanchieh Jay Yang, Ariel M. Greenberg, and Mica Endsley (eds.), *Social Computing, Behavioral-Cultural Modeling and Prediction*. Berlin: Springer, Berlin, Heidelberg.

Weisburd, David. 2015. "The Law of Crime Concentration and the Criminology of Place." *Criminology* 53(2): 133–157.

Weisburd, David, Shawn Bushway, Cynthia Lum, and Sue-Ming Yang. 2004. "Trajectories of Crime at Places: A Longitudinal Study of Street Segments in the City of Seattle." *Criminology* 42(2): 283–322.

Weisburd, David, Elizabeth R. Groff, and Sue-Ming Yang. 2012. *The Criminology of Place: Street Segments and Our Understanding of the Crime Problem*. Oxford: Oxford University Press.

Weisburd, David, Cody W. Telep, Breanne Cave, Kate Bowers, John E. Eck, Gerben Bruinsma, Charlotte Gill, Elizabeth Groff, Julie Hibdon, and Joshua C Hinkle. 2016. *Place Matters*. Cambridge: Cambridge University Press.

Wooldredge, John. 2002. "Examining the (Ir)relevance of Aggregation Bias for Multilevel Studies of Neighborhoods and Crime with an Exanple Comparing Census Tracts to Official Neighborhoods in Cincinnati." *Criminology* 40(3): 681–710.

Wyant, Brian R., Ralph B. Taylor, Jerry H. Ratcliffe, and Jennifer Wood. 2012. "Deterrence, Firearm Arrests, and Subsequent Shootings: A Micro-Level Spatio-Temporal Analysis." *Justice Quarterly* 29(4): 524–545.

2

Chronic *and* Temporary Crime Hot Spots

Wilpen Gorr and YongJei Lee

Introduction

The literature defines crime hot spots in terms of crime concentration. Indeed, Weisburd (2015) has proposed the *law of crime concentration at places*, which states that urban crimes concentrate in micro geospatial units, hot spots, within a narrow band of high percentages. For example, in large cities around 50% of crime occurs in only roughly 5% of a city's block-long street segments. This chapter adds a second dimension to the definition of crime hot spots, *duration* of high crime concentrations in micro geospatial places, leading to a spectrum of crime hot spots from (1) spatially random crimes (non-hot spots), to (2) temporary hot spots (one-time, infrequent, and regularly recurring), and to (3) chronic hot spots (Gorr and Lee 2015).

Chronic hot spots last for years and, with their steady stream of crimes, should have constant crime prevention programs by police such as directed patrols and problem-oriented policing on a daily basis. Recurring temporary hot spots have an on-and-off behavior, being hot for weeks or months, then cold for weeks or months, then hot again, and so forth. One-time and infrequent temporary hot spots are by definition less important than recurring temporary hot spots but may also be targets for crime prevention. Temporary hot spots should have dynamic crime prevention programs with allocations of police crime prevention resources, "on and off," matching hot spot behavior.

To be effective and efficient, temporary hot spots need prediction models that have acceptably low prediction errors. A prediction model forecasts future crime flare-ups in micro locations (emergence of hot spots) a short time, days or weeks, before they occur. Certain criminal behaviors in micro geospatial areas, namely, near-repeat crimes and the fact that crimes tend to harden over time, give rise to temporary hot spots and patterns in crime data that can be modeled and used to predict temporary hot spots with acceptable accuracy.

Given two kinds of hot spots, chronic and temporary, police need criteria to optimally deploy resources to one, the other, or both. While the hot spot literature has focused primarily on effectiveness of crime prevention (number of crimes prevented), it is *equity* of crime prevention that makes temporary hot spots, in combination with chronic hot spots, particularly valuable for hot spot programs. Allocating all available police crime prevention resources to a relatively small number of chronic hot spots, which remain fixed for a year or more, is simply unfair to the residents in the widely scattered locations with temporary hot spots.

The second section of this chapter reviews effectiveness and equity criteria applied to crime prevention at hot spots. The third section reviews chronic hot spots in terms of their theory, prediction models, police interventions, and crime prevention policies. The fourth section has a similar review of temporary hot spots. The final section includes a summary of the chapter and suggestions for future work.

Crime Hot Spot Criteria

The three major criteria for designing and evaluating public goods are effectiveness, equity, and efficiency (Culyer 2001). Effectiveness measures the degree to which policies provide the benefits they are supposed to achieve (Nagel 1986). Equity means that the persons or groups who need public goods get them at least at some minimal level (Culyer 2001). Efficiency is the degree to which total costs are minimized, as can be measured with benefit/cost ratios (Nagel 1986). The next two subsections cover effectiveness and equity measures for hot spot programs. Efficiency is not a major criterion for comparing chronic versus temporary hot spot programs because both types of programs use the same types of police interventions. Also, computer programs can make crime predictions and produce crime maps with hot spot locations for distribution to field officers who carry out crime prevention work, thereby reducing the extra costs of operating dynamic temporary hot spot programs.

Effectiveness

The primary measures for chronic and temporary hot spot effectiveness are the number of crimes exposed to crime prevention on input and the number prevented on output. In particular, input effectiveness is a function of the accuracy of hot spot prediction models, and output effectiveness is a function of both prediction accuracy and the effect size of police interventions in preventing crimes at hot spots. This section focuses on prediction accuracy, which has not had a great deal of attention in the literature, while only noting that a growing number of randomized field trials have demonstrated the effectiveness of hot spot policing on preventing crimes (e.g., Braga, Papachristos, and Hureau 2014).

Therefore, this chapter turns to the question of which prediction accuracy measures to use. There are three alternatives. The first is traditional forecast accuracy measures that use the mean or median error of numerical forecast of quantities, in this case the number of future crimes. Commonly used measures for demand forecasting in industry are the mean squared error, mean absolute error, and mean absolute percent error.

The second prediction accuracy measure is based on receiver operating characteristic (ROC) curves (Swets 1988). ROC analysis provides a well-developed set of measures and decision-making tools for predicting abnormal conditions, such as disease in a patient, given results of imprecise diagnostic tests. The corresponding problem in this chapter is predicting temporary hot spots, a kind of societal disease, with imprecise models. Given that hot spots make up only a small percentage of a city's area, they can be considered abnormal conditions.

The underlying ROC construct is the contingency table that tabulates prediction errors over a sample of cases: true positives, false positives, true negatives, and false negatives. In terms of disease prediction, true positives are patients for whom a diagnostic test predicted disease and the patients were later found to have the disease. False positives are patients predicted to have the disease but who did not have it. Likewise true negatives and false negatives are defined. True positives plus false negatives sum to all positives in a sample (e.g., all diseased patients or hot spots). False positives plus true negatives sum to all negatives in the sample (healthy individuals or non-hot spots). The true positive rate is a measure of benefits from prediction, the fraction of all positives predicted. The false positive rate is a measure of costs of predictions, the fraction of negatives that are falsely predicted as positives. The ROC curve plots the true positive rate on the vertical axis and the false positive rate on the horizontal axis. The curve is increasing but downward sloping between (0,0) and (1,1). The larger the area under an ROC curve, the more accurate the diagnostic test. Better than total area under the curve as a performance measure is partial area under the curve for false positive rates from 0 up to a maximum after which false positive costs are prohibitive (e.g., see Gorr and Schneider 2013).

Traditional forecast measures and ROC curves are for two different kinds of forecasting or prediction problems, and it is important to match measures to the correct problem. Consider two kinds of forecast models. The first is for usual conditions, such as demand for a manufactured good. In this case, a simple extrapolative time series model with time trend and seasonality is widely used in industry. The second kind of forecast model is for abnormal conditions, such as disease in a population or crime flare-ups at micro geospatial units in a city. One such model reviewed later in this chapter is a leading-indicator model. If leading-indicator crimes have flared up recently, chances are the target crimes of interest will flare up in the near future. Gorr (2009) showed that, for forecasting temporary hot spots in Pittsburgh, extrapolative methods are by far the most accurate using simple extrapolative models and traditional forecast measures, but that the leading-indicator model is by far the most accurate using ROC measures. The reason for this contradiction on accuracy is that traditional forecast error measures provide the wrong lens for exceptional conditions such as flare-up of crimes at a temporary hot spot. Traditional measures are applicable to "business as usual" where the mean of distributions is relevant. ROC, however, concerns the tails of behavior in populations, whether the populations be persons or geospatial units.

Therefore, we might conclude that partial area under the ROC curve is the favored accuracy measure for predicting hot spots. There is, however, one problem: ROC is not directly related to sizing crime hot spot programs (deciding how many hot spots to include). A hot spot program designer using ROC analysis would need to translate true positive and false positive rates into the number of hot spots that police are able to patrol with crime prevention dosages high enough to prevent crimes.

Much better and more easily related to hot spot program design is an effectiveness curve based on the Predictive Accuracy Index (PAI) of Chainey, Tompson, and Uhlig (2008):

$$PAI = (n/N)/(a/A)$$

Where
n = number of crimes in hot spots
N = number of crimes in total study area
a = area of hot spots
A = area of total study area

If crime were uniformly distributed over a city, then PAI = 1: we would expect 1% of land area to have 1% of the city's crime. If a certain 0.5% area chronic hot spot program exposes 10% of part 1 violent crimes (P1V: homicides, rapes, robberies, and aggravated assaults) to prevention, the corresponding PAI is 10/0.5 = 20. The PAI is interpreted as a crime concentration 20 times higher than random or uniform crime locations of the same area. PAI is unitless, and therefore allows comparisons across cities. The law of crime concentration finds generally a PAI of 50/5 = 10 for the hottest 5% area of cities.

To optimize a chronic (or temporary) hot spot program, one needs to rank order hot spots by PAI and then allocate high-enough dosages of crime prevention measures by police to hot spots in order by rank until resources are exhausted. A PAI *effectiveness curve* (Mohler 2014; Gorr and Lee 2015) is a chart of PAI values in rank order with the PAI numerator on the vertical axis and denominator on the horizontal axis. The PAI effectiveness curve is an increasing but downward sloping curve from (0,0) to (100,100), like the ROC curve, with a benefit of crime prevention (percentage of crimes treated with prevention) on the vertical axis and a cost of crime prevention (percentage area of a city under treatment) on the horizontal axis. The percentage area of a city under treatment is easily converted to percentage of street network length under treatment, which is easily converted to hours of demand per day of police time for patrol using average patrol speeds.

Figure 2.1 shows an example effectiveness curve for chronic hot spots in Pittsburgh, Pennsylvania (Gorr and Lee 2015). The data used to estimate the curve is from a time interval without hot spot programs in Pittsburgh (2004 through 2010) to match time periods for temporary hot spots in Figure 2.4 later in this chapter. The vertical axis is the predicted percentage of total P1V that could be exposed to crime prevention interventions at chronic hot spots, and

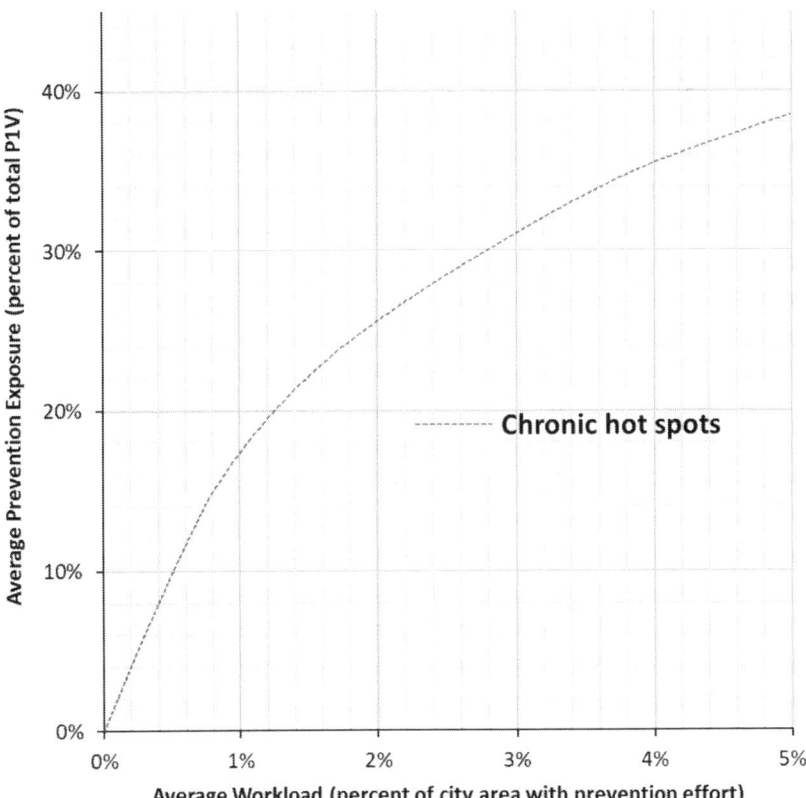

Figure 2.1 Effectiveness curve for part 1 violent crime (P1V) chronic hot spots in Pittsburgh: 2004 through 2010.

the horizontal axis is the corresponding average percentage of Pittsburgh's area with constant police interventions. (See Figure 2.3 and its discussion in the text later in this chapter to understand chronic hot spot prediction.)

Equity

How important are the crime prevention services of police in society? We believe that public safety, and especially crime prevention, is a primary good, like health and education, that is essential for individuals and families to flourish in all other endeavors and activities of life (see Culyer 2001 for this definition of primary goods). Hence the citizens of cities are particularly sensitive to distributional equity of crime prevention services by police, and hot spot programs had better be equitable.

Eck and Rosenbaum (1994) reviewed community-oriented policing programs in terms of effectiveness, efficiency, and equity. Their essay includes two forms of police equity. The first is that equity is obtained if police follow the rules as laid down in law and procedures, applying them uniformly across neighborhoods and groups of people. Following the long history of excessive police force against nonwhite citizens, for example, any crime prevention program must be implemented using this form of equity.

The second form of policing equity is in regard to the distribution of input police resources, that the distribution is in proportion to need across communities. To date, only Gorr and Lee (2015) have addressed equity of crime hot spot programs in regard to the distribution of resources. All other hot spot research has focused solely on effectiveness.

While certain measures exist that are designed to measure equity, such as the Gini Coefficient (Gini 1921) and Herfindahl index (Hirschman 1964), our efforts to date have not found such measures insightful for designing hot spot programs. Instead, maps of the urban footprint of chronic and temporary hot spots in programs and simple tabulations of areas receiving prevention services are currently the best and most persuasive means for assessing equity. Sample footprint maps and statistics are presented in the "Temporary Hot Spots" section of this chapter.

Chronic Hot Spots

Sherman (1995) defined crime hot spots as "small places in which the occurrence of crime is so frequent that it is highly predictable, at least over a one year period." Sherman and Weisburd (1995) ran a controlled experiment on "very small clusters of high-crime addresses" to show that adequately high dosages of police-provided crime prevention can prevent crimes. Many crime hot spot papers have appeared in the literature between then and now shedding much light on the nature of hot spots and effectiveness of crime prevention at hot spots (e.g., see Telep and Weisburd 2014).

Weisburd, Groff, and Yang (2014) labeled the hottest 1% of street segments "chronic hot spots" because they consistently had the highest crime concentrations over a 16-year period in Seattle and accounted for 23% of all crime incidents. Gorr and Lee (2015), using kernel density estimation (see the "Prediction" subsection later in this chapter), similarly found chronic hot spots in Pittsburgh for 1% of land area persisting over a 21-year period and accounting for 18% of predicted P1V.

In this chapter we define chronic hot spots as those with high-enough crime concentrations persisting continuously over time to merit a constant police prevention program, for example, daily targeted patrols and stops in high-enough dosages to prevent crime. As one increases the size of a hot spot program, in terms of percentage of a city's street network or area, chronic hot spots become larger or more numerous with added areas approaching temporary hot spots in behavior (Figure 2.6 later in this chapter illustrates this behavior). In Gorr and Lee (2015), after the first 1% area chronic hot spots are assigned to a program, increasing the size of the program beyond 1% is more effective using temporary hot spots (Figure 2.4 later in this chapter illustrates this behavior).

Figure 2.2 is a sample chronic hot spot map, showing predicted hot spots with 1% of the areas of Pittsburgh. Also shown in the map are areas zoned

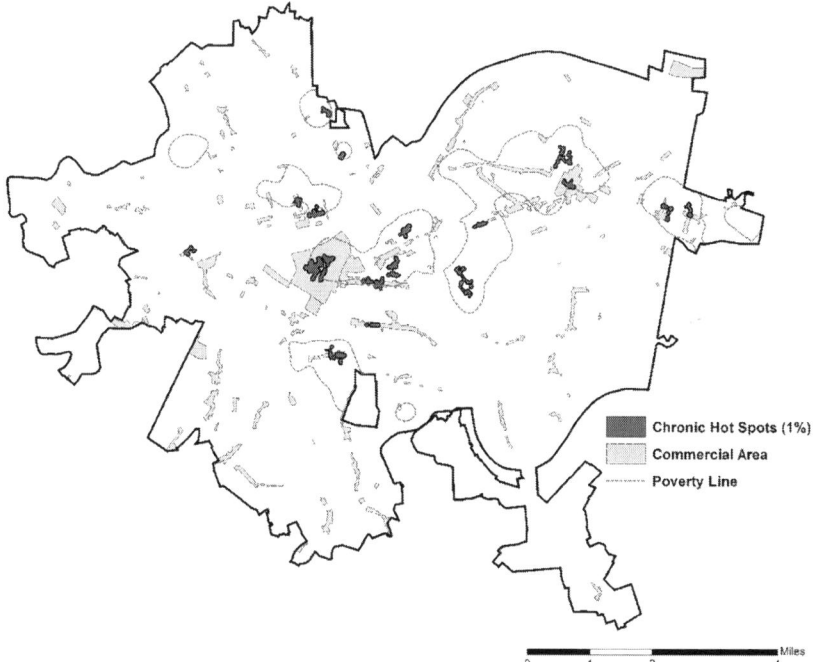

Figure 2.2 1% area chronic hot spot map of Pittsburgh with poverty and commercial areas shown: for 2009 estimated using 2006–2008 crime data.

commercial, and areas with high levels of poverty (some commercial areas are not visible because they are covered by hot spots, but nearly every chronic hot spot is in a commercial area, and most are also in poverty areas).

Note that as currently configured, police in the U.S. spend much of their time responding to 911 calls, leaving a limited amount of discretionary time for prevention work, around an hour per unit and shift. This limitation translates to small hot spot programs of at most a few percentage of a city's street network or area. For example, two recent field trials for crime hot spots (Mohler et al. 2015; Barak, Weinborn, and Sherman 2016) had hot spot programs of about 1% area.

Theory

There is a large and growing literature on the criminality of places. The review here provides only a brief outline of two major theories of that literature, social disorganization theory and opportunities for crime theory.

Social disorganization theory (e.g., Kubrin and Weitzer 2003; Shaw and McKay 1942) is based on the contribution of certain kinds of places on the development of criminals. It states that ecological conditions within certain neighborhoods, such as low educational attainment, high unemployment, and deteriorating housing stock, decrease the ability of communities to control the behavior of people in public places, thus leading to delinquency and crime. This theory was first advanced by Shaw and McKay (1942) when they found that high rates of delinquency persisted in certain inner-city Chicago neighborhoods despite changes in racial and ethnic makeups of those neighborhoods over long periods of time. The occurrence of chronic hot spots within Figure 2.2's poverty areas is predicted by social disorganization theory. The poverty areas are defined from an index that equally weights populations that have low educational attainment, that have female-headed households, that have high levels of unemployment, and that are below the poverty income level.

Theories on opportunities for crime—rational choice, routine activity theory, and crime pattern theory—use data on criminal events in micro-area locations such as addresses, buildings, and block faces to explain location-based crime (e.g., see Eck and Weisburd 1995). Rational choice theory (e.g., see Cornish and Clarke 1986) assumes that criminals are rational actors who make decisions to commit crimes on a cost-benefit basis. Routine activities theory (Cohen and Felson 1979) further states that the routine activities of life generate crime events where and when motivated offenders meet accessible targets under conditions of low guardianship. Crime pattern theory (Brantingham and Brantingham 1993) combines rational choice and routine activities to explain the distribution of crime across space. The prevalence of chronic hot spots in and around commercial areas of Figure 2.2 is predicted by these theories. Criminals have acceptable reasons, as do citizens, to be in and around commercial areas; whereas informal guardianship provided by vigilant residents of residential areas detects strangers and suspicious behavior. Shoppers in commercial areas have cars parked in parking lots with goods in them, have money and goods on their persons, and sometimes may have to be in places where there is low guardianship such as parking lots. Commercial areas in poor neighborhoods tend to have especially low guardianship.

Prediction

The law of crime concentration at places is stated in terms of criminal behavior, for example, that in large cities about 50% of crime occurs in 5% of its street network. For police to run a crime prevention program at crime hot spots, however, it is necessary to *predict* the boundaries or locations of crime hot spots. Prediction has errors, so we can expect less than 50% of crime to occur in the *predicted* 5% of the street network or area that comprises hot spots.

Prediction is relatively easy with chronic hot spots. One tabulates the number of target crimes for prevention by block-long street segment (block face) over a recent multi-year sample of data and then uses the desired percentage of street segments with the highest crime counts as future hot spots. Crimes that have street intersections as incident locations (e.g., Grant St and Forbes Ave), however, are not easily included in such tabulations. The question is, which of the four street segments making up the intersection is attributed to the crime? One approach is simply to ignore crimes at intersections and not include them in analysis, but that can lead to errors in ranking street segments for designation as hot spots. For example, more than 25% of part 1 violent crimes in Pittsburgh have intersection locations. Another approach is to allocate 0.25 to tabulations for each intersecting street of such a crime.

A second prediction method is based on a grid system for a city under study. For example, Mohler et al. (2015) use square grids 500 feet on a side, on the order of a city block. For prediction, one simply tabulates the number of target crimes per cell for a recent multi-year data sample. An advantage of this approach over street segments is that crimes at intersections are easily counted. A disadvantage is that generally some street segments cross boundaries of cells, thereby possibly splitting a block-face hot spot between two adjacent cells (and diluting the concentration of the hot spot). City blocks are poor representations of hot spots because they split every street segment in half, likely diluting all hot spots.

Kernel density estimation (KDE) is a third approach to predicting chronic hot spots, and one that has been found to be more accurate for crime hot spot prediction than others in one study (Chainey et al. 2008). It accounts for spatial errors in location (e.g., from geocoding or using street intersections as locations) and for sampling errors of events (e.g., that future events may not occur exactly where historical events occurred but will be close by).

Most commonly, the kernel of KDE is a bell-shaped surface with unit area that is centered over each event's location. The kernel spreads out a crime event from a point to the area of the kernel's footprint. The KDE surface is simply the sum of kernels for all events, including events at intersections. The result is a smooth concentration surface (e.g., with events per square mile) with peaks and valleys where each incident has been spread out according to a parameter called the search radius or bandwidth of the kernel. The larger the search radius, the flatter the peaks and the shallower the valleys. Regardless of the search radius selected, KDE preserves the original number of events smoothed. If one integrates any KDE surface over the area of estimation (e.g., a city), one gets back the input number of incidents. Integration can be easily accomplished by multiplying the average event density of the KDE surface (provided as a statistic by ArcGIS 10.3) by the area of the city.

Because crime hot spots are micro locations on the order of a block-long street segment, KDE estimates for crime hot spots should have a search radius of about the average block length of commercial and residential areas of a city. This parameterization leads to highly peaked surfaces that can run the length of a commercial corridor or include a portion of a city's central business district. To obtain hot spot boundaries from a KDE surface, one chooses a crime concentration level and obtains corresponding contours that define the boundaries as seen in Figure 2.2. Gorr and Lee (2015) remove KDE hot spots that do not attain a threshold number of target crimes per month (average of one per month), thereby eliminating many small-size artifact areas.

Figure 2.3 shows the time trend of estimated and predicted chronic hot spot crimes for the 1% area, the hottest hot spots in Pittsburgh (estimated using KDE) over ten years. The height of each bar represents the total number of serious violent crimes per year as estimated using KDE applied to that year's data. Those values are indicative of criminal behavior in chronic hot spots. There was a downward trend in crime density over the period shown with a reduction of about a third. If we had extended the chart backward to 1990, there would have been a steady decline over the entire period of more than 50% for the hottest 1% area chronic hot spots, accompanied by an increasing number of temporary hot spots (Gorr and Lee 2012).

To predict criminal behavior for the 1% hottest chronic hot spots for crime prevention, we estimated a kernel density map from the three years' data prior to each bar's year and assumed that the corresponding 1% boundary persisted in the following year as a prediction. The darkly shaded portion of each bar is the resulting number of predicted serious crimes that then occurred within the predicted chronic hot spot boundaries. On average 74% of the estimated target crimes of a year were captured by predictions. Thus while chronic hot spots are mainly fixed for years, their boundaries vary to some extent from year to year. These hot spots are not single street segments, but areas such as business districts and corridors made up of small subsets of street networks in cities.

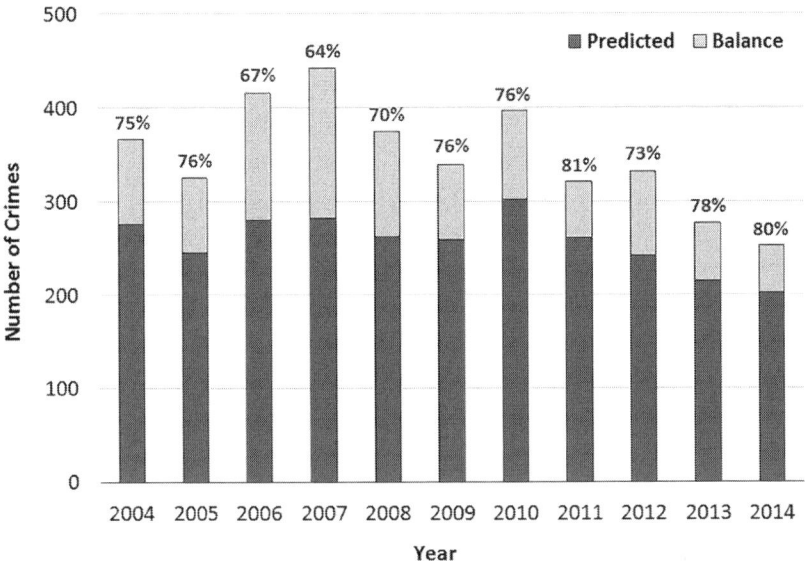

Figure 2.3 Time trend of estimated and predicted crimes for the 1% hottest chronic hot spots in Pittsburgh.

Corresponding to 50% estimated crime for the hottest 5% area of a city, we can thus expect that about 0.74*50% = 38% of crime can be predicted for the 5% hottest area of a city. Prediction error is the likely explanation for Figure 2.1 earlier in the chapter showing that 38% of Pittsburgh's serious violent crimes fall within 5% of *predicted* hot spots, instead of 50%. Note that the 95% prediction error for the darkly shaded predicted bars in Figure 2.3 is about plus or minus 5% of the number of predicted crimes.

Police Interventions

The two main police interventions for crime hot spots are (1) frequent, randomly timed directed patrols and (2) problem-oriented policing. For directed patrols, generally officers are given the locations of hot spots and instructed to patrol them as often as possible, in their cars and on foot. Exactly what to do while on patrol is left to the discretion of the officers.

Starting with Sherman and Weisburd (1995) a major issue has been designing patrol-based hot spot programs with a sufficiently high dosage of police presence in hot spots to cause crime prevention. Koper (1995), Telep et al. (2014), and Barak et al. (2016) among others have found short visit times per hot spot, 15 minutes, to be effective. Koper (1995) is well known for his experiment to estimate the residual deterrence of patrol after officers leave a hot spot, with 14 to 15 minute patrols providing the maximum residual deterrence. The hot spot design by Telep et al. (2014) called for 15 minute patrols every two hours from 9:00 AM until 1:00 AM, a total of eight patrols per hot spot and day (although the actual number of patrols was less). Officers were encouraged to get out of their cars while patrolling hot spots. Barak et al. (2016) found that three foot patrols in each hot spot per day, during high-crime times of day, reduced crime in treatment areas by 64.8% over control areas. While the program had a design duration of 15 minutes per hot spot, the average was only eight minutes.

Problem-oriented policing (or POP, Goldstein 1979, 1990) attempts to identify underlying problems causing crime and disorder and to design responses to prevent crimes. Eck and Spelman (1987) developed the SARA model for implementing POP, which has four steps: scanning for problems, analysis of problems, development and implementation of responses, and assessment of results. Numerous studies have evaluated POP applied to hot spots (e.g., see Taylor, Koper, and Woods 2011), finding reductions of some forms of crime and disorder, and mixed results for violent crimes. POP promises to yield medium- or long-term solutions for crime problems, but POP is costly in terms of crime analyst and field officer time to carry out the SARA process. For example, in the Jacksonville, Florida hot spot experiment using POP, officers spent an average of 95 hours per week per hot spot in addition to time spent by four crime analysts who worked full time supporting POP. If resulting crime prevention has a long-enough duration in hot spots, then such expenditures would be worthwhile and superior perhaps to directed patrols. Needed are benefit/cost studies to compare the efficiencies of the two approaches.

Police Policy

In absence of a temporary hot spot program, the public policy recommendation for a chronic hot spot program is to allocate some portion or all of field officers' discretionary time to directed hot spot patrol using an effectiveness curve such as in Figure 2.1 for design of the program. Given the somewhat dynamic behavior of even chronic hot spots, as seen in Figure 2.3, we recommend that chronic hot spots be estimated and predicted at least annually.

If there are more worthwhile chronic hot spots than police resources allow for crime prevention, then we suggest rotating hot spots for treatment, using random selection. Rotation serves two purposes. First, it provides a program with higher equity than a program with fixed hot spots. Second, it allows for continuous evaluation of effectiveness in preventing crimes, using untreated hot spots as controls.

Temporary Hot Spots

While temporary hot spots exist, and one can find them in historical data, to prevent crimes at temporary hot spots it is necessary to predict their occurrence or to predict their persistence after being detected. Then patrols can be directed to temporary hot spots to prevent crimes. In addition it is necessary to have rules to stop directed patrols at hot spots. Much of this section is concerned with crime hot spot prediction methods and their application to crime prevention.

Theory

Two criminological theories are the basis for predicting temporary hot spots: (1) crimes tend to harden from public disorder soft crimes to serious hard crimes in the same area, and (2) after a first crime of a certain type additional crimes of the same type tend to occur nearby (i.e., they are "near-repeat" crimes). Both of these types of criminal behavior yield data and patterns for building predictive models.

Broken windows theory suggests that crime hardens over time as neighborhoods decay, and can occur over a variety of time-scales including short time intervals (Doran and Burgess 2012, p. 13). Also supporting the notion that crime hardens in the short term is that criminals tend to be generalists and commit a wide range of disorder and other lesser crime types, and occasionally a serious crime (Blumstein, Cohen, and Farrington 1988; Piquero 2000; DeLisi 2001). Consider the case of a newly active criminal or group of criminals (e.g., gang members). Public disorder crimes are on the order of ten times more prevalent than serious crimes, so even if chance alone were allocating crime types, lesser crimes would be likely to lead to serious crimes (Gorr 2009). Additionally, the distance to crime literature (e.g., Rengert, Piquero, and Jones 1999; Bernasco 2010) supports formation of temporary hot spots. This literature finds that criminals tend to commit crimes near their residences, suggesting that if there is a new criminal element in a neighborhood, we can expect to have a variety of crime types occurring in a relatively small area.

Morgan (2001), Townsley, Ross, and Janet (2003), Johnson and Bowers (2004a, 2004b), Mohler, Short, Brantingham, Schoenberg, and Tita (2011), and others studied near-repeat burglaries, namely, that residences near an initial burglary are likely to be targeted for burglaries soon after the initial burglary. Burglars, car thieves, and other criminals are "creatures of habit" (Phillips and Lee 2009) who have favorite crime hunting grounds and return to locations where they had earlier successes. In part this behavior is reflected in the distance to crime literature in that criminals generally commit crimes near to where they live, and there may only be a limited number of good targets in areas near to home. Among other causes of near-repeat crimes is retaliation among criminals. For example, Ratcliffe and Rengert (2008) found near-repeat behavior in shootings, likely due to retaliation for earlier gang shootings (Cohen and Tita 1999; Tita and Ridgeway 2007).

Gorr and Lee (2015) introduced a theory on the geography of chronic and temporary hot spots, that chronic hot spots tend to be in large commercial areas and corridors, while temporary hot spots are widely scattered including at the edges of chronic hot spots, but mostly in outlying small commercial and residential areas. Chronic hot spots are optimal locations for crimes, in terms of routine activities, with a steady stream of crimes. Temporary hot spots have conditions less optimal than those of chronic hot spots, but are still favorable with intermittent high crime densities.

Clearly a goal of city leaders is to have crime-free and vibrant commercial areas, so crime prevention is certainly desirable in chronic hot spots. Gorr and Lee (2015), however, speculated that fear of crime is much higher in temporary hot spots than in chronic hot spots. Citizens expect high crime concentrations in chronic hot spots and therefore can take precautions to prevent being victimized (e.g., parking cars in safe parking lots, avoiding walking alone). Residents in and around temporary hot spots, in contrast, do not expect high crime concentrations on a steady basis or at all. Informal communication networks quickly spread information about crimes in neighborhoods (Skogan 1986) so that residents become fearful for themselves and their children when crimes occur near to where they live.

Prediction

Olligschlaeger (1997a, 1997b) was the first researcher to build and promote short-term crime forecasting models that led to the field of predictive policing. He developed a leading-indicator crime forecast model that included a lagged dependent variable, temporally and spatially lagged leading-indicator variables, and control variables with data aggregated to uniform grid cells and with models estimated by regression, Poisson, Tobit, and neural network models. His model specification eclipses all crime predictive modeling that has occurred since his seminal work. With a leading-indicator model, if a small spatial cluster of leading-indicator crimes (selected lesser crimes and emergency calls for service) has flared up recently, then the same area is likely to have a flare-up of serious crimes in the near future. Cohen, Gorr, and Olligschlaeger (2007) extensively tested the crime leading-indicator model. The leading-indicator model predicts temporary hot spots, either entirely new or of the recurring nature, *before* a target crime occurs.

Neill and Gorr (2007) applied a spatial scan statistic to the leading-indicator model in which early detection of leading-indicator space-time clusters predicts target crime clusters. Instead of using fixed cells for data aggregation, the spatial scan statistic aggregates grid cells to build a custom area for each hot spot by searching all relevant aggregations.

From a time series forecasting perspective, near-repeat prediction methodology is similar to an autoregressive, univariate model consisting of the dependent variable (e.g., burglaries) and time-lagged dependent variables (also burglaries) as independent variables but with the extension of weights decaying with distance as well as time. Near-repeat prediction is an example of early detection (a target crime has already occurred and is known to police) with a prediction of persistence (additional crimes of the same type in nearby locations in the near future). Bowers, Johnson, and Pease (2004) developed a simple method, prospective hot-spotting, for near-repeat predictions. Mohler et al. (2011) introduced a non-parametric, self-exciting point process model for burglaries with localized background and aftershock events, taken from seismic prediction known as Epidemic Type Aftershock-Sequences (ETAS) modeling. This model simultaneously estimates both chronic and temporary hot spots as short-term dynamic and long-term static crime densities using exponential smoothing extended to time and space decay of weights for past crime points, and with smoothing parameters optimally estimated. Mohler (2014) extended the near-repeat ETAS model with a parametric (Gaussian) version including leading-indicator variables, but apparently the randomized field trials conducted by Mohler et al. (2015) applied an ETAS model without leading indicators.

Gorr and Lee (2015) designed a simple detection-based crime prediction system using grid cells for P1V crime. To become a candidate for a new deployment of police crime prevention services, a cell needs to (1) have a current P1V crime occurrence (a detection) and (2) have a prediction of being a cell that in the short term will have additional P1V crimes. The prediction is intended for recurring temporary hot spots and is the simplest conceivable: if the previous 12 months had a prediction level threshold number of months or higher with at least one P1V crime then a positive prediction is made. A more sophisticated prediction method would include clustering in time for P1V crimes to identify past temporary hot spots of a cell. Deployments at a cell are stopped when the number of time periods without a target crime after the most recent target crime exceeds a stopping threshold. An alternative stopping rule used by Mohler et al. (2015) is to stop a deployment when a hot spot is no longer predicted to be in the top k where k is the number of desired cells in a hot spot program. Yet another alternative is to select a fixed time interval for length of deployments, following Sherman's alternating scheme (Sherman 1990).

Example of Effectiveness Curves

Using the first three years of a ten-year data set for calibration of temporary hot spot models, we optimized the prediction level threshold, grid cell size, and stopping rule threshold for points along the horizontal axis of an effectiveness curve. Then with decision rules fixed at the so-determined optimal levels, the prediction and deployment scheme was run in simulation mode for the last seven years of data to produce the temporary hot spot tradeoff curves shown in Figure 2.4. Chronic hot spots, as in Figure 2.2, were predicted using KDE with the most recent three years' data on part 1 violent crime. The alternative hot

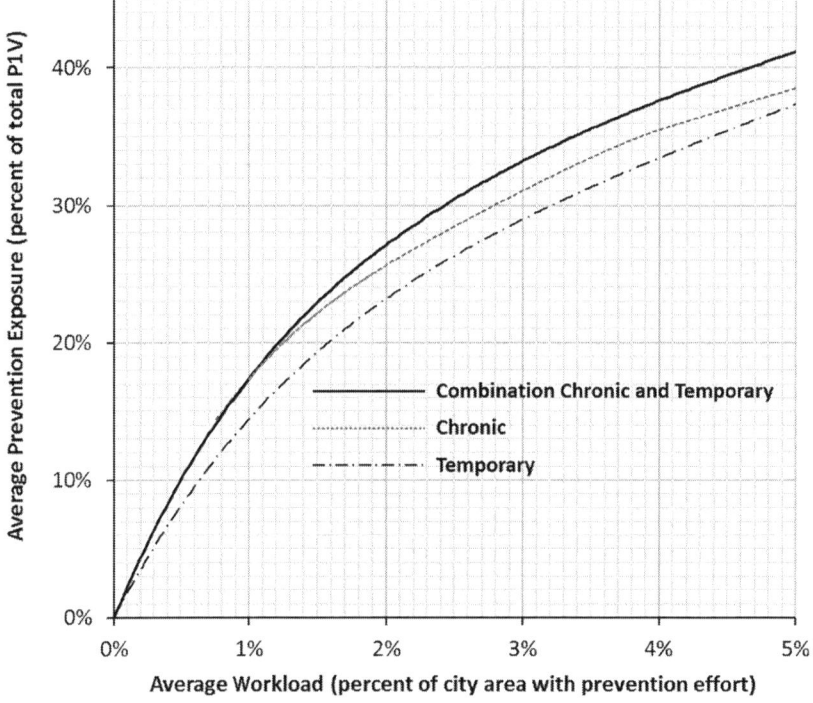

Figure 2.4 Effectiveness curve for chronic, temporary, and combination hot spot programs in Pittsburgh: 2004 through 2010.

spot programs considered in Figure 2.4 are (1) all chronic with constant police deployment, (2) temporary with on-and-off police deployment, and (3) a combination program with the first 1% area allocated to chronic hot spots and the remaining areas with temporary hot spots. The temporary hot spot program, by itself with no chronic hot spots, is dominated by the other two programs. The chronic hot spot program by itself is most effective from 0% to 1% area, but thereafter temporary hot spots added outside of allocated chronic hot spots are most effective, making the combination program the most effective overall. Apparently after 1% area, treating chronic hot spots with constant crime prevention workload is less efficient than treating temporary hot spots with dynamic workload, even though temporary hot spot predictions have errors.

Figure 2.5 is a sample map for July 2009 corresponding to the 2% average workload area combination program of Figure 2.4. From Figure 2.4, that program exposes 27% of Pittsburgh's P1V crime to prevention workload with a PAI of 13.5. The map in Figure 2.5 displays all predicted chronic and temporary hot spots with models estimated on data prior to June 2009. The map also

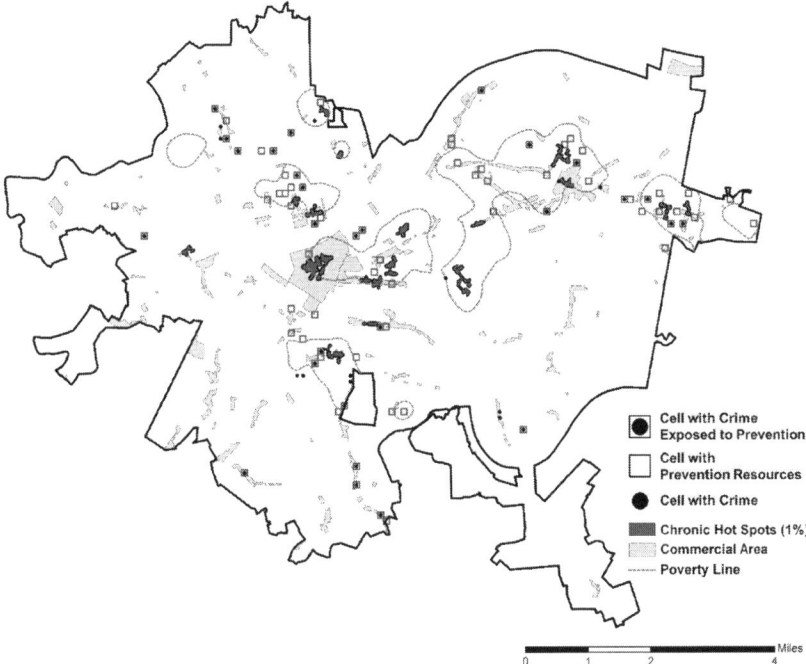

Figure 2.5 Sample map for a combination 1% area chronic and 1% area temporary hot spot program: predicted hot spots for July 2009.

displays all actual July 2009 P1V crimes outside of chronic hot spot areas, so it is possible to calculate the true positive rate for temporary hot spots, which equals 100*number of true positives (boxes enclosing small black circular markers)/(number of true positives plus false negatives) [small black circular markers not enclosed by boxes] = $100*27/(27+11) = 71\%$, which is quite good. About half of the temporary hot spots are in or intersect with commercial areas, and the other half are in residential areas.

Equity Performance Measure

The measure of equity used in this section is the area of Pittsburgh receiving appropriate input crime prevention services from police. So, for example, a 0.009 square mile (same as a grid cell with 500 feet on a side) chronic hot spot getting 12 months per year of crime prevention is the same as a 0.009 square mile temporary hot spot cell getting any number of months per year greater than 0. The inhabitants of each such area should feel fairly treated and have the same level of equity. A visualization of this equity is possible by mapping the footprints of predicted chronic and temporary crime hot spots for a year. A footprint map displays all locations of hot spots that occur during the year. Chronic hot spots are fixed for a calendar year, and for temporary hot spots, the footprint includes all locations of temporary hot spots that occurred during the year.

Figure 2.6 shows maps comparing footprints of two 2% area hot spot programs in 2009, created using the effectiveness curve of Figure 2.4. The top map is for a combination 1% chronic hot spot program with a 1% temporary hot spot program added on. The bottom map is an all chronic, 2% area hot spot program. From Figure 2.4 the all chronic program exposes 25.5% of Pittsburgh's P1V crimes to prevention services, whereas the combination program exposes 28%, a 10% increase in effectiveness for the combination program.

In the combination program map, almost every chronic hot spot is in an identifiable major commercial area of Pittsburgh: the central business district, Oakland, East Liberty, Shadyside, Beltzhoover, South Side, Homewood, North Side, etc. The temporary hot spots are widely scattered, with some adjacent to chronic hot spots but most in outlying areas of Pittsburgh.

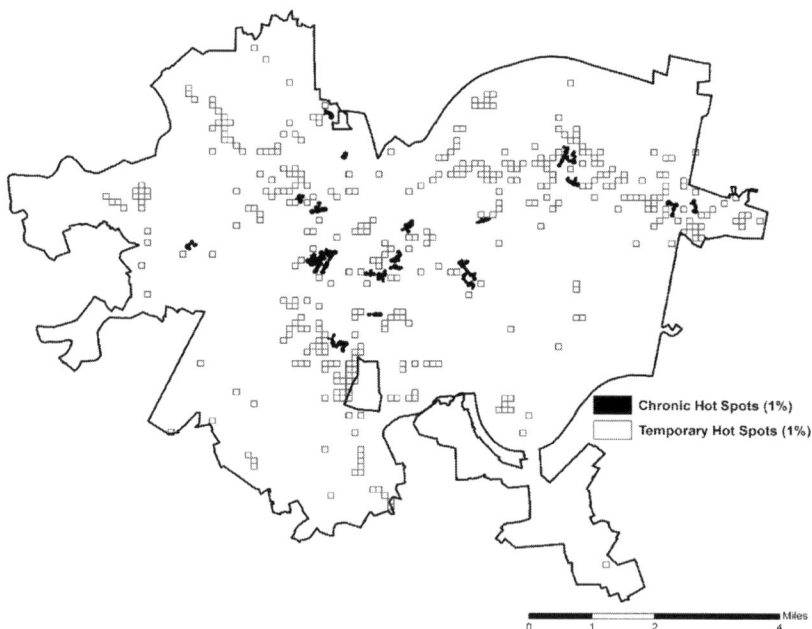

Figure 2.6a and 2.6b Comparison of the footprints of 2% combination versus 2% all chronic programs: 2009.

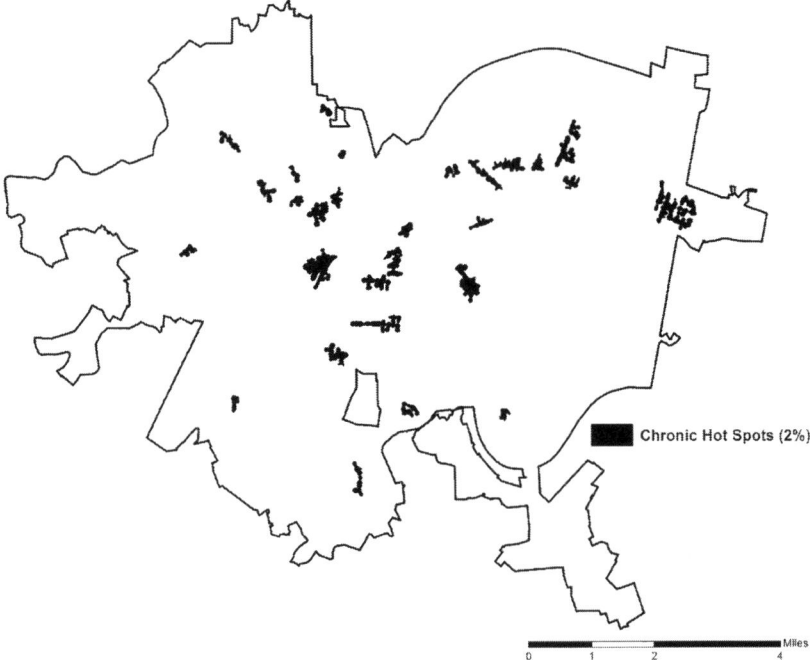

Figure 2.6a and 2.6b (Continued)

The total footprint area of the combination program is 4.07 square miles, whereas that of the all chronic program is only 1.31 square miles. So the combination program is 4.07/1.31 = 3.11 times more equitable than the all chronic program. Of the 4.07 square mile combination program, 3.42 square miles (84%) consist of temporary hot spots. In the bottom map, the original 1% area chronic hot spots of the top map are expanded in size, plus there are new chronic hot spots including many that are temporary hot spot cells from the top map converted to chronic hot spots (now with constant police deployment). The combination program has 0.65 square miles of chronic hot spots, and of course the all chronic program has twice as large an area of chronic hot spots, 1.31 square miles. In effect, the "off" times with no crimes of the chronic hot spots of the 0.65 square miles in the all chronic program from the 1% to 2% area of the effectiveness curve of Figure 2.4 are converted into the 3.42 square miles of temporary hot spots of the combination program. Each unit area of chronic hot spots is converted to 3.42/0.65 = 5.26 units of temporary hot spot footprint when moving from the all chronic to combination program. The gains in equity of the combination program over the all chronic program are very large.

Conclusion

The decomposition of crime hot spots into chronic and temporary hot spots of this chapter raises several prospects as well as questions for crime prevention by police. Even with the very simple temporary hot spot method of Gorr and Lee (2015), temporary hot spots increase both effectiveness and equity of crime prevention when used in combination with chronic hot spots. More sophisticated temporary hot spot prediction models would make this case even stronger.

Equity needs to be included as a criterion, along with effectiveness, in the design of crime hot spot programs as a matter of public policy and because crime prevention, as a key element of public safety, is a primary good essential for the well-being and flourishing of urban populations in all endeavors of life. The increases in equity by including temporary hot spots in a program are dramatic.

The first issue to address with future research is designing and determining the most accurate predictive models, for both chronic and temporary hot spots. While kernel density estimation (KDE) is a leading simple method for accuracy of predicting chronic hot spots, if a hot spot program is cell-based, then simple tabulations of target crimes by cell are likely as accurate as KDE. A question remains if complex models for chronic hot spots can improve accuracy and include dynamic predictions to the extent of determining which part of a chronic hot spot is about to flare up with more crimes.

Several models and methods are available for predicting temporary hot spots. Needed are a series of retrospective studies, replicated in many cities, comparing prediction accuracy of alternative models and methods. A primary accuracy measure for effectiveness is the Predictive Accuracy Index (PAI) as implemented through PAI effectiveness curves with the numerator of the PAI on the vertical axis (percentage of target crimes predicted) and the denominator on the horizontal axis (average percentage of area under prevention workload).

Another issue for future research is the geography of chronic versus temporary hot spots in cities. In Pittsburgh, chronic hot spots tend to be in large commercial areas and corridors, whereas temporary hot spots are widely scattered, with some near chronic hot spots but most in outlying areas away from chronic hot spots. Does this pattern hold in other cities? A related issue is the fear of crime in chronic hot spots compared to the fear in temporary hot spots. We hypothesize that fear of crime is much higher in temporary hot spots, because the expectations are for low numbers of crimes close to home, and informal communication networks quickly spread news of local crimes.

The last issue to address is the design of randomized field trials with control and treatment hot spots in a combined program. Trials will need to be stratified by duration of hot spot (chronic and temporary) and by type of crime (e.g., part 1 violent crimes, part 1 property crimes, and selected public disorder crimes that affect perceptions of fear of crime). As such it may be difficult to have trials powerful enough to show significant prevention of crimes, although at least total number of crimes prevented may be shown with significance. Trials need to be designed to avoid contamination of controls from treatment benefit spill-overs or crime displacement of adjacent treatment hot spots. Some form of crossover experimental design (e.g., Johnson 2010) may be desirable, with the same hot spots alternating as treatment and control cells. Crossover experiments are commonly used for cases analogous to crime prevention at hot spots, namely, to test drugs that relieve symptoms of chronic diseases. In this case the same patient can be treated for a period of time, then be not treated as a control, and then treated again, etc. Recurring temporary hot spots present the same conditions, except that the experimenter cannot schedule recurrences of hot spots.

References

Barak, Ariel, Cristobal Weinborn, and Lawrence W. Sherman. 2016. "'Soft' Policing at Hot Spots—Do Police Community Support Officers Work? A Randomized Controlled Trial." *Journal of Experimental Criminology* 12: 277–317.

Bernasco, Wim. 2010. "A Sentimental Journey to Crime: Effect of Residential History on Crime Location Choice." *Criminology* 48: 389–416.

Blumstein, Alfred, Jacqueline Cohen, and David P. Farrington. 1988. "Criminal Career Research: Its Value for Criminology." *Criminology* 26: 1–35.

Bowers, Kate J., Shane D. Johnson, and Ken Pease. 2004. "Prospective Hot-Spotting: The Future of Crime Mapping?" *British Journal of Criminology* 44: 641–658.

Braga, Anthony, Andrew Papachristos, and David M. Hureau. 2014. "The Effects of Hotspots Policing on Crime: An Updated Systematic Review and Meta-Analysis." *Justice Quarterly* 31: 633–663.

Brantingham, Paul J., and Patricia L. Brantingham. 1993. "Environment, Routine and Situation: Toward a Pattern Theory of Crime." *Advances in Criminological Theory* 5: 259–294.

Chainey, Spencer, Lisa Tompson, and Sebastian Uhlig. 2008. "The Utility of Hotspot Mapping for Predicting Spatial Patterns of Crime." *Security Journal* 21: 4–28.

Cohen, Jacqueline, Wilpen L. Gorr, and Andreas M. Olligschlaeger. 2007. "Leading Indicators and Spatial Interactions: A Crime-Forecasting Model for Proactive Police Deployment." *Geographical Analysis* 39: 105–127.

Cohen, Jacqueline, and George Tita. 1999. "Diffusion in Homicide: Exploring a General Method for Detecting Spatial Diffusion Processes." *Journal of Quantitative Criminology* 15: 451–493.

Cohen, Lawrence E., and Marcus Felson. 1979. "Social Change and Crime Rate Trends: A Routine Activity Approach." *American Sociological Review* 44: 588.

Cornish, Derek B., and Ronald V. Clarke. 1986. *The Reasoning Criminal: Rational Choice Perspectives on Offending*. New York, NY: Springer.

Culyer, Anthony J. 2001. "Equity—Some Theory and Its Policy Implications." *Journal of Medical Ethics* 27: 275–283.

DeLisi, Matt. 2001. "Extreme Career Criminals." *American Journal of Criminal Justice* 25: 239–252.

Doran, Bruce J., and Melissa B. Burgess (eds.). 2012. "Why Is Fear of Crime a Serious Social Problem?" Pp. 9–23 in *Putting Fear of Crime on the Map*. New York, NY: Springer New York.

Eck, John E., and Dennis Rosenbaum. 1994. "The New Police Order: Effectiveness, Equity, and Efficiency in Community Policing." Pp. 3–23 in Dennis P. Rosenbaum (ed.), *The Challenge of Community Policing: Testing the Promises*. Thousand Oaks, CA: Sage.

Eck, John E., and William Spelman. 1987. "Problem-Solving: Problem-Oriented Policing in Newport News." Washington, DC: Police Executive Research Forum.

Eck, John E., and David L. Weisburd. 1995. "Crime Places in Crime Theory." Pp. 1–33 in John E. Eck and David L. Weisburd (eds.), *Crime and Place: Crime Prevention Studies*. Monsey, NY: Criminal Justice Press.

Gini, Corrado. 1921. "Measurement of Inequality of Incomes." *The Economic Journal* 31: 124.

Goldstein, Herman. 1979. "Improving Policing: A Problem-Oriented Approach." *Crime & Delinquency* 25: 236–258.

Goldstein, Herman. 1990. *Excellence in Problem-Oriented Policing*. New York, NY: McGraw-Hill.

Gorr, Wilpen L. 2009. "Forecast Accuracy Measures for Exception Reporting Using Receiver Operating Characteristic Curves." *International Journal of Forecasting* 25: 48–61.

Gorr, Wilpen L., and Yong Jei Lee. 2012. "Longitudinal Study of Crime Hot Spots: Dynamics and Impact on Part 1 Violent Crime." Proceedings of the 32nd International Symposium on Forecasting, March 27, 2012. Boston, MA.

Gorr, Wilpen L., and Yong Jei Lee. 2015. "Early Warning System for Temporary Crime Hot Spots." *Journal of Quantitative Criminology* 31: 25–47.

Gorr, Wilpen L., and Matthew J. Schneider. 2013. "Large-Change Forecast Accuracy: Reanalysis of M3-Competition Data Using Receiver Operating Characteristic Analysis." *International Journal of Forecasting* 29: 274–281.

Hirschman, Albert O. 1964. "The Paternity of an Index." *The American Economic Review* 54: 761–762.

Johnson, Dallas E. 2010. "Crossover Experiments." *WIREs Comp Stat* 2: 620–625.

Johnson, Shane D., and Kate J. Bowers. 2004a. "The Burglary as Clue to the Future: The Beginnings of Prospective Hot-Spotting." *European Journal of Criminology* 1: 237–255.

Johnson, Shane D., and Kate J. Bowers. 2004b. "The Stability of Space-Time Clusters of Burglary." *British Journal of Criminology* 44: 55–65.

Koper, Christopher S. 1995. "Just Enough Police Presence: Reducing Crime and Disorderly Behavior by Optimizing Patrol Time in Crime Hot Spots." *Justice Quarterly* 12: 649–672.

Kubrin, Charis E., and Ronald Weitzer. 2003. "New Directions in Social Disorganization Theory." *Journal of Research in Crime and Delinquency* 40: 374–402.

Mohler, George. 2014. "Marked Point Process Hotspot Maps for Homicide and Gun Crime Prediction in Chicago." *International Journal of Forecasting* 30: 491–497.

Mohler, George O., Martin B. Short, P. Jeffrey Brantingham, Frederic Paik Schoenberg, and George E. Tita. 2011. "Self-Exciting Point Process Modeling of Crime." *Journal of the American Statistical Association* 106: 100–108.

Mohler, George O., Martin B. Short, Sean Malinowski, Mark Johnson, George E. Tita, Andrea L. Bertozzi, and P. Jeffrey Brantingham. 2015. "Randomized Controlled Field Trials of Predictive Policing." *Journal of the American Statistical Association* 110: 1399–1411.

Morgan, Frank. 2001. "Repeat Burglary in a Perth Suburb : Indicator of Short- Term or Long-Term Risk?" *Crime Prevention Studies* 12: 83–118.

Nagel, Stuart S. 1986. "Efficiency, Effectiveness, and Equity in Public Policy Evaluation." *Review of Policy Research* 6: 99–120.

Neill, Daniel B., and Wilpen L. Gorr. 2007. "Detecting and Preventing Emerging Epidemics of Crime." *Advances in Disease Surveillance* 4: 1.

Olligschlaeger, Andreas M. 1997a. "Artificial Neural Networks and Crime Mapping." Pp. 313–348 in David L. Weisburd and Tom McEwen (eds.), *Crime Mapping and Crime Prevention*. Monsey, NY: Criminal Justice Press.

Olligschlaeger, Andreas M. 1997b. *Spatial Analysis of Crime Using Gis-Based Data: Weighted Spatial Adaptive Filtering and Chaotic Cellular Forecasting with Applications to Street-Level Drug Markets*. Ph.D. Dissertation, Carnegie Mellon University, Pittsburgh.

Phillips, Peter, and Ickjai Lee. 2009. "Mining Top-K and Bottom-K Correlative Crime Patterns through Graph Representations." 2009 IEEE International Conference on Intelligence and Security Informatics, Dallas, TX, IEEE, 25–30.

Piquero, A. 2000. "Frequency, Specialization, and Violence in Offending Careers." *Journal of Research in Crime and Delinquency* 37(4): 392–418.

Ratcliffe, Jerry H., and George F. Rengert. 2008. "Near-Repeat Patterns in Philadelphia Shootings." *Security Journal* 21: 58–76.

Rengert, George F., Alex R. Piquero, and Peter R. Jones. 1999. "Distance Decay Reexamined." *Criminology* 37: 427–446.

Shaw, Clifford R., and Henry D. McKay. 1942. *Juvenile Delinquency and Urban Areas*. Chicago, IL: University of Chicago Press.

Sherman, Lawrence W. 1990. "Police Crackdowns: Initial and Residual Deterrence." *Crime and Justice* 12: 1–48.

Sherman, Lawrence W. 1995. "Hot Spots of Crime and Criminal Careers of Places." *Crime and Place* 4: 35–52.

Sherman, Lawrence W., and David Weisburd. 1995. "General Deterrent Effects of Police Patrol in Crime 'Hot Spots': A Randomized, Controlled Trial." *Justice Quarterly* 12: 625–648.

Skogan, Wesley. 1986. "Fear of Crime and Neighborhood Change." *Crime and Justice* 8: 203–229.

Swets, John A. 1988. "Measuring the Accuracy of Diagnostic Systems." *Science* 240: 1285–1293.

Taylor, Bruce, Christopher S. Koper, and Daniel J. Woods. 2011. "A Randomized Controlled Trial of Different Policing Strategies at Hot Spots of Violent Crime." *Journal of Experimental Criminology* 7: 149–181.

Telep, Cody W., Renée J. Mitchell, and David Weisburd. 2014. "How Much Time Should the Police Spend at Crime Hot Spots? Answers from a Police Agency Directed Randomized Field Trial in Sacramento, California." *Justice Quarterly* 31: 905–933.

Telep, Cody W., and David Weisburd. 2014. "Hot Spots and Place-Based Policing." Pp. 2352–2363 in Bruinsma, Gerben, and David Weisburd (eds.), *Encyclopedia of Criminology and Criminal Justice*. New York, NY: Springer.

Tita, George, and Greg Ridgeway. 2007. "The Impact of Gang Formation on Local Patterns of Crime." *Journal of Research in Crime and Delinquency* 44: 208–237.

Townsley, Michael, Homel Ross, and Chaseling Janet. 2003. "Infectious Burglaries: A Test of the Near Repeat Hypothesis." *British Journal of Criminology* 43: 615–633.

Weisburd, David. 2015. "The Law of Crime Concentration and the Criminology of Place." *Criminology* 53: 133–157.

Weisburd, David, Elizabeth R. Groff, and Sue-Ming Yang. 2014. "Understanding and Controlling Hot Spots of Crime: The Importance of Formal and Informal Social Controls." *Prevention Science* 15: 31–43.

Part II

Frameworks for Understanding Crime and Place

3

The Added Value of the Criminology of Place to the Research Agenda of Environmental Criminology: The Necessity of Mechanism-Based Frameworks

Gerben J.N. Bruinsma and Lieven J.R. Pauwels

Introduction

The criminology of place is a recent development in geographical criminology that draws on a rich tradition of two hundred years of spatial research on crime rates (Bruinsma 2017). The focus of study has been centered on the spatial distribution of crime and its variations at several levels of aggregation like countries, provinces, cities or neighborhoods. During these two centuries the unit of analysis of geographical criminology gradually shifted from countries and regions to micro places today (Weisburd, Bruinsma, and Bernasco 2009). Micro places can be street segments, shops, restaurants, railway stations or shopping malls. Since 1980 a growing number of empirical research efforts have demonstrated that crimes cluster at micro places (Telep and Weisburd 2017; Weisburd 2015; Weisburd, Groff, and Yang 2012; Weisburd and Telep 2014). A small number of crime places are accountable for the majority of crime counts of larger areas. This clustering of crime at places seems to be a universal empirical 'fact'. That is why Weisburd proclaimed the 'law of crime concentration' stating that 'for a defined measure of crime at a specific micro geographic unit, the concentration of crime will fall within a narrow bandwidth of percentages for a defined cumulative proportion of crime' (Weisburd 2015: 138). However, the theoretical development of the criminology of crime places is still in its early stages. The next step in the criminology of place is to address the issue of explaining *why* there is a clustering of crime at micro places. To achieve this goal one can rely on existing spatial theories like (various versions of) social disorganization theory or opportunity theory (see chapter 3 of Weisburd et al. 2016), or one can make use of promising insights from other disciplines such as (the psychology of) geography or sociology.

This chapter aims at contributing to theorizing on crime place by introducing fundamental ideas from philosophers of science and methodologists to the criminology of place that can be very fruitful to the understanding of why crimes cluster. These innovative ideas are centered on the concepts of 'causal mechanisms' and 'emergence'. We submit that these concepts are very useful to understand and to explain why crimes are concentrated at micro places. These ideas are borrowed from well-known philosophers like Bunge (2004); Hedström (2005); Elster (2007); Manzo (2010); Coleman (1990); Wan (2011); and Thagard (1998). They have in common their focus on the complex notion of causality, a highly debated concept in the philosophy of science and a long avoided topic in criminology in which a majority of the theoretical thinking is limited to correlational relationships (Wikström 2007). In the next section, we first discuss key questions and a selection of core propositions of the criminology of place (formulated as 'if, then' sentences). Many of these statements originated from US research, however, *claiming universal validity*. We will discuss the status of general propositions in the third section, demonstrating that the traditional deductive-nomological method (DN-model) of covering law-like (universal) explanations (Hempel 1965; Hempel and Oppenheim 1948; Popper 1975) in its original application led to confusion. A lot of scholars became dissatisfied with this model and were convinced that such explanations would not lead to scientific progress in our discipline. Nowadays many philosophers of science (Hedström 2005) are dissatisfied with the DN-model and have offered a powerful alternative causal explanation. This alternative is strongly based on the complex concepts of causal mechanisms and emergence, the central topics of this section. We then continue the discussion of examples of core propositions in the criminology of place that are based on mechanisms. We try to show how these mechanisms can be linked to crime generators and crime attractors of micro places. We conclude that the explanation of the clustering of crimes cannot be done properly without the presence of individual agents who are triggered to make action decisions at these settings. Places are merely passive entities, not active agents. They cannot commit crimes; only human actors can do so. But places may have detrimental causal effects on some individuals under some circumstances. For the sake of convenience we limit ourselves in this chapter to public crimes. However, it should be clear that the ideas presented here can be transposed to other micro places and crime types.

The chapter will be closed by a discussion of what the advantages and disadvantages are when working with core propositions to explain why crimes cluster at micro places that are based on the elaboration of causal mechanisms and emergence.

Key Questions and Core Propositions of Criminology of Crime and Place

The criminology of places is grounded on two hundred years of spatial research at various levels of aggregation (Bruinsma 2017; Bruinsma and Weisburd 2014a, 2014b). In the beginning in the 1830s, French, Belgian and English mathematicians and cartographers started to study empirically the distribution of crime across countries and counties (Greg 1835; Guerry 1832, 1833; Quételet 1847, 1848, 1984[1831]; Rawson 1839). By using officially recorded crime data, these scholars in general revealed unequal spatial distributions of crime across countries and large areas. Guerry (1833), for instance, found more violent crimes in the southern part of France and more property crimes in the northern provinces of France (and displayed these findings on maps). The 1920s marked a second period of heydays in spatial criminology. US sociologists and criminologists (ignoring the European geographic literature of the 19th century) studied the impact of neighborhood characteristics of big cities on crime rates (with Chicago as the most researched city) (Burgess 1967 [1925]; Park and Burgess 1967 [1925]; Shaw and McKay 1969 [1942]; Shaw, Zorbaugh, McKay, and Cottrell 1929). Leading theory in those days was the social disorganization theory as developed by Thomas (1966) and Shaw and McKay (1969 [1942]).

After a period of criticism (Kornhauser 1978; Robinson 1950) that led to a decline in spatial research in our discipline, a new period of spatial criminology emerged in the 1980s in which Paul and Patricia Brantingham in Canada and Ralph Taylor in Philadelphia called attention to micro places in criminology (Brantingham and Brantingham 1978, 1981; Taylor 1987, 1988; Taylor, Gott-fredson, and Brower 1981, 1985). The Brantinghams introduced the notion of the geometry of crime and elaborated a crime site selection model that can be seen as a predecessor of their crime pattern theory. They sought to explain how targets come to the attention of individual offenders, how that influences where they offend and how the collective activity patterns of offenders affect the distribution of crime events over time and across places. Taylor focused on the micro level physical environment (micro-ecology) and its influence on an individual's behavior.

This development affected an entire new generation of scholars who started to readdress the study of crime in neighborhoods (Reiss and Tonry 1986). Especially the question of whether communities have crime careers (Reiss 1986) was vividly discussed. Bursik revisited crime rates in Chicago neighborhoods over long time periods and found that stability or instability in the social characteristics of neighborhoods would lead to stability or instability in crime rates (Bursik 1984, 1986; Bursik and Grasmick 1993).

Later, Sampson developed the collective efficacy theory, in which he unraveled why poverty and residential mobility are positively related to crime and victimization rates (Sampson 2010, 2012). His theory stressed the importance of a community that is characterized by social trust and the willingness to intervene on commonly identified problems, such as crime and safety concerns.

At the time when computerized crime mapping and more sophisticated geographical statistical tools were about to emerge, a new group of theorists challenged traditional criminological (ecological) interest. Cohen and Felson put forward their routine activity theory, arguing that variations in crime rates were caused by the routine nature of targets and guardianship, irrespective of criminal motives of offenders (Cohen and Felson 1979; Felson 2008). The Canadians Patricia and Paul Brantingham developed their crime pattern theory focusing on places by asking why and how targets came to the attention of offenders and how that influenced the distribution of crime over time and across places (Brantingham and Brantingham 1984, 2008, 1981). When an offender's awareness space (cognitive map of activity nodes and paths) overlaps with crime opportunities, crime will be more likely to occur. In 1989, Sherman and his colleagues Gartin and Buerger coined the term of 'criminology of place' to emphasize the dawn of an exciting new era in criminology that focuses on micro places (previously called hot spots) (Sherman, Gartin, and Buerger 1989). In a study in Seattle fifteen years later, Weisburd and his colleagues reported that between 4% and 5% of street segments in the city accounted for 50% of the crimes for each year over fourteen years (Weisburd, Bushway, Lum, and Yang 2004). Since then, a great number of empirical studies have been carried out in various cities in search of concentrations of crime at small spaces, followed by a substantial number of publications to answer the question of why studying crime clusters at micro places is important for criminology (Groff, Weisburd, and Yang 2010; Weisburd 2015; Weisburd, Bernasco, and Bruinsma 2009; Weisburd et al. 2016; Weisburd et al. 2012; Weisburd and Telep 2014). These and other empirical results (Bernasco and Steenbeek 2016; Steenbeek and Weisburd 2016) allow Weisburd to conclude that there is a 'law of crime concentration' in criminology: 'for a defined measure of crime at a specific micro geographic unit, the concentration of crime will fall within a narrow bandwidth of percentages for a defined cumulative proportion of crime' (Weisburd 2015: 138). Studying micro places is important because larger areas can hide large underlying variations in crime (Glyde 1856), or can hide underlying differences in social worlds of residents or passers-by (Zorbaugh 1929); individuals have a limited space-awareness (Brantingham and Brantingham 1984, 2008); offenders commit their crimes at specific locations, not in large areas (Bernasco 2010a, 2010b); and specific features of locations influence the choices of offenders (Johnson 2014; Townsley et al. 2015; Wikström 2014).

What are the key questions of the criminology of places? According to Weisburd (Weisburd 2015; Weisburd et al. 2016; Weisburd et al. 2012) the key questions of criminology of places are:

1. Is the law of crime concentrations at places valid?
2. Is the law of crime concentrations at places valid across time?
3. Is the law of crime concentrations at places valid across cities?
4. Why is crime clustered at places?
5. Do crime opportunities, victimization and guardianship at places vary in significant ways across a city?
6. Do variations of crime opportunities, victimization and guardianship at places vary in significant ways across time or are they stable?
7. Are characteristics of crime places correlated with social disorganization?

To classify the key questions, one could argue that most of them are *empirical* questions in the Humean sense: they are questions on the existence of *constant conjunctions* in reality (1, 2, 3, 5 and 6). To answer these key questions, further empirical research needs to be carried out (next to the already existing empirical evidence). Questions 6 and 7 however also suggest that opportunities, victimization and guardianship are relevant (causal) factors when studying crime concentrations at micro places. Nevertheless, they are also empirical issues to be solved in the future. Question 7 is more ambiguously formulated: it is an empirical question to be answered, but suggests also some theoretical significance. The question implies what Wikström has called 'the causes of the causes' research. It is not directed to explain why crimes cluster at micro places. The theory of social disorganization might be an interesting theory to explain these features of micro places. However, there is no argument offered as to why social disorganization theory is presumed the most promising spatial theory. Considering the numerous versions of social disorganization theory that have flourished in the criminological literature, the reader has to make a guess about which version is the most promising.

More interesting for our contribution is question 4 in which the open why-question is raised: the search for causal explanations of crime concentration at places (Bruinsma 2010; Opp 2002; Taylor 2015; Ultee 1977). We focus on that key question, while stressing that much research has already been carried out to establish empirically concentrations in crime at micro places (similar to other levels of aggregation during the last two centuries). Recent studies have demonstrated without any doubt an empirical regularity of the clustering of crimes justifying criminologists—by using the principle of induction—to proclaim the universality of this given in a law of crime concentration (Weisburd 2015: 139).

This law of crime concentration as formulated by Weisburd can be classified as an empirical law, not a causal law. If it was a causal law, the law should have been worded like 'if X, then Y' (a concentration of crimes at micro places), in which X is the explanans and Y is the explanandum and micro place the unit of analysis (to which the statement would apply). That is not the case here. To answer the why-question we cannot fall back on this law. We have to explore the existing theoretical literature to search for core propositions. Spatial criminology has been productive the last forty years and produced about forty different theories on crime concentrations (see for a list Bruinsma 2010). Obviously, they cannot all be true at the same time (Bruinsma 2016). The current state of spatial criminology however does not allow for distinction between the theories based on true and false explanations, neither by conclusive empirical findings nor by assessing them with methodological standards. There is more or less a situation of what Lakatos called pseudo-pluralism not pluralism (Lakatos 1970). To give an example: spatial theories have different units of analysis, reflecting historical developments of research traditions in criminology (Weisburd, Bruinsma, et al. 2009) and use concepts that resemble each other and in many cases overlap (Bruinsma 2013). To discuss them all goes beyond the scope of this contribution. Therefore, we limit ourselves to the most popular and inspiring spatial theory nowadays: the routine activity theory (RAT) developed by Cohen and Felson (Cohen and Felson 1979; Felson 2008; Felson and Cohen 1980). Felson (2008) later called it an approach, not a theory, but we better ignore his judgment for this moment. RAT had originally a macro scope version to explain temporal variations in crime rates in one country (US) by using characteristics like the level of technology or the social organization of households. We put that macro version aside because it is unsuitable to explain concentrations of crime at micro places. In the micro version of RAT, the most popular version in spatial criminology, daily routines of people play an essential role: "These routines deliver temptations and controls and thus organize the type and amount of crime in society" (Felson 1994: 42). Three factors play a role in influencing why crimes happen at a location: (1) motivated offenders must be present; (2) suitable targets must be available; and (3) capable guardians must not be present. Physical characteristics of the location are not mentioned in RAT (unless physical characteristics are part of the suitable targets). Nevertheless, they are important: you can only shoplift in a store.

We can formulate RAT as follows:

If and only if the following factors are all valid at the same time at a location:

Motivated offenders are present;
Suitable targets are available; and
Capable guardians are not present,

Then a crime is likely to happen at that location.

The issue here is that the dependent variable of this theory is not a concentration of crimes at micro places. Assuming that a location can be subsumed under micro places, we can solve a first problem by stating that RAT has a similar unit of analysis as the law of crime concentration at micro places. Next, we have to decide whether the explanans 'crimes happen at location' is similar to concentrations of crime. Literally that is not the case. RAT is only stating that crimes will occur when the elements of the crime triangle are combined. There are no indications that locations with motivated offenders, attractive targets and no capable guardians have disproportionally more crimes than other locations.[1] We have to reformulate RAT to make it suitable to explain concentrations of crimes. With the contemporary state-of-the art knowledge that is not possible. The theory is not clear enough about how many numbers of attractive targets, motivated offenders or guardians, the kind of attractiveness of targets or the kind of motivated offenders are needed to be a meaningful tipping point to affect crime concentrations. Furthermore, it is likely that variations in guardianship might be more relevant than just the absence of it (Reynald 2009; 2011).

Given this example, it would be advisable to find out if and, if yes, how other disciplines such as philosophy of science, methodology and sociology might be helpful to improve our theory of explaining spatial concentrations of crimes at micro places.

Unraveling Mechanisms to Provide Causal Explanations in the Crime Place Theories

Before delving into the problem of mechanisms and the necessity of mechanism-based explanations in crime place theories and research, we point to the fact that in criminology a lot of misunderstandings exist regarding the complex notion of causation (Sampson, Winship, and Knight 2013). To fully understand the complex notion of causation, scholars can learn a lot by studying the philosophy of causation (for an overview, see Beebee, Hitchcock, and Menzies 2009). No single theory of causation has been discovered that is free of counter-examples. This says a lot about the complexity of the concept. Philosophers have understood for ages the complexities surrounding the notion of causation. In the past century, many efforts have been undertaken to get a grip on that vague, dubious but nevertheless very important concept. While social scientists in general—and crime place theorists are probably no exception to the rule—take different stances toward the notion of causation, it may be good to give a broad overview of influential notions of causations that have fostered inquiries into the causes of criminality, acts of crime or criminal events, depending on the dependent variable that is of interest.

While the famous philosopher of science Bertrand Russell (2013) declared the concept of causation dead and denounced it as a relic of a bygone age, we shall argue that a thorough understanding of causation is pivotal for the development of explanations of crime concentrations. The concept of causation was strongly criticized by David Hume, who argued that causation, no matter how important, faced an ultimate problem: it could never be observed, and even the most stable regular observation could not guarantee that the observation could be repeated, let alone that it could be understood causally (Morris and Brown 2016). We should be clear on one thing: Hume was not against causation; quite on the contrary, he strongly believed the world was full of causal events, only the causal process itself could never be demonstrated (Tacq 1984). For Hume, collapsing billiard balls were highly suggestive of causal forces being at work, but these 'dark' forces are not observable. Therefore, Hume developed a regularity view of causation. In that view, causation is restricted to constant conjunction, nothing more and nothing less (correlations are all that matter; all the rest is chatter). It may be clear that many scholars did not agree. Although all philosophers of causation clearly understood that Hume hit the bull's eye by unraveling a key problem, many felt that there was a shortcoming in the Humean notion of causation. Applying the Hume problem to the study of crime concentrations at micro places makes clear that criminologists are not learning much more than the fact that factors by varying degrees of necessity or sufficiency are regularly observed together.

The influence of Hume's view cannot be neglected. The concept of constant conjunction (i.e. the regularity definition) ultimately gave rise to the idea of a tradition that aimed at detecting such regularities, which was at the time called the DN-model, i.e. the deductive-nomological model of explanation (Hempel 1965). The DN-model was based on the idea that science grows by finding law-like explanations and that the role of the scientist is to observe regularities (e.g. settings that have a high level of physical disorder and dilapidation also are settings where many drugs are sold).

According to this explanatory model, the deductive-nomological model, as developed by Hempel and Oppenheim, the researcher was supposed to observe the initial condition, which was stated as follows (Hempel and Oppenheim 1948):

> *Law 1*: The higher the level of physical disorder at specific micro places in comparison to other micro places in a city, the higher the attraction of those micro places for drug dealers in comparison to other places in that city.
>
> *Law 2*: The higher the number of drug dealers at micro places in comparison to other micro places in a city, the higher the number of customers at those micro places in comparison to other micro places in that city and the higher number of 'economic transactions'.
>
> *Initial condition*: At places with higher levels of physical disorder also high numbers of drug deals are being observed compared to the case at other micro places with low physical disorder.

Explanandum: The high number of drug deals can be explained by the attraction of places with high levels of physical disorder for drug dealers.

The DN-model resulted in so-called *covering laws*. Although these covering laws were sometimes highly informative (Opp 2002), the DN-model has since been discarded as it was not waterproof. According to opponents, the major problem with the DN-model (there are many problems, but for the sake of conceptual parsimony we only refer to some) is that the formulation of explanations in terms of initial conditions, an explanans and a law does not guarantee that causes are identified.

The DN-model was thus restricted to observation that indeed could be regularly conducted. But a regularity view does not necessitate causation. Another issue at stake is the determinist view of the DN-model. The model was originally and preferably stated in if and only if terms, leaving no room for error. While the latter issue could easily be solved by a variant of the DN-model, the inductive statistical (IS) model, the problems here become even more clear: the IS model is not based on deductive reasoning but merely on statistical laws, which have inductive character, thus weakening the assumptions of the DN-model.

Many philosophers of causation were dissatisfied with the DN-model, and while the model was predominant in social sciences, at least during the time when Popper's critical rationalism was a major paradigm (Popper 1974, 1975), it has been largely abandoned. An increasing number of both philosophers and social scientists started to discuss the notion of causation and increasingly acknowledged that the DN-model fell short. One philosopher of science, Mario Bunge, has strongly criticized the DN-model and offered a powerful alternative definition of causation (Bunge 1979). Causation, he argued, is about *relations between events*. An event is an object that can change from one state to another. Events can take place in micro places: an object in a micro place can be victimized or not. From this, it follows that only changes can be considered as causes. Bunge further stressed (1) the notion of production (an effect needs to be brought about by a mechanism) and (2) the notion of law-likeness (each unique causal connection should be observed at a regular basis, i.e. it is impossible to observe a causal relationship only once).[2] Bunge (1979) originally borrowed examples from regular and quantum physics, and distinguished between causation (causal determination) and auto-determination ('spontaneity'), which he considered a random term (which we argue is highly comparable to what Sampson and Laub referred to as random 'developmental noise'). Of major interest for the criminology of micro places is the way Bunge (1999) reflected on causation for the social sciences in his *Finding Philosophy in Social Sciences*. He stressed that the world is multicausal and full of causal interaction, and argued that social scientists should pay attention to causes ('external events') in two forms: energy transfers (e.g. the observation of disorder at a micro place causes the actor to decide whether to commit a crime at the micro place; brain processes are examples of energy transfers) and triggering events (e.g. one actor convinces another actor to commit a crime at a micro place). Causes (system-extern events) can thus have proportional or chaos-like effects (small causes, huge consequences, like when a terrorist selects a micro place). Bunge realized that even when causal production would lie behind observed correlations, studies of causal relations would ultimately be restricted to the detection of probabilistic relations, because he recognized how improbable it would be to detect all the relevant mechanisms, and acknowledged that in the situations where events are caused by more than one factor, all relations were bound to result in probabilistic equations. He stressed that causation (under the right circumstances) would lead to production of an outcome via one or more mechanisms. In later works, philosophers of science stressed the notion of conditionality (i.e. searching for the right conditions under which productive, law-like events could be brought about by some mechanism).

In short, many philosophers of causation who did not agree with the Humean notion of causation felt that law-like explanations were too dangerous (restricted for social science), and these philosophers provided strong alternative perspectives on causation. While it is impossible to discuss them all, it is essential to stress the consequences of these philosophical works for the criminology of crime places and the study of our understanding of the law of crime concentration. Clearly, the law of crime concentration cannot be understood as a mere statistical probability affecting law, because it does not teach us anything with regard to the multiple mechanisms (at multiple levels) that are involved, let alone what kinds of mechanisms: social mechanisms, developmental mechanisms or situational mechanisms.

However, we believe that for a thorough understanding the law of crime concentration requires that we must be aware of the nature of the causal events. We submit the thesis that event causation (the type of causation philosophers usually talk about) is not very fruitful in criminology. Event causation is commonly studied in (quantum) physics, biology, etc., but in social science, acts of crimes (events) are always caused by actors. While causal processes take place in humans (changes in brain states and changes in decision-making), event causation does not stress the actor and suggests that all humans passively undergo the causal cement of the universe. The necessity of recognizing the actor as an active person, able to bring about events, has already been stressed by George Henrik von Wright in the 1970s (Von Wright 2004), but only a very few scholars in criminology picked up the notion of 'action' (i.e. acts in deliberate or spontaneous mode), while its consequences were huge. Von Wright provided scholars with a revolutionary idea at that time. He argued that it was by doing things that humans brought about events, and thus, he introduced actor-causation in several sciences. Von Wright was responsible for (re) introducing notions of 'agency' in causal theories in social sciences, thereby also influencing a lot of 'rational choice thinking' (in both narrow and wide versions, and even influencing reasonable actor thinking, which is paramount to the analytical tradition in sociology).

What is the major consequence of recognizing actor causation for the criminology of crime places? It is clear that not every property that is related to the commission of a criminal act (e.g. at the micro place level) can be an external causal event or internal mechanism. Not all properties of micro places can be interpreted as having a strong causal effect for several reasons: micro places are not actors; they are small areas whose effect depends on the perception of opportunities (e.g. temptation, provocation) of the setting to commit an act, deliberately or habitually.[3] This notion of dual processes is increasingly being applied in crime causation theories, e.g. situational action theory (Wikström 2014) and the model of frame selection (Kroneberg, Heintze, and Mehlkop 2010).

Action causation refers to the commitment of an act as a consequence of an individual deliberating on the act or as a consequence of triggering and habitual response. This distinction is necessary when we try to understand what is going on. When we want to know why some places are crime ridden, we must understand the consequences of our choices: when we restrict ourselves to the study of the criminal event, we risk ignoring that a criminal event at a micro place is the result of humans that perceive action alternatives and make decisions in an environment (of micro place).

The productivity element in causation made some philosophers of science think about how production could be translated and tested, and this discussion led to the idea of interventionism. A key supporter of the interventionist causality notion is James Woodward (Woodward 2003). He argues his vision in his book *Making Things Happen*:

> I favour a broad notion of causation according to which, roughly, any explanation which proceeds by showing how an outcome depends (where the dependence in question is not logical or conceptual) on other variables or factors counts as causal. I suggest that the distinguishing feature of causal explanations, so conceived, is that they are explanations that furnish information that is potentially relevant to manipulation and control; they tell us how, if we were able to change the value of one or more variables, we could change the value of other variables (Woodward 2003: 6).

He continued:

> My idea is that one ought to be able to associate with any successful explanation a hypothetical or counterfactual experiment that shows us that and how manipulation of the factors mentioned in the explanation (the explanans, as philosophers would call it) would be a way of manipulating or altering the phenomenon explained (the explanandum) . . . [A]n explanation ought to be such that it can be used to answer what I call a what-if-things-had-been-different question (Woodward 2003: 11).

Now that we have explained, albeit in a nutshell and being somewhat selective, the elements of causation that are quintessential to crime place theories, the notion of causation and the fact that studying laws may not be enough, we need to delve further into the notion of mechanisms. A crucial element is the presence of a mechanism or a series of mechanisms that bring about the event (or the act of crime). The attention to mechanisms is not new in social sciences, but was latently embedded in the theories of the founders of sociology such as Durkheim and Merton. Therefore, we can still learn important lessons from these founding fathers today, which, as the sociologist Peter Hedström (2005) stated, go further than mere historical lessons. Although these founders were not always theoretically sophisticated, and they did not have the most sophisticated analytical techniques available, their merit lies exactly in their approach to and their vision of science. Merton's research program concerned the development and testing of theories of the medium-range scope. Merton (1996) saw analysis in terms of mechanisms as a good compromise between the unattainable (Hempelian) covering laws, on the one hand, and, on the other hand, the non-explanatory descriptions that many theoretical and empirical analyses have restricted themselves to. In his view, the main task of the sociologist is to identify social mechanisms and to determine under what conditions they arise and fail (Hedström and Swedberg 1998: 6). Merton (1968: 43) wrote about social mechanisms as fundaments of sociological middle-range theories and defined the word 'mechanism' as 'social processes having designated consequences for designated parts of the social structure'. In contemporary sociology the concept of 'social mechanism' is prominent in the writings of Mario Bunge (2003), James Coleman (1986) and Peter Hedström (2005). A mechanism is internal to a system; it explains how something works, and can therefore contribute to increasing insights into the relationship between micro places and crime.

A major shortcoming of covering law-based theorizing is that it excludes from the explanation exactly these processes that make it possible to really understand why social entities, such as micro places, exhibit the regularities they do. The problem is basically that referring to a state of affairs is not enough to provide a causal explanation. In this respect, covering law theories are blackbox explanations that exclude from focus those processes that would allow us to understand why a specific causal factor is likely to be of explanatory relevance.

This problem has plagued the ecological school for too long: what was lacking in the ecological approach of Shaw and McKay, but also of Blau and Blau (1982) and Stark (1987), other early scholars of crime place theories, and also of those who considered themselves to be methodological 'holists', was their failure to theorize and empirically demonstrate the basic *entities* and *activities* that generate these correlations. The most reasonable ontological hypothesis we can formulate in order to make sense of the social world as we know it is that it is individuals in interaction with others in settings that generate the social regularities we observe.

In many disciplines great efforts are made to understand what a cause would produce were it to act alone, with no other causes at work. For example, in econometrics parameters are estimated that represent what a single cause by itself contributes to an overall effect (see Cartwright 2007); the same happens in quantitative criminology. Philosophers of science, especially those who work from the 'powerful particulars' perspective, argue that certain characteristics (dispositions) of objects (and actors) need to be taken into account when we want to understand causation (Mumford and Anjum 2011). This perspective supposes the information gained is useless since in the practical world no cause ever acts alone, while all causes generally act in interaction with each other. This is recently also acknowledged in criminology (Wikström 2007). Why do scholars spend great effort to learn what causal events do in circumstances that rarely if ever occur in isolation? Because it seems natural to expect that action is always the outcome of exposure to micro places and actors perceiving action alternatives, defining situations and habitually or volitionally deciding between action alternatives, it is hard to make sense of laws (such as the law of crime concentration) using only the regularity law itself. The view of micro places as 'passive powerful particulars' may be of help to understand the law. Micro places have the ability to trigger perception-choice processes in some persons who are exposed to a micro place, and have the ability of being attractive to certain kinds of persons, i.e. selection effects (Taylor 2015). These abilities are attributed to specific entities in micro places. The question, from a micro place perspective, is what kinds of micro place characteristics have the ability to trigger perception-choice processes in individuals and what properties cause individuals to self-select themselves in a micro place. This example makes it clear how important it is not to exclude the individual from crime place theories. While the criminology of place raises extremely important questions, it is the individual who is triggered, and the individual actor alone has the real causal power to commit an offense. A micro place cannot produce or spawn crime without an actor.

Criminologists often define mechanisms as intermediate variables that are necessary to make an observed correlation between characteristics plausible. Blalock (1964) described this relationship as an indirect effect. There is however one danger that one should be aware of when following this interpretation. One cannot consider a variable that represents a mediator of another variable to be equal to the underlying mechanisms behind a known association, without having given serious thought to cause-and-effect relationships. The definition of 'causal mechanism' is usually associated with the analogy of the operation of machinery. Take, for example, the following definition of Paul Thagard (1998: 106–107): 'A mechanism is a system of parts that operate or interact like those of a machine, transmitting forces, motion and energy to one another . . . Mechanical systems are organised hierarchically, in that mechanisms at lower levels (e.g., molecules) produce changes that take place at higher levels (e.g., cells)'.

The Norwegian sociologist Jon Elster was one of the most important socio-logical advocates for a renewed focus on mechanisms (Elster 1989). Elster wrote that the state of an event or action is tantamount for giving a plausible reason for why an event or action took place.

Having compared multiple mechanism definitions as developed by Bunge (2004); Hedström (2005); Elster (1989); and Wikström (2007) we cannot but conclude that no consensus exists about precise definitions of mechanisms. While Wikström argues that a mechanism is the process that connects a cause and an effect, and Elster (2007) refers to frequently occurring easily recogniz-able patterns that are brought about under certain conditions, it is Bunge's defi-nition that provides the most interesting explanation of a mechanism, not only for the study of crime at place but for criminology as a whole. Bunge (2004) defines a mechanism as a process in a definite system that is able to bring about or to prevent an effect in that system. Bunge's definition is important because of its link to systems. Micro places can be studied like systems, and in systems emergent processes are likely to happen. Environmental criminology is about *spatial systems and spatial mechanisms* and thus needs to study actors and actions at specific places that bring about their effects. Thinking of mechanisms in this way reveals that mechanisms are more than just intermediate variables. Explanation is thus not about detecting laws, while this may be a very important step, but should ultimately deal with an increase in our understanding of the mechanisms at work. By explaining things, we increase our understanding of the social fact. Theories of crime places should not be seen as just intellectual constructions useful for making predictions and controlling criminal events. If we translate the ideas of analytical sociologist Ylikoski (2011) to our under-standing of the law of crime concentration, the primary epistemic goal is to represent the causal processes that generate the observable phenomena.

It is an important theoretical task for environmental criminology to state why a geographical unit of analysis plays an important theoretical role in the explanation of events (action). We submit that Bunge's (1999) ideas on mech-anism-based explanations, which he developed as an integral part of his emer-gent systemist approach (which he often refers to as the CESM-model), can be a helpful tool to explain crime as individual action and crime as social fact (crime concentrations at places) by looking at:

1. The *composition* of the micro place as a system, i.e. the collection of parts of the system;
2. The *environment* of the micro place as a system or the collection of entities that are not a part of the system but do have an influence on parts of the system;
3. The *structure* of the micro place as a system, i.e. the whole of structural relationships between the parts of a system;[4] and
4. The *mechanisms* that generate actions in a system and may stop generating actions in the system.

Systemism is a way of non-reductionist theorizing that goes beyond the so-called methodological individualist approach (and especially the atomist approach, which argues that societies are *only* made up of individual actors, i.e. the notion that society is nothing more than a membership) and the holist approach, which overemphasizes the oversocialized conception of humans. Systemism is about individuals (biosocial organisms or systems) that are taking part in multiple systems. Micro places are systems, so a systemism (meta-theoretical) framework can be a powerful blueprint for further unraveling the generative processes behind the law of crime concentration. The systemic approach is so important because it allows for theorizing across levels, and no other framework has been more fruitful for the study of emergence. Some contemporary scholars, such as social scientists (Manzo 2010; Sawyer 2001), criminologists (Taylor 2015; Wikström 2014) and philosophers of science (Bunge 2003; Wan 2011), are clearly influenced by the systemic approach (see also McGloin, Sullivan, and Kennedy 2012).

Toward a Better Understanding of Emergence

The idea of emergence and emergent properties is especially important if we want to increase our understanding of the emergence of crime places. The concept of emergence is often used in an inaccurate or ambiguous way to show something 'new' appearing through the interaction of different parts that the (complex) entity has, properties that cannot be reduced to the parts of which the entity consists. Emergent systemism provides an ontological definition to emergence.

Figure 3.1 is based on the ideas that are developed in Jepperson and Meyers (2011) and can be seen as an elaboration of the famous Boudon-Coleman

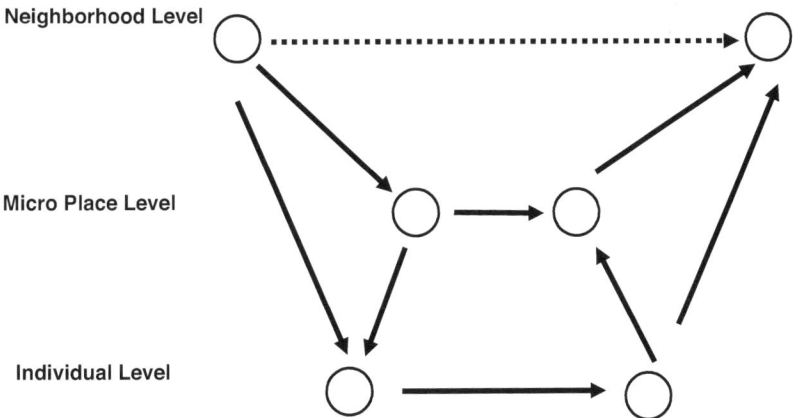

Figure 3.1 Relationships between the actor characteristics and action at multiple levels.

diagram. The only difference is that we have drawn three levels to socially give micro places a causal place and a context in the emergent systemic framework. Applying the study of emergence to the study of crime at micro places, we need to know what status the properties (at the individual/target level, micro place level and neighborhood level) have in a criminological explanation. What causal force can we ascribe to them, if any?

First, with regard to the debate about the (in)dependence of macro properties (neighborhood level) in relation to micro place level objects and individual/target level properties: Are these neighborhoods compiled from actions of individuals? Reductionists state that the properties are not different, and they will derive from it that we should formulate our explanations on the micro level.

Three key problems should be addressed when we look for explanations of micro place concentrations: (1) is supervenience the mechanism behind micro place correlations, (2) to what extent is multiple realization possible and (iii) is there heterogeneous disjunction?

> *Supervenience* suggests that there can be no difference in the higher (social) level without there being a difference in the lower (individual) level, which is dominated by the higher level. The dependency relationship (a component of non-reductionist individualism) can, therefore, be expressed on the basis of supervenience. For example, a turf war between gangs in a micro place L supervenes with regard to the behavior of gang members in that micro place. This means that the nature of the turf war R will only change if there is a change at the lower level, in particular, in the behavior of gang members I.
>
> *Multiple realization*: an attribute on the highest level (i.e. in the present example a neighborhood level crime count) can be achieved in several different ways by attributes and objects (i.e. individuals) on the lower, individual level, but also in micro places at the meso-level. For example, the number of acts of crime in a micro place can be established in multiple ways, i.e. different individual behavior (either a different number of individuals or the same returning individuals) can ensure that a micro place has a high level of crime counts, which in turn may increase the likelihood that neighborhoods have high crime rates (if there are no problems of overlapping boundaries). The level of crime counts of a micro place is not only determined by the behavior of the residents, but also by that of visitors, students, commuters, tourists, etc. Multiple realization is of major importance to evidence-based practices in reducing the number of crime counts in a micro place.
>
> *Heterogeneous disjunction*: a characteristic on the higher level can be achieved by a heterogeneous-disjunctive combination of properties at the lower level, and, therefore, these heterogeneous-disjunctive combinations can be related to each other in a useful (and even lawful)

way. For example, if there are a high number of crime counts in a micro place one could suggest that these counts may not be explained by a law or by a rational-choice (or suboptimal choice by selection of frames and scripts) statement that relates to the behavior of residents, passers-by and by-standers. The heterogeneity of the behavior of different individuals hinders this. As crime is generally and most often the result of complex interactions between the individual who perceives action alternatives at a setting, and chooses among alternatives through his or her senses, Sawyer's argument can be used. At some micro places conditions can be present that interact more strongly and at shorter intervals with intrapersonal characteristics of people.

These three characteristics of the relationship between the higher (micro place) level and lower (individual) level form the arguments for the existence of social mechanisms (contextual effects), i.e. causation at the level of the micro place ecological setting. In addition, these characteristics are strong arguments for non-reductive individualism: supervenience clarifies the dependency relationship (ontological individualism), and multiple realization and heterogeneous disjunction offer the arguments against a reductionist approach (against methodological individualism and against atomism). Sawyer (2001: 573) refers to social causation as being supervening causation: 'Emergentism does not claim that all higher-level properties are irreducible; some of them are predictable and derivable from the system of lower-level components. Only in cases where the relation between higher-level and lower-level properties is wildly disjunctive beyond some threshold of complexity will the higher-level property not be lawfully reducible' (Sawyer 2001: 558). Sawyer, just like Bunge, developed a powerful argument for an ontological definition of the concept of emergence. Ontological emergence means that new, real and non-reducible properties (on the higher level) exist.

Disentangling the Propositions Into Mechanisms in Spatial Criminology

As stressed before, spatial criminology has at its disposal a great number of theories aiming at the explanation of the concentration of crime at spaces. Some have been tested in empirical studies, others are still waiting to be researched and others have been used to explain observed concentrations of crimes at micro places (Pratt and Cullen 2005; Wilcox et al. 2003). Especially (various versions of) social disorganization theories have been researched empirically for decades. Nevertheless, the theoretical development of the criminology of place is still in its early stages (Weisburd 2015). This kind of ecological research has some structural (methodological) limitations, but criminology of place can be helpful because of its focus on smaller units of analysis (Weisburd, Bernasco, et al. 2009).

To increase our understanding of the ways micro place concentrations occur, we can make use of the blueprint of emergent systemism and fill out the blanks at multiple levels (see Figure 3.1). It is clear that we should be guided by theoretical integration at different levels (vertical and end-to-end integration). Drawing on the integration between environmental criminology and the social disorganization tradition, we can expect micro place concentrations to be the outcome of complex interactions between processes of informal control, the presence of crime attractors and generators, the moral climate of the micro place, the presence of gang activities (provocation), disorderly processes and so on. While each of these factors can be thought of to influence concentrations at micro places, it seems a valuable approach to search for specific combinations that have the largest impact on micro place concentrations. Identifying the specific combinations of elements that have the largest effect on concentrations may be of relevance for situational crime prevention. In Figure 3.2 an extended version of Figure 3.1 is presented. Each line must be elaborated to explain why at certain micro places concentrations of crime occur. It is a different strategy than using e.g. social disorganization theory and opportunity theory as competitors to explain the same phenomena (Braga and Clarke 2014).

Figure 3.2 is inspired by Manzo's schematic representation of the development of macro-micro interactions over time. As actors are responsible for the commission of criminal acts, we submit that micro place studies will also highly benefit from studies of selection processes and studies of land use. Understanding who makes use of the public and semi-public space at micro places should allow for functional differentiation of preventing activities (such as POP [Problem, Observation and Proposition]). Just like Sampson (2012)

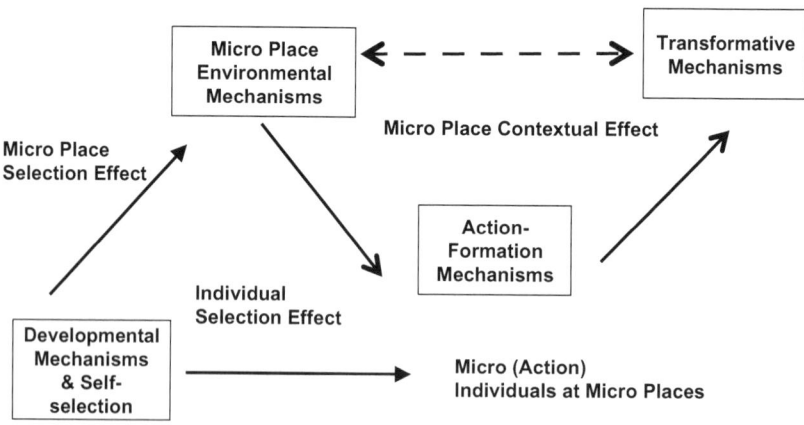

Figure 3.2 Extended relationships between actor characteristics and the actor's environment (elaboration of Manzo [2010]).

and Taylor (2015) have argued in their respective work on neighborhoods and communities, we should treat selection (both self-selection and social selection) as a real problem and not just some problem that one needs to control for. Selection can turn into causation and vice-versa, in a bottom-up and top-down cycle of feedback loops over time. Individuals (as a result of their daily routine activities) 'self-select' habitually or deliberately places in an urban environment where they want to be; offenders may live near micro places because of social selection mechanisms (e.g. segregation at the housing market); potential offenders may create kinds of niches. Niches are places selected by (potential) offenders as bases for their criminal activities such as dealing hard drugs or picking pockets. As Felson (2006) argued, taking a human ecological (or micro-ecological; see Taylor [2015]) approach can be a valuable way of thinking about a micro place's spatial mechanisms and an individual's behavior in micro-ecological settings. Such an approach can add up to the mechanism-based approach by simultaneously looking for functions.

Notwithstanding all that relevant information, it cannot be denied that locations are essentially *passive* agencies that can trigger perception-choice processes of individuals. Individuals have certain characteristics that may allow them morally to commit criminal acts, given that the chance to be apprehended (by guardians or law enforcement) is as low as possible. Classic environmental criminology has neglected the fact that individuals can be offenders or become offenders when at certain locations. The past focus of environmental criminology on large areas or neighborhoods is probably the consequence of an overestimation of the effect of large areas. However, individuals do not commit crimes in large areas or neighborhoods but at certain locations (micro places). The criminology of place can be the next step in explicitly elaborating the complex spatial mechanisms that lead to crime concentrations at micro places. With special empirical data, as collected by Wikström and his colleagues (Wikström, Oberwittler, Treiber, and Hardie 2012) or by the NSCR in Amsterdam (Bernasco, Bruinsma, Pauwels, and Weerman 2013; Bernasco, Ruiter, Bruinsma, Pauwels, and Weerman 2013; Hoeben, Bernasco, Weerman, Pauwels, and van Halem 2014), these propositions can be adequately tested. These data fit the micro places and can be extended by systematic observations. These data also allow testing why certain individuals with particular characteristics may commit a crime at a certain setting (location) and not at another setting (Bruinsma, Pauwels, Weerman, and Bernasco 2015; Weerman et al. 2015).

In order to empirically test the ideas we outlined previously, we suggest the following strategy. *First*, environmental criminologists could study the empirical literature on settings/places (outside the realm of criminology). However, this might be a disappointing endeavor because we expect not very much literature to be found in which empirically tested causal mechanisms at places have been researched. Nevertheless, the existing literature may be helpful in tracking down interesting results or uncovering causal mechanisms that can be used as thoughtful propositions for the next step. *Second*, a long-lasting research program can be developed to investigate step by step the presence or non-presence of causal mechanisms at places. We do not advocate one 'grand theory' in which all theoretical propositions can be tested empirically in one study, but we need informative meta-theoretical frameworks as a guide to research. We opt for a *trial and error strategy* in which step by step, during subsequent empirical studies, the propositions about causal mechanisms can be tested empirically one by one (Popper 1974). Additionally, we submit the thesis that it remains important to be able to compare theories, in the spirit of Lakatos's research program of comparing theories. This research program (see Lakatos 1970; Opp 2013) should of course take into account the problems and prospects that have been described by proponents of the analytical school in sociology (Hedström 2005) and proponents of the analytical traditions in criminology (Taylor 2015; Wikström et al. 2012). However, general, detailed and highly informative guidelines of analytical criminology as a distinct research paradigm are not available at the moment. The similarities are often larger than the differences between analytical criminology and Opp's (2009) structural-individualist research program of comparative testing of macro-micro theories: the elaboration and fine-tuning of the DN-model by including generative mechanisms is difficult to distinguish in its empirical form from the activities of the analytical tradition (Opp 2013). Both traditions make use of carefully stated propositions. Often straw hypotheses lead scholars to embrace one research program above another. In line with Taylor (2015), we argue that micro place criminology may become stronger when various methods and data in several distinct contexts can be used and when various methodological issues are resolved, before hypotheses are vigorously tested. On some occasions experiments can be applied; in other cases observations in combination with interviews or administrative data are more fruitful (with recognition of all the limitations administrative data have). Triangulation is of critical importance here.

A research program for micro place criminology should also design tests in different contexts, e.g. not only in American cities, but also in European, African or Asian cities, to get insight into the universality of those causal mechanisms at places. Whatever the focus of the studies, criminologists should not (exclusively) depend on existing (administrative or police) data, but should collect their own designed data by choosing step by step the 'best' (empirical) operational measures for the (theoretical) variables and phenomena under study. Special attention should also be paid to two topics when testing empirically causal mechanisms at places. *First*, researchers should develop clearly formulated propositions that connect places, actors and contexts as we have discussed. Elucidation is the goal of stating hypotheses (Bunge 1999). Existing theories can be used as a source of inspiration, but a fresh new start can be fruitful as well. *Second*, the empirical research should not only focus on the attractive circumstances to commit crimes at places, but should also not neglect or ignore selection processes as elaborated by Taylor (2015). One should keep in mind in all designs that even frequent or habitual offenders do not commit a crime every time when being present at particular places. Criminologists sometimes forget that crime is still a rare phenomenon in the everyday life of people.

To end, we try to give a preliminary answer to the question addressed by Taylor (2015). Are there meta perspectives that could be used besides the Boudon-Coleman approach? In this chapter we have argued for a complex variant of the Boudon-Coleman diagram, namely Manzo's complex structuralism, which is almost equivalent to Bunge's systemism. The focus on micro places and the methodological and theoretical problems that are addressed in detail by Taylor may not lead to a reductionist approach, ignoring context and social selection. Adopting a full emergent systemic approach, or a complex structural-individualist approach, allows for a fine-tuning or fine-graining of the ideas that are already outlined in the classic Boudon-Coleman diagram. This way of thinking has been successfully applied in situational action theory, where it has proven to be a productive 'road map for building integrative frameworks that each explain a part of a complex interactive chain of events and mechanisms', but the systemic approach of Bunge may also be useful to study the acts of individuals in groups (gangs) in micro places; these are different non-hierarchically overlapping settings that all produce individual-environment interactions that bring about criminal events.

From the aforementioned remarks it becomes clear that micro place criminology awaits a lot of challenges. The key theoretical and methodological questions that Ralph Taylor asks about community criminology should be taken into account because they are straightforwardly applicable to micro place criminology; the only serious difference we observe is the level of aggregation. Methodologically, micro place criminology awaits a lot of exciting challenges as the units of analyses are becoming increasingly smaller, which we suspect will raise concerns regarding the ecological reliability and validity of measures (Taylor 2015). Scaling issues relate to how large micro places should be, what are boundaries (natural or not), and can reliable and valid indicators be developed at such a small level? This problem is not restricted to micro place criminology but to criminological theorizing in general: several indicators can be interpreted as indicators for different concepts (collective efficacy's dimension of informal control versus guardianship is meanwhile a known problem). Therefore, comparative testing of competing integrative models using multiple valid indicators is a daunting task for micro place criminology. Finally, and often neglected, although it has been stressed elsewhere (Taylor 2015; Wikström and Sampson 2003), the study of both self-selection and social processes as separate non-causal processes that bear causal consequences, which in turn can affect the perception of action alternatives or the choices that actors make deliberately or habitually in micro places, should be part of an emergent research program that may advance our current knowledge on micro places as systems in criminology.

Conclusion

The goal of the present chapter is to stimulate theorizing on spatial mechanisms to increase our understanding of crime concentrations at micro places. The study of crime at multiple levels of analysis requires a mechanism-based approach. Social and micro-ecological processes that connect causes and effects at different levels of analysis are being studied within this approach. These levels should be explicated, and the theoretically relevant mechanisms that operate at each level should be clearly dissected and defined. The answer to these 'why' questions can best be given when four principles are taken into account: the principles of explanation, dissection, precision and clarity, and action. These principles force environmental criminologists to study crime as a social phenomenon at small levels of aggregation (micro-ecology) and give an explanation that goes beyond the relations between variables. We should keep in mind also that, when it comes to crime prevention at the micro place level, causality does not operate at the variable level. Micro places are not active causal agents, but that does not mean that they have no causal effect. They can bring about judgments and (consciously or unconsciously) trigger action strategies in individuals in micro places as action is always a consequence of perceiving an action alternative and choosing an act of crime as a viable action alternative. Advanced theoretical development in environmental criminology is necessary if we want to improve our insight into the complexity of a spatially skewed phenomenon such as crime, and if we want to develop better (i.e. more successful, evidence-based) prevention projects that achieve crime reduction at the micro place levels.

One strong point of this approach is that it appeals for the study of crime as action at multiple levels of analysis from a theoretical point of view. To illustrate the existence of crime at multiple levels, Boudon-Coleman's approach toward the study of macro-micro relations was given as an example. Bunge's CESM-model can help to determine the nature of observed correlations at multiple levels. This framework can easily be extended to the study of other topics in environmental criminology while still using the same principles of analytical precision.

Notes

1. In practice, many criminologists or crime analysts studying the spatial distribution of crimes first observe a number of locations with high crime counts, and afterward assume that those locations 'thus' must have attractive targets, motivated offenders and no guardians. This practice is called ad-hoc explanation, but has no empirical or theoretical validity. Despite its popularity and simplicity, the empirical status of

RAT is anyway not very impressive (Mustaine and Tewksbury 1997; Pratt and Cullen 2005; Wilcox, Land and Hunt 2003). In most research, RAT is not empirically tested by measuring the propositions of the theory as well as the concepts that figure in it.

2. Bunge (1979) recognized that causation is a complex notion and was one of the first to argue that a causal explanation needs to be mechanism-based. Bunge has previously been accused of being deterministic, but that is a consequence of wrong reading of the first edition of his opus magnum on causation. Scholars originally tended to equate causation with causal determinism, but causal determination simply means that something is determined by something else. Determination is thus not determinism (the idea that everything is caused by something else—causalism), and even determinism is not the same as fatalism. These conceptual misunderstandings are truly a consequence of a lack of insight in the philosophical literature on causation.

3. See system 1 versus system 2 thinking by Kahneman (2011).

4. Structure should not be confused with the composition of the system. Structure refers to the relations between actors in a system.

References

Beebee, Helen, Christopher Hitchcock, and Peter Menzies. 2009. *The Oxford Handbook of Causation*. Oxford: Oxford University Press.

Bernasco, Wim. 2010a. "Modeling Micro-Level Crime Location Choice: Application of the Discrete Choice Framework to Crime at Places." *Journal of Quantitative Criminology* 26: 113–138.

Bernasco, Wim. 2010b. "A Sentimental Journey Tot Crime: Effects of Residential History on Crime Location Choice." *Criminology* 48: 389–416.

Bernasco, Wim, Gerben J. N. Bruinsma, Lieven J. R. Pauwels, and Frank M. Weerman. 2013. "Adolescent Delinquency and Diversity in Behavior Settings." *Australian & New Zealand Journal of Criminology* 46: 357–378.

Bernasco, Wim, Stijn Ruiter, Gerben J. N. Bruinsma, Lieven J. R. Pauwels, and Frank M. Weerman. 2013. "Situational Causes of Offending: A Fixed-Effects Analysis of Space—Time Budget Data." *Criminology* 51: 895–926.

Bernasco, Wim, and Wouter Steenbeek. 2016. "More Places than Crimes: Implications for Evaluating the Law of Crime Concentration at Place." *Journal of Quantitative Criminology*: 1–17.

Blalock, Hubert M. 1964. *Causal Inferences in Nonexperimental Research*. Chapel Hill, NC: The University of North Carolina Press.

Blau, Judith R., and Peter M. Blau. 1982. "The Cost of Inequality: Metropolitan Structure and Violent Crime." *American Sociological Review*: 114–129.

Braga, Anthony A., and Ronald V. Clarke. 2014. "Explaining High-Risk Concentrations of Crime in the City: Social Disorganization, Crime Opportunities, and Important Next Steps." *Journal of Research in Crime and Delinquency* 51: 480–498.

Brantingham, Paul J., and Patricia L. Brantingham. 1978. "A Theoretical Model of Crime Site Selection." Pp. 105–118 in M. D. Krohn and R. L. Akers (eds.), *Crime, Law and Sanctions*. Beverly Hills, CA: Sage.

Brantingham, Paul J., and Patricia L. Brantingham. 1981. *Environmental Criminology*. Beverly Hills, CA: Sage.

Brantingham, Paul J., and Patricia L. Brantingham. 1984. *Patterns in Crime*. New York, NY: Macmillan.

Brantingham, Paul J., and Patricia L. Brantingham. 2008. "Crime Pattern Theory." Pp. 78–94 in R. Wortley and L. Mazarolle (eds.), *Environmental Criminology and Crime Analysis*. Devon: Willan Publishing.

Bruinsma, Gerben J.N. 2010. "Pleidooi voor een interactionistische criminologie. Over de rol van de omgeving bij de spreiding en het ontstaan van criminaliteit." Den Haag: Boom Juridische uitgevers.

Bruinsma, Gerben J. N. 2013. "Fuzzy Pluralism in Theoretical Criminology." Pp. 51–60 in A. Kuhn, P. Margot, M. F. Aebi, C. Schwarzenegger, A. Donatsch, and D. Jositsch (eds.), *Criminology, Criminal Policy and Criminal Law in International Perspective: Essays in the Honour of Martin Killias*. Bern: Stämpfli Verlag.

Bruinsma, Gerben J. N. 2016. "Proliferation of Crime Causation Theories in an Era of Fragmentation: Reflections on the Current State of Criminological Theory." *European Journal of Criminology* 13: 659–676.

Bruinsma, Gerben J. N. 2017. "From Countries to Micro Places: A Brief History of 200 Years of Geographical Criminology." *Jerusalem Review of Legal Studies*: 14.

Bruinsma, Gerben J. N., Lieven J. R. Pauwels, Frank M. Weerman, and Wim Bernasco. 2015. "Situational Action Theory: Cross-Sectional and Cross-Lagged Tests of Its Core Propositions." *Canadian Journal of Criminology and Criminal Justice* 57: 363–398.

Bruinsma, Gerben J. N., and David Weisburd. 2014a. "History of Geographic Criminology Part I: Nineteenth Century." Pp. 2159–2163 in Gerben J. N. Bruinsma and D. Weisburd (eds.), *Encyclopedia of Criminology and Criminal Justice*. New York, NY: Springer.

Bruinsma, Gerben J.N., and David Weisburd. 2014b. "History of Geographic Criminology Part II: The 20th Century." Pp. 2164–2172 in Gerben J. N. Bruinsma and D. Weisburd (eds.), *The Encyclopedia of Criminology and Criminal Justice*. New York, NY: Springer.

Bunge, Mario. 1979. *Causality and Modern Science*. New York, NY: Courier Corporation.

Bunge, M. 1999. *The Sociology-Philosophy Connection*. New Brunswick, NJ: Transaction Publications.

Bunge, Mario. 2003. *Emergence and Convergence: Qualitative Novelty and the Unity of Knowledge*. Toronto: University of Toronto Press.

Bunge, Mario. 2004. "How Does It Work? The Search for Explanatory Mechanisms." *Philosophy of the Social Sciences* 34: 182–210.

Burgess, Ernest W. 1967 [1925]. "The Growth of the City: An Introduction to a Research Project." Pp. 47–62 in R. E. Park and E. W. Burgess (eds.), *The City: Suggestions for the Investigation of Human Behaviour in the Urban Environment*. Chicago, IL: The University of Chicago Press.

Bursik, Robert J. 1984. "Urban Dynamics and Ecological Studies of Delinquency." *Social Forces*. 63: 393.

Bursik, Robert J. 1986. "Ecological Stability and the Dynamics of Delinquency." Pp. 35–66 in A. J. Reiss Jr. and M. Tonry (eds.), *Communities and Crime: Crime and Justice: A Review of Research*. Chicago, IL: The University of Chicago Press.

Bursik, Robert J., and Harald G. Grasmick. 1993. *Neighborhoods and Crime: The Dimensions of Effective Community Control*. New York, NY: Lexington.

Cartwright, Nancy. 2007. *Hunting Causes and Using Them: Approaches in Philosophy and Economics*. Cambridge: Cambridge University Press.

Cohen, Lawrence E., and Marcus Felson. 1979. "Social Change and Crime Rate Trends: A Routine Activity Approach." *American Sociological Review* 44: 588–608.

Coleman, James S. 1986. "Social Theory, Social Research, and a Theory of Action." *American Journal of Sociology* 91: 1309–1335.

Coleman, James S. 1990. *Foundations of Social Theory*. Cambridge and London: The Belknap Press and Harvard University Press.

Elster, Jon. 1989. *Nuts And Bolts for the Social Sciences*. Cambridge: Cambridge University Press.

Elster, Jon. 2007. *Explaining Social Behaviour: More Nuts and Bolts for the Social Sciences*. Cambridge: Cambridge University Press.

Felson, Marcus. 1994. *Crime and Everyday Life: Insight and Implications for Society*. Thousand Oaks, CA: Pine Forge Press.

Felson, Marcus. 2006. *Crime and Nature*. Thousand Oaks, CA: Sage.

Felson, Marcus. 2008. "Routine Activity Approach." Pp. 70–77 in Richard Wortley and Lorraine Mazarolle (eds.), *Environmental Criminology and Crime Analysis*. Devon: Willan.

Felson, Marcus, and Lawrence E. Cohen. 1980. "Human Ecology and Crime: A Routine Activity Approach." *Human Ecology* 8: 389–406.

Glyde, John. 1856. "Localities of Crime in Suffolk." *Journal of the Statistical Society of London* 19: 102–106.

Greg, William R. 1835. *Social Statistics of the Netherlands*. London Ridgway: Harrison and Crosfield.

Groff, Elizabeth R., David Weisburd, and Sue-Ming Yang. 2010. "Is It Important to Examine Crime Trends at a Local 'Micro' Level?: A Longitudinal Analysis of Street to Street Variability in Crime Trajectories." *Journal of Quantitative Criminology* 26: 7–32.

Guerry, André-Michel. 1832. "La Statistique Comparée de l'Etat de l'Instruction et du Nombre des Crimes." *Revue Encyclopédique* 55: 414–424.

Guerry, André-Michel. 1833. *Essai sur la Statistique Morale de la France*. Paris: Crochard.

Hedström, Peter. 2005. *Dissecting the Social: On the Principles of Analytical Sociology*. Cambridge: Cambridge University Press.

Hedström, Peter, and Richard Swedberg. 1998. *Social Mechanisms: An Analytical Approach to Social Theory*. Cambridge: Cambridge University Press.

Hempel, Carl G. 1965. *Aspects of Scientific Explanation and Other Essays in the Philosophy of Science*. New York, NY: The Free Press.

Hempel, Carl G., and Paul Oppenheim. 1948. "Studies in the Logic of Explanation." *Philosophy of Science* 15: 135–175.

Hoeben, Evelien M., Wim Bernasco, Frank M. Weerman, Lieven Pauwels, and Sjoerd van Halem. 2014. "The Space-Time Budget Method in Criminological Research." *Crime Science* 3: 12.

Jepperson, Ronald, and John W. Meyer. 2011. "Multiple Levels of Analysis and the Limitations of Methodological Individualisms." *Sociological Theory* 19: 2954–2973.

Johnson, Shane D. 2014. "How Do Offenders Choose Where to Offend? Perspectives from Animal Foraging." *Legal and Criminological Psychology* 19: 193–210.

Kahneman, Daniel. 2011. *Thinking, Fast and Slow*. New York, NY: Farrar, Strauss, Giroux.

Kornhauser, Ruth R. 1978. *Social Sources of Delinquency: An Appraisal of Analytic Models*. Chicago, IL: University of Chicago Press.

Kroneberg, Clemens, Isolde Heintze, and Guido Mehlkop. 2010. "The Interplay of Moral Norms and Instrumental Incentives in Crime Causation." *Criminology* 48: 259–294.

Lakatos, Imre. 1970. "Falsification and the Methodology of Scientific Research Programmes." Pp. 91–196 in I. Lakatos and A. Musgrave (eds.), *Criticism and the Growth of Knowledge*. Cambridge: Cambridge University Press.

Manzo, Gianluca. 2010. "Analytical Sociology and Its Critics." *European Journal of Sociology* 51: 129–170.

McGloin, Jean M., Christopher J. Sullivan, and Leslie W. Kennedy. 2012. *When Crime Appears: The Role of Emergence*. London: Routledge.

Merton, Robert K. 1968. *Social Theory and Social Structure* (Enlarged ed.). New York, NY: Free Press.

Merton, Robert K. 1996. *On Social Structure and Science*, edited by P. Sztompka. Chicago and London: The University of Chicago Press.

Morris, William E., and Charlotte R. Brown. 2016. "David Hume." In E. N. Zalta (ed.), *The Stanford Encyclopedia of Philosophy*. Retrieved from http://plato.stanford.edu/archives/spr2016/entries/hume/

Mumford, Stephen, and Rani Lill Anjum. 2011. *Getting Causes from Powers*. Oxford: Oxford University Press.

Mustaine, Elizabeth Ehrhardt, and Richard Tewksbury. 1997. "Obstacles in the Assessment of Routine Activities Theory." *Social Pathology* 3: 177–194.

Opp, Karl-Dieter. 2002. Methodologie der Sozialwissenschaften. *Einführung in Probleme ihrer Theoriebildung und praktischen Anwendung* (5., überarbeitete Auflage ed.). Wiesbaden: Westdeutscher Verlag.

Opp, Karl-Dieter. 2009. *Theories of Political Protest and Social Movements: A Multidisciplinary Introduction, Critique, and Synthesis*. London: Routledge.

Opp, Karl-Dieter. 2013. "What Is Analytical Sociology? Strengths and Weaknesses of a New Sociological Research Program." *Social Science Information* 52: 329–360.

Park, Robert, and Ernest Burgess. 1967 [1925]. *The City: Suggestions for Investigation of Human Behavior in the Urban Environment*. Chicago: The University of Chicago Press.

Popper, Karl. 1974. *Conjectures and Refutations: The Growth of Scientific Knowledge* (4th ed.). London: Routledge and Kegan Paul.

Popper, Karl. 1975. *The Logic of Scientific Discovery* (8th ed.). London: Hutchinson.

Pratt, Travis, and Francis T. Cullen. 2005. "Assessing Macro-Level Predictors and Theories of Crime." Pp. 373–450 in Michael Tonry (ed.), *Crime and Justice: A Review of Research*. Chicago: The University of Chicago Press.

Quételet, Adolphe. 1847. "Statistique morale de l'influence du libre arbiter de l'homme sur les faits sociaux, et particulierement sur le nombre des marriages." *Bulletin de la Commission Centrale de Statistique* 3: 135–155.

Quételet, Adolphe. 1848. *Sur la Statistique Morale et les Principes qui Doivent en Former la Base*. Bruxelles: Hayez.

Quételet, Adolphe. 1984 [1831]. *Research on the Propensity for Crime at Different Ages* (trans. and with an introduction by S. F. Sylvester). Cincinnati, OH: Anderson Publishing.

Rawson, Rawson W. 1839. "An Inquiry into the Statistics of Crime in England and Wales." *Journal of the Statistical Society of London*: 316–344.

Reiss, Albert J. 1986. "Why Are Communities Important in Understanding Crime?" Pp. 1–34 in A. J. Reiss and M. Tonry (eds.), *Communities and Crime: Crime and Justice: A Review of Research*. Chicago: The University of Chicago Press.

Reiss, Albert J., and Michael Tonry. 1986. *Communities and Crime*. Chicago: The University of Chicago Press.

Reynald, Danielle M. 2009. *Guardianship in Action: A Theoretical and Empirical Elaboration of the Routine Activity Concept*. Ph.D. Dissertation. Vrije Universiteit, Amsterdam.

Reynald, Danielle M. 2011. *Guarding against Crime: A Theoretical and Empirical Elaboration of the Routine Activity Concept*. London: Ashgate Publishers.

Robinson, William S. 1950. "Ecological Correlations and the Behavior of Individuals." *American Sociological Review* 15: 351–357.

Russell, Bertrand. 2013. *History of Western Philosophy: Collectors Edition*. New York, NY: Routledge.

Sampson, Robert J. 2010. "Collective Efficacy Theory." Pp. 802–812 in Francis T. Cullen and Pamela Wilcox (eds.), *Encyclopedia of Criminological Theory*. Thousands Oaks, CA: Sage.

Sampson, Robert J. 2012. *Great American City: Chicago and the Enduring Neighborhood Effect*. Chicago, IL: The University of Chicago Press.

Sampson, Robert J., Christopher Winship, and Carly Knight. 2013. "Translating Causal Claims." *Criminology & Public Policy* 12: 587–616.

Sawyer, R. Keith. 2001. "Emergence in Sociology: Contemporary Philosophy of Mind and Some Implications for Sociological Theory 1." *American Journal of Sociology* 107: 551–585.

Shaw, Clifford R., and Henry McKay. 1969 [1942]. *Juvenile Delinquency and Urban Areas: A Study of Rates of Delinquency in Relation to Differential Characteristics of Local Communities in American Cities*. Chicago, IL: The University of Chicago Press.

Shaw, Clifford R., Harvey M. Zorbaugh, Henry D. McKay, and Leonard S. Cottrell. 1929. *Delinquency Areas: A Study of the Geographic Distribution of School Truants, Juvenile Delinquents, and Adult Offenders in Chicago*. Chicago, IL: University of Chicago Press.

Sherman, Lawrence W., Patrick R. Gartin, and Michael E. Buerger. 1989. "Hot Spots of Predatory Crime: Routine Activities and the Criminology of Place." *Criminology* 27: 27–56.

Stark, Rodney. 1987. "Deviant Places: A Theory of the Ecology of Crime." *Criminology* 25: 893–910.

Steenbeek, Wouter, and David Weisburd. 2016. "Where the Action Is in Crime? An Examination of Variability of Crime across Different Spatial Units in the Hague, 2001–2009." *Journal of Quantitative Criminology* 32: 449–469.

Tacq, Jacques. 1984. *Causaliteit in sociaal wetenschappelijk onderzoek*. Antwerpen: Van Loghum Slaterus.

Taylor, Ralph B. 1987. "Toward an Environmental Psychology of Disorder: Delinquency, Crime, and Fear of Crime." Pp. 951–986 in D. Stokols and I. Altman (eds.), *Handbook of Environmental Psychology*. New York, NY: John Wiley and Sons.

Taylor, Ralph B. 1988. *Human Territorial Functioning*. Cambridge: Cambridge University Press.

Taylor, Ralph B. 2015. *Community Criminology: Fundamentals of Spatial and Temporal Scaling, Ecological Indicators, and Selectivity Bias*. New York, NY: New York University Press.

Taylor, Ralph B., Stephen D. Gottfredson, and Sidney Brower. 1981. "Territorial Cognitions and Social Climate in Urban Neighborhoods." *Basic and Applied Social Psychology* 2: 289–303.

Taylor, Ralph B., Stephen D. Gottfredson, and Sidney Brower. 1985. "Attachment to Place: Discriminant Validity, and Impacts of Disorder and Diversity." *American Journal of Community Psychology* 13: 525–542.

Telep, Cody, and David Weisburd. 2017. "The Criminology of Places." In G. J. N. Bruinsma and S. D. Johnson (eds.), *The Oxford Handbook on Environmental Criminology*. Oxford and New York, NY: Oxford University Press (in press).

Thagard, Paul. 1998. "Explaining Disease: Correlations, Causes, and Mechanisms." *Minds and Machines* 8: 61–78.

Thomas, William I. 1966. *On Social Organization and Social Personality: Selected Papers* (ed. and with an Introduction by M. Janovitz). Chicago, IL: The University of Chicago Press.

Townsley, Michael, Daniel Birks, Wim Bernasco, Stijn Ruiter, Shane D. Johnson, Gentry White, and Scott Baum. 2015. "Burglar Target Selection: A Cross-National Comparison." *Journal of Research in Crime and Delinquency* 52: 3–31.

Ultee, Wouter C. 1977. *Groei van kennis en stagnatie in de sociologie. Een aantal regels van de methode en een kritische doorlichting van enkele sociologische tradities.* Dissertation UU. Groningen: VRB Drukkerijen.

Von Wright, Georg H. 2004. *Explanation and Understanding.* Ithaca: Cornell University Press.

Wan, Poe Yu-Ze. 2011. *Reframing the Social: Emergentist Systemism and Social Theory.* Farnham: Ashgate.

Weerman, Frank M., Wim Bernasco, Gerben J. N. Bruinsma, and Lieven J. R. Pauwels. 2015. "When Is Spending Time with Peers Related to Delinquency? The Importance of Where, What, and with Whom." *Crime & Delinquency* 61: 1386–1413.

Weisburd, David. 2015. "The 2014 Sutherland Address: The Law of Crime Concentrations and the Criminology of Place." *Criminology* 53: 133–157.

Weisburd, David, Wim Bernasco, and Gerben J.N. Bruinsma. 2009. *Putting Crime in Its Place.* New York, NY: Springer.

Weisburd, David, Gerben J. N. Bruinsma, and Wim Bernasco. 2009. "Units of Analysis in Geographic Criminology: Historical Development, Critical Issues, and Open Questions." Pp. 3–31 in David Weisburd, Wim Bernasco, and Gerben J. N. Bruinsma (eds.), *Putting Crime in Its Place: Units of Analysis in Geographic Criminology.* New York, NY: Springer.

Weisburd, David, Shawn Bushway, Cynthia Lum, and Sue-Ming Yang. 2004. "Trajectories of Crime at Places: A Longitudinal Study of Street Segments in the City of Seattle." *Criminology* 42: 283–322.

Weisburd, David, Elizabeth R. Groff, and Sue-Ming Yang. 2012. *The Criminology of Place: Street Segments and Our Understanding of the Crime Problem.* Oxford: Oxford University Press.

Weisburd, David, and Cody Telep. 2014. "Law of Crime Concentrations at Places." Pp. 2827–2834 in Gerben J. N. Bruinsma and David Weisburd (eds.), *The Encyclopedia of Criminology and Criminal Justice.* New York, NY: Springer.

Weisburd, David, John E. Eck, Anthony A. Braga, Cody Telep, Breane Cave, Kate J. Bowers, Gerben J. N. Bruinsma, Charlotte Gill, Elizabeth R. Groff, Joshua C. Hinkle, Julie Hibdon, Shane D. Johnson, Brian Lawton, Cynthia Lum, Jerry H. Ratcliffe, George Rengert, Travis Taniguchi, and Sue-Ming Yang. 2016. *Place Matters.* Cambridge: Cambridge University Press.

Wikström, Per-Olof H. 2007. "In Search of Causes and Explanations of Crime." Pp. 117–140 in Roy King and Emma Wincup (eds.), *Doing Research on Crime and Justice.* Oxford: Oxford University Press.

Wikström, Per-Olof H. 2014. "Why Crime Happens: A Situational Action Theory." Pp. 74–94 in G. Manzo (ed.), *Analytical Sociology.* Hoboken, NJ: John Wiley and Sons.

Wikström, Per-Olof H., Dietrich Oberwittler, Kyle Treiber, and Beth Hardie. 2012. *Breaking Rules: The Social and Situational Dynamics of Young People's Urban Crime.* Oxford: Oxford University Press.

Wikström, Per-Olof H., and Robert J. Sampson. 2003. "Social Mechanisms of Community Influences on Crime and Pathways in Criminality." Pp. 118–148 in B. B. Lahey, T. E. Moffitt, and A. Caspi (eds.), *Causes of Conduct Disorder and Juvenile Delinquency.* New York, NY: The Guilford Press.

Wilcox, Pamela, Kenneth Land, and Scott Hunt. 2003. *Criminal Circumstance: A Dynamic Multicontextual Criminal Opportunity Theory.* New York, NY: Aldine de Gruyter.

Woodward, James. 2003. *Making Things Happen: A Theory of Causal Explanation.* New York, NY: Oxford University Press.

Ylikoski, Petri. 2011. "Social Mechanisms and Explanatory Relevance." Pp. 154–172 in P. Demeulenaere (ed.), *Analytical Sociology and Social Mechanisms*. Cambridge: Cambridge University Press.

Zorbaugh, Harvey W. 1929. *The Gold Coast and the Slum: A Sociological Study of Chicago's Near North Side*. Chicago, IL: The University of Chicago Press.

4

The Relationship Between Social Disorganization and Crime at the Micro Geographic Level: Findings From Tel Aviv-Yafo Using Israeli Census Data[1]

David Weisburd, Maor Shay, Shai Amram, and Roie Zamir

Introduction

Traditionally, research and theory in criminology have focused on individuals and communities (Nettler 1978; Sherman 1995). Recently, however, criminologists have begun to explore crime at micro units of geography (Eck and Weisburd 1995; Sherman et al. 1989). While concern with the relationship between crime and place is not new and indeed goes back to the founding generations of modern criminology (Guerry 1833; Quetelet 1831), the "micro" approach to places suggested by recent theories has only begun to be examined by criminologists.[2] Places in this micro context are specific locations within the larger social environments of communities and neighborhoods (Eck and Weisburd 1995). They are sometimes defined as buildings or addresses (e.g. see Green 1996; Sherman et al. 1989), sometimes as block faces or street segments (e.g. see Smith et al. 2000; Taylor 1997), and sometimes as clusters of addresses, block faces or street segments (e.g. see Sherman and Weisburd 1995; Weisburd and Green 1995; Weisburd et al. 2012).

Perhaps the key finding in this area of study is that there is a very significant clustering of crime at places, irrespective of the specific unit of analysis that is defined (e.g. see Andresen and Malleson 2011; Braga et al. 2014; Brantingham and Brantingham 1999; Crow and Bull 1975; Curman et al. 2015; Pierce et al. 1988; Roncek 2000; Sherman et al. 1989; Weisburd and Amram 2014; Weisburd and Green 1994; Weisburd et al. 2009; Weisburd et al. 1992). Such concentrations have been found not only across time within cities, but also across cities (Weisburd 2015). Weisburd argues that the consistency of such concentrations is so strong that they lead to confirmation of a "law of crime concentration at places."

Research supported by the US National Institute of Justice that examined the distribution of crime at micro places over time has further reinforced the relevance of hot spots approaches. Examining crime at street segments in Seattle over a 14-year period, Weisburd et al. (2004) found that there were distinct developmental trends at street segments, which suggested significant variability in the nature of crime trends over time at micro levels of geography. Using group-based trajectory analysis (Nagin 1999, 2005; Nagin and Land 1993) they identified 18 separate developmental trajectories (Weisburd et al. 2004). Despite the fact that Seattle, like other major American cities at the time (see Blumstein and Wallman 2000), had experienced a 24% crime drop during the study period, the bulk of these trajectories and the vast majority of the street segments in the city experienced little change in the 14 years examined. The crime "drop" in Seattle was driven by only 14% of the street segments in the study. And despite the overall crime decline, some 2% of street segments in the city evidenced stark increases in crime. These increasing trajectory segments experienced a rise in crime of fully 42%, while crime for the city overall declined 24% (Weisburd et al. 2004).

A follow up study on Seattle street segments has reinforced the earlier findings, and added important new information about the factors that influence crime trends over time (Weisburd et al. 2012, 2014). Examining 16 years of data, Weisburd, Groff and Yang found that both situational opportunities and social characteristics of places strongly distinguish chronic crime hot spots from areas with little crime. The finding that situational opportunities for crime were strongly related to crime trends at a micro geographic level did not surprise researchers in this area. But the finding that variables reflecting social disorganization were related to crime at this level opened a new area of inquiry. Weisburd et al.'s (2012) findings have been challenged because the measures used often did not directly capture social disorganization variables at the street segment level (Braga and Clark 2014). Such data are not available from the US Census because of privacy questions, and so Weisburd et al. (2012) drew from student data at schools and voting data to construct demographic background characteristics of streets. While Weisburd et al. (2012) use a variety of approaches to validate their measures, they remain for the most part proxies for direct measures of the social backgrounds of individuals living on the streets examined.

In this paper we report on findings from a study in Tel Aviv-Yafo in which we were able to gain data on social and demographic characteristics at the micro geographic level from the Israeli Central Bureau of Statistics (CBS). In a previous study we had found that crime at street segments in Tel Aviv-Yafo exhibits very similar trends to those identified in Seattle and other cities (see Weisburd 2015; Weisburd and Amram 2014). In Seattle, for example, between 4% and 6% of street segments (two block faces between intersections) produced 50% of crime each year over the 16-year study period, and 1% of street segments produced almost a quarter of reported crime at street segments (Weisburd et al. 2012; see also Weisburd et al. 2014 for a similar distribution of crime in New York City). In Tel Aviv-Yafo in 2010, about 5% of the street segments included about 50% of crime incidents and 1% of street segments produced almost 25% of crime incidents (Weisburd and Amram 2014).

Our present work extends crime trends in Tel Aviv-Yafo at street segments to 35 years focusing on residential streets, which makes our study the longest longitudinal analysis of crime trends at micro places we are aware of. Using group-based trajectory analysis (see Nagin 1999, 2005; Nagin and Land 1993; Nagin and Tremblay 1999, 2001, 2005) we have identified developmental patterns of crime at place over time (discussed later in this chapter). In this paper we focus on characteristics of people at places related to theories of social disorganization, and link those characteristics with crime trajectories. We received CBS data at the street segment level for the 1983 and 1995 censuses, as well as administrative data including social characteristics from 2000 until 2012. Our access to these data has allowed us to provide the first direct examination of the relationship between social disorganization factors at the street segment level and crime.

Social Disorganization and Crime at Place

Study of crime at higher geographic levels has placed emphasis on the social characteristics of places, emphasizing what is often termed "social disorganization" (see Sampson and Groves 1989; Shaw and McKay 1942 [1969]). Social disorganization theories suggest responses to the crime problem that are focused "on the effectiveness of informal mechanisms by which residents themselves achieve public order" (Sampson et al. 1997: 918). Sources of the differential ability of communities to regulate their residents are reflected in structural characteristics such as poverty and residential mobility.

If social disorganization theory is relevant at the street segment level, it would be expected that economic advantage would act as a protective factor against crime, and poverty as a risk factor for crime (Connolly et al. 2010; Kubrin and Weitzer 2003; Smargiassi et al. 2006). Theorists have assumed that poorer and more disadvantaged populations will have more difficulty in exercising informal social controls.

It is often argued that such social disorganization theories have little relevance for understanding crime at micro levels of geography. This seems to be the position of many scholars in this area. Sherman et al. (1989: 30), for example, argue that "traditional collectivity theories [termed here as social disorganization theories] may be appropriate for explaining community-level variation, but they seem inappropriate for small, publicly visible places with highly transient populations" (see also Braga and Clarke 2014).

But the geographies of crime hot spots may also be seen in many cases as small-scale communities. For example, a number of hot spots studies (including our own) use street segments or street blocks as a key unit for examining the distribution of crime. Taylor (1997, 1998) argues that such micro geographic units function as "behavior settings" (Wicker 1987: 614). They have many of the traits of communities that have been seen as crucial to social disorganization theory, in that these physical units function also as social units with specific routines. This approach is reinforced by Weisburd et al. (2012) in their examination of social disorganization characteristics in Seattle. For example, they collected data on public housing and Section 8 vouchers (housing) at street segments in Seattle, finding that there are "public housing assistance hot spots." Indeed, 50% of housing assistance is consistently found on approximately 0.4% of the street segments in Seattle. There is also strong street-by-street variability, emphasizing the importance of hot spot segments rather than larger area concentrations. Within 250 meters of the public assistance hot spots, 84.3% of street segments do not have any public housing assistance recipients. And such social disorganization characteristics at the street segment level are related to crime trajectories (Weisburd et al. 2012).

Weisburd et al. (2012) found that there was a strong relationship between social disadvantage and crime hot spots. Using housing values and vouchers for public assistance in housing, they report that higher levels of social disorganization are correlated with the likelihood of a street being in the chronic crime hot spot category. But these measures were indirect measures of social disadvantage because Weisburd et al. could not gain direct street level measures of such social factors as race, educational achievement, family status and income. Braga and Clarke (2014) raise this as a key issue in establishing the relevance of social disorganization theory to micro geographic patterns of crime. Absent direct measures it is difficult to establish a clear relationship between social characteristics of places and crime.

In this chapter we examine the relationship between social, demographic, educational and economic variables and crime at micro levels of geography based on direct measurement of these social characteristics. We extend upon prior research through access to social and demographic characteristics of streets that have been provided by the Israeli Central Bureau of Statistics.[3]

Unit of Analysis

The geographic unit of study for these analyses is the street segment, including both block faces between two intersections. The choice of street segments as a micro geographic unit of analysis reflects both theoretical and practical concerns. Scholars have long recognized the relevance of the street segment in organizing life in the city (Appleyard 1980; Jacobs 1961; Smith et al. 2000; Taylor 1997; Weisburd and Amram 2014; Weisburd et al. 2004, 2012). Taylor (1997), for example, argued that the visual closeness of block residents, inter-related role obligations, acceptance of certain common norms and behavior, common regularly recurring rhythms of activity, the physical boundaries of the street and the historical evolution of the street segment make the street block or street segment a particularly useful unit of analysis of place (see also Hunter and Baumer 1982; Taylor et al. 1984; Weisburd et al. 2004). Weisburd et al. (2012) and Weisburd et al. (2014) argued that the street segment is a type of micro community, forming a first layer in the complex arrangements of com-munity life at varying levels of community in a city (Sampson 2012). In this sense, the street segment is an important theoretical unit for studying crime at place (Weisburd et al. 2012).

The choice of street segments over smaller units, such as addresses, also mini-mizes the error likely to develop from miscoding of addresses in official data (see Klinger and Bridges 1997; Weisburd and Green 1994; Weisburd et al. 2004, 2012). It is one thing to get the specific address of a crime wrong, but it is another to miscode the fact that a crime occurred on a street between two intersections. Following Weisburd et al. (2012) we operationalize the definition of street seg-ments by referring directly to the geography of streets in Tel Aviv-Yafo. In Tel Aviv-Yafo, as contrasted with many other cities, the police do not code crime incidents to intersections, but rather attach all crimes directly to street addresses.

We estimate that there are 16,446 street segments in the city based on a geo-graphic file provided by MAPI (the Survey of Israel) for the year 2014. How-ever, many of these streets are not residential streets. The 1995 census, which is the most recent census survey that includes a full census of all residents of Tel Aviv-Yafo, includes only 5,781 residential street segments (i.e. that include a residential household).[4] In the current study we examine data only on people 18 years and older. In addition, to prevent identification of specific families or individuals the CBS only provided information on street segments that had a minimum of three households in the 1995 census survey.[5] This left us with 4,781 street segments in 1995, which forms the main sample for our study. While this is less than 30% of all estimated streets, they include 42% of crime in Tel Aviv-Yafo for the study period. The mean length of our street segments is 60 meters. The majority of the street segments (roughly 75%) are between 25 and 70 meters, and only 2% of the street segments are more than 200 meters.

Data

We examine computerized records of crime incident reports for a period of 35 years, from 1/1/1980 to 31/12/2014. Crime incident reports are gener-ated by police officers after an initial response to a request for police service. The total number of incidents for the 35-year period in all of Tel Aviv-Yafo is 2,382,536 (which includes all crime types). We excluded reports that lacked a street address or a house number, and records that could not be geocoded. We were left with 2,035,865 incident reports over the 35 years of police data (1980–2014) or about 85% of all crime incidents. Our average geocoded percentage hit rate was 85% and was between 77% and 91% across the years. This sample of 4,781 residential street segments includes 1,013,417 crime incidents during the study period.

Israel Population Census

The Israeli census survey is conducted approximately every decade, having been carried out six times since the state's founding: 1948, 1961, 1972, 1983, 1995 and 2008. Our research is based on the census data for the years 1983 and 1995. The surveys conducted in 1983 and 1995 were "traditional census surveys" in that they included all households in Tel Aviv-Yafo and therefore provide the opportunity for examination of street segment characteristics. However, the 2008 census is an "integrated census" in which the CBS first defined sampling areas (enumeration areas) and then took a random sample of those areas. The average enumeration area included 270 households. Twenty percent of the enumeration areas were included in the census in 2008. This approach naturally leads to a large number of street segments being excluded from the sample.[6] Accordingly, we do not include in our study the 2008 population census.

Because we are interested in detailed information about people living on streets in Tel Aviv-Yafo, we rely in this chapter primarily on the "long form" census survey. The sample is taken by going to every fifth household included in the short form (which includes the entire population of households). This dataset contains information on 4,362 street segments and 50,256 individuals 18 or older in 1995. The 4,362 street segments include 954,481 crime incidents over the study period. The number of street segments with census data in 1983 that we were able to cross-reference with the 1995 data base was 3,847, which includes 54,807 individuals 18 or older.[7]

Administrative Registry

The Administrative registry includes data from the "Education" and "Employer-Employee" data base. The Employer-Employee data base is drawn from "Internal Revenue Service—IRS" files of salaried employees. This dataset refers to the employee population over the years 2000–2012. It is important to mention that we received this data only for individuals ages 18–65. Also, the file for the year 2007 was missing in the CBS documents. The Education files include information about formal and non-formal education tracks.

Overall, for the years 2000–2012, we have the full sample of streets with three or more households in the 1995 census, with small deviations that are likely due to street segments that were demolished, or in which there is no evidence of employment or education among residents. The N varies between 4,641 and 4,654 street segments.

Trajectory Analysis

We applied group-based trajectory analysis developed by Nagin (1999, 2005) and Nagin and Land (1993) to our crime data. This approach provides the opportunity to identify common trends of crime at street segments over the 35-year observation period. Group-based trajectory analysis is designed to identify latent groups of individuals with similar developmental pathways (Nagin 2005). Initially, trajectory analysis was used primarily to examine individual criminal careers (e.g. Kreuter and Muthén 2008; Nagin and Odgers 2010), and the focus of the analysis was mostly on individual criminality (e.g. Blokland 2005; Broidy et al. 2003; Nagin and Odgers 2010; Piquero et al. 2010). More recently it has also been applied to crime places at different levels of geography (e.g. Griffiths and Chavez 2004; Hipp 2011; Weisburd et al. 2004, 2012).

We started by testing three trajectory groups, then four, five, six, etc. To identify the best model we began by comparing the Bayesian Information Criteria (BIC).[8] The final model included 12 groups.[9] While trajectory analysis is useful to reduce complicated phenomenon into some manageable patterns, some scholars have criticized its utility as a theory-testing tool to support crime typologies (Laub 2006; Moffitt 2006; Skardhamar 2010). These criticisms center on the issue of whether the latent groups extracted from trajectory analysis are "real and distinct." It is possible, and even likely, that the boundaries of such groups are not precise. Following this, we collapsed the trajectory groups from 12 groups into nine to increase interpretability and because the groups combined were substantively similar (see Figure 4.1).

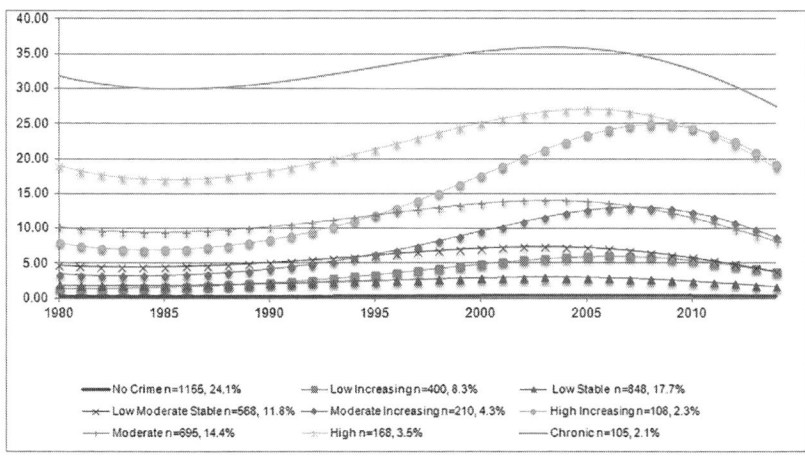

Figure 4.1 Group-based trajectory model—nine trajectory patterns.

As in prior studies, low crime streets form the large majority of streets in the city (e.g. see Weisburd et al. 2004, 2012). The "No Crime" street segments represent about 24% of the residential street segments in our sample. This 24% of streets produced just 1.7% of crime in the sample. Three other low crime pattern trajectories also emerge: we have termed these "Low Stable," "Low Moderate Stable" and "Low Increasing" patterns. They represent almost 50% of the residential street segments but include only 23% of crime across the study period.

In contrast to these low crime groups we identify a "Chronic" crime street pattern that includes just 2.1% of the residential streets but 18% of the crime in the study period. Similarly, we identify a "High" crime group and a "High Increasing" crime group. These two groups include only 6% of the street segments in the sample but 20% of the crime. Finally, there are two moderate groups, representing "Moderate" and "Moderate Increasing" patterns. These two groups include about 19% of the sample streets, and about 33% of the crime in the study period.

Levels of Crime and Levels of Social Disorganization

We begin by examining how levels of crime are related to levels of the social disorganization. For this analysis we examine only the stable crime trajectories (No Crime, Low Stable, Low Moderate Stable, Moderate, High, Chronic). Following social disorganization theory and prior work by Weisburd et al. (2012) we would expect that higher crime level trajectories would evidence greater economic and social disadvantage. We use Analysis of Variance to estimate statistical significance. Because the N of cases is so large in our study, we only note comparisons in the tables that are not statistically significant at the 5 percent level. We use the 1983 and 1995 census surveys, and take an average of the 2000–2006 and 2007–2012 Administrative surveys to gain averages for the two recent time periods.

There is not a strong relationship between minority/majority status and crime trajectories (see Table 4.1). In the case of percentage of Muslim residents on the street, two of the time periods are not statistically significant. In turn, Chronic crime streets have lower proportions of minorities than low crime streets. At the same time the proportion of minority Muslim residents in Tel Aviv-Yafo is very small. Consistent with social disorganization theory, we find that the highest crime streets include higher proportions of people born abroad compared to the case with the lower crime streets. The mean number of years lived in Israel (for immigrants) is also shorter on higher crime streets, at least after 1983.

Marital status follows what we would expect according to social disorganization theory. As crime levels increase, the proportion of married residents decreases (see Table 4.2). This relationship is fairly strong and follows the same pattern across the four time periods examined in our data. We also find linear and positive relationships with divorce. As the crime level increases at street segments, the proportion of divorced residents also increases. Again the

Table 4.1

Stable trajectory groups and disadvantaged communities

Trajectory	Jewish (%)				Muslims (%)			
	1983	1995	2000–2006[NS]	2007–2012[NS]	1983[NS]	1995	2000–2006[NS]	2007–2012[NS]
No Crime	95.70	92.43	90.69	89.48	2.61	3.94	4.06	4.22
Low Stable	97.20	95.25	91.57	90.28	1.58	2.45	3.02	3.34
Low Moderate Stable	96.14	94.88	90.30	89.14	2.78	1.80	3.71	4.31
Moderate	97.99	95.07	90.74	89.13	1.47	1.80	3.12	3.60
High	99.23	91.42	88.81	87.22	0.36	1.74	3.06	3.65
Chronic	99.00	92.00	89.71	87.95	0.87	0.54	1.71	2.17

[NS] No significant difference between the trajectories p >0.05

Trajectory	Years in Israel (Mean)[10]				Born Abroad (%)			
	1983[NS]	1995	2000–2006	2007–2012	1983	1995	2000–2006	2007–2012
No Crime	34.93	38.63	39.93	40.12	56.20	42.28	45.29	40.94
Low Stable	34.93	38.51	38.20	38.39	59.45	45.26	44.98	41.05
Low Moderate Stable	34.90	36.19	36.20	36.18	61.27	46.94	46.79	42.82
Moderate	34.47	35.78	34.37	34.38	62.94	48.81	48.64	44.49
High	33.51	33.32	32.75	32.57	69.63	52.39	52.76	48.09
Chronic	34.16	31.40	31.14	30.77	70.53	53.46	53.76	49.54

[NS] No significant difference between the trajectories p >0.05

Table 4.2

Stable trajectory groups and family measures

Trajectory	Married (%)				Divorced (%)				Number of Children (Mean)	
	1983	1995	2000–2006	2007–2012	1983	1995	2000–2006	2007–2012	1983	1995
No Crime	67.38	55.38	49.64	47.27	3.59	6.28	9.46	10.64	2.72	2.88
Low Stable	65.78	53.81	47.84	45.55	4.29	7.33	10.29	11.37	2.59	2.71
Low Moderate Stable	62.21	49.49	44.17	41.11	4.63	8.04	10.93	11.91	2.41	2.57
Moderate	61.67	49.50	42.69	40.01	5.04	8.45	11.59	12.00	2.27	2.52
High	61.71	50.11	41.28	38.13	5.03	8.86	12.10	12.16	2.41	2.45
Chronic	54.83	39.73	35.83	32.44	6.86	10.83	14.21	14.33	2.19	2.39

relationships are similar across the four time periods. A very interesting finding is identified in the number of children that residents of street segments report. In the 1983 and 1995 censuses there is a trend showing that larger families (number of children) are found on street segments with less crime. This is not what would have been expected based on social disorganization theory, and we will return to this finding in more detail in our discussion.

Looking at economic variables there are generally clear linear negative relationships between crime at street segments and measures of social disadvantage (see Table 4.3). High crime streets evidence higher disadvantage as would be predicted by social disorganization theory. A key measure of economic status in Israel is home ownership. We have home ownership data from the 1983 and 1995 censuses. Thirty-seven percent of the residents of Chronic crime trajectory street segments owned their own homes in 1995, while more than 65% of the residents owned their homes on No Crime streets for that year. Home ownership in the sample is higher overall in 1983, but again there is a large difference on Chronic crime streets (47%) as contrasted with No Crime streets (75%). Apartments (number of rooms) are also larger on lower crime street segments compared to the high crime street segments. Finally, car ownership

Table 4.3
Stable trajectory groups and economic measures

Trajectory	Home Ownership (%)		# Rooms (Mean)		Car Ownership (%)	
	1983	1995	1983	1995	1983	1995
No Crime	75.14	65.22	3.01	3.33	56.19	78.33
Low Stable	74.48	64.63	2.92	3.16	55.58	75.09
Low Moderate Stable	67.80	55.51	2.79	3.20	48.04	66.54
Moderate	65.19	55.99	2.78	3.15	47.07	61.45
High	60.19	51.17	2.72	2.96	39.48	52.62
Chronic	47.46	36.80	2.59	2.96	35.09	39.79

Trajectory	Monthly Salary (NIS)		Annual Salary (NIS)		No Income (%)	
	1983[11]	1995	2000–2006	2007–2012	2000–2006	2007–2012
No Crime	4545.14	10729.01	97603.05	122204.74	29.49	28.84
Low Stable	4412.28	10631	97514.91	115290.74	31.09	31.8
Low Moderate Stable	3978.24	10053.31	86801.89	107191.22	32.07	29.93
Moderate	3868.66	9687.49	86128.16	104727.7	33.57	28.84
High	3412.44	8559.6	76816.09	95423.25	36.71	30.71
Chronic	3252.93	7458.77	69661.67	90569.81	38.98	35.07

follows a similar negative linear pattern in the 1983 and 1995 censuses. For instance, in 1995 the proportion of car ownership on No Crime streets (78%) was nearly twice that on Chronic crime street segments (40%).

The relationship between income and crime is particularly strong (see Table 4.3). For the years 2007–2012 the average annual salary per family on the Chronic crime streets was almost 91,000 NIS per year. In contrast, on the No Crime street segments the annual average salary was about 122,000 NIS per year. Similar patterns are found in the 1983 and 1995 censuses and 2000–2006 Administrative data. The proportion of unemployed residents, indicated by "no income," also follows this pattern, with the chronic crime streets having the highest level of residents with "no income."[12]

Contrary to the trend of our analyses of other socio-economic measures, we find little relationship between educational levels on street segments and crime levels (see Table 4.4). Despite the large samples, none of the comparisons across the years are statistically significant.

Increasing Trajectories and Social Indicators

Weisburd et al. (2012) report a strong relationship in multivariate analyses between social disorganization measures and increasing and decreasing trajectory patterns. The question we turn to now is whether increasing crime patterns at street segments are related to changes in the social measures we examine. We look at three trajectory patterns: Low Increasing, Moderate Increasing and High Increasing. The No Crime trajectory is used to establish a bench mark for this analysis. It may be for example that a factor is increasing in the expected direction for increasing trajectories, but that is just part of a secular trend of

Table 4.4
Stable trajectory crime levels and educational levels

Trajectory	B.A. (%)		M.A., Ph.D., M.D. (%)		Matriculation (BAGRUT) (%)	
	2000–2006[NS]	2007–2012[NS]	2000–2006[NS]	2007–2012[NS]	1983[NS]	1995[NS]
No Crime	62.71	65.47	35.02	32.58	15.29	22.11
Low Stable	63.21	64.71	34.8	33.52	16.7	20.91
Low Moderate Stable	62.38	64.49	35.83	34.15	16.66	22.2
Moderate	61.5	65.55	36.55	32.93	18.34	22.6
High	60.96	66.18	37.28	32.65	17.15	22.06
Chronic	59.74	63.56	39.01	35.21	15.42	22.24

[NS] No significant difference between the trajectories p>0.05

the data in the city. Our presentation of the No Crime category allows us to distinguish whether the trends observed are specific to increasing trajectories or relate to a more general trend in the data. In this case statistical significance is measured using t tests comparing the first and last periods measured for each trajectory group. Only non-significant results are noted.

In line with social disorganization theory the largest increases in minority populations at street segments over time are found for the High Increasing and Moderate Increasing patterns (see Table 4.5). We also find that the number of years in Israel (for immigrants) decreases for the higher increasing patterns relative to the no crime pattern. Looking at the proportion of residents born abroad, however, there are similar decreases across all groups, including the No Crime trajectory.

Looking at the family measures we do observe patterns consistent with social disorganization theory (see Table 4.6). In the case of marriage there

Table 4.5
The relationship between increasing crime patterns and disadvantaged communities

	Jewish (%)					Muslims (%)				
Trajectory	1983	1995	2000– 2006	2007– 2012	% Change	1983	1995	2000– 2006	2007– 2012	% Change
No Crime	95.7	92.43	90.69	89.48	−6.50	2.61	3.94	4.06	4.22	61.69[NS]
Low Increasing	94.17	90.89	87.08	85.34	−9.38	4.42	4.11	6.49	6.87	55.43
Moderate Increasing	95.66	90.44	87.2	83.82	−12.38	3.05	3.77	4.66	6.34	107.87
High Increasing	98.63	87.41	88.15	84.77	−14.05	0.81	3.12	3.27	4.36	438.27

[NS] No significant difference between the first and last observation years p >0.05

	Years in Israel (Mean)					Born Abroad (%)				
Trajectory	1983	1995	2000– 2006	2007– 2012	% Change	1983	1995	2000– 2006	2007– 2012	% Change
No Crime	34.93	38.63	39.93	40.12	14.86	56.2	42.28	45.29	40.94	−27.15
Low Increasing	35	35.9	36.07	36.43	4.09	57.82	47.63	49.49	45.13	−21.95
Moderate Increasing	33.35	32.32	33.03	32.75	−1.80	63.52	47.93	53.96	50.46	−20.56
High Increasing	36.46	32.4	32.63	32.81	−10.01	66.44	57.65	53.87	49.79	−25.06

Table 4.6
The relationship between increasing crime patterns and family measures

Trajectory	Married (%)					Divorced (%)					Number of Children (Mean)		
	1983	1995	2000–2006	2007–2012	% change	1983	1995	2000–2006	2007–2012	% change	1983	1995	% change
No Crime	67.38	55.38	49.64	47.27	−29.85	3.59	6.28	9.46	10.64	196.38	2.72	2.88	5.88
Low Increasing	65.63	57.19	48.74	45.45	−30.75	3.34	6.98	10.83	12.05	260.78	2.98	2.92	−2.01[NS]
Moderate Increasing	58.51	50.44	43.69	40.44	−30.88	5.86	10.31	13.67	15.33	161.60	2.72	2.95	8.46[NS]
High Increasing	63.64	51.8	41.41	37.63	−40.87	4.64	9.05	15.55	16.1	246.98	2.89	2.86	−1.04[NS]

[NS] No significant difference between the first and last observation years p >0.05

is a decrease of more than 40 percent for the High Increasing pattern, and a decrease of only 30 percent for the No Crime pattern. In the case of divorce, the proportion doubles for the No Crime pattern, but is 2.5 times higher for the High Increasing pattern. There is not a consistent pattern for number of children.

We do not observe patterns strongly consistent with social disorganization in looking at socio-economic measures (see Table 4.7). In the case of home ownership and size of apartments (number of rooms), the trends are similar both for the no crime and crime increasing patterns. Similar findings emerge looking at income and other economic measures. Incomes rise strongly across all of the groups. If anything there is an indication that incomes are rising faster on the High Increasing pattern streets.

Finally, as in our earlier analyses of levels of crime, the education variables do not show a strong trend consistent with social disorganization theory

Table 4.7
The relationship between increasing crime patterns and economic measures

	Monthly Salary (NIS)			Annual Salary (NIS)			No Income (%)		
Trajectory	1983	1995	% Change	2000–2006	2007–2012	% Change	2000–2006	2007–2012	% Change
No Crime	4545.14	10729.01	136.05	97603.05	122204.74	25.21	29.49	28.84	–2.20
Low Increasing	3667.3	10140.21	176.50	86591.64	107713.95	24.39	32.23	31.25	–3.04
Moderate Increasing	2915.78	7817.31	168.10	74330.54	92506.21	24.45	35.98	35.57	–1.14
High Increasing	3159.97	8694.52	175.14	68422.1	87527.68	27.92	38.09	36.52	–4.12

	Home Ownership (%)			Number of Rooms (Mean)			Car Ownership (%)		
Trajectory	1983	1995	% Change	1983	1995	% Change	1983	1995	% Change
No Crime	75.14	65.22	–13.20	3.01	3.33	10.63	56.19	78.33	39.40
Low Increasing	71.04	61.29	–13.72	2.87	3.04	5.92	48.08	75.09	56.18
Moderate Increasing	62.18	57.07	–8.22	2.48	2.89	16.53	37.26	53.62	43.91[NS]
High Increasing	70.39	58	–17.60	2.55	2.87	12.55	32.95	50.41	52.99[NS]

[NS] No significant difference between the first and last observation years p >0.05

Table 4.8
The relationship between increasing crime trends and educational levels

	B.A. (%)			M.A., Ph.D., M.D. (%)			Matriculation (BAGRUT) (%)		
Trajectory	2000–2006	2007–2012	% Change	2000–2006	2007–2012	% Change	1983	1995	% Change
No Crime	62.71	65.47	4.40	35.02	32.58	–6.97	15.29	22.11	44.60
Low Increasing	59.33	65.53	10.45	37.63	32.45	–13.77	13.98	18.39	31.55
Moderate Increasing	56.49	64.05	13.38	40.24	33.26	–17.35	13.52	19.91	47.26[NS]
High Increasing	57.52	64.26	11.72	39.86	34.66	–13.05	13.86	17.05	23.02[NS]

[NS] No significant difference between the early and late observation years p >0.05

(see Table 4.8). The percentage of residents with a B.A. increases at twice the rate in the High Increasing streets as in the No Crime trajectory from 2000, though the proportion of those with a higher degree decreases at twice the rate in the High Increasing pattern. In the High Increasing pattern the increase in matriculation exams (though not statistically significant) is twice that in the No Crime streets between 1983 and 1995.

This latter finding raises an important issue with regard to interpreting our data about change over time. Tel Aviv-Yafo, like many other high tech and cultural centers, has attracted large numbers of young, well educated professionals over the last two decades. In this context, gentrification of streets may be having an important impact on our data. Many very high crime streets in less attractive areas have become the locus of young men and women who are attracted to Tel Aviv-Yafo but cannot afford the very high rents on nicer streets in the city. In this context, it may be that in the earlier periods on increasing crime trajectory streets, better educated individuals were moving out. But in the later period, gentrification was leading to better educated and higher salaried residents moving in. While we can only speculate about these issues here, we think this is an important set of questions to examine in future studies.

Discussion

Social disorganization is one of the most important theoretical contributions of modern criminology. But as we noted at the outset, this perspective has generally not been seen as relevant for understanding the patterns of crime at a micro geographic level (e.g. see Braga and Clarke 2014; Sherman et al. 1989). Weisburd et al. (2014) in a longitudinal study of crime at street segments in

Seattle, however, found a strong relationship between social disorganization measures and crime in the context of a multivariate analysis. Overall, their study showed a strong link between variables representing social organization at street segments such as housing assistance and housing value and chronic crime hot spots. But that study has been criticized because of its use of proxy variables, rather than direct measurement of social structural variables at the street segment level. Our study overcomes this limitation through use of data from the Central Bureau of Statistics in Israel.

Looking at levels of crime and measures of family status and socio-economic status we find a strong bivariate relationship between social disorganization and crime. The Chronic Crime trajectory group street segments have higher divorce rates, lower incomes and lower home ownership rates than the lower crime level trajectories. This appears to confirm the findings of Weisburd et al. (2012, 2014), and more generally the relevance of social disorganization theory to micro geographic studies. What is important here is that these are not neighborhood or area-wide measures of social disorganization. They are measures at the street segment level. At the street segment level we find that structural indicators of social disorganization are directly related to crime levels.

Weisburd and Amram (2014) found that there was strong street to street variability in crime patterns in Tel Aviv. Very high crime streets were often near to low crime streets. Those findings mirrored earlier work in Seattle, Washington (Weisburd et al. 2012), which showed a great deal of street to street variability of crime levels. In that study they found that streets of different crime levels were often intermixed. This suggests more generally that we need to sharpen our focus when looking at crime in the city. We need to look beyond the average characteristics of large areas to the characteristics of specific streets. Our data here suggest that when we get to a very micro geographic level of resolution, high crime streets have strong evidence of social disorganization.

The fact that social disorganization on a micro geographic level is strongly related to crime levels suggests that we need to think more about micro geographic communities and how they influence crime. How do lower incomes or home ownership on a street affect informal social controls of people who live on high crime streets? Ordinarily, criminologists have considered informal social controls as being developed in larger communities. Church groups or other community organizations are seen to play key roles in enabling informal social controls to develop. But our findings suggest that more intimate relationships developed among neighbors may be equally important. If the specific environment of a street leads to crime, our data suggest that structural characteristics of the people on that street influence their ability to marshall social controls. In this case it may simply be the extent to which neighbors socialize, or whether they organize block parties, or come together when specific problems are encountered. Perhaps it is simply that poverty and disadvantage make it less likely that individuals will be able to engage their neighbors.

It certainly makes sense that the ability of people on a street to marshall informal social controls would affect crime directly on that street. Street segments are the building blocks of social life in cities. They are places where we have informal contacts with our neighbors simply in the everyday routine activities of life. If crime is common on that street, then we would expect people who live there to feel it most directly. What our data lead us to ask is how structural factors indicated in social disorganization theory affect the ability of neighbors on a street to marshall such informal social controls. What are the mechanisms through which specific people on specific streets influence crime? While criminologists have considered the broad ways in which communities influence crime, they have largely neglected the very immediate and specific ways in which micro communities influence crime rates.

Turning our attentions to this phenomenon is important not simply for theoretical reasons but also for practical crime prevention. Social prevention programs are often expensive and unwieldy. Trying to improve structural characteristics of communities is generally unrealistic. It simply costs too much to change the structural characteristics of large areas. But affecting individual streets and the people who live there provides a much more manageable focus for social interventions. Targeting a large amorphous area with high levels of social disorganization is costly. Focusing on a small number of hot spot streets is not only more realistic economically, but it would also allow us to bring very high "dosages" of changes to those streets. Such high levels of intervention seem particularly likely to affect the realities of crime on chronic crime hot spot streets.

While our examination of levels of crime (as indicated by trajectory patterns) overall affirms relationships that would be expected in social disorganization, when we examined increasing trajectory patterns we did not observe a consistent relationship. Or at least, such changes were not consistently evident to a greater degree than that observed in the stable No Crime pattern. In some cases patterns were consistent with social disorganization theory, but in others they seemed to indicate either no specific trend or even trends contrary to the social disorganization perspective.

Our observations, especially regarding economic variables, may be confounded more generally by secular trends in Tel Aviv-Yafo over the last 30 years. Israel has experienced an "economic miracle" over the last few decades, moving from a struggling socialist economy to one of the wealthiest countries in the world per capita. This is reflected in our data in the overall patterns of decreasing social disorganization over time in Tel Aviv-Yafo. It may simply be that the overall changes in Tel Aviv-Yafo are so large that it is difficult to observe trends that might be related to increasing crime patterns.

Moreover, we think it important to recognize that bivariate descriptive analyses like those conducted here may not be nuanced enough to identify longitudinal relationships, especially given the radical economic and structural changes that occurred during the study period. What is needed is more sophisticated statistical analyses of the trends we examine. Such analyses would have to take into account how factors interact and how confounding may be affecting our observations. For example, we noted earlier that gentrification may be confounding our bivariate observations regarding education levels. Our data suggest that the longitudinal relationships between crime and social disorganization in Tel Aviv-Yafo are complex and warrant more nuanced statistical analyses.

An intriguing finding in our data is that number of children is related to levels of crime in the reverse direction of what social disorganization theory would predict at the street segment level. Very high crime streets have on average more children per family than No Crime streets, raising the question of the specific mechanism through which children are related to crime. In social disorganization theory more children per family is seen as an indicator of poverty or social disorganization. But looking at this from the opportunity perspective, one might wonder whether children increase the level of guardianship on a street, because of either increased parental social controls, or third parties such as baby sitters. More generally this finding suggests the relevance of Braga and Clarke's (2014) contention that traditional social disorganization measures may also reflect opportunity mechanisms.

Finally, we did not find a strong relationship between education and stable trajectory patterns. This seems perhaps contradictory to our more general finding that economic measures are strongly related to crime levels. We suspect that this finding, however, may be a function of the large young adult population drawn to Tel Aviv-Yafo because of both its work opportunities and leisure time venues. It would be interesting to examine whether these relationships are similar in other Western cities experiencing similar influxes of young professionals.

Conclusion

Our study is the first we know of that allowed identification of social structural variables at the street segment level. Examination of the relationship of such factors to crime trajectories at street segments overall reinforces earlier work by Weisburd et al. (2012, 2014). Using direct measures of social backgrounds of street residents, rather than proxy measures as was the case in the prior studies, we also find evidence of the salience of social disorganization measures at a micro geographic level. High levels of social disorganization are correlated with high crime trajectory patterns in our study. For most measures, the higher the level of social disorganization the higher the crime level observed. But having shown that social disorganization variables are related to crime levels, we also find challenges to this approach when examining the relationship between longitudinal trends in crime and structural characteristics of street segments. We note that the nature of our analyses and structural changes in Israel (such as gentrification) more generally may be masking such relationships in our analyses, and call for further study.

We need more studies that expand the theoretical view of crime and place research. If we simply ignore alternative theories, such as social disorganization, then we cannot benefit from the ways in which they may expand our understanding of the crime problem. And of course, we cannot begin by arguing that such theories have little relevance without looking to observe empirical data reflecting those theories. It is time for crime and place researchers to explore more carefully the role of social disorganization in the production of crime at the micro geographic level. Our data suggest a strong relationship, but we need much more theorizing about the mechanisms through which structural characteristics of street segments impact crime.

Notes

1. We would like to express our thanks to Dan Nagin, who visited Israel and helped us to develop the trajectory models reported upon in this article. This research was supported by the Israel Science Foundation (grant No. 793\14).
2. For a notable example of an early approach that did place emphasis on the "micro" idea of place as discussed here, see Shaw (1929).
3. It is important to note that we were provided access to these data only within the secure environment of the CBS's data room. No data on street segments were released outside this room.
4. The CBS now takes a sample of streets within areas for the full census survey conducted each decade, as discussed later in the chapter.
5. A household refers to one person or a group of people living together in one apartment permanently during most of the week, and having common expenses such as a budget for food. Households can include people that are not relatives or family (see www.cbs.gov.il/house/reka.pdf).
6. Retrieved from the CBS site: www.cbs.gov.il/census/census/pnimi_sub_page. html?id_topic=2&id_subtopic=1.
7. It is important to note that the number of households increased between the years 1983 and 1995, from 23,439 to 28,296.
8. Before determining the final trajectory model, we had to make three choices: (1) for the distribution of the model we chose the Zero-Inflated Poisson (ZIP) distribution since the data have many observations of zero crime in street segments; (2) because of the shape of the trend of our data we chose a third-order polynomial that defines a cubic trajectory (3, 3, 3, 3) model; (3) to determine the number of groups, a key decision of this analysis, we tested all the possible combinations (Nagin 2005).
9. At 13 trajectories the BIC did not decrease; indeed it increased at 13 trajectories. A second criterion we used was to examine the "posterior probabilities" of the group assignment for group membership. The validity of the 12 trajectory model is confirmed by the posterior probabilities for the different trajectories. Nagin (2005) suggests that posterior probabilities higher than 0.7 indicate that the model fits well for the groups. The value of the group posterior probabilities for our 12 group model was more than 0.9 for each group. We merged street segments with zero crime events across the 35-year period (N=714) with the lowest crime trajectory (N=441), centered at zero crimes.

10. For "new immigrants."
11. Initially we received the income data for 1983 according to the old shekel (IS) currency that has a different value than the New Shekel (NIS). In order to compare 1983 data to the NIS we converted the figures taking into account inflation.
12. For the years 1983 and 1995 there is no information about unemployment.

References

Andresen, Martin A., and Nicolas Malleson. 2011. "Testing the Stability of Crime Patterns: Implications for Theory and Policy." *Journal of Research in Crime and Delinquency* 48: 58–82.

Appleyard, Donald. 1980. "Livable Streets: Protected Neighborhoods?" *The ANNALS of the American Academy of Political and Social Science* 451: 106–117.

Blokland, Arjun. 2005. *Crime over the Life Span: Trajectories of Criminal Behavior in Dutch Offenders.* Netherlands Institute for the Study of Crime and Law Enforcement, Faculty of Law, Leiden University, the Netherlands.

Blumstein, Alfred, and Joel Wallman. 2000. "The Recent Rise and Fall of American Violence." Pp. 1–12 in Alfred Blumstein, and Joel Wallman (eds.), *The Crime Drop in America.* Cambridge, UK: Cambridge University Press.

Braga, Anthony A., and Ronald V. Clarke. 2014. "Explaining High-Risk Concentrations of Crime in the City: Social Disorganization, Crime Opportunities, and Important Next Steps." *Journal of Research in Crime and Delinquency* 51: 480–498.

Braga, Anthony A., Andrew V. Papachristos, and David M. Hureau. 2014. "The Effects of Hot Spots Policing on Crime: An Updated Systematic Review and Meta-Analysis." *Justice Quarterly* 31: 633–663.

Brantingham, Patricia L., and Paul J. Brantingham. 1999. "A Theoretical Model of Crime Hot Spot Generation." *Studies on Crime & Crime Prevention* 8:7-26.

Broidy, Lisa M., Daniel S. Nagin, Richard E. Tremblay, John E. Bates, Bobby Brame, Kenneth A. Dodge, David Fergusson, John L. , Robert Laird, Terrie E. Moffitt, Daniel Nagin, John E. Bates, Kenneth A. Dodge, Rolf Loeber, Donald R. Lynam, Gregory S. Pettit, and Frank Vitaro. 2003. "Developmental Trajectories of Childhood Disruptive Behaviors and Adolescent Delinquency: A Six-Site, Cross-National Study." *Developmental Psychology* 39: 222.

Connolly, Sheelah, Dermot O'Reilly, and Michael Rosato. 2010. "House Value as an Indicator of Cumulative Wealth Is Strongly Related to Morbidity and Mortality Risk in Older People: A Census-Based Cross-Sectional and Longitudinal Study." *Journal of Epidemiology* 39: 383–391.

Cohen, Lawrence E., and Marcus Felson. 1979. Social change and crime rate trends: A routine activity approach. *American Sociological Review,* 588–608.

Crow, Wayman J., and James L. Bull. 1975. *Robbery Deterrence: An Applied Behavioral Science Demonstration: Final Report.* La Jolla, CA: Western Behavioral Sciences Institute.

Curman, Andrea S. N., Martin A. Andresen, and Paul J. Brantingham. 2015. "Crime and Place: A Longitudinal Examination of Street Segment Patterns in Vancouver, BC." *Journal of Quantitative Criminology* 31: 127–147.

Eck, John E., and David Weisburd. 1995. "Crime Places in Crime Theory." Pp. 1–33 in John E. Eck and David Weisburd (eds.), *Crime and Place: Crime Prevention Studies*, vol. 4. Monsey, NY: Willow Tree Press.

Green, Lorraine. 1996. *Policing Places with Drug Problems.* Thousand Oaks, CA: Sage Publications.

Griffiths-, Elizabeth, and Jorge M. Chavez. 2004. "Communities, Street Guns and Homicide Trajectories in Chicago, 1980–1995: Merging Methods for Examining Homicide Trends across Space and Time." *Criminology* 42: 941.

Groff, Elizabeth R., David Weisburd, and Sue-Ming Yang. 2010. "Is It Important to Examine Crime Trends at a Local 'Micro' Level?: A Longitudinal Analysis of Street to Street Variability in Crime Trajectories." *Journal of Quantitative Criminology* 26: 7–32.

Guerry, André-Michel. 1833. *Essai sur la statistique morale de la France.* Paris: Crochard.

Hipp, John R. 2011. "Spreading the Wealth: The Effect of the Distribution of Income and Race/Ethnicity across Households and Neighborhoods on City Crime Trajectories." *Criminology* 49: 631–665.

Hunter, Albert, and Terry L. Baumer. 1982. "Street Traffic, Social Integration, and Fear of Crime." *Sociological Inquiry* 52: 122–131.

Jacobs, Jane. 1961. "The Death and Life of Great American." New York, NY: Vintage.

Klinger, David A., and George S. Bridges. 1997. "Measurement Error in Calls-for-Service as an Indicator of Crime." *Criminology* 35: 705–726.

Kreuter, Frauke, and Bengt Muthén. 2008. "Analyzing Criminal Trajectory Profiles: Bridging Multilevel and Group-Based Approaches Using Growth Mixture Modeling." *Journal of Quantitative Criminology* 24: 1–31.

Kubrin, Charis E., and Ronald Weitzer. 2003. "New Directions in Social Disorganization Theory." *Journal of Research in Crime and Delinquency* 40: 374–402.

Laub, John H. 2006. "Edwin H. Sutherland and the Michael-Adler Report: Searching for the Soul of Criminology Seventy Years Later." *Criminology* 44(2): 235–257.

Moffitt, Terrie E. 2006. "Life-Course-Persistent versus Adolescence-Limited Antisocial Behavior." Pp. 570–598 in Cicchetti Dante and Cohen J Donald (eds.), *Developmental Psychopathology* (2nd ed). New York, NY: Wiley.

Nagin, Daniel S. 1999. "Analyzing Developmental Trajectories: A Semiparametric Group-Based Approach." *Psychological Methods* 4: 139–157.

Nagin, Daniel S. 2005. *Group-Based Modeling of Development over the Life Course.* Cambridge, MA: Harvard University Press.

Nagin, Daniel S., and Kenneth C. Land. 1993. "Age, Criminal Careers, and Population Heterogeneity: Specification and Estimation of a Nonparametric, Mixed Poisson Model." *Criminology* 31: 327–362.

Nagin, Daniel S., and Candice L. Odgers. 2010. "Group-Based Trajectory Modeling in Clinical Research." *Annual Review of Clinical Psychology* 6: 109–138.

Nagin, Daniel, and Richard E. Tremblay. 1999. "Trajectories of Boys' Physical Aggression, Opposition, and Hyperactivity on the Path to Physically Violent and Nonviolent Juvenile Delinquency." *Child Development* 70: 1181–1196.

Nagin, Daniel S., and Richard E. Tremblay. 2001. "Parental and Early Childhood Predictors of Persistent Physical Aggression in Boys from Kindergarten to High School." *Archives of General Psychiatry* 58: 389–394.

Nagin, Daniel S., and Richard E. Tremblay. 2005. "Developmental Trajectory Groups: Fact or a Useful Statistical Fiction?" *Criminology* 43: 873–904.

Nettler, Gwynn. 1978. *Explaining Crime* (2nd ed.). Montreal: McGraw-Hill.

Pierce, Glenn L., Susan Spaar, and LeBaron R. Briggs. 1988. *The Character of Police Work: Strategic and Tactical Implications.* Boston, MA: Center for Applied Social Research, Northeastern University.

Piquero, Alex R., David P. Farrington, Daniel S. Nagin, and Terrie E. Moffitt. 2010. "Trajectories of Offending and Their Relation to Life Failure in Late Middle Age: Findings from the Cambridge Study in Delinquent Development." *Journal of Research in Crime and Delinquency* 47(2): 151–173.

Quetelet, Adolphe. 1831. *Research on the Propensity to Crime of Different Ages Brussels: Hayez*. Translated by Sawyer F. Test Sylvester. Cincinnati, OH: Anderson Publishing Co.

Roncek, Dennis W. 2000. "Schools and Crime." Pp. 153–165 in Victor Goldsmith, Philip. G. McGuire, John. H. Mollenkopf, and Timothy. A. Ross (eds.), *Analyzing Crime Patterns: Frontiers of Practice*. Thousand Oaks, CA: Sage Publications.

Sampson, Robert J. 2012. *Great American city: Chicago and the Enduring Neighborhood Effect*. Chicago, IL: University of Chicago Press.

Sampson, Robert J., and Byron W. Groves. 1989. "Community Structure and Crime: Testing Social-Disorganization Theory." *American Journal of Sociology* 94: 774–802.

Sampson, Robert J., Stephen W. Raudenbush, and Felton Earls. 1997. "Neighborhoods and Violent Crime: A Multilevel Study of Collective Efficacy." *Science* 277: 918–924.

Shaw, Clifford R. 1929. *Delinquent Areas: A Study of the Geographical Distribution of School Truants, Juvenile Delinquents, and Adult Offenders in Chicago*. Chicago, IL: University of Chicago Press.

Shaw, Clifford R., and Henry D. McKay. 1942 [1969]. *Juvenile Delinquency and Urban Areas: A Study of Rates of Delinquency in Relation to Differential Characteristics of Local Communities in American Cities* (rev. ed.). Chicago, IL: University of Chicago Press.

Sherman, Lawrence. W. 1995. "Hot Spots of Crime and Criminal Careers of Places." Pp. 35–52 In John Eck and David Weisburd (eds.), *Crime and place: Crime Prevention Studies*, vol. 4. Monsey, NY: Willow Tree Press.

Sherman, Lawrence W., Patrick R. Gartin, and Michael E. Buerger. 1989. "Hot Spots of Predatory Crime: Routine Activities and the Criminology of Place." *Criminology* 27: 27–56.

Sherman, Lawrence W., and David Weisburd. 1995. "General Deterrent Effects of Police Patrol in Crime 'Hot Spots': A Randomized, Controlled Trial." *Justice Quarterly* 12: 625–648.

Skardhamar, Torbjørn. 2010. "Distinguishing Facts and Artifacts in Group-Based Modeling." *Criminology* 48: 295–320.

Smargiassi, Audrey, Khalid Berrada, Isabel Fortier, and Tom Kosatsky. 2006. "Traffic Intensity, Dwelling Value, and Hospital Admissions for Respiratory Disease among the Elderly in Montreal (Canada): A Case-Control Analysis." *Journal of Epidemiology and Community Health* 60: 507–512.

Smith, William R., Sharon Glave Frazee, and Elizabeth L. Davison. 2000. "Furthering the Integration of Routine Activity and Social Disorganization Theories: Small Units of Analysis and the Study of Street Robbery as a Diffusion Process." *Criminology* 38: 489–524.

Taylor, Ralph B. 1997. "Social Order and Disorder of Street Blocks and Neighborhoods: Ecology, Microecology, and the Systemic Model of Social Disorganization." *Journal of Research in Crime and Delinquency* 34: 113–155.

Taylor, Ralph B. 1998. "Crime and Small-Scale Places: What We Know, What We Can Prevent, and What Else We Need to Know." Pp. 1–22 in Ralph B. Taylor, Gordon Bazemore, Barbara Boland, Todd R. Clear, Ronald. P. J. Corbett, John Feinblatt, Greg Berman, Michele Sviridoff, and Christopher Stone (eds.), *Crime and Place: Plenary Papers of the 1997 Conference on Criminal Justice Research and Evaluation*. Washington, DC: National Institute of Justice.

Taylor, Ralph B., Stephen D. Gottfredson, and Sidney Brower. 1984. "Block Crime and Fear: Defensible Space, Local Social Ties, and Territorial Functioning." *Journal of Research in Crime and Delinquency* 21: 303–331.

Weisburd, David. 2015. "The Law of Crime Concentration and the Criminology of Place." *Criminology* 53: 133–157.

Weisburd, David, and Shai Amram. 2014. "The Law of Concentrations of Crime at Place: The Case of Tel Aviv-Jaffa." *Police Practice and Research* 15: 101–114.

Weisburd, David, Shawn Bushway, Cynthia Lum, and Sue-Ming Yang. 2004. "Trajectories of Crime at Places: A Longitudinal Study of Street Segments in the City of Seattle." *Criminology* 42: 283–322.

Weisburd, David, and Lorraine Green. 1994. "Defining the Drug Market: The Case of the Jersey City DMA System." Pp. 61–76 in Doris. L. MacKenzie, and Craig D. Uchida (eds.), *Drugs and Crime: Evaluating Public Policy Initiatives*. Thousand Oaks, CA: Sage Publications.

Weisburd, David, and Lorraine Green. 1995. "Policing Drug Hot Spots: The Jersey City Drug Market Analysis Experiment." *Justice Quarterly* 12: 711–735.

Weisburd, David, Elizabeth R. Groff, and Sue-Ming Yang. 2012. *The Criminology of Place: Street Segments and Our Understanding of the Crime Problem*. Oxford: Oxford University Press.

Weisburd, David, Elizabeth R. Groff, and Sue-Ming Yang. 2014. "Understanding and Controlling Hot Spots of Crime: The Importance of Formal and Informal Social Controls." *Prevention Science* 15: 31–43.

Weisburd, David, Lisa Maher, and Lawrence Sherman. 1992. "Contrasting Crime General and Crime Specific Theory: The Case of Hot Spots of Crime." Pp. 45–69 in Freda Adler, and William Laufer (eds.), *New Directions in Criminological Theory, Advances in Criminological Theory*, vol. 4. New Brunswick, NJ: Transaction Press.

Weisburd, David, Nancy A. Morris, and Elizabeth R. Groff. 2009. "Hot Spots of Juvenile Crime: A Longitudinal Study of Arrest Incidents at Street Segments in Seattle, Washington." *Journal of Quantitative Criminology* 25: 443.

Wicker, Allan W. 1987. "Behavior Settings Reconsidered: Temporal Stages, Resources, Internal Dynamics, Context." Pp. 613–653 in Daniel Stokels, and Irwin Altman (eds.), *Handbook of Environmental Psychology*. New York, NY: Wiley-Interscience.

5

Place and Neighborhood Contexts[1]

Pamela Wilcox and Marie Skubak Tillyer

Introduction

The study of neighborhood-level variation in crime is an enduring aspect of the field of criminology (e.g., Bursik and Grasmick 1993; Shaw 1929; Shaw and McKay 1942; Sampson 2012). Conceptually speaking, "neighborhood" studies have largely been interested in areas that approximate an "urban village" (Boessen and Hipp 2015), though a variety of units have been used for such approximation—including census tracts, census block groups, police districts, political wards, or locally demarcated areas defined on the basis of within-area homogeneity and/or natural barriers.

In the past several decades, however, a different approach to understanding the spatial distribution of crime has taken hold. This contemporary approach emphasizes variation in crime events at relatively small geographic units of analysis, thus making it "micro-spatial" in focus. Advocates of this micro-spatial approach point to discernible *within-neighborhood* clusters of crime, suggesting the importance of *immediate* settings for understanding crime events and implying that a focus on problem places (e.g., hot spots) offers greater crime prevention precision and efficiency than neighborhood-based interventions (e.g., Sherman, Gartin, and Buerger 1989; Taylor 1998; Weisburd, Bushway, Lum, and Yang 2004; Weisburd and Telep 2010). Simply put, neighborhoods are considered "too big" a unit of analysis, and sub-neighborhood "places" such as street segments or specific addresses are deemed more appropriate (e.g., Braga 2012; Madensen and Eck 2013; Weisburd, Groff, and Yang 2012). Though place-based researchers have tended to ignore neighborhood influences, this chapter argues that the utility of place-based thinking would be enhanced if it, instead, recognized the value of considering the broader neighborhood contexts in which places are situated. Specifically, we propose a theoretical approach that emphasizes the embeddedness of places in larger neighborhoods, or a "place in neighborhood" approach. We build toward this approach by, first, providing a brief overview of two major theoretical traditions in criminology useful for understanding the geographic distribution of crime at the neighborhood and place levels—the social disorganization tradition and the opportunity perspective, respectively. Second, we review work that has integrated these two traditions, including research on neighborhood- and individual-level influences on personal victimization as well as research on crime at single, small-scale units of analysis. We next present an alternative, hybrid integrative approach that focuses on neighborhood- and place-level influences on crime at places. Finally, we discuss the implications of our proposed "place in neighborhood" approach for addressing key issues regarding crime at places in future research.

The Geography of Crime: Ecological Theory and Criminology

The Chicago School Tradition—Social Disorganization Theory

Scholarship focused on the geographic distribution of crime events enjoys a long history, including mid-nineteenth century work done outside the United States (Guerry 1883; Quetelet 1842). Nonetheless, the ecological perspective has been dominated, until fairly recently, by work in the "Chicago School tradition." This tradition has roots in the early days of the University of Chicago's Department of Sociology (founded in 1892). In the late nineteenth and early twentieth centuries, the scholars associated with this department embraced the view that human behavior, including criminal behavior, developed and changed due to pathological forces within the social and physical environments.[2] Neighborhoods, in particular, were thought to be a fundamental organizational unit regarding social life in urban areas (Park, Burgess, and McKenzie 1925 [1967]).

Chicago School criminology became especially known for scholarship highlighting the geographic distribution of gangs and crime, with the highest rates clustering in transitional neighborhoods just outside the central business district (e.g., Shaw 1929; Shaw and McKay 1942; Thrasher 1927). To account for this spatial patterning, Chicago-school scholars underscored the ill-effects of urban neighborhood *social disorganization*, in particular. More specifically, Chicago-school scholars articulated a view that physically deteriorated and socially disorganized slum areas (indicated by poverty, ethnic heterogeneity, and residential instability) lacked the institutional means for adequately controlling the formation of gangs and/or the commission of delinquency (see, e.g., Kornhauser 1978).

Numerous contemporary scholars have continued this important tradition, noting that crime is highest in neighborhoods that have weak capacity for informal social control due to weak friendship and kinship ties, weak secondary/organizational ties, and/or weak ties to extra-community agents that foster control, such as police (e.g., Bellair 1997; Bursik 2000; Bursik and Grasmick 1993; Sampson and Groves 1989; Velez 2001; Warner 2003; Warner and Wilcox Rountree 1997; see also Warner and Clubb 2013 for a review). Most recently, scholarship in the Chicago-school tradition has focused on the importance of neighborhood-level *collective efficacy* in controlling crime (Morenoff, Sampson, and Raudenbush 2001; Sampson 2002, 2006, 2012; Sampson, Raudenbush, and Earls 1997). Rather than assuming that crime is more effectively controlled when intra- and extra-community institutional ties are strong, the collective efficacy perspective focuses on the extent to which community members have shared expectations about collectively activating control against crime and disorder.

Environmental Criminology—Opportunity Perspectives

Environmental criminology is a set of theories and perspectives that focus on *crime events* and the immediate circumstances surrounding them (Wortley and Mazerolle 2008). Most criminological theories are explanations of *criminality* and therefore identify factors that create a criminal offender. In contrast, environmental criminologists view the offender as one of many elements of the crime event, and little emphasis is placed on distal factors related to his or her background. Crime events are seen as "confluences of offenders, victims or criminal targets, and laws in specific settings at particular times and places" (Brantingham and Brantingham 1991: 2), and emphasis is placed on proximal factors that create *opportunities* for such confluences.

Environmental criminology holds that criminal opportunity plays a role in causing all crime (Felson and Clarke 1998). Opportunities for crime are created by ordinary, everyday routine activity patterns that bring motivated offenders into contact with suitable targets in the absence of capable guardians (Cohen and Felson 1979; Brantingham and Brantingham 1991). Therefore, crime opportunities, and in turn crime events, are temporally and spatially patterned. Crime opportunities are also highly specific (Felson and Clarke 1998; Cornish and Clarke 2008); the conditions that create an opportunity for armed street robbery, for example, are distinctly different from those necessary for embezzlement.

Environmental criminological theories assume that bounded rationality guides offender decision making, with offenders attempting to maximize rewards and minimize risks based on their perceptions of environmental cues (Clarke and Cornish 1985; Brantingham and Brantingham 1982). Criminal behavior is thus viewed as the result of a person-situation interaction (Wortley and Mazerolle 2008), and in fact, criminal motivation itself may be situationally dependent, with some environments encouraging or inducing individuals to commit crimes they would not otherwise commit (Wortley 2001). Given the role of routine activities in shaping opportunities for crime *and* the influence of the immediate environment on criminal decision making, environmental criminology assumes that characteristics of places—including how they are designed (Cozens 2008; Jeffery 1971; Newman 1973), their function and the people they attract (Brantingham and Brantingham 1995), and the way they are managed (Eck 1994)—are important to understanding the spatial patterning of crime.

Crime Patterns and Integrative Theory

As suggested earlier, environmental criminology and the social disorganization tradition share an overlapping focus on the spatial patterning of crime. Further, both emphasize the importance of social and physical aspects of the environment in understanding the non-random geographic distribution of crime. Yet, as alluded to earlier, scholars working in these traditions have largely ignored one another.

One reason that Chicago-school criminologists and environmental criminologists have engaged in mutual disregard for one another is that social disorganization theory, as a macro-level control theory, has most typically been conceptualized as being a theory of offending behavior, or criminality; in contrast, opportunity theories explicitly offer explanations for crime events (see, e.g., Hirschi 1986; see also Bursik 1988). Additionally, these two perspectives often focus on different units of analysis. Again, social disorganization scholars have traditionally held the neighborhood unit up as the fundamental organizational unit for social life. In contrast, environmental criminologists view micro-scale places within neighborhoods as the more realistic unit for serving as "behavioral settings" (Taylor 1997, 1998; Weisburd et al. 2012). Furthermore, environmental criminologists point out that small-scale places are much more appropriate and manageable from a crime policy standpoint—police and other prevention agents can more readily tackle specific crime hot spots than they can entire neighborhoods (see, e.g., Eck and Guerette 2012; Taylor 1997, 1998; Telep and Weisburd 2012; Sherman et al. 1989; Weisburd et al. 2012).

Despite these noted differences, a growing number of scholars have begun to chisel away at the divide between social disorganization theory and environmental criminology by offering analyses of crime and victimization events that integrate both perspectives. These integrative studies stress the compatible rather than contradictory nature of the theories. Their compatibility is expressed in a couple of different ways (Miethe and Meier 1994). First, some have noted compatibility by actually playing up a traditional distinction often made in comparing social disorganization and crime opportunity theories—that social disorganization explains aggregate variation in criminal offending, whereas opportunity explains ecological variation in the opportunity for crime events. Some scholars have therefore suggested that integration of the two perspectives offers a more comprehensive explanation of crime—a perspective capable of addressing "elements of the offender, the victim, and those features of the social environment that facilitate or inhibit the expression of criminal motivation and the opportunity for crime" (e.g., Miethe and Meier 1994: 27–28; see also Smith, Frazee, and Davison 2000).

Another view claims compatibility between social disorganization theory and opportunity theory on the grounds that areas plagued by disorganization provide cues to offenders about the supply of criminal opportunities. For instance, disorganization can signal the (low) likelihood of surveillance and informal social control on the part of residents, while also providing cues about aggregate levels of target suitability (i.e., how target-rich is the environment?) and general levels of exposure or accessibility of potential targets (e.g., Sampson and Wooldredge 1987; Wilcox, Land, and Hunt 2003; Wilcox, Gialopsos, and Land 2013; Wilcox, Madensen, and Tillyer 2007; Wright and Decker 1997; see also Tillyer, Fisher, and Wilcox 2011). Viewed from this lens, "social disorganization" and other neighborhood characteristics are seen less as indicators of aggregate criminality and more as indicators of general levels of opportunity in an area. That is, social disorganization theory essentially serves as a situational theory of crime events rather than a theory of criminality. The lines between social disorganization theory and opportunity theory thus become especially blurred, as "social disorganization" and all that it entails is treated as a facet of opportunity. In fact, scholars invoking this sort of rationale for integration refer to resulting models as ones of "general opportunity" (e.g., Sampson and Wooldredge 1987; Wilcox et al. 2003, 2007, 2013).

Empirical studies that integrate social disorganization and opportunity theories, often using one of the viewpoints on compatibility outlined earlier, fall into distinct types: (1) studies of victimization that measure neighborhood-level and individual-level variables most traditionally associated with social disorganization and opportunity traditions, respectively, *using multiple, hierarchically embedded levels of analysis*; and (2) studies of crime that measure variables from social disorganization and opportunity theories *at a sub-neighborhood, or "place," level*. We review each of these types of integration in more detail next.

Multilevel Models of Victimization Risk

Multilevel models of victimization risk have been used in recent decades to reflect the variation in opportunities for criminal victimization that exists at multiple levels (e.g., Miethe and McDowall 1993; Sampson and Wooldredge 1987; Wilcox Rountree, Land, and Miethe 1994; Wilcox et al. 2003, 2007). These models—which recognize that individual victims are situated within broader contexts, such as neighborhoods—are grounded in work suggesting that offenders make decisions about crime events in a multi-staged fashion

(Taylor and Gottfredson 1986; Wilcox et al. 2013; Wright and Decker 1994, 1997). More specifically, multilevel victimization research suggests that the characteristics of neighborhoods are important, as offenders first choose general areas of a city/town in which to offend. Once appropriate neighborhoods are selected, offenders then focus on characteristics of individual targets/victims. Thus, multilevel victimization studies estimate the effects of both individual-level and neighborhood-level characteristics related to victimization, with the idea that neighborhood-level indicators of "social disorganization" serve to indicate contextual opportunity for crime events.

Sampson and Wooldredge (1987) were among the first to link the micro- and macro-level dimensions of victimization risk, arguing that the human ecological roots of the lifestyle-routine activity approach to victimization implicates both individual *and* community influences in creating opportunities for criminal victimization. Individual lifestyles and routine activities that are associated with proximity to potential offenders and low guardianship were presumed to create risk for victimization. At the same time, the broader community context was thought to structure routine activities and opportunities for victimization, as well as shape offender perceptions of weak informal control. Their multilevel study using data from the British Crime Survey confirmed that both individual and contextual factors contribute to victimization risk for burglary, household theft, and personal theft. For example, single-person households and households that were frequently left empty were at greater risk for burglary, thus demonstrating that lifestyles and routine activities can create opportunities for criminal victimization. In addition, households in communities marked by family disruption, single-person households, low social cohesion, VCR ownership, unemployment, and a high proportion of apartments were at greater risk for burglary, thus providing support for the idea that community context can structure real and perceived criminal opportunities, and in turn, influence burglary risk (Sampson and Wooldredge 1987).

Subsequent multilevel studies of victimization risk have supported the micro-macro dimensions of criminal opportunity (e.g., Kennedy and Forde 1990; Miethe and McDowall 1993; Smith and Jarjoura 1989; Wilcox Rountree et al. 1994; Wilcox Rountree and Land 2000).[3] Smith and Jarjoura's (1989) study of household burglaries in residential neighborhoods across Rochester, Tampa-St. Petersburg, and St. Louis, for example, found that both household characteristics and the neighborhood social context were associated with burglary victimization. Households comprised of single parents, single males, two males, non-whites, more residents, and younger residents were at greater risk for burglary victimization. Neighborhood characteristics such as racial heterogeneity, residential instability, single-parent households, age, median income, and social integration were also associated with burglary risk. Miethe and McDowall's (1993) study of adults living on city blocks in Seattle found that both individual and contextual variables were related not only to burglary victimization, but violent victimization as well. For example, their measure of "dangerous activity"—which taps the extent to which respondents frequent bars, nightclubs, places where teenagers hang out, and public transit—was associated with an increased risk for violent victimization, as was block-level land use and socioeconomic conditions.

Beyond the direct effects of community context and individual indicators of criminal opportunity, multilevel studies have explored the ways in which neighborhood context might *moderate* the influence of individual opportunity on victimization risk. Studies that have modeled these *cross-level interactions* provide some support for the idea that individual lifestyles and routine activities do not uniformly influence risk for victimization across all settings, but rather that neighborhood structural characteristics can interact with individual indicators of opportunity to affect victimization risk (Miethe and McDowall 1993; Miethe and Meier 1994; Wilcox et al. 2007; Wilcox Rountree et al. 1994). Wilcox Rountree et al. (1994) found that the crime prevention effect of individual-level guardianship (in the form of safety precautions such as locked doors, burglar alarm, extra locks, dog ownership, etc.) on burglary victimization risk was weakened in areas with high levels of disorder. Similarly, Wilcox et al. (2007) found that the protective effects of individual-level guardianship on burglary victimization risk were significantly strengthened by neighborhood-level indicators of target-hardening, informal social control, and defensible space. Finally, Miethe and Meier (1994) found that the negative influence of family income on stranger assault victimization risk was significantly stronger in residential areas with low socioeconomic decay, low public activity, high levels of safety precautions, and low levels of living alone. Conversely, the positive relationship between living alone and stranger assault victimization risk was primarily observed in areas with high levels of socioeconomic decay, high rates of public activity, low levels of safety precautions, and higher rates of single-person households.

Place-Based Social Disorganization and Opportunity

A great deal of important work in the last several decades has championed small geographic units of analysis, or "places," for the study of crime (see, e.g., Eck et al. 2005; Eck and Guerette 2012; Taylor 1997, 1998; Taylor, Koons, Kurtz, Greene, and Perkins 1995; Weisburd, Bernasco, and Bruinsma 2000; Weisburd et al. 2004; Weisburd et al. 2012; see also Sherman et al. 1989). "Place" is operationalized differently by various scholars, ranging from a specific address to an entire street block or two, but most place-level research is united in its focus on opportunity theories to account for crime patterning. However, according to some place scholars, place-level patterns should be understood as a function of processes of *both* social disorganization and opportunity. For instance, Taylor (1998) claims that street blocks are settings in which people can realistically get to know one another, share norms about standards for behavior, and observe behavior (thus exhibiting social organization). At the same time, they are clearly bounded units that have distinct, regularly occurring activity patterns that provide more or less opportunity (Taylor 1998: 10).

Place-based empirical work exists to support Taylor's claims that places are important units for understanding both social (dis)organization and crime opportunities. For example, beginning in the early 1980s, Dennis Roncek and his colleagues published a series of studies that showed that street blocks with certain *non-residential land uses*, including on-premise alcohol outlets and high schools, experienced higher crime (Roncek and Bell 1981; Roncek and Faggiani 1985; Roncek and LoBosco 1983; Roncek and Maier 1991). Roncek and colleagues argued that schools and bars generated crime on street blocks containing them by fostering a convergence of motivated offenders and suitable, unguarded targets. Adjacency to such facilities exerted strong effects on various types of crime in Roncek and colleagues' work, and the effects were consistent in block-level analyses across very different types of cities. At the same time, however, variables theoretically aligned with block-level social disorganization—including racial heterogeneity and/or percentage black and population density—also exhibited strong effects in their various analyses.

In discussing their findings, Roncek and colleagues generally emphasize the value in focusing on the crime opportunity offered by facilities rather than explicitly embracing an integrated approach focusing on *both* opportunity and social disorganization. Despite this general tenor in their discussions, there are instances where they imply the value of better specifying the way in which processes of opportunity and social disorganization work in conjunction with one another. For instance, Roncek and LoBosco (1983: 608–609) considered the interaction between school adjacency and variables traditionally associated with "social disorganization" for a block in San Diego as follows:

> Blocks which were adjacent to public schools and had crimes on them tended to have a significantly higher concentration of minority residents, lower housing values, greater densities, more young male residents, and more total residents than blocks near schools without crime. . . . Thus, proximity to public high schools further increased crime on those adjacent city blocks which had the demographic and housing characteristics linked with high crime levels.

Since Roncek's pathbreaking work, contemporary crime research has continued to examine the effects of non-residential land uses in combination with social characteristics of places, with more explicit attention to the theoretical integration behind such analyses (e.g., Kurtz, Koons, and Taylor 1998; Rice and Smith 2002; Smith et al. 2000). For example, Smith and colleagues borrow from work examining the interactions between individual routine activities and characteristics associated with neighborhood disorganization (reviewed earlier), and suggest that the interaction of such processes is perhaps best observed at the place (street block) level. They explicate their posited interactions in the following way:

> The basic hypothesis is that proximity to motivated offenders, as measured by the number of single-parent heads of household and distance to the downtown area (where would-be robbers presumably visit and near where many also live), interacts with land use variables, which measure the availability of attractive targets and what draws motivated offenders to a face block. It is hypothesized that where more single-parent households exist in the presence of land uses that attract victims as well as would-be robbers, street robbery is more likely. As distance from the center of the city increases, the criminogenic effect of various land uses is hypothesized to decline.
>
> (Smith et al. 2000: 506)

Many of their findings were supportive of these proposed interaction effects. As single-parent households on blocks increased, the effect of the presence of motels/hotels, bars, restaurants, and gas stations on robbery all increased. Distance from the central city attenuated the effects of multifamily residences, bars, restaurants, gas stations, and vacant/parking lots on robbery.

Rice and Smith (2002) conducted a similar follow-up study of auto theft on the same set of street blocks. Rice and Smith (2002) found that 13 of 22 possible interactions between land uses and indicators of social disorganization were significantly related to block-level auto theft. Similar to Smith et al.'s (2000) findings, the percentage of single-parent households tended to exacerbate the auto theft risk associated with opportunity-generating land uses, while distance from downtown tempered the risks associated with such land uses. Furthermore, the effect of stores/shops and commercial places was enhanced as the percentage of buildings on the block of less than median value increased. Similarly, Stucky and Ottensmann's (2009) analysis of violent crime among 1,000-feet grid squares in Indianapolis showed that the effects of several measures of land uses and traffic routes on violence were moderated by the level of economic disadvantage within the surrounding area.

More recently, Weisburd et al. (2012) put forth a comprehensive, 16-year longitudinal analysis of street segments in Seattle that incorporated opportunity- and disorganization-related risk and protective factors. Their study revealed strong stability in patterns of crime concentration (i.e., hot spots) at the street segment level of analysis across the time period examined, 1989–2004. Furthermore, the largely stable developmental trends they observed regarding crime at street segments was well-predicted by the characteristics of these places that they measured. In particular, size of residential population, number of employees, presence of arterial roads, and level of physical disorder all increased crime on street segments. In contrast, socioeconomic status and collective efficacy served to protect street segments from crime. While stability in crime on street blocks was the clear normative pattern in their data, Weisburd et al. (2012) did also explore the characteristics of street segments most associated with significant changes in crime (i.e., the causes of crime waves or crime drops). Crime waves and crime drops were most strongly associated with variables at the street segment level aligned with the social disorganization perspective: physical disorder, socioeconomic status, number of unsupervised teens, and collective efficacy. The authors conclude, "It is time to include both opportunity and social disorganization in our understanding of the criminology of place" (Weisburd et al. 2012: 180–181).

A New Approach: "Place in Neighborhood" Theory

We follow Weisburd et al.'s (2012) suggestion and extend previous work incorporating aspects of both opportunity and social disorganization theories to better understand crime at places. In doing so, we merge important components of the two major integrative lines of inquiry reviewed in the previous section to offer a similar, yet distinct, perspective. Drawing from multilevel research on victimization risk, we see value in considering multiple, hierarchically nested units of analysis in theory on crime events. Yet, extant multilevel theory and research have almost exclusively focused on individuals, as potential victims, nested within neighborhood contexts (see Deryol, Wilcox, Logan, and Wooldredge 2016 for an exception). As such, multilevel work has heretofore largely ignored the important phenomenon of micro-ecological crime places, which we view as an important omission. In contrast, "crime and place" research, including that which integrates concepts and measures from social disorganization and opportunity traditions, puts such small-scale places front-and-center. However, this emphasis on place is at the expense of other contextual units, even in place-based research that integrates "neighborhood" (i.e., social disorganization) theory. We thus advocate a "place in neighborhood" (PIN) approach that recognizes both the value in studying, understanding, and preventing crime at small-scale places *and* the value in situating those places in broader neighborhood contexts.

Rationale and Underpinnings of a Place in Neighborhood Theory

Implicit support for such an approach to crime has actually been around for decades. For example, collectively, research has shown that crime clusters at numerous, embedded, and increasingly narrow levels of resolution, including neighborhoods, streets, and places on streets (e.g., see Brantingham, Dyreson, and Brantingham 1976; Eck et al. 2005). As mentioned previously, work describing how offenders search for crime targets, including places, supports the clustering we see on maps at different levels of resolution. This literature suggests that target search and selection involve multilevel, sequential pro- cesses whereby offenders engage in multiple decisions about crime opportu- nities at progressively smaller units of analysis—for instance, first selecting neighborhoods and then selecting places within neighborhoods (e.g., Brant- ingham and Brantingham 1991, 1993; Taylor and Gottfredson 1986; Wright and Decker 1994, 1997). Indeed, there is evidence in prominent scholarship emphasizing place-level influences and that the broader context also affects the crime potential of particular places. For example, Weisburd et al. (2012) emphasize the block-to-block variability in crime in their data and conclude that block-level variation *cannot* be *primarily* attributed to higher-level influ- ences. At the same time, they do note some clustering of hot blocks: "we do find cases in our data where several adjacent street segments, one after another, evidence similar developmental trends of crime" (Weisburd et al. 2012: 173). They suggest that this provides some evidence that higher geographic influ- ences, such as neighborhoods, play a role in understanding crime on street blocks. More recently, Deryol and colleagues provided more direct evidence of contextual influences on crime at places (addresses, in their study). They found that the proximity of addresses to drinking/liquor establishments and bus stops was more strongly related to crime in neighborhoods with higher overall com- mercial density (Deryol et al. 2016).

Despite evidence of the value in a place-neighborhood integrative perspec- tive, an explicit statement of such a framework is still needed. In offering such a perspective, we draw heavily upon the market framework utilized by Wilcox et al. (2003) in theorizing about multilevel main and moderating effects in the study of crime events (see also Cook 1986). Wilcox et al. (2003) put forth their "multicontextual opportunity theory" by integrating micro- and macro-level routine activities theories with control theories (including social disorganiza- tion theory) to explain crime and victimization events, though they did not apply their perspective to events at places, specifically. In this theory, con- cepts from both theoretical traditions were used to indicate individual-level and broader contextual opportunity. At the individual level, exposure to moti- vated offenders, target suitability, and a lack of capable guardianship define criminal opportunity, which is hypothesized to directly influence crime and victimization. Indicators of individual-level opportunity include variables from lifestyle-routine activities theory and individual-level control theories (i.e., social bond theory). At contextual levels, opportunity is created by area- level features that reflect a concentration of motivated offenders, the supply of attractive targets, and collective levels of guardianship, according to Wil- cox et al.'s (2003) perspective. They suggest that indicators of such contex- tual opportunity include variables traditionally linked to macro-level routine activities theory as well as macro-level control theories (i.e., social disorgani- zation theory, deterrence theory). These features combine to create a "market context" for crime (Wilcox et al. 2003: 104–112; see also Cook 1986). Like individual-level opportunity, contextual opportunity is assumed to influence crime events (Wilcox et al. 2003).

Beyond the main influences of individual and contextual opportunity, Wilcox et al. (2003) further draw on principles of economic theory of markets to develop specific predictions about how opportunity structures interact across individual and contextual levels. In particular, they focused on how contexts vary in terms of their market exposure (i.e., supply of offenders), market value (i.e., supply of targets), and market costs (i.e., macro-level control) and how each of these contextual factors can serve to moderate the effects of individual-level indicators of opportunity on crime events. For instance, in theorizing about how opportunity in the form of individual levels of exposure to motivated offenders, target suitability, and guardianship might vary in their effects on crime events across contexts, they suggest the following: (1) contexts characterized by large supplies of offenders increase market demand for targets; such contexts make individual-level exposure and suitability all the more important in defining criminal opportunity, while reducing the importance of individual guardianship; (2) contexts characterized by a large aggregate supply of suitable targets diminish the value of any one target; such contexts make individual exposure and guardianship all the more important, while making suitability less important; and (3) contexts with strong aggregate guardianship increase the market costs of criminal acts, thus deterring crime; such contexts make individual-level exposure and target suitability less important, while enhancing the effects of individual-level guardianship (Wilcox et al. 2003:106–112).

We extend Wilcox et al. (2003) in offering a multilevel approach to understanding *crime places in neighborhood context*, specifically. This place in neighborhood approach is summarized below in what we refer to as "PIN propositions".

1. Crime events occur non-randomly at particular places as a result of offenders making decisions about opportunity. In particular, offenders consider the effort, risk, and rewards of crime.
2. Perceptions of effort, risk, and reward (i.e., perceived opportunity) are defined by characteristics of places—such as their density of users, the activities they support, the sort of street on which they sit, the effectiveness of their management, and so on. These factors thus help account for the non-random patterning of crime across places.
3. Perceptions of effort, risk, and reward (i.e., perceived opportunity) are also defined by characteristics of the broader contexts in which places are situated. In particular, neighborhoods in which places are embedded have varying levels of exposure to offenders, varying supplies of targets, and varying macro-level control. Hence, neighborhoods provide variable market contexts for crime, and specific places embedded within are influenced by these broader neighborhood crime markets.

4. Characteristics of places and the broader neighborhood crime markets in which they are situated can work jointly to influence crime at places in several different ways: they might exert independent simultaneous effects, or, more likely, they might exhibit interdependent, or interaction, effects.

4a. Both characteristics of places AND characteristics of the neighborhoods can influence the rates of crime events at places.

4b. Opportunity-related characteristics of places can influence the rates of crime events differentially across places, depending on the crime market characteristics of neighborhoods in which places are situated.

4b-i. Neighborhoods that have large supplies of offenders provide to places within them high levels of market exposure to crime. Thus, the effects of place-level indicators of (high) reward are enhanced in such contexts, while the effects of place-level indicators of (high) effort and (high) risk/control (i.e., place management) are reduced in such contexts.

4b-ii. Neighborhoods that offer large supplies of targets have high market values, with the value of individual target-places within diminished. Place-level distinctions in terms of effort and risk will matter more in such contexts, whereas place-level distinctions in terms of rewards will matter less.

4b-iii. Neighborhoods that offer strong collective guardianship (in the form of both formal and informal control) produce a risky market in which to offend. Place-level distinctions in terms of effort and reward matter less in such well-controlled contexts, whereas the effects of place-level risk to offenders (i.e., place management) are enhanced by the market risk.

To summarize, our PIN approach identifies micro-places as relevant units of analysis and concepts from environmental criminological theories as key to understanding spatial variation in crime. Micro-places, however, are embedded within broader neighborhood crime markets that can directly contribute to crime at places. Further, the effects of place-level opportunity characteristics on crime may vary depending on the neighborhood crime market characteristics. In fact, these potential moderating effects of neighborhood-level crime market context are perhaps the most integral features of the PIN perspective. The posited moderating effects—stated in Propositions 4b-i, 4b-ii, and 4b-iii earlier in the chapter—are also summarized in Figure 5.1.

In laying out the PIN perspective, we implicitly assume that our propositions hold across the various definitions of "neighborhood" and "place," yet we raise as a question for future elaborations of this perspective (or empirical tests thereof) whether that assumption is justified. We recognize that there is ongoing debate in the community literature about whether the effects of various neighborhood units are substantively distinct, but conclusions are mixed

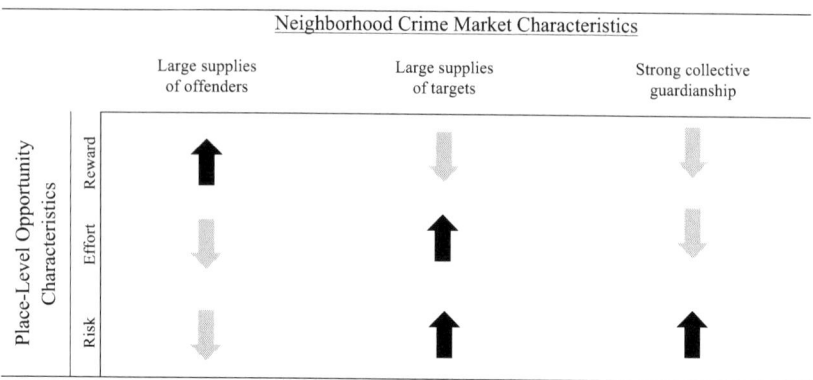

Figure 5.1 The influence of neighborhood crime market characteristics on the importance of place-level opportunity characteristics.

Note: Bold arrows pointing up indicate that the importance of the place-level opportunity characteristics is increased when the neighborhood crime market characteristic is present. Gray arrows pointing down indicate that the importance of the place-level opportunity characteristics is reduced when the neighborhood crime market characteristic is present.

across studies (c.f., Boessen and Hipp 2015; Steenbeek and Weisburd 2016). Likewise, we recognize the possibility that various sub-neighborhood, micro-spatial units may be distinct conceptually. In short, it is possible that the interactive relationships posited here might vary depending on the definition and nature of "neighborhoods" and "places," but we do not yet have strong enough evidence about the unique nature of various units to provide unit-specific propositions. Thus, generalizability remains a question for future theoretical elaboration or empirical exploration.

A PIN-Based Agenda for Crime and Place Research

In light of our PIN-based approach to understanding crime, we propose an agenda to guide future research. This agenda emphasizes the importance of both neighborhood- and place-level main effects as well as potential interactions between neighborhood and place characteristics. Similar to research that accounts for the fact that potential victims are embedded within neighborhood contexts, we encourage research on crime at places to explore both the main and interactive effects of neighborhood and place characteristics in multilevel models so that the relative contributions of each can be observed. In particular, future research should consider how a PIN approach might apply across various crime types. Environmental criminological perspectives emphasize the crime-specific nature of offender decision making (Felson and Clarke 1998; Cornish and Clarke 2008); applying a PIN approach requires that the general neighborhood market characteristics and place-level opportunity characteristics described earlier be tailored to specific crimes to develop hypotheses about crime at places. To illustrate, we apply a PIN approach to the spatial distribution of open-air drug dealing.

PIN and Specific Crime Events at Places: The Case
of Open-Air Drug Dealing

First, a PIN approach assumes that drug dealing occurs non-randomly at particular places as a result of offenders making decisions about opportunity provided by various places (Proposition 1). The characteristics of places contribute to drug dealers' perceptions about the efforts, risks, and rewards associated with dealing drugs at specific locations. In particular, their density of users, the activities they support, the sort of street on which they sit, and the effectiveness of their management affect perceptions about opportunities across places and thus contribute to the non-random patterning of open-air drug dealing across places (Proposition 2). In addition, neighborhood-level drug market characteristics can influence offenders' perceptions about opportunities for drug dealing at places. All else being equal, places embedded within neighborhood crime markets with a large supply of drug dealers, a large supply of drug users, and low collective guardianship will be more vulnerable to open-air drug dealing (Proposition 3). In short, both the characteristics of places and the broader neighborhood market for drug dealing influence drug dealers' perceptions of opportunities and, in turn, the geographical distribution of open-air drug dealing (Proposition 4a).

Beyond these main effects, a PIN approach posits that the neighborhood crime market influences the importance of place-level opportunity characteristics; in other words, the two interact to influence the spatial distribution of open-air drug dealing (Proposition 4b). For example, perhaps the characteristics of a particular street corner offer high rewards for drug dealers: ideal traffic flow from two busy intersecting streets provides optimal drug sales. This same corner, however, leaves the drug dealer in plain view of many potential witnesses, thus increasing risk for the dealer. A PIN approach suggests that the importance of these place-level characteristics will vary depending on the neighborhood crime market.

Neighborhood crime markets with a large supply of drug dealers have a heightened market demand for drug buyers. The risks and efforts associated with any particular place will be less important in such neighborhoods; it is the profit potential (i.e., rewards) a place offers that will be of greatest importance to drug dealers. Therefore, the aforementioned street corner with its high earning potential will be viewed as a favorable location for dealing drugs (Proposition 4b-i; see also column 1 of Figure 5.1).

On the other hand, a large supply of drug *users* in a neighborhood diminishes the value of any single buyer, thus making it easier for dealers to avoid risky places that may leave them exposed, even if such places might allow them to meet more buyers. The profit potential of a particular place (i.e., rewards) matters less in such neighborhoods, while the detection potential (i.e., risk) matters more. The street corner described earlier, therefore, would be viewed as less favorable for drug dealing in such neighborhood contexts (Proposition 4b-ii; see also column 2 of Figure 5.1).

Finally, neighborhood crime markets with strong collective guardianship create risky markets for drug dealing. In such neighborhoods, residents are likely to call the police when they witness suspicious behavior, act as witnesses, and provide informal social control more generally. The natural surveillance associated with the street corner described earlier will be perceived as particularly risky in neighborhoods with strong collective guardianship, whereas a similar street corner in neighborhoods with weak collective guardianship would not be viewed as risky, given that there is little expectation of third party intervention in such neighborhood contexts (Proposition 4b-iii; see also column 3 of Figure 5.1).

PIN and Other Crime-Related Outcomes

Beyond exploring the main and interactive effects of neighborhood- and place-level characteristics on the distribution of crime, we believe a PIN approach to understanding crime at places can be expanded to study other crime-related outcomes. Neighborhood crime market characteristics and place-level opportunity characteristics might also influence crime events as they unfold, thus affecting the *severity* of the crime with respect to victim injury or death, property damage or loss, length of time of the offense, etc. (see Baumer, Horney, Felson, and Lauritsen 2003). The PIN approach we have presented clearly suggests that the perceived opportunities associated with place-level characteristics influence the likelihood of crime. Recent arguments by Tillyer and colleagues describe how place-level characteristics could influence crime events in at least two other ways (Tillyer, Miller, and Tillyer 2011; Tillyer and Tillyer 2014).

First, place characteristics may affect the perceived risk of third party intervention, so offenders limit the severity of their crimes—they do not injure victims, they quickly take the goods that are readily available and leave to avoid apprehension, they limit the extent of property damage, and so forth. In other words, the perceived threat of third party intervention—which is a function of place-level opportunity characteristics—limits the harm associated with a crime event. Second, offenders might proceed to commit their crimes despite the risks associated with a particular place, but third parties intervene during the event to limit the severity—they assist victims, they call the police, they confront the offender, etc. Each of these scenarios would still be recorded as a crime in most studies, thus masking the influence of place-level opportunity characteristics on crime events (Tillyer et al. 2011; Tillyer and Tillyer 2014).

The influence of place-level opportunity characteristics that are assumed to contribute to offender perceptions of risk and, in turn, the severity of a crime might also be moderated by the neighborhood crime market. For example, a recent study found that robberies occurring in semi-public places (shops, bars, etc.) were less likely to result in victim injury relative to robberies occurring in public and private locations (Tillyer and Tillyer 2014). One explanation for this finding is that such locations offer a certain degree of real or perceived place management. The study also found that the relationship between location type and victim injury was weakened in contexts with high levels of concentrated disadvantage, potentially because there is little expectation of third party intervention in such contexts. One interpretation of these findings is that place-level factors associated with offender risk reduce the likelihood of victim injury during robberies in contexts with strong collective guardianship, but the effect is tempered when collective guardianship is low.

Conclusion

The position advanced here is that studying crime places does not have to exclude the possibility for neighborhood-level influences. Theory and research to date suggest that both place-level and neighborhood-level influences help us understand crime places; they should therefore be used together to understand crime places more fully. The PIN approach advanced here identifies micro-places as relevant units of analysis and concepts from environmental criminological theories as key to understanding the spatial distribution of crime. This approach, however, recognizes that places are situated within broader neighborhood crime markets that can directly affect crime at places. In addition, neighborhood crime market characteristics can interact with place-level opportunity characteristics to influence crime at places.

We encourage future research to apply a PIN-based approach when studying crime at places. To do so will require researchers to consider how the neighborhood crime market and place-level opportunity operate for specific crime types (as demonstrated earlier in the example of open-air drug dealing). We also encourage researchers to explore how a PIN approach might be applied to research examining the severity of crime events. A PIN approach assumes that crimes are dynamic events that can involve many actors, including place managers and other third parties who may try to stop or at least limit the severity of the crime as it unfolds. Examining crime-related outcomes that tap the severity of crime may shed light on additional neighborhood crime market and place-level opportunity effects that are overlooked in studies that simply measure whether or not a crime occurred.

Notes

1. Address all correspondence to Pamela Wilcox, School of Criminal Justice, University of Cincinnati, 660NA Dyer Hall, Box 201389, Cincinnati, OH 45220–0389, pamela.wilcox@uc.edu.
2. At the time, this view of crime was quite novel, as criminology had largely been approaching criminal behavior as an individual rather than environmental pathology.
3. Additional studies have examined the multilevel dimensions of criminal opportunity in settings other than neighborhoods, such as universities and schools (see, for example, Fisher, Sloan, Cullen, and Lu 1998, Tillyer et al. 2011).

References

Baumer, Eric, Julie Horney, Richard Felson, and Janet L. Lauritsen. 2003. "Neighborhood Disadvantage and the Nature of Violence." *Criminology* 41: 39–71.

Bellair, Paul. 1997. "Social Interaction and Community Crime: Examining the Importance of Neighbor Networks." *Criminology* 35: 677–703.

Boessen, Adam, and John R. Hipp. 2015. "Close-Ups and the Scale of Ecology: Land Uses and The Geography of Social Context and Crime." *Criminology* 53: 399–462.

Braga, Anthony A. 2012. "High Crime Places, Times, and Offenders." Pp. 316–336 in Brandon C. Welsh and David P. Farrington (eds.), *The Oxford Handbook of Crime Prevention*. New York, NY: Oxford University Press.

Brantingham, Patricia L., and Paul J. Brantingham. 1982. "Mobility, Notoriety, and Crime: A Study in the Crime Patterns of Urban Nodal Points." *Journal of Environmental Systems* 11: 89–99.

Brantingham, Patricia L., and Paul J. Brantingham. 1993. "Nodes, Paths, and Edge Considerations on the Complexity of Crime and the Physical Environment." *Journal of Environmental Psychology* 13: 3–28.

Brantingham, Patricia L., and Paul J. Brantingham. 1995. "Criminality of Place: Crime Generators and Crime Attractors." *European Journal on Criminal Policy and Research* 3: 5–26.

Brantingham, Paul J., and Patricia L. Brantingham. 1991. *Environmental Criminology* (2nd ed.). Prospect Heights, IL: Waveland Press.

Brantingham, Paul J., Delmar A. Dyreson, and Patricia L. Brantingham. 1976. "Crime Seen Through a Cone of Resolution." *American Behavioral Scientist* 20: 261–273.

Bursik, Robert J., Jr. 1988. "Social Disorganization and Theories of Crime and Delinquency: Problems and Prospects." *Criminology* 26: 519–551.

Bursik, Robert J., Jr. 2000. "The Systemic Theory of Neighborhood Crime Rates." Pp. 87–103 in Sally Simpson (ed.), *Of Crime and Criminality*. Thousand Oaks, CA: Pine Forge Press.

Bursik, Robert J., Jr., and Harold B. Grasmick. 1993. *Neighborhoods and Crime: The Dimensions of Effective Community Control*. New York, NY: Macmillan.

Clarke, Ronald V., and Derek B. Cornish. 1985. "Modeling Offenders' Decisions: A Framework for Research and Policy." *Crime and Justice: A Review of Research* 6: 147–185.

Cohen, Lawrence E., and Marcus Felson. 1979. "Social Change and Crime Rate Trends: A Routine Activities Approach." *American Sociological Review* 44: 88–100.

Cook, Philip J. 1986. "The Demand and Supply of Criminal Opportunities." Pp. 1–27 in Michael Tonry and Norval Morris (eds.), *Crime and Justice: A Review of Research*, vol. 7. Chicago, IL: University of Chicago Press.

Cornish, Derek B., and Ronald V. Clarke. 2008. "The Rational Choice Perspective." Pp. 21–47 in Richard Wortley and Lorraine Mazerolle (eds.), *Environmental Criminology and Crime Analysis*. Cullompton, UK: Willan Publishing.

Cozens, Paul. 2008. "Crime Prevention Through Environmental Design." Pp. 153–177 in Richard Wortley and Lorraine Mazerolle (eds.), *Environmental Criminology and Crime Analysis*. Cullompton, UK: Willan Publishing.

Deryol, Rustu, Pamela Wilcox, Matthew Logan, and John Wooldredge. 2016. "Crime Places in Context: An Illustration of the Multilevel Nature of Hotspot Development." *Journal of Quantitative Criminology* 32: 305–325 (Erratum, pp. 327–328).

Eck, John E. 1994. *Drug Markets and Drug Places: A Case-Control Study of the Spatial Structure of Illicit Drug Dealing*. Unpublished Doctoral Dissertation. College Park, MD: University of Maryland, College Park.

Eck, John E., Spencer Chainey, James G. Cameron, Michael Leitner, and Ronald E. Wilson. 2005. *Mapping Crime: Understanding Hot Spots*. Washington, DC: U.S. Department of Justice, National Institute of Justice. NCJ 209393.

Eck, John E., and Rob T. Guerette. 2012. "Place-Based Crime Prevention: Theory, Evidence, and Policy." Pp. 354–383 in Brandon C. Welsh and David P. Farrington (eds.), *The Oxford Handbook of Crime Prevention*. New York, NY: Oxford University Press.

Felson, Marcus, and Ronald V. Clarke. 1998. *Opportunity Makes the Thief: Practical Theory for Crime Prevention*. Police Research Series, Paper 98, edited by B. Webb. London: Home Office.

Fisher, Bonnie S., John J. Sloan, Francis T. Cullen, and Chunmeng Lu. 1998. "Crime in the Ivory Tower: The Level and Sources of Student Victimization." *Criminology* 36: 671–710.

Guerry, Andre-Michel. 1883. *Essai Sur La Statistique Morale De La France*. Paris: Crochard.

Hirschi, Travis. 1986. "On the Compatibility of Rational Choice and Social Control Theories of Crime." Pp. 105–118 in Ronald V. Clarke and Derek B. Cornish (eds.), *The Reasoning Criminal: Rational Choice Perspectives on Offending*. New York, NY: Springer-Verlag.

Jeffery, C. Ray. 1971. *Crime Prevention Through Environmental Design*. Beverly Hills, CA: Sage.

Kennedy, Leslie W., and David R. Forde. 1990. "Routine Activities and Crime: An Analysis of Victimization in Canada." *Criminology* 28: 137–152.

Kornhauser, Ruth Rosner. 1978. *Social Sources of Delinquency: An Appraisal of Analytic Models*. Chicago, IL: University of Chicago Press.

Kurtz, Ellen, Barbara Koons, and Ralph B. Taylor. 1998. "Land Use, Physical Deterioration, Resident-Based Control, and Calls for Service on Urban Streetblocks." *Justice Quarterly* 15: 121–149.

Madensen, Tamara D., and John E. Eck. 2013. "Crime Places and Place Management." Pp. 554–578 in Francis T. Cullen and Pamela Wilcox (eds.), *The Oxford Handbook of Criminological Theory*. New York, NY: Oxford University Press.

Miethe, Terance D., and David McDowall. 1993. "Contextual Effects in Models of Criminal Victimization." *Social Forces* 71: 741–759.

Miethe, Terance D., and Robert F. Meier. 1994. *Crime and Its Social Context: Toward an Integrated Theory of Offenders, Victims, and Situations*. Albany, NY: State University of New York Press.

Morenoff, Jeffrey D., Robert J. Sampson, and Stephen W. Raudenbush. 2001. "Neighborhood Inequality, Collective Efficacy, and the Spatial Dynamics of Urban Violence." *Criminology* 39: 517–560.

Newman, Oscar. 1973. *Defensible Space, People and Design in the Violent City.* London: Architectural Press.

Park, Robert E., Ernest W. Burgess, and Roderick Duncan McKenzie. 1925 [1967]. *The City.* Chicago: University of Chicago Press.

Quetelet, Adolphe. 1969 [1842]. *A Treatise on Man and the Development of His Facilities.* Edinburgh, Scotland: William and Robert Chambers.

Rice, Kennon J., and William R. Smith. 2002. "Socioecological Models of Automotive Theft: Integrating Routine Activity and Social Disorganization Approaches." *Journal of Research in Crime and Delinquency* 39: 304–336.

Roncek, Dennis W., and Ralph Bell. 1981. "Bars, Blocks, and Crimes." *Journal of Environmental Systems* 11: 35–47.

Roncek, Dennis W., and Donald Faggiani. 1985. "High Schools and Crime: A Replication." *Sociological Quarterly* 26: 49–505.

Roncek, Dennis W., and Antoinette LoBosco. 1983. "The Effect of High Schools on Crime in Their Neighborhoods." *Social Science Quarterly* 64: 598–613.

Roncek, Dennis W., and Pamela A. Maier. 1991. "Bars, Blocks, and Crimes Revisited: Linking the Theory of Routine Activities to the Empiricism of 'Hot Spots'." *Criminology* 29: 725–753.

Sampson, Robert J. 2002. "Transcending Tradition: New Direction in Community Research, Chicago Style." *Criminology* 40: 213–230.

Sampson, Robert J. 2006. "Collective Efficacy Theory: Lessons Learned and Directions for Future Research." Pp. 149–167 in Francis T. Cullen, John Paul Wright, and Kristie R. Blevins (eds.), *Taking Stock: The Status of Criminological Theory: Advances in Criminological Theory*, vol. 15. New Brunswick, NJ: Transaction.

Sampson, Robert J. 2012. *Great American City: Chicago and the Enduring Neighborhood Effect.* Chicago, IL: University of Chicago Press.

Sampson, Robert J., and W. Byron Groves. 1989. "Community Structure and Crime: Testing Social Disorganization Theory." *American Journal of Sociology* 94: 774–802.

Sampson, Robert J., Stephen W. Raudenbush, and Felton J. Earls. 1997. "Neighborhoods and Violent Crime: A Multilevel Study of Collective Efficacy." *Science* 277: 918–924.

Sampson, Robert J., and John Wooldredge. 1987. "Linking the Micro- and Macro-Level Dimensions of Lifestyle-Routine Activity and Opportunity Models of Predatory Victimization." *Journal of Quantitative Criminology* 3: 371–393.

Shaw, Clifford R. 1929. *Delinquency Areas.* Chicago, IL: University of Chicago Press.

Shaw, Clifford R., and Henry D. McKay. 1942. *Juvenile Delinquency and Urban Areas.* Chicago, IL: University of Chicago Press.

Sherman, Lawrence W., Patrick R. Gartin, and Michael E. Buerger. 1989. "Hot Spots of Predatory Crime: Routine Activities and the Criminology of Place." *Criminology* 27: 27–55.

Smith, Douglas A., and G. Roger Jarjoura. 1989. "Household Characteristics, Neighborhood Composition, and Victimization Risk." *Social Forces* 68: 621–640.

Smith, William R., Sharon G. Frazee, and Elizabeth L. Davison. 2000. "Furthering the Integration of Routine Activity and Social Disorganization Theories: A Socio-Ecological Analysis of Street Robbery as a Diffusion Process." *Criminology* 38: 489–524.

Steenbeek, Wouter, and David Weisburd. 2016. "Where the Action Is in Crime? An Examination of Variability of Crime Across Different Spatial Units in The Hague, 2001–2009." *Journal of Quantitative Criminology* 32: 449–469.

Stucky, Thomas. D., and John R. Ottensmann. 2009. "Land Use and Violent Crime." *Criminology* 47: 1223–1264.

Taylor, Ralph B. 1997. "Social Order and Disorder of Street Blocks and Neighborhoods: Ecology, Microecology, and the Systemic Model of Social Disorganization." *Journal of Research in Crime and Delinquency* 34: 113–155.

Taylor, Ralph B. 1998. "Crime and Small-Scale Place: What We Know, What We Can Prevent, and What Else We Need to Know." Pp. 1–22 in *Crime and Place: Plenary Papers of the 1997 Conference on Criminal Justice Research and Evaluation*. Washington, DC: National Institute of Justice.

Taylor, Ralph B., and Stephen D. Gottfredson. 1986. "Environmental Design, Crime, and Prevention: An Examination of Community Dynamics." Pp. 387–416 in Albert J. Reiss, Jr. and Michael Tonry (eds.), *Communities and Crime: Crime and Justice: A Review of Research*, vol. 8. Chicago, IL: University of Chicago Press.

Taylor, Ralph B., Barbara A. Koons, Ellen M. Kurtz, Jack R. Greene, and Douglas D. Perkins. 1995. "Street Blocks with More Nonresidential Land Use Have More Physical Deterioration." *Urban Affairs Review* 31: 120–136.

Telep, Cody, and David Weisburd. 2012. "What Is Known About the Effectiveness of Police Practices in Reducing Crime and Disorder?" *Police Quarterly* 15: 331–357.

Thrasher, Frederic M. 1927. *The Gang: A Study of 1,313 Gangs in Chicago*. Chicago, IL: University of Chicago Press.

Tillyer, Marie Skubak, Bonnie S. Fisher, and Pamela Wilcox. 2011. "The Effects of School Crime Prevention on Students' Violent Victimization, Risk Perception, and Fear of Crime: A Multilevel Opportunity Perspective." *Justice Quarterly* 28: 249–277.

Tillyer, Marie Skubak, J. Mitchell Miller, and Rob Tillyer. 2011. "The Environmental and Situational Correlates of Victim Injury in Non-Fatal Violent Incidents." *Criminal Justice and Behavior* 38: 433–452.

Tillyer, Marie Skubak, and Rob Tillyer. 2014. "Violence in Context: A Multilevel Analysis of Victim Injury in Robbery Incidents." *Justice Quarterly* 31: 767–791.

Velez, Maria B. 2001. "The Role of Public Social Control in Urban Neighborhoods: A Multilevel Analysis of Victimization Risk." *Criminology* 39: 837–864.

Warner, Barbara D. 2003. "The Role of Attenuated Culture in Social Disorganization Theory." *Criminology* 41: 73–97.

Warner, Barbara D., and Audrey C. Clubb. 2013. "Neighborhood Ties, Control, and Crime." Pp. 333–351 in Francis T. Cullen and Pamela Wilcox (eds.), *The Oxford Handbook of Criminological Theory*. New York, NY: Oxford University Press.

Warner, Barbara D., and Pamela Wilcox Rountree. 1997. "Local Social Ties in a Community and Crime Model: Questioning the Systemic Nature of Informal Social Control." *Social Problems* 44: 520–536.

Weisburd, David, Wim Bernasco, and Gerben J. N. Bruinsma. 2000. "Units of Analysis in Geographic Criminology: Historical Development, Critical Issues, and Open Questions." Pp. 3–31 in David Weisburd, Wim Bernasco, and Gerben J. N. Bruinsma (eds.), *Putting Crime in Its Place: Units of Analysis in Spatial Crime Research*. New York, NY: Springer-Verlag.

Weisburd, David, Shawn Bushway, Cynthia Lum, and Sue-Ming Yang. 2004. "Trajectories of Crime at Places: A Longitudinal Study of Street Segments in the City of Seattle." *Criminology* 42: 283–321.

Weisburd, David, Elizabeth R. Groff, and Sue-Ming Yang. 2012. *The Criminology of Place: Street Segments and Our Understanding of the Crime Problem*. New York, NY: Oxford University Press.

Weisburd, David, and Cody W. Telep. 2010. "The Efficiency of Place-Based Policing." *Journal of Police Studies* 17: 247–262.

Wilcox, Pamela, Brooke Miller Gialopsos, and Kenneth C. Land. 2013. "Multilevel Criminal Opportunity." Pp. 579–601 in Francis T. Cullen and Pamela Wilcox (eds.), *The Oxford Handbook of Criminological Theory*. New York, NY: Oxford University Press.

Wilcox, Pamela, Kenneth C. Land, and Scott A Hunt. 2003. *Criminal Circumstance: A Dynamic, Multi-Contextual Criminal Opportunity Theory*. New York, NY: Aldine de Gruyter.

Wilcox, Pamela, Tamara. D. Madensen, and Marie Skubak Tillyer. 2007. "Guardianship in Context: Implications for Burglary Risk and Prevention." *Criminology* 45: 771–804.

Wilcox Rountree, Pamela, and Kenneth C. Land. 2000. "The Generalizability of Multilevel Models of Burglary Victimization: A Cross-City Comparison." *Social Science Research* 29: 284–305.

Wilcox Rountree, Pamela, Kenneth C. Land, and Terance D. Miethe. 1994. "Macro-Micro Integration in the Study of Victimization: A Hierarchical Logistic Model Analysis across Seattle Neighborhoods." *Criminology* 32: 387–414.

Wortley, Richard. 2001. "A Classification of Techniques for Controlling Situational Precipitators of Crime." *Security Journal* 14: 63–82.

Wortley, Richard, and Lorraine Mazerolle. 2008. "Environmental Criminology and Crime Analysis: Situating the Theory, Analytic Approach and Application." Pp. 1–18 in Richard Wortley and Lorraine Mazerolle (eds.), *Environmental Criminology and Crime Analysis*. Cullompton, UK: Willan Publishing.

Wright, Richard T., and Scott H. Decker. 1994. *Burglars on the Job: Streetlife and Residential Breakins*. Boston, MA: Northeastern University Press.

Wright, Richard T., and Scott H. Decker. 1997. *Armed Robbers in Action: Stickups and Street Culture*. Boston, MA: Northeastern University Press.

Part III

Managing Places and the
Control of Crime

6

Place Manager Motivations and Crime Prevention

Troy C. Payne

Introduction

As the expanding crime prevention and environmental criminology literature demonstrates, the opportunity for crime is not ubiquitous. Criminal opportunities vary across both time and space, and opportunity for crime can be manipulated for the purpose of crime prevention. While traditional criminology has ignored places in favor of individuals and large aggregates such as neighborhoods, the criminology of place has frequently ignored the importance of property owners. The decisions of place managers have a material impact on crime at their properties. Decisions that owners make can inhibit, facilitate, or ensure crime. These decisions are often not made with crime prevention in mind, as property owners balance a large constellation of concerns when making place management decisions. Just as the motivations behind offender decision-making vary within categories of crime—not all automobiles are stolen for the same reason—the motivations of place managers also likely vary considerably within facility types. Understanding the motivations of place managers has obvious implications for policy and practice. Place managers implement nearly all crime prevention at places; we must understand place manager decision-making if we are to entice place managers to make decisions likely to reduce crime. Understanding that the incentive structure for place managers likely provides few (or no) incentives for reducing crime through place management has implications for theory as well. Criminology has explored the motivations and drives of both offenders and victims—but very little attention has been paid to what motivates place managers. This chapter explores this idea, using the motivations of owners of one facility type (rental housing) as an illustration of the importance of owner motivation for crime prevention.

Crime Is Concentrated at Places and Within Facilities

The criminology of place literature argues that geographic aggregations such as nations, cities, and neighborhoods are too large for the purpose of preventing criminal acts. If a crime is the result of a motivated offender interacting with a target that lacks capable guardianship at a place (Cohen and Felson 1979; Eck 1994), then *place* is a logical intervention point. The definition of "place" often depends on the research question and on pragmatic concerns such as data availability and degree of error in the data. Entire volumes have been devoted to choosing the correct geographic unit of analysis in crime and place studies (e.g. Weisburd, Bernasco, and Bruinsma 2008). The general advice is that smaller units of analysis are often better, though accuracy of geolocatable data frequently determines the smallest unit of analysis with reliable and valid data (Weisburd et al. 2008; Gill, Wooditch, and Weisburd 2016).

Increasing computing power and access to analysts trained in geospatial analysis has led to a proliferation of tools to examine geographic concentrations of crime. Yet crime is also concentrated in nongeographic ways. Eck, Clarke, and Guerette hypothesize that crime is highly concentrated within *any* homogenous facility type (apartments, bars, convenience stores, motels, etc.), with a relative handful of places within that facility type producing a large percentage of crime. The risky facilities hypothesis is frequently misread as *some facility types are inherently risky*. That is true to some extent, however, Eck, Clarke, and Guerette (2007) provide a commentary on the distribution of crime within a facility type. Eck et al. (2007) suggest that the concentration of crime persists no matter how facilities and crime are subdivided, provided that adequate numbers of facilities and crime exist to facilitate analyses. Wilcox and Eck describe this skewed distribution of crime within facility types as the "iron law of troublesome places" (2011: 476), while Weisburd (2015) describes it as "the law of crime concentration" (133). This distribution of crime at places would not be surprising to most police officers—nearly every jurisdiction has a handful of "problem" bars (for example), while the majority of bars rarely come to the attention of the police.

Place Management and Crime Concentration

Place features can attract criminals or generate crime—and most place features are the end result of decisions made by the individuals who own or manage the place (Eck 1994; Eck 2002; Madensen 2007). Places tend to be fixed in space—but there are exceptions such as buses or online communities (Reyns 2010). Places are also often the site of repeated problems, making the place a good starting point for problem-oriented solutions because the location of offenders and victims is frequently unknown (Clarke and Eck 2005; Goldstein

1990). Perhaps more useful for crime prevention practice is that *who should control* a place should be readily identifiable in most circumstances. A lack of effective place management for crime prevention creates crime opportunities and attracts offenders. Place management consists of the organization of space, regulation of conduct, control of access, and acquisition of resources conducted by property owners or their agents (Madensen 2007; Eck 1994).

Owners (or agents of the owners) are responsible for place management, much in the same way owners are responsible for ensuring the property is in continued compliance with various building codes. Owners of bars, for example, make many decisions that affect the types of criminal opportunities available in and around their bars. Among those decisions are what type of bar (pool hall, gastro-pub, dance club, etc.), the type and price of drinks available, the type and price of food available, the vessels the drinks are served in (bottles vs. cans vs. glassware), the target clientele (bikers, after-work crowd, weekend partiers, etc.), where and how the bar is advertised, operating hours of the bar, whether there are cameras and if so placement of cameras, whether there is an employee at the door, lighting (both inside and outside), how many employees are on duty, how employees are trained, and how disturbances at the bar are handled (Madensen 2007). These decisions and many others are made by owners or their agents—place managers of the bar.

If criminologists are going to suggest that place managers make changes, or if we are going to suggest regulatory schemes that require changes such as those suggested by Eck and Eck (2012), we should have a better understanding of what motivates place managers. Place management should be studied in the context of particular facility types and, perhaps, subtypes, (Madensen 2007; Payne 2010) just as crime is studied in types and subtypes in environmental criminology. Crime script analysis, for example, studies the decision-making of offenders committing specific offenses in detail (Haelterman 2016; Levi and Maguire 2004). Such scripting analysis could be useful in the examination of place management. Each facility type is likely to have a different set of economic incentives for a variety of decisions made by place managers. A need for facility-specific and sub-facility-specific theory and data could explain why place management is frequently ignored, even in criminological studies of crime and place.

The Competing Concerns of Property Owners:
An Example Using Rental Property

The idea that motivation of place managers is key is not new. One of the critiques of Shaw and McKay (1972) was that social disorganization ignored that property owners in the transitional zone "refrained from making new investments in construction and refused to make 'wasteful' repairs" because the owners knew that the central business district would eventually encroach on the zone in transition (Snodgrass 1976: 10). There was no sense in investing in these properties because doing so carried little economic benefit. Owners may not be part of the community in any sociologically meaningful way; instead, they could be engaged in profit-taking and real estate speculation. This critique assumes that property owners always take the long view and are perfectly rational. There is good reason to suspect that neither of these is true for many owners.

Consider the example of rental housing. Relatively few residential rental properties are owned by non-profit organizations and the public sector. It is probably fair to assume that most property owners engage in rental housing to make a profit in some way. The profit motive may be simple and obvious, such as collecting more in rents than the property costs to own. The profit motive may be expressed in other, less obvious ways. Property may be rented to offset a loss, such as renting a property that cannot be sold for one reason or another. Property ownership can also carry tax benefits that offset profits in other business ventures. Yet the literature suggests the motives of landlords are more complex than a simple economic calculation, and even among those landlords who are motivated primarily by economics there are a variety of economic factors at play.

In creating a typology of landlords, Allen and McDowell (1989) took into account the landlord's (1) reasons for originally entering the market; (2) source of funding and financial liabilities; (3) amount of capital available, including investments outside of the rental market; (4) social meaning attached to being a landlord; and (5) attitudes toward government regulation. Using this framework as a starting point, Andersen (1998) developed a more detailed typology of landlord motivations. Its use here is illustrative; there may be other motivations for landlords, and these motivations may be market-specific. Andersen (1998) described landlord motivations as:

> *Long-term economic.* These are the type of motives most commonly associated with landlords. The value of improvements is assessed by these owners with the assumption that short-term losses may be necessary to realize long-term gains. These owners are frequently able to raise capital to finance losses, potentially years-long losses, and year-to-year profitability is a secondary goal to enhancing the property's long-term potential for profit.
>
> *Short-term economic.* These landlords are also driven by profit and loss, but the motives are on a shorter time scale. For some landlords, it is business-critical that their property remain profitable at all times. Such landlords may be living off the proceeds of the rental property, or using its profits to fund other business ventures. Landlords motivated primarily by short-term economic gain may be unable to raise capital for substantial improvements or to finance a temporary loss. Investments in rental housing that negatively impact short-term profitability would be fiercely resisted by owners in this category.

Speculative economic. These motives are fueled by the real estate market, with little concern for the maintenance and improvement of the property itself except as it impacts real estate valuation. For these owners, rental housing is one of many investment possibilities. Projected short-term changes in market prices drive the decisions of these owners, while long-term profitability concerns are minimized unless they impact the property's valuation in the real estate market. This is the type of owner motivation discussed by Snodgrass (1976).

Property as a personal possession. This is an emotional motivation, with the property becoming "a kind of personal belonging" (Andersen 1998). These owners attach importance to the maintenance and management of their rental property that defies pure economic motives. This may take the form of pride in ownership, or pride in *control* over the property.

Service or social. These motives push some landlords to ensure that rental housing be of good quality or as inexpensive as practicable. This could include non-profit organizations, or corporations that exist solely or partially to ensure affordable housing exists (perhaps for specific segments of the market or specific demographic groups).

In examining the distribution of motivations among owners of rental property in Denmark, Andersen (1998) found that most landlords were not large businesses enterprises. They were, instead, small investors (with fewer than four properties) or informal landlords (with one property having fewer than seven dwellings). Andersen (1998) found that short-term financial motives were more common among landlords in his sample than long-term motives. Similarly, Eck and Wartell (1995) found that landlords were frequently not able to afford improvements. Anecdotally, consulting work by this author in several mid-size US cities suggests that small investors or informal landlords who own just one or two properties are far more common than landlords with deep pockets. For these owners, short-term profitability is more important than long-term profitability, if for no other reason than because they frequently lack the financial resources to absorb even temporary losses.

Ignoring Crime Is Rational for Most Owners

We can think of owner motivations for failing to implement effective place management similar to how we commonly think of offender motivations in situational crime prevention: in terms of effort, risk, reward, provocation, and excuses (Clarke 1997; Cornish and Clarke 2003). The effort (or cost) associated with effective place management strategies can be substantial. Adding staff to manage tenant requests for maintenance, for example, incurs significant costs. In many circumstances, poor place management carries little perceived risk for owners. This is especially true when owners are not motivated by long-term economics. Rewards for effective place management can be indirect and may not be immediately perceptible by owners. Excuses for failing to implement effective place management are legion: costs are too high, profits are too low, and crime is the job of the police are common examples.

The truth of the matter is that *ignoring crime is probably a rational business decision for most property owners most of the time*. Crime is so rare it can effectively be ignored by many property owners. Particularly for property owners who are running a business, the immediate cost of crime is frequently lower than the cost of preventing it. In a longitudinal analysis of police incidents at addresses in Cincinnati, for example, Payne and Gallagher (2016) found that while most addresses in the city had one or more police incidents in the 15 years covered by their analysis, only about one third of addresses had one or more police incidents in any given year. The typical property therefore will eventually experience crime, but only rarely. Were crime prevention a higher priority among typical property owners, most owners would likely spend more on crime prevention efforts than they would save—especially in the short-term. This is critical in a market like Cincinnati, where many rental properties are four- or six-unit apartment buildings owned by small businesses or individuals (Payne 2010). For these buildings, a single vacancy can be the difference between profit and loss.

Crime prevention and control are rarely the primary goals of place managers. Crime prevention is one of many competing goals of place managers and is easily overlooked or devalued in favor of other priorities during decision-making processes (Eck 1994; Felson 1986; Madensen 2007). This should not be surprising. Managing for crime prevention is often considered by place managers only *after* having to deal with crime (Campbell 2000). Returning to the example of landlords, landlords may be in business for years before having a serious crime problem—and some landlords could go their entire professional careers without a crime problem merely by chance.

The constellation of competing concerns for property owners is complex. Using Madensen's (2007) model of bar management and key informant interviews with apartment owners in Cincinnati, Payne (2010) diagrammed a theory of place management at apartments. This model is reproduced as Figure 6.1. While the discussion here is specific to apartment managers, similar thinking could expand it to other facility types, much as Payne adapted Madensen's work.

The decisions of rental property owners are constrained at purchase by the availability and condition of the property, property location, financing, and the value of existing tenants. Some place management decisions are more easily altered than others. For example, changes to staff, tenant screening, or marketing are likely easier to implement than changes to the physical characteristics of the building or amenities. Physical changes vary in difficulty as well. Changing the locks is easier than replacing windows, which is easier than changes to

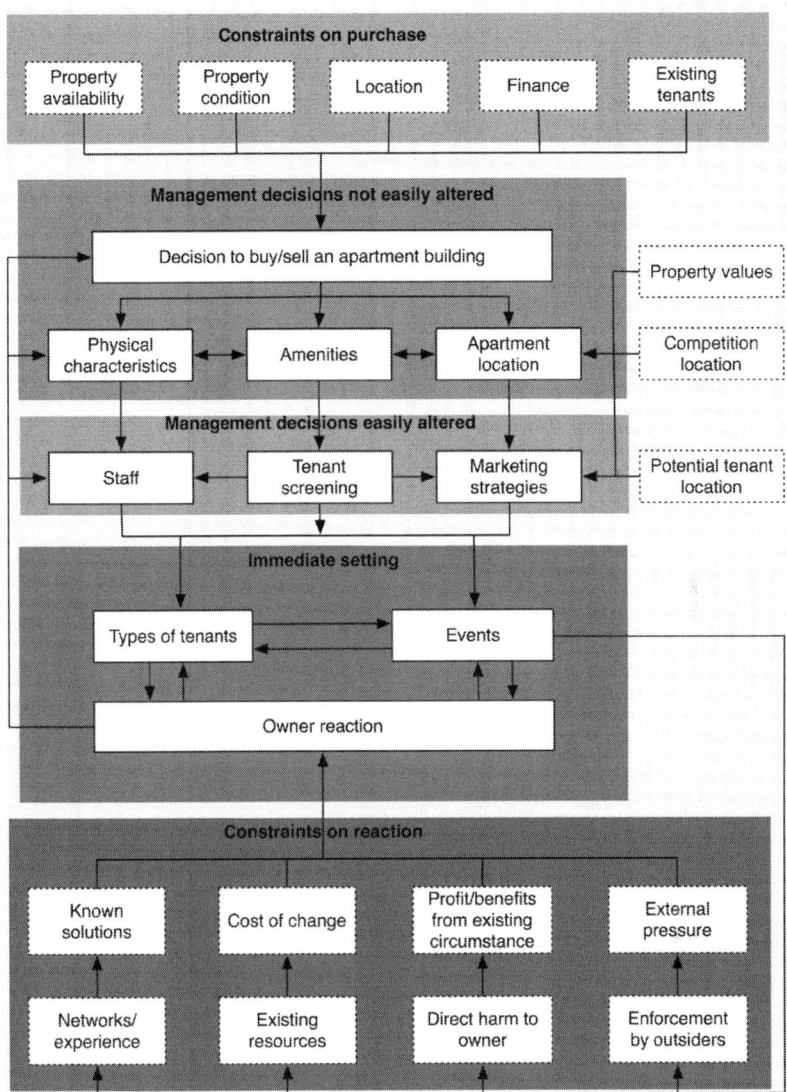

Figure 6.1 Theory of place management at apartments.

exterior or load bearing walls. The ability of owners to react to events at the property is constrained by the owners' knowledge of solutions, cost of change, and degree of direct harm to the owner (among other constraints).

Programs that seek to reduce crime by intervening at places should acknowledge that owners have concerns other than crime. Many owners do not have capital available to make even minor changes to the physical characteristics of a property (Eck and Wartell 1998). Poor place management practices for crime at one property are likely to be practiced at other properties owned by the same owner. Place management is not the only variable on which there could be more variation between rather than within owners. Owners also vary in their ability to evaluate the profitability of a property prior to purchase and frequently learn through experiencing losses. Each future purchase is informed by experiences with past properties, and this experience becomes a part of the constraints on both purchasing property and reacting to events at a property. Even within one facility type, there are differing levels of experience and different motivations among owners. Moreover, the decisions place managers make are likely not independent among the various properties and businesses they own. In fact, it is likely that decisions made regarding one property impact other properties held by the same owner(s)—if for no other reason than owners' resources, time, and attention are finite. Improvements made to one property may forestall improvements to others for small businesses with limited resources.

Concerns other than crime can manifest in many ways. Consider the problem of shoplifting of a particular product at one retail location that is part of a large national retail chain. For a large retail chain, seemingly small changes in place management may incur substantial costs or carry other risks when replicated across all locations. As an example, changing how a product is displayed may be a trivial cost in one retail outlet but could be a large cost when multiplied across hundreds of locations. This is especially true after considering employee time spent designing a new display, communicating the change, effecting the change, and ensuring the change occurs. Such a change could also impact the retailer's relationship with the manufacturer, particularly if the troublesome product's placement was part of a larger business plan between the retailer and manufacturer. It could be substantially less risky for such a retailer to simply continue tolerating shoplifting of the product.

Implications for Policy and Practice

An understanding of place managers' motivations is critical to encouraging behavior that is likely to reduce crime. This is particularly true when discussing owners who are likely motivated by profit. A better understanding of the type of profit motive (long-term vs. speculation vs. short-term) is needed to craft regulations likely to address those motivations. Careful calibration of regulatory schemes is also needed to ensure compliance. In discussing how housing policies can impact crime, Sampson (1990) describes how concentrated disadvantage can be shaped by public housing policy. Sampson (1990: 531) off-handedly comments that it is frequently "more profitable for slum operators to go to court [regarding housing code violations] even if they lost than it was to repair their properties." In situational crime prevention terms, the cost of regulatory compliance was less than the risk of regulatory sanctions.

Unintended consequences can be surfaced by examining place management motivations as well. Policies such as fees or fines for excessive police services are one policy instrument that has been used to ensure owners incur short-term costs of crime as an incentive to improve place management (Payne 2015). Payne (2015) found that notifying owners of potential civil fine liability for chronic nuisance police calls for service resulted in fewer future police calls for service at properties. In unpublished analyses from that study, however, only half of notified owners bothered to respond to the Municipality of Anchorage despite an official requirement to do so. Of those who responded, half evicted a tenant or otherwise made the tenant vacate.[1] Eviction is incentivized in the Anchorage chronic nuisance ordinance by allowing landlords to escape liability after an eviction, with no further examination of the landlord's business practices and how they might contribute to crime at the property. Vacancy rates are low enough that landlords have little trouble finding new tenants in the Anchorage market. Eviction is low-effort, low-risk, and high-reward—it is little wonder it is a common response by landlords.

The model described in Figure 6.1 earlier in the chapter has not been subjected to a strenuous empirical test. Even before testing, however, we can use a logic model like this combined with the literature on motivations of property owners within a facility type to guide policy and practice. One way this could guide policy is to recognize the different experiences of place managers when implementing policy. The idea is, in many ways, similar to the concept of responsivity of offenders to treatment. The risk-need-responsivity (RNR) model has proven to be a useful framework for correctional rehabilitation (Bonta and Andrews 2007). Broadly speaking, risk addresses *who* to treat, need addresses *what* to treat, and responsivity addresses *how* to deliver the treatment. In crime prevention, much work has focused on risk (hot spots, risky facilities) and need (patrol dosage, crime prevention through environmental design, place management), but little work has addressed responsivity especially as it relates to place managers: How amenable to this particular treatment is this particular place manager?

Again returning to landlords as an example, Andersen (1998) found that the landlord motivations impacted different types of landlords differently. Small investors and informal landlords (those who owned only one small property) were motivated by short-term economics, property as a personal possession, and service. Long-term economics did not motivate these landlords. Just like correctional rehabilitation effectiveness is impacted by an offender's responsivity to treatment, encouragement to engage in better place management-based crime prevention efforts among these landlords is unlikely to work unless they address the landlord's strengths, personality, motivation, and resources available. Small investors and informal landlords are unlikely to be responsive to place management that comes at short-term cost, even if there is a long-term gain. Even where such landlords recognize the potential for long-term gain, they may lack the resources to physically improve their properties or change place management practices. Any change that impacts (or potentially impacts) short-term profitability will likely be met with resistance from these owners. Combined, small investors and informal landlords were 77.8% of landlords, holding 58% of properties and 40% of dwellings in Andersen's (1998) study of landlords in Denmark.

The ability of property owners to assimilate and use crime prevention knowledge likely varies considerably among owners, and is probably related to the core motivations of the owners. Crime at the property may be unknown to the current owner and may be unknowable by potential buyers. Particularly well-connected and savvy buyers may be able to determine the frequency of crime through public records requests. But the cost of crime at the property may not be included in its market price, and unsophisticated buyers may not be aware of the potential costs of crime. This is problematic because unsophisticated buyers are also less likely to have experience managing properties with crime prevention in mind. The results could be disastrous: a property is purchased by a naïve buyer who cannot make enough profit to maintain and manage the property, resulting in selling the property—likely at a loss. Perhaps an even *more* naïve buyer purchases the property, and the cycle repeats, with physical and social conditions deteriorating with each sale.

One potential way to stop such a cycle of decline is to make crime data part of the available information on a property. In most jurisdictions, address or land-parcel level crime data are not readily available to the public. Even a relative ranking of properties is not available. Despite some jurisdictions moving toward open data (e.g. Seattle), data are usually not compiled at a unit of analysis that would be useful to place managers. Place managers generally cannot, for example, see how many crimes have occurred at their properties. Moreover, they cannot easily see how many crimes have occurred at similar properties that they own, or at properties similar to theirs that others own. Whether such information would reduce crime in the aggregate depends on how property owners incorporate information regarding crime at their properties into their place management decisions—and that, in turn, is likely determined at least in part by their motivations in the first place.

The motivations of property owners are less well-studied than the motivations of offenders and victims in criminology. Both police and academic crime prevention specialists would be well-served by conducting research that more closely examines the motivations of property owners. For commercial properties and businesses, profit is a common motive—but on what time scale? How will place managers perceive the effort, risks, and rewards of managing their places for crime prevention? Are motivations similar for all owners of particular types of facilities? Are there particular motivations that are common to owners of high-crime properties (or of low-crime properties)? Those who would prevent crime can craft better interventions when the motivations of property owners are understood.

Note

1. Month-to-month rental leases are common in Anchorage, particularly after the first 12 months of a lease. In most instances, 30-day notices to vacate properties can be served to tenants with no cause required. While not legally "evictions," the result is the same.

References

Allen, John, and Linda McDowell. 1989. *Landlords and Property: Social Relations in the Private Rented Sector*. Cambridge, UK: Cambridge University Press.

Andersen, Hans Skifter. 1998. "Motives for Investments in Housing Rehabilitation among Private Landlords Under Rent Control." *Housing Studies* 13: 177–200.

Bonta, James, and Donald A. Andrews. 2007. "Risk-Need-Responsivity Model for Offender Assessment and Rehabilitation." *Rehabilitation* 6: 1–22.

Campbell, John. 2000. *Keeping Illegal Activities Out of Rental Property: A Police Guide for Establishing Landlord Training Programs*. Washington, DC: U.S. Department of Justice, Bureau of Justice Assistance.

Clarke, Ronald. 1997. *Situational Crime Prevention: Successful Case Studies* (2nd ed.). Guiderland, NY: Harrow and Heston.

Clarke, Ronald, and John Eck. 2005. *Crime Analysis for Problem Solvers in 60 Small Steps*. Washington, DC: U.S. Department of Justice.

Cornish, Derek Blaikie, and Ronald V. Clarke. 2003. "Opportunities, Precipitators and Criminal Decisions: A Reply to Wortley's Critique of Situational Crime Prevention." Pp. 41–96 in *Crime Prevention Studies: Theory for Practice in Situational Crime Prevention*. Monsey, NY: Criminal Justice Press.

Cohen, Lawrence E., and Marcus Felson. 1979. "Social Change and Crime Rate Trends: A Routine Activity Approach." *American Sociological Review*: 588–608.

Eck, John E. 1994. *Drug Markets and Drug Places: A Case-Control Study of the Spatial Structure of Illicit Drug Dealing*. Ph.D. Dissertation. Research directed by Institute of Criminal Justice and Criminology, College Park, MD: University of Maryland at College Park.

Eck, John E. 2002. "Preventing Crime at Places." Pp. 241–294 in Lawrence Sherman, David P. Farrington, Brandon Welsh, and Doris Layton MacKenzie (eds.), *Evidence-Based Crime Prevention*. New York, NY: Routledge.

Eck, John E., Ronald V. Clarke, and Rob T. Guerette. 2007. Risky Facilities: Crime Concentration in Homogeneous Sets of Establishments and Facilities. In Graham Farrell, Kate J. Bowers, and Shane D. Johnson (eds.), *Imagination for Crime Prevention: Essays in Honour of Ken Pease: Crime Prevention Studies*, vol. 21. Monsey, NY: Willan Publishing.

Eck, John E., and Emily B. Eck. 2012. "Crime Place and Pollution." *Criminology & Public Policy* 11: 281–316.

Eck, John E., and Julie Wartell. 1998. "Improving the Management of Rental Properties with Drug Problems: A Randomized Experiment." Pp. 161–185 in Lorraine Green Mazzerolle and Jan Roehl (eds.), *Crime Prevention Studies: Civil Remedies and Crime Prevention*. Monsey, NY: Criminal Justice Press.

Felson, Marcus. 1986. "Linking Criminal Choices, Routine Activities, Informal Control, and Criminal Outcomes." Pp. 119–128 in Derek B. Cornish, and Ronald V. Clarke (eds.), *The Reasoning Criminal: Rational Choice Perspectives on Offending*. New York, NY: Springer-verlag.

Gill, Charlotte, Alese Wooditch, and David Weisburd. 2017. "Testing the 'Law of Crime Concentration at Place' in a Suburban Setting: Implications for Research and Practice." *Journal of Quantitative Criminology*: 33(3): 519–545.

Goldstein, Herman. 1990. *Problem-Oriented Policing*. New York, NY: McGraw-Hill, Inc.

Haelterman, H. 2016. *Crime Script Analysis: Preventing Crimes Against Business*. Palgrave Macmillan UK.

Levi, M., and M. Maguire. 2004. "Reducing and Preventing Organized Crime: An Evidence-based Critique." *Crime, Law & Social Change* 41: 397–469.

Madensen, Tamara D. 2007. *Bar Management and Crime: Toward a Dynamic Theory of Place Management and Crime Hotspots*. Ph.D. Dissertation. Cincinnati, OH: University of Cincinnati.

Payne, Troy C. 2010. *Does Changing Ownership Change Crime? An Analysis of Apartment Ownership and Crime in Cincinnati*. Ph.D. Dissertation. Cincinnati, OH: University of Cincinnati.

Payne, Troy C. 2017. "Reducing Excessive Police Incidents: Do Notices to Owners Work?" *Security Journal* 30(3): 922–939.

Payne, Troy C., and Kathleen Gallagher. 2016. "The Importance of Small Units of Aggregation: Trajectories of Crime at Addresses in Cincinnati, Ohio, 1998–2012." *Criminology, Criminal Justice, Law & Society* 17: 20.

Reyns, Bradford W. 2010. "A Situational Crime Prevention Approach to Cyberstalking Victimization: Preventive Tactics for Internet Users and Online Place Managers." *Crime Prevention & Community Safety* 12: 99–118.

Sampson, Robert J. 1990. "The Impact of Housing Policies on Community Social Disorganization and Crime." *Bulletin of the New York Academy of Medicine* 66: 526.

Shaw, Clifford, and Henry McKay. 1972. *Juvenile Delinquency and Urban Areas: Revised Edition*. Chicago, IL: University of Chicago Press.

Snodgrass, Jon. 1976. "Clifford R. Shaw and Henry D. McKay: Chicago Criminologists." *The British Journal of Criminology* 16: 1–19.

Weisburd, David. 2015. "The Law of Crime Concentration and the Criminology of Place." *Criminology* 53: 133–157.

Weisburd, David, Wim Bernasco, and Gerben Bruinsma, eds. 2008. *Putting Crime in Its Place*. New York, NY: Springer.

Wilcox, Pamela, and John E. Eck. 2011. "Criminology of the Unpopular." *Criminology & Public Policy* 10: 473–482.

7

The Opportunity Structure for Bad Place Management: A Theory to Assist Effective Regulation of High Crime Places

John E. Eck

The Need for a Theory for Practice

If the concentration of crime at a relatively few properties is due to the way these properties are managed, then focusing on the owners of properties can help reduce crime overall. Regulation of these gate-keeper third parties—people and institutions who control opportunity structures that facilitate crime but are not direct participants (Kraakman 1986)—has been widely used to control crime, though it has only recently received much attention (Eck and Eck 2012; Mazerolle and Ransley 2005; Quirk, Seddon, and Smith 2014). It has several potential advantages over police responses, including hot spots policing. These include greater impact on crime at the hot spots; the ability to produce a long term reduction in crime by addressing the underlying circumstances that make a place hot, rather than repeatedly returning to the hot spot; less use of criminal sanctions to reduce crime along with reduced attendant financial and social costs; less displacement of crime and more diffusion of prevention benefits (Bowers, Johnson, Guerette, Summers, and Poynton 2011; Clarke and Weisburd 1994); and shifting the responsibility and costs of crime reduction from the tax payer to those who create conditions for crime (Scott 2004).

There are two difficulties with this optimistic forecast. First, regulatory approaches have received little systematic study, though a number of evaluations show promising results. Bichler, Schmerler, and Enriquez (2013) showed that regulating the management of high calls for service motels reduced calls to the police and costs to the public. Similarly, Payne (2015) showed that two cities that implemented regulations on landlords with excessive calls from their properties reduced these calls. Eck and Wartell (1998) and Mazerolle, Roehl, and Kadleck (1998) showed in separate randomized controlled trials that threatening civil sanction against landlords of properties with chronic drug dealing helped reduce crime and drug dealing in these properties. Because the police led the interventions in these examples, these are examples of "third-party policing" (Mazerolle and Ransley 2005) as well as examples of the use of regulation.

Non-police regulatory interventions are less well known, but nevertheless important. The most obvious example of non-police regulation of places is the regulation of bars, drinking establishments, and alcohol sales outlets (Graham and Homel 2008). Despite increasing interest in this broad area, most attention has been focused on how policing can apply civil law as part of a third-party, community-oriented, or problem-oriented approach. The focus on the police might seem natural, but it is a manifestation of what Goldstein (1979) called the "means over ends syndrome" as it assumes, prematurely, that the police are the best institution for regulating places to reduce crime. We should first ask, "How can we best reduce crime?" and then, once we have some answers, ask "Who should be doing this?" Even before we ask how, we must ask a deeper set of questions. These deal with how high crime place problems arise. An understanding of the reasons for high crime places helps us determine what we can do about it, and helps us avoid policies that do not work or make things worse. This brings us to the second difficulty with a regulatory approach.

The second difficulty is that we know little or nothing about the reasons some place owners choose to manage their properties in ways that facilitate crime. To date, most attention has been paid to ways of identifying place hot spots and testing interventions for their effectiveness. There is little research on the circumstances that give rise to high crime locations with the intent of using the research to craft effective and fair interventions. One reason we do not have a body of research examining why some places are criminogenic is the question has not been raised. And since the question has not been raised, there is no theory to guide policy analysis and research into the causes of "bad places."

The purpose of this paper is to describe a theory of why high crime places arise. There are three types of places—addresses, street segments, and areas (Madensen and Eck 2013)—and my theory directly applies to only the first. This is because my theory hinges on property ownership and property rights: concepts that are not applicable to the other two. If the theory I propose is a reasonable approximation of what creates high crime places, then this will help develop useful regulatory (and perhaps other) interventions.

I have divided this paper into five parts. This introduction is the first part. The second part describes the assumptions, framework, and definitions for the theory. I first describe two assumptions that guided my development of the theory: a rational choice perspective and the need for the theory to have the potential to be useful, practically. I also define the type of places that the theory will address. The term "place" has several meanings in the study of crime, and the theory applies only to one of them, so called "proprietary places," commonly known as addresses (Madensen and Eck 2013). Finally, I distill the place research into six questions and their answers. The answers are the principles—foundational, empirically based assumptions—that my theory rests upon; if any of them are shown later to be false, my theory is likely to need major revisions or discarding.

The third part examines a peculiarity of high crime places: they cluster. Though many researchers have noted this phenomenon, it has received little attention. I think it provides a major clue as to the opportunity structure for bad property management, and I explain why.

The fourth and longest part describes my theory. I propose that there are two different opportunity structures for high crime places. The first explains why we have so many high crime places in poor areas. The second explains why we have some high crime locations in other areas. I also introduce three processes—economic, political, and social—that shape the two opportunity structures. Of the three, economics is the dominant influence. However, they do not act independently or additively. Rather, economics interacts with social and political influences, so in practice it is difficult to partition the influence of each process relative to the other two. Economics is only dominant in the sense that it will operate even in the absence of the other two processes.

The final part examines the policy and research implications of the theory. I first discuss how the theory of the opportunity structure of bad place management interacts with other theories of neighborhoods. Then I turn to policy. The policy implications are, of course, based on the assumption that my theory is reasonably true. Consequently, I am not strongly advocating them. Rather, I use them to show why tests of this theory are important. I also show how this theory has implications for how we link places to neighborhoods. Many place researchers, including myself, have been highly skeptical of the utility of continuing to examine crime at the neighborhood level and conclude that we should downgrade the importance of neighborhoods, if not abandon them when studying crime. I suggest that neighborhoods have utility for understanding the opportunity structure of high crime locations.

Foundations and Assumptions

Types of Places

The term "place" is used in a variety of ways in criminology and in the wider world. The theory I will propose applies to some types of place, but not to other types. Using the classification scheme proposed by Madensen and Eck (2013), regulation makes sense for *proprietary places*—land parcels with owners—rather than *proximal places*—street segments (e.g., see Weisburd,

Groff, and Yang 2013)—or *pooled places*—areas such as neighborhoods (e.g., see Sampson, Raudenbush, and Earls 1997). This is because it is the owner who is held accountable by regulation. Proximal and pooled places do not have singular, or even identifiable, owners. Owners can be people, public or private organizations, or other legal entities (e.g., a trust or a limited liability partnership). The fact that places and their associated property rights can be bought and sold is critical as ownership of property rights conveys control and power over the use of the space. In countries that promote private ownership of property there is seldom a single entity or consortium that has property rights over an entire street segment or neighborhood. Rather, segments and neighborhoods contain multiple owners. This means that control over activities in these spaces is diffuse and usually uncoordinated. There is no person, agency, business, or other organization who is responsible for the use of segments and neighborhoods, or who can be held accountable for harmful activities throughout.

Consequently, the theory I will describe does not apply to proximal or pooled places. However, because proprietary places are nested within proximal and pooled places, these larger units of analysis do play an important contextual role.

Assumptions

I take a rational choice perspective and apply it to property owners and to the people to whom they delegate responsibility (e.g., employees and contractors). Collectively, these people are "place managers." Place managers are not synonymous with guardians, though the two concepts overlap (Madensen and Eck 2013). Place managers can provide guardianship, or make sure it is provided by others. But place managers do far more than create guardianship, as can be seen by examining place management's functions.

As proposed by Madensen (2007), place managers have four functions. They *organize space*. The most fundamental way they do this is by selecting the site (e.g., placing a parking garage on one location rather than another). Space organization also includes the creation of landscaping outside and arranging the space inside (e.g., locating walls, creating passages, securing doors, and so forth). In retail stores, the placement of merchandise, cash registers, and display cabinets falls within this function.

Place managers *regulate conduct*, including encouraging some behaviors (e.g., shopping, drinking, sleeping, and so forth) and discouraging other behaviors (e.g., taking things without payment, parties, drinking, and so forth). What is encouraged and what is discouraged depend on the place's function. Sleeping is encouraged in college dormitories, but not in college classrooms, for example. Place managers may promote guardianship in various ways to regulate conduct. It is in the carrying out of this function that guardianship most clearly overlaps with place management. However, it should be clear that regulation of conduct is not just protecting people and things; it involves a host of other activities.

Place managers also *control access*. This means they encourage some people to enter the place and discourage others. This may vary by time of day, or week. So a public library will encourage almost everyone to come in and use the place, but only during open hours. A shelter for battered women encourages abused women to enter the place, but probably has restrictions on access by men. A high end women's apparel store will encourage women of means to enter, but through pricing, advertising, staff behavior, and window displays it will discourage women who have little discretionary income.

Finally, place managers are concerned with the *acquisition of resources*. For businesses, this includes revenues and profits. For a public agency, this might include user fees or annual budget allotments. For places of worship and charitable organizations, this includes donations from place users and others. These resources influence how place managers can carry out the first three functions.

Resource acquisition is critical to my theory. Place managers are sensitive, to varying degrees, to the costs of operating their facilities and to the resources they glean from their environment. In environments where resource acquisition is relatively easy through legitimate activities, place managers will avoid creating chronic crime places. In environments where resource acquisition through illegitimate means is more productive than strict adherence to rules and norms, hot places are more likely. And in contexts where the costs of crime and prevention can be avoided—usually by shifting these costs onto others, including tax payers—place managers will tolerate operating a chronic crime location.

In short, I assume that place managers make numerous choices to carry out these functions, and they do so reasonably rationally. Place managers may not be the hyper-rational optimizers of classical economic theory. But they are not making arbitrary or consistently irrational decisions either. They are boundedly rational as individuals, as they respond to their environments.

Empirical Principles Underlying Theory

There is a considerable body of research on crime places. The vast majority of the research was published following the works of Pierce, Spaar, and Briggs (1988) and Sherman's team (1989), though there are a few studies that predate the late 1980s (see Lee, Eck, Martinez, and O 2017 for a systematic review). The primary interest in place research over the last quarter century has been the improvement of police operations. Pierce's group (1988) was interested in describing police work, and Sherman's team (1989) was creating the empirical foundation for a randomized experiment of police hot spots patrolling (Sherman and Weisburd 1995).

Place researchers have investigated a wide variety of questions. For the purposes of this paper, I am interested in the answers to six overlapping questions:

1. How is crime distributed over tiny geographic units?
2. Are high crime places chronically high crime, and do low crime places stay low crime places?
3. How effective are interventions at places; do these interventions reduce crime?
4. Does crime displace from high crime places following these interventions? Or, do prevention benefits diffuse outward from formerly high crime locations where interventions have been applied?
5. Do the owners of places have a role in the creation of chronic high crime locations, and can changes in place management reduce crime at these places?
6. Would regulation of managers of high crime places reduce crime at these places?

Fortunately, there are multiple studies addressing all these questions, and most of the questions have been the subject of standard and systematic reviews. This body of research is covered in the recent book authored by the Crime and Place Research Group (Weisburd et al. 2016), so I will not examine it in depth here. Rather, I have summarized the answers to these six questions in the second column of Table 7.1. Prominent studies that provide the answers are listed in the third column.

I will treat this body of research findings as an established set of facts: empirically based assumptions. As they form the foundations upon which my theory is built, if a body of future research substantially contradicts these six foundations, then my theory is at risk of being invalid. Though a solid foundation, this body of research does not provide many clues as to how to build the theory. So I turn to another set of findings that has not been fully exploited by place researchers, but provides some useful clues. I turn to that literature next.

Clusters of Clusters of Crime

The geography of high crime places can provide useful clues as to how to build the theory. If high crime places are evenly distributed across jurisdictions, then the factors that give rise to them is likely to be evenly distributed. However, if high crime places cluster, then factors that give rise to high crime places are likely to be unevenly distributed. What is the distribution of high crime places?

High crime places are themselves clustered. A number of researchers have remarked on this, including Sherman and colleagues (1989). A diverse set of studies in the United States and Great Britain show clustering of crime clusters. This literature is summarized in Table 7.2. It includes two studies of repeat victimization. Much of property crime victimization (burglary and theft) are place-based. Unless victimization survey respondents are highly mobile, reports of repeated victimization of these crimes can also be interpreted as crimes at the same addresses.

I have omitted a substantial body of research showing that high crime proximal places (street segments) cluster also (Weisburd, Bushway, Lum, and Yang

Table 7.1
Six empirical foundations of place regulation

	Description	Selected Sources of Evidence
1. Concentration	Crime is highly concentrated at a small proportion of places.	Lee, et al. (2017)**
		Pierce et al. (1988)
		Sherman, Gartin, and Buerger (1989)
		Weisburd (2015)*
		Weisburd et. al. (2016)*
		Wilcox and Eck (2011)*
2. Stability	High crime and low crime places are reasonably stable over time.	Andresen and Malleson (2010)
		Braga, Hureau and Papachristos (2010)
		Weisburd et al. (2004)
		Spelman (1995)
3. Effectiveness	Intervening at places, to change place characteristics, is often an effective strategy. Situational crime prevention is effective in a wide variety of places.	Braga, Papachristos, and Hureau (2014)**
		Eck (2002)**
		Eck and Guerette (2012)**
4. Dislocation	Displacement of crime from high crime places following interventions is not inevitable and is less likely than crime reductions around intervention sites (diffusion of benefits).	Braga, Papachristos, and Hureau (2014)**
		Guerette and Bowers (2009)**
		Bowers et al. (2011)**
		Weisburd et al. (2006)
5. Management	The people and institutions that own and operate places (place managers) have considerable control over place conditions that make them safe from crime or facilitate crime.	Clarke and Bichler-Robertson (1998)
		Eck (2002)**
		Eck and Guerette (2012)**
		Madensen and Eck (2013)*
6. Regulation	Interventions on place managers of high crime locations can reduce crime at places.	Bichler et al. (2013)
		Eck and Wartell (1998)
		Mazerolle, Roehl, and Kadleck (1998).
		Eck and Eck (2012)*
		Mazerolle and Ransley (2005)**
		Payne (2015)

* Standard review of multiple studies.
** Systematic or meta-analytic review of multiple studies.

Table 7.2
Studies showing a clustering of high crime places

Study	Study Location	Summary of Findings
Sherman et al. (1989)	Minneapolis, USA	"We do not claim that hot spots are completely unrelated to each other. To the contrary, they are clearly bunched on major thoroughfares, at least in Minneapolis. They are also bunched near each other" (p. 43).
Trickett, Osborn, Seymour, and Pease (1992)	England & Wales	High crime areas are characterized by higher numbers of people with multiple victimizations, relative to low crime areas. "(W)hen people are victimized, they experience about three times as many crimes on average in the highest crime areas compared to the lowest" (p. 85).
Trickett, Ellingworth, Hope, and Pease (1995)	England & Wales	Confirmation of findings from earlier article (previous row of table). "Victim concentration—that is, the rate of victimization and the resulting proportion of repeat victims—cannot be denied a central role in understanding either the distribution of crime incidence at one time, or changes over time in that distribution. In England and Wales between 1982 and 1988, both property and, to a lesser extent, personal crime became more uneven in their distribution across constituencies. Particularly for property crime, this was attributable to an increasing inequality in victim concentration. It seems constituencies diverged during the 1980s primarily in the number of victimizations their victims sustained, rather than the number of victims among their citizens" (p. 357).
Sherman and Weisburd (1995)	Minneapolis, USA	Identified 5,538 addresses and intersections with more than three calls to police about incidents that they defined as "hard crime." "Inspection of the computer printouts for each map [revealed] what appeared to be visually connected clusters of these addresses. Using this technique, we identified and mapped 420 address clusters with 20 or more hard crime calls" (p. 631).
Eck, Gersh, and Taylor (2000)	New York, USA / Baltimore, USA	Examination of the distribution of crime in an area of the Bronx, New York and a neighborhood in Baltimore. Comparing maps with all crimes plotted to maps with only hot spots plotted reveals hot spot clusters that are not apparent when all crimes are shown. This was true in both cities.
Groff, Weisburd, and Yang (2010)	Seattle, USA	"More specifically, chronic high street segments have the greatest degree of local clustering." "In sum, street segments of the same temporal trajectory group to be generally more clustered at distances of less than a half-mile than would be expected as compared to either the intrinsic clustering in the street network or under CSR [complete spatial randomness]" (pp. 19–20).
Payne and Gallagher (2016)	Cincinnati, USA	Used group-based trajectory models to identify stable high crime addresses. Though these are interspersed among low crime addresses, they are also distinctly clustered in low income neighborhoods.

2004; Weisburd et al. 2013). These studies (summarized in Weisburd and colleagues 2016) provide indirect support for the clustering of high crime proprietary places. If most addresses on a street segment have few or no crimes, but a few addresses have most of the crime, then segment clustering points to address clustering. YongJei Lee has closely examined more than 13,500 street segments in Cincinnati, including more than 1,800 that had seven or more crimes (they were among the 10 percent most crime prone segments). More than half of these segments had high levels of crime at four or fewer addresses on the segment. Less than 10 percent of these hot segments had high levels of crime at ten or more addresses. This suggests street segments' crime problems may be largely due to a few places (Lee et al. 2017). However, it is possible that some segment level crime is due to street activity—traffic flow and pedestrian movement—rather than address characteristics. There is little research to help sort this out, so I do not rest my theory upon clustering of proximal places.

To illustrate the concentration of crime concentration at proprietary places, I applied Repeat Address Mapping (Eck, Gersh, and Taylor 2000) to crimes in Cincinnati for the year 2014. For simplicity, I defined a high crime place as being within the top 10 percent of the places with regard to crime. Then I looked for the minimum number of crimes necessary to account for the most crime ridden 10 percent of the addresses. This turned out to be three: 12.7 percent of the addresses had three or more crimes. All addresses with three or more crimes were then plotted on a map. These locations account for more than 40 percent of the crime in Cincinnati that year (shown in Figure 7.1).

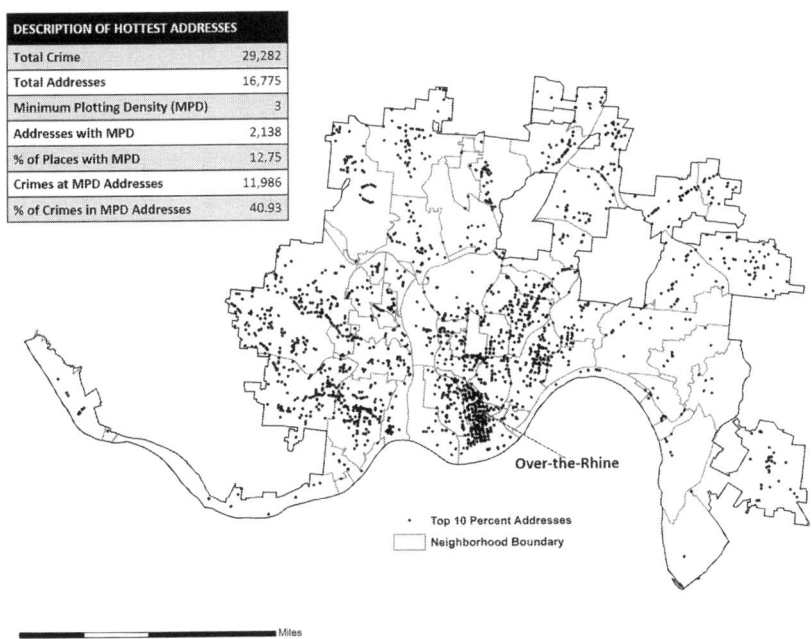

DESCRIPTION OF HOTTEST ADDRESSES	
Total Crime	29,282
Total Addresses	16,775
Minimum Plotting Density (MPD)	3
Addresses with MPD	2,138
% of Places with MPD	12.75
Crimes at MPD Addresses	11,986
% of Crimes in MPD Addresses	40.93

Figure 7.1 Distribution of hot addresses across Cincinnati neighborhoods, 2014.

As is often reported in the literature on high crime places, the high crime places are spread all over the city: from the wealthier east side neighborhoods to the poorer neighborhoods in the lower center of the map.[1] Almost all neighborhoods have some of the worst crime places. Just as important, and as reported in the literature reviewed in Table 7.2, the figure shows clustering of high crime locations. These clusters have two basic shapes: blobs and strings. The blobs are two dimensional clusters; the Over-the-Rhine neighborhood has high crime locations (seemingly) covering almost all of its area, for example (the most prominent cluster identified in Payne and Gallagher 2016). The strings mark major thoroughfares. Interestingly, Sherman and his team (1989) pointed out this dichotomy of crime place clustering types at the beginning of crime and place research. This distinction will be important.

As Trickett and colleagues noted in two separate papers (Trickett et al. 1992; Trickett, Ellingworth, Hope, and Pease 1995), repeats drive much of the total crime volume in neighborhoods: those areas with numerous repeat

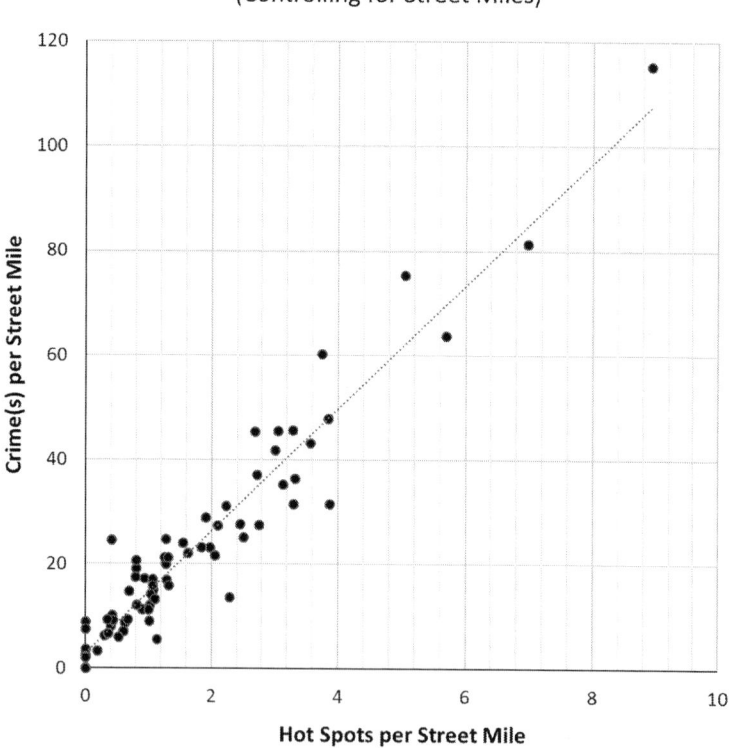

Figure 7.2 High crime places (with three or more crimes) and crimes in Cincinnati neighborhoods, 2014 (n = 75).

victimizations have more crime overall. The same is true in Cincinnati, using police reports of crime at addresses. This is illustrated in Figure 7.2.

Here we show a scatter plot of Cincinnati's 75 neighborhoods[2] depicting the relationship between crime volume and high crime places (the 12.75 percent of the places with a minimum plotting density [MPD] of 3). Because the 75 neighborhoods vary in size, and this could confound the results, I standardized the crime and place numbers by the street miles in each neighborhood.[3] The number of street miles has the advantage of being associated with physical size, and the number of people using the area. The regression line shown is almost superfluous, as the linear relationship of the dots is very prominent.

This example, and the research literature, show that we need to design a theory that takes into account differences among areas. The strong association between relatively rare high crime locations and the volume of crime tells us something else as well: because crime is associated with poverty areas, it is quite likely that high crime locations are also associated with poverty areas. In the next part, I will build on this point.

Though crime is associated with poverty in general, there are other factors associated with crime. It is instructive that the two highest crime locations in Cincinnati, in 2014, were two big box stores (a Walmart and a Target located two miles apart) that were not in high poverty areas. Wolfe and Pyrooz (2014) provide evidence that Walmarts contribute to crime. One reason, described in a lengthy article in the *Tampa Bay Times*, may be that store operations encourage theft, and store managers report many shoplifters to the police (Sampson, Morel, and Murray 2016). Consequently, my theory needs to account for high crime locations that may be in other than high poverty areas.

In the next part, I will describe a theory built on these findings. In keeping with the findings in this part, it will have two subsections. The first describes why high crime locations cluster in urban neighborhoods with high poverty. The second describes why some high crime places are not in these areas.

A Theory of How High Crime Places Arise

Property is costly, and so are the facilities built on it. It is not just the purchase costs that matter, but the costs of upkeep, management, insurance, and taxes. Therefore, all place managers will need to have some resources to cover these costs. If the property is a single family residence, then homeowners' jobs usually provide the revenue. For other property, the revenue comes directly or indirectly through the management of the property: renting apartments, selling shoes, hawking bicycles, retailing eyeglasses, peddling tickets to sporting events, pouring beer, serving meals, and so on. Even if the property is not a business, the property has some role in covering its costs: to maintain a church, for example, members of the congregation donate money; a free drug clinic must entice members of the public or government agencies to donate money to maintain the services; a non-profit theater not only relies on ticket sales, but the largess of wealthy donors. This is the resource acquisition function of place management identified by Madensen (2007).

Crime prevention is one of the costs. It will vary depending on the type of facility—banks will invest more in prevention than will stores selling used vintage clothing, for example. Place managers will not invest more in prevention than they think is necessary. And this depends on the costs of crime.

Crime creates numerous costs. First, there is the loss of goods and cash. Second, there is the repair necessary to address damage from crime. Third, there are reputational costs; the more crime the more the reputation of a place suffers and the fewer people who will want to use the place. Fourth, there are insurance costs that can rise after crimes are reported. And fifth, there are costs associated with litigation if a place user or employee is hurt or killed during a crime at the location.

The salience of these costs varies. It varies across place types; a homeowner is probably less concerned about reputational costs, compared to an apartment owner, for example. A small shopkeeper may be very concerned about the shoplifting of a three-dollar item, but the same theft in a big box store is of less concern. It varies across crime types; litigation costs may be low for burglary, but high for a rape or murder, for example. Further, place managers have some discretion as to how they can handle costs: they may replace a broken window so that it is better than before it was shattered; they can undertake cosmetic repairs; they can simply board it up; or they can ignore it. The costs of crime can be borne by different people or institutions. Most obviously, the costs of a break-in to a single family home are borne by the owner and her insurance company (if any). However, the owner of a rental apartment complex might bear little of the costs of a break-in to one of his units—these may be borne by the renter, mostly—and none of the costs stemming from a tenant's car being vandalized in the complex's parking area.

Place management will entail a balancing of costs, risks, and available resources. These are economic decisions. For some places, the economics of crime and its prevention are sufficient to explain why most places have no crime but a few have a great deal. But in other circumstances there are also political and social considerations that influence prevention decision making. Economic, political, and social considerations are not completely separable in practice, and might not be distinguishable. Nevertheless, for theory they are useful indicators of possible sources of motivation for actions.

Further, these considerations vary by the contexts of the places. The principal contexts will be the income and race or ethnicity of the primary place users in an area. However, geographic areas, such as neighborhoods, are often quite heterogeneous; they comprise numerous micro-environments. An apartment building located on a major thoroughfare will operate in a somewhat different context than a similar building a block away on a side street, for example. A small grocery store located next to a bar and a payday lender has a different context than a similar store located adjacent to a church and a hair salon. The theory I propose suggests the risks of becoming a high crime location depend, in many respects, on street and neighborhood contexts. But this risk is an average over numerous micro-environments.

Crime imposes costs on place managers, so one can expect them to take steps to avoid it. Prevention of crime also comes with a cost. So while most place managers will take steps to prevent crime at their locations, they will typically only take prevention measures that can address pressing crime concerns, or that are mandated by insurance companies, the threat of litigation, or regulatory requirements. Usually, this is sufficient, as evidenced by the fact that most places have little or no crime, regardless of place type. There are two important exceptions, and these create high crime places.

One exception creates mostly crime attractors, and the other exception creates mostly crime generators. Crime attractors attract persistent offenders (Brantingham and Brantingham 1995). Crime generators have numerous targets, thus create large scale crime opportunities (Brantingham and Brantingham 1995). Ronald Clarke and I (2003) suggested that there is a third type: crime enablers where the managers fail to block crime opportunities. These are not mutually exclusive types. Crime enablers interact with generators and attractors. That is, it is possible to imagine a place with numerous possible targets that is managed so that crime is kept down. And it is possible to imagine a well-managed place with many potential offenders that has little crime.

Crime Attractors

I will describe three broad influences on the opportunity structure for bad place management that create crime attractors. I separate them into economic, social, and political influences, but in reality these interact. For example, mortgage availability is an economic factor property buyers and sellers must take into account, but there is documented evidence of racial discrimination in mortgage lending (Massey, Rugh, Steil, and Albright 2016): a social influence. And the degree of regulatory enforcement to prevent such discrimination is largely due to politics, which is in turn influenced by economics and social prejudices.

Economics. Within a short walk of my home there is an old multistory hotel that used to cater to the wealthy. It currently houses the very poor, some of whom have drug or mental health problems. The owners have deferred maintenance and residents are living in squalor (Bernard-Kuhn 2015). In 2014 and 2015 the building had 34 and 37 serious crimes, respectively. In 2014, 33 of the residents were victims of crime, which is approximately a 10 percent victimization rate.

Most crime attractors are not this large. They will include the corner grocery store that stocks paraphernalia useful for smoking crack or shooting heroin, the apartment building where gang members have taken over one or more units to use as comfort spaces (Hammer 2011), the motel that is the site for sex work or houses parolees (Bichler et al. 2013), and the inexpensive cell phone store that caters to drug dealers and gang members.

Crime attractors of this type are likely to be concentrated in low income areas where businesses have very low profit margins and have difficulty paying the costs of adequate prevention. Further, to the extent that such neighborhoods also have a larger percentage of offenders than other higher income areas, offender concentration will interact with economic incentives for poor place management to create high crime locations. There is a chicken-and-egg process here: the opportunities for potential offenders to concentrate at a few places help create the offenders, and a concentration of potential offenders in an area facilitates the creation of crime attractors.

Incentives for low place management have not been explored in criminology (Payne, in this volume, is an exception), but some researchers have come close to identifying the role of property owners. Burgess (1925) noted that the interstitial areas of cities (the zones between the industry and middle class neighborhoods), where delinquency proliferated, were created by property owners holding property of speculative purposes: waiting for the expansion of the nearby industrial zone so the property could be resold. For such speculators, it makes little economic sense to invest in their properties. Instead, they can exploit the restricted ability of residents to find housing by offering cheap rents but very few services (Drake and Cayton 1945; Duneier 2016). So owners do not make repairs, they do not screen tenants, and they do not create or consistently enforce rules (Desmond 2016). Shaw and McKay (1942), when describing the origins of delinquency, failed to follow-up on this initial link between place management and crime (Snodgrass 1976). One reason for this is that Burgess as well as Shaw and McKay thought of the processes that created neighborhoods as "natural" rather than intentional (Duneier 2016).

From a place management perspective, what might appear to be "natural" in aggregate is made up of numerous decisions, intentionally made. Sternlieb's (1966) singular book on landlords in low income areas of Newark is instructive. Through the use of surveys and interviews, Sternlieb shows that "weak resale and financial markets definitely inhibit rehabilitation efforts" (1966: xix). He also shows that vacancy rates are critical for the financial viability of most landlords, and is of great concern to those operating in very low income areas. Further, he notes, "The worst housing areas have the highest concentration of major owners," and these areas are dominated by "white large scale slum landlords"; these "multiple-slum parcel owners are specialists in slum properties" (1966: xviii). And faced with high vacancy rates, "the typical, large-scale landlord reaction has been to reduce maintenance expenditures rather than to reduce rents, with a minority making improvements to secure tenantry" (p. xix). Desmond's (2016) study of Milwaukee landlords and tenants shows that 50 years after Sternlieb's work, these incentives and processes are still at work.

Landlords with property in areas where tenants have very low incomes and where vacancies are endemic have three options, according to Sternlieb. They can sell their property. This can be difficult, and whoever buys it will face the same three options. Second, they can hold onto the property until its value improves, but in the meantime invest as little as possible in the property. Or, third, they can invest more in the property in the hopes of attracting tenants who can afford higher rents and are more stable. This last option can be very risky, so this is unlikely unless there is clear evidence that the housing market has reversed directions. The Goldilocks solution is obvious: option two.

Peter Salins (1980) makes a related point about property management. Salins was addressing the creeping destruction of residential property in some New York City neighborhoods during the 1970s, and examined the market, racial, and government policy forces behind this destruction. He wrote,

> The absence or depression of asset value on the part of residential property in or near the city's zones of housing destruction creates the following distortions in property owner behavior, distortions, that is, from the norm that prevails where there is some appreciable asset or resale value. Property owners have little incentive to:
>
> "a.   invest in maintenance, repair, let alone improvement of the property beyond what is required . . .
>
> b.   honor such obligations as tax and mortgage payments beyond the period necessary to obtain some predetermined optimal return on investment . . .
>
> c.   screen the potential tenantry to weed out potentially destructive, irresponsible, or otherwise undesirable households; especially if such discrimination would result in an appreciable number of vacancies in a slack market . . ."
>
> (Salins 1980: 93)

Neither Salins nor Sternlieb make much reference to crime, but their references to the lack of investment in property, and lack of tenant screening in particular, are telling. If a landlord is unwilling or unable to address his property's physical plant, or to control access, then we would expect him to pay little attention to addressing crime or disorder on his property. After all, much of the costs of crime will be borne by tenants, not him.

Most people writing about places in impoverished areas write about residential places. However, there are other places in these areas. Their owners and operators too face difficulties. The grocery store will have customers, but there will be fewer, and most will not be able to afford high profit margin items, so the store's viability will be at risk. The items for sale will be more expensive than if sold elsewhere, and the quality of goods will be lower (Economic Research Service 2009). If a neighborhood is undergoing outmigration, then most of these stores will go out of business. But as the store owners struggle to stay in business, they will be less attentive to curbing misbehavior on and nearby their properties, and may engage in practices that facilitate crime. It is not surprising, therefore, that stolen goods markets are concentrated in impoverished areas (Sutton 2010). To varying extent, all businesses in the areas will be under pressure to ignore crime, and even to facilitate it, if the costs of addressing crime far outweigh the costs of tolerating or promoting it.

In contrast, place managers in high and moderate income areas are less likely to face this pressure. The place users have sufficient incomes to make the place economically viable. And because crime threatens this viability fighting crime is a more likely response than tolerating it.

The economics of places provides the basic mechanism for the creation of clusters of high crime locations. However, there are two other mechanisms that can come into play.

Social Mechanisms. Historically, in the United States, race matters. Segregation has been and continues to be a fact in metropolitan regions (Briggs 2005; Meyer 2000). It influences property management decisions by restricting access to places for racial minorities and forcing individuals belonging to such minority groups to live in particular neighborhoods. This has been extensively documented in Chicago (Hirsch 1983), New York (Osofsky 1971), Cleveland (Kusmer 1976), Cincinnati (Miller and Tucker 1998), Denver (James and Tynan 1986), and Detroit (Sugrue 2005), among other cities.

The form racial discrimination takes has varied over the years. Throughout slavery Blacks were denied the ability to own property in many states. Even after slavery the right to own property was often neither honored nor enforced, and frequently denied. Through the late 1940s restrictive covenants prevented white homeowners from selling to African-American and other minority buyers (Rose and Brooks 2016). White mobs used physical violence and threats to prevent African-Americans from moving into some neighborhoods (Green, Strolovitch, and Wong 1998; Hirsch 1983). The threat of racial attacks has not completely disappeared (Moore 2016). Racial steering has been widely documented: real-estate agents show African-American buyers fewer houses in white areas than they show to white buyers (Galster 1990; List 2004). And there is continued evidence of discrimination in the availability of mortgages (Apgar and Calder 2005; Massey et al. 2016).

The resistance of whites to live, shop, and work in largely minority areas of cities restricts the income place owners can obtain from businesses in these areas, and suppresses home prices. For those individuals living in these areas, discrimination has resulted in overcrowding in two ways. First, area residents have fewer housing, shopping, and recreation options. Transportation restrictions aggravate the difficulties: low income residents are less likely to own cars, and their neighborhoods often are poorly served by public transportation. Second, the reluctance of whites to use the area diminishes the economic viability of businesses, including rental apartments, and increases the abandonment of property, which reduces the supply of usable places (Desmond 2016; Moore 2016; Salins 1980).

When a group can dwell only in a restricted area then the owners of property in that area have an incentive to charge higher rents. When coupled with higher costs of transportation, local merchants have an incentive to charge more for goods and services than they would charge in areas where people earn more money and have better transportation options. At the same time, place managers do not feel the market pressure to deliver the same quality of services they would to other economically comparable place users of the majority race or ethnicity (Sternlieb 1966). One of the services is the protection of tenants and other place users from crime.

Thus, racial and other forms of discrimination compound the problems of low income residents by further disincentivizing good place management. In addition to compounding the economic difficulties of place managers, when racial bias is a norm place managers have an excuse to reduce services in these areas that they cannot use in areas populated by people who are not discriminated against.

Political Mechanisms. The economic and social influences on poor place management can be further augmented by the lack of political power. Compared to higher income areas, used by people from the majority population, low income minority neighborhoods will get fewer and lower quality government services (Bonds 2007). Much has been made of differential police, schooling, and other government services (Mladenka and Hill 1978; Building Education Success Together 2006). It is quite likely this extends to code enforcement, building and health regulations, and other government services that directly influence how places are managed (Nivola 1978).

Throughout the latter part of the twentieth century, local, state, and federal governments have influenced property ownership through the construction of highways, public housing, government facilities, and other projects in low income areas. One of the biggest influences on low income neighborhoods in urban areas has been urban renewal. This public-private effort resulted in the removal of buildings in low income and often African-American neighborhoods, the replacement of some housing for the poor, and the displacement of most of the poor to other areas (Pritchett 2003). The consequence has been that property owners face greater uncertainty about their property in such areas, and have therefore more incentive not to invest in them. One of the reasons poor and non-white neighborhoods become afflicted with such developments is the lack of political influence that keeps such projects out of higher income white neighborhoods (Hirsch 1983; Miller and Tucker 1998).

There is very little research on the political influence of property owners in low income areas on elected officials. But given how much local and state governments can do to influence property values, it would be surprising if property owners did not try to exert political muscle. Such efforts can include seeking financial incentives to serve low income residents without much oversight or accountability, lobbying against enforcement and sanctions for health and safety code violations, and pushing for redevelopment efforts that would allow property sales at higher prices (e.g., arguing for a highway interchange that would require land purchases and raise the commercial value of property near the interchange).

The consequences will be that the political forces that might offset the economic and social influences on bad place management will be reduced or completely negated. In the extreme, vice activities that would not be tolerated anywhere else in the city will be allowed in low income minority areas (Drake and Cayton 1945). Some place managers, with limited ability to make money in the legitimate economy, will allow illicit activities (Eck 1994). Occasionally, they will actively promote such activities. More often, it is simpler and less risky to pretend ignorance and allow illicit activities to flourish. Routine vice activity can become a crime attractor. On the occasion that the police or other government agencies decide to take action, the place manager can plead ignorance, make a superficial attempt to comply with regulatory orders, and then quietly allow the illicit behavior to begin again, once the furor dies down. It is not surprising that vice activity is often located in economically depressed neighborhoods housing people who are discriminated against and who have little political power.

The role of economic, social, and political mechanisms in creating an opportunity structure for bad place management can be described within a situational crime prevention framework (Cornish and Clarke 2003). This framework suggests that decision makers (criminal offenders as originally described, but property owners in this application) take into account five incentives: reward, risk, effort, provocations, and excuses. The three mechanisms I have described influence these perceived incentives in a variety of ways. This interaction is illustrated in Table 7.2.

Crime Generators

Not all high crime places are located in high poverty areas, even if most are. Place managers may forgo crime prevention to facilitate mass scale business to reduce the unit costs of goods or services sold. The low cost of goods or services draws in a large volume of place users. A relatively small proportion

Table 7.3
Incentives for the creation of high crime places in low income areas

	Reward	Risk	Effort	Provocations	Excuses
Economic	Seeking higher return from property—curbing actions that could prevent crime	Risk of default loss requires higher rate of return, which justifies higher charges and lower costs		Expecting losses provokes cut backs in services	"I cannot afford to . . ."
Social	Exacting higher rate than justified. Reduce costs by providing less service, including crime prevention	Members of stigmatized groups less likely to have complaints heard by regulators	Suppressing reporting makes exploitation easier	Status differential invites exploitation	"These people don't care; they destroy the place. . . ."
Political	Lobbying for redevelopment in order to sell at profit, and for lower sanctions for poor service	Blocking enforcement of violations	Violations are easier if they do not need to be hidden		"We are providing services to people no one else will serve."

• Economic—financing and profiting
• Social—discrimination and segregation
• Political—the political capital of owners

of these users can exploit the place or other place users to create a high volume of crime. The place manager can internalize some of the costs of crime. But much of the cost can be exported to the public through high demands for police services (e.g., to handle shoplifters or disorderly patrons, or respond to false alarms), or to place users (e.g., victims of thefts or robberies). Some big box store operations function in this way (Sampson et al. 2016; Clarke and Eck 2003). So do some large nightclubs (BBC Newsbeat 2016; Forsyth, Cloonan, and Barr 2005) with low staffing (Scott and Dedel 2006).

Crime generators of this type are not restricted to any particular area. Nevertheless, area characteristics may have some influence. Crime generators may be less common in very high income neighborhoods where there are tight restrictions on what businesses can locate in the area. Further, well-to-do residents with political influence often can keep high volume facilities out of their neighborhoods. At the opposite extreme, low income areas might not have enough consumers with sufficient incomes to create the conditions necessary for crime generation. Consequently, crime generators will be less common in very low income areas than in other areas (except for very high income areas).

It is in areas between the two extremes where crime generators are most likely to flourish. But area incomes and zoning are not sufficient conditions for crime generators.

Clusters of high crime locations due to generation will follow arterial routes, as first proposed by Patricia and Paul Brantingham (1981, 1993). The large volume of potential place users using arterial routes attracts businesses and other facilities catering to large numbers of people. This in turn attracts more traffic on the arterial route. Many, though not all, of these places along these arterial routes provide crime targets: either goods or cash that can be stolen, vehicles that can be broken into or stolen, or pedestrians who can be robbed. In Figure 7.1, evidence of this can be seen in the string-like clusters found on the map. Many of these strings of hot places are along arterial routes radiating out from the center of the city.

The concentration of crime among proximal places (street segments) can be easily explained by two loosely coupled conditions described by Marcus Felson (1987). First, traffic flow and pedestrian use create varying crime opportunities. This alone might explain some very high crime proximal places. But within a high crime segment, a few addresses are likely to have most of the crime. It seems highly unlikely that crime is typically spread evenly, or randomly, down the length of a street segment.

The second condition is place management variation along the segment. Location on the segment, place type, building age, property configuration, and other specific features make some places easier to manage against crime than others. Also, poor place management, by itself, is unlikely to generate crime if there are few place users or targets. It is the combination of high volumes of place users and poor place management along with the presence of offenders that creates the crime generators.

Place managers can be more that passive exploiters of the prevalence of place users. Some place managers intentionally create high volumes of users. Large nightclubs, sporting venues, big box stores, and shopping centers are all examples of efforts by property owners to create high volumes of place users. Shopping centers are particularly interesting as they often contain passive and active exploiters. There are usually one or two anchor stores that draw in high volumes of users, and a host of smaller stores that can exploit the presence of such users.

In summary, the clustering of high crime places is explainable by the incentives areas offer place managers to curtail crime. In low income areas combinations of economic, social, and political incentives create blob-like clusters of mostly crime attractors. Crime generators will cluster as strings along arterial routes along which place users travel. Some crime generators will be on arterial routes within low income areas, but as Figure 7.1 illustrates, the string clusters of high crime locations will be most visible elsewhere.

Implications

Yes, most crime is found at a few places, and these places are found throughout cities; they are not restricted to a few high crime neighborhoods. This basic finding has been cited to suggest that places—proprietary and proximal—matter more than pooled places (neighborhoods). However, considerable evidence shows that high crime places are clustered at the neighborhood level.

I contend that the spatial clustering of high crime places is due to a combination of economic, social, and political factors that create opportunity structures for place management. In some areas, the opportunity structure provides strong incentives for good place management. In these areas, the number of high crime places will be small. In other areas, the opportunity structure provides fewer incentives for good place management and more incentives for bad place management. It is in these areas that high crime places will cluster. In low income areas, particularly those inhabited by people who have historically been discriminated against, a larger proportion of these high crime places will be crime attractors. Outside of such areas, the clusters will be strings of crime generators along arterial routes, for the reasons first articulated by Brantingham and Brantingham (1981, 1993, 1995).

Explanations for high crime areas (pooled places) have usually relied upon some variation on the ideas of social disorganization—the inability or unwillingness of local residents to act informally and collectively to maintain order and suppress crime. The theory I have proposed departs from the explanations originating in Shaw and McKay's (1942) work. Rather, my point of departure is the work of two African-American sociologists, who worked and wrote down the hall from Shaw and McKay at the University of Chicago, St. Clair Drake and Horace Clayton. The following passage from their extensive study of Chicago's largest African-American area is particularly relevant as it points to two opposing explanations: the inability of poor non-white residents to choose better living conditions versus the choices available to wealthier property owners who live elsewhere.

The areas in which these groups are concentrated become stigmatized as "slum neighborhoods," and there is a tendency to blame the group for the condition of the area. One factor that complicates this whole matter of land-values—for the areas in question *are* predominately slums—is the fact that the "undesirable" groups usually inherit sections of the city that the older, more well-to-do inhabitants have abandoned and thus "the undesirable racial factor is so merged with other unattractive features, such as proximity to factories, poor transportation, old and obsolete buildings, poor street improvements, and the presence of criminal or vice elements, that the separate effect of race cannot be disentangled" (emphasis in original).

(Drake and Cayton 1945: 175; and quoting Hoyt 1933: 317)

This perspective was echoed by Snodgrass (1976) in a piece both praising and criticizing Shaw and McKay:

> The transitional zone, Shaw and McKay noted, came about through the expansion of the central business district. Owners of land and property in the interstitial area retained ownership knowing that land values would go up and that eventually wealthy enterprises would pay handsome prices for the territory as more and more of it was required for expansion. They refrained from making new investments in construction and refused to make "wasteful" repairs on the property since the buildings would be demolished sooner or later to make way for the expansion. Land values remained high, but property rentals stayed comparatively low. Over time the areas deteriorated. Into these slums were drawn impoverished migrants and immigrants who struggled for an existence by performing the menial work in the central city, whose meagre wages enriched the absentee landlords and whose children in large numbers became the "notorious" delinquents."
>
> (Snodgrass, 1976: 10)

Broken Windows Theory (Wilson and Kelling 1982) also draws upon the understanding that crime is created when informal social controls fail. It too points at the residents' inability to stem crime. The broken window is a metaphor for the decline in informal social controls. Whereas standard social disorganization champions suggest that government policy should be directed at creating stronger cohesion among neighborhood residents through various social interventions, advocates of Broken Windows Theory suggest that the police should enforce social norms, until residents can resume their informal social controls (Wilson and Kelling 1982).

Broken Windows Theory comes tantalizingly close to recognizing the role of the place manager. What if Wilson and Kelling had taken broken windows as real, instead of as metaphors? What if instead of focusing upon how the unrepaired broken window influences the perceptions of people in the area, the authors had asked: Who owns those windows? Why don't they repair them? What can cities do to get owners to reglaze their broken windows? Asking these questions leads not to intensive police enforcement against minor incivilities, but to government interactions with business owners, landlords, and other property owners.

Although academic criminological teaching and writing, including Broken Windows Theory, has emphasized the social disorganization perspective it has generally failed to notice the alternative suggested by Drake and Cayton and other scholars (Duneier 2016). The study of high crime places, and the behavior of their owners, suggests that it is time to reconsider their insights. Fortunately, there is interest in the interactions of place managers and place users. Specifically, Desmond (2016) provides a riveting set of accounts of how owners of low income properties in Milwaukee manage their properties, and as important, how their clients cope with these management practices. Though not overtly a study of crime, Desmond (2016) notes how place management can concentrate criminal activity:

> [Landlords] decide who got to live where. And their screening practices (or lack thereof) revealed why crime and gang activity or an area's civic engagement and its spirit of neighborliness could vary drastically from one block to the next. They also helped explain why on the same block in the same low-income neighborhood, one apartment complex but not another became familiar to the police."
>
> (Desmond 2016: 89)

No theory of the spatial arrangement of crime can be valid at the neighborhood level if it does not account for the high degree of heterogeneity of crime involvement with neighborhoods at the place level. For this reason, Wilcox and Tillyer (in this volume) are correct in calling for a "place in neighborhood" perspective. The theory I have proposed fits within their conception of a valid theory. My theory differs from extant theories of crime in that it focuses on those who own property and control crime facilitating settings, rather than on the offenders or the victims, or even how residents informally coproduce safety (or fail to) through social arrangements. Why do some people prey upon others repeatedly? Because some third parties create facilitating conditions that allow this to occur. And these third parties are responding to neighborhood level characteristics driven by economics, segregation, and politics.

The hierarchical arrangement of influences, I suspect, is far more complex than the place in neighborhood perspective implies. To begin with, there may be at least four levels: neighborhood, proximal place, proprietary place, and individual. But there is also an extra-geographical level that further complicates this hierarchy: the place manager. This is because a small proportion of property owners control a relatively large proportion of the properties (Payne and Eck 2007; Payne, Gallagher, Eck, and Frank 2013), and their properties may be scattered over several neighborhoods.

Is the theory I propose antithetical to social disorganization type theories? No. There is no logical reason why place management and social disorganization cannot coproduce crime in neighborhoods. They may do this as completely separate processes, or as processes that interact and reinforce each other. For example, bad place management could further erode informal social controls or collective efficacy. Or, weak collective efficacy could create exploitation vulnerabilities that some property owners use (managing their properties in ways they could not in middle class or wealthy neighborhoods). If one subtracts from neighborhoods' crime levels the crime at the worst addresses, the remaining crime level differences among neighborhoods may be due, at least in part, to social disorganization processes.

Policy

Shifting our attention from local residents to property owners is also important for policy. The reason I began this enquiry was to help determine how we should structure regulatory policies toward high crime places. Policy implications for addressing high crime places have focused almost exclusively on police policy. After a quarter of a century we should have a broader view of the policy implications of high crime locations. High crime places are indeed important for policing, but that does not mean that the policy implications stop there, particularly as it is unclear if police agencies are willing to move beyond hot spots patrols (Eck 2015). So these implications are not merely directed at improving police effectiveness. Rather, these implications are directed at local government officials above the level of the police chief, those who head other local agencies, as well as police officials.

The theory I have proposed suggests the following guidance with regard to regulating high crime places:

- Focus on the worst places first. It is at these predictably high crime places that the most benefit can be achieved, in contrast to intermittently crime afflicted locations. Structure regulatory policies to impose no or very light burdens on owners of properties with no crime.
- Consider the possibility that crime generators and crime attractors should be treated differently. Many crime generators are caused by high economic activity, whereas many crime attractors have their roots in the absence of legitimate economic activity and the presence of segregation.
- Be sensitive to the slender economic threads by which many businesses in low income areas hang. This is particularly the case with crime attractors.
- Be cognizant of the possible interplay between economics and race-based decisions. The fact that areas have been abandoned, as Drake and Cayton (1945) state, is not just a consequence of economics, but also a consequence of racial and other forms of discrimination, often supported by public policies.
- Recognize the inherently political nature of regulation. The fact that some property owners in low income neighborhoods get away with management policies that would not be tolerated in other neighborhoods suggests a lack of enforcement. If political power were equally distributed, such disparities in management practices would not be as great. The political nature of high crime places is likely to be a serious impediment to crafting and implementing regulatory policies to address these concentrations.

- Do not expect spontaneous development of community norms and enforcement to address crime. The theory I propose implies that efforts to inject social order or jumpstart informal social controls are far less useful than is focusing on the powers of property owners. Perhaps, once property owners manage their places in ways that provide little or no crime opportunities, informal social norm enforcement might be useful. In the absence of positive place management, however, local residents are unlikely to make much headway against disorder and crime. Local residents might have more impact lobbying local governments for more controls over property owners than by attempting to step up informal social controls.
- Consider alternatives to policing individuals who make use of places that facilitate crime. The concentration of crime at a few places has been used by police to focus patrol efforts. This does nothing to address the crime opportunities that place managers have created, so the police need to return often. It also increases racial disparities in police stops and arrests. Focusing on the property owner has the potential to reduce the need for intensive patrolling of hot spots. And it has the potential to reduce some of the racial disparity in police enforcement. Until police or others address chronic high crime places, playing whack-a-mole by attempting to predict the location of the next crime is likely to be a misuse of resources.
- Beware of unanticipated negative consequences of penalizing place owners for reported offenses. Desmond and Valdez (2012), for example, show how police efforts to reduce calls for service from high call rental properties have prompted landlords to evict victims of domestic violence who repeatedly call the police. This reduces the women's willingness to report domestic violence, thus imperiling their safety. Unless carefully tailored, place-based interventions on place managers could create other harms and racial disparities in these harms.
- Consider efforts to reduce crime at high crime locations to be part of a larger effort to improve living and business conditions in communities. Property owners can more easily exploit tenants when housing is scarce for those who have the least ability to afford market-based rents (Desmond 2016).

The ideas expressed in this theory arose from considering a practical problem: how to best reduce crime by addressing the relatively small number of places where most crime is located. Regulating the owners of such places, rather than just going after offenders, appeared to be a logical step, as it is these owners who control the opportunities for crime at their places. This led to the question: Why do some property owners allow crime although most do not?

The evidence suggested the opportunity structure for bad place management had to be at a geographic level above the place itself. That is, at street and neighborhood levels. The mechanisms for crime at these levels commonly considered—social organization, social capital, and collective efficacy among residents—did not seem meaningful to explain property owners' behaviors, particularly in low income neighborhoods where crime and high crime places are concentrated and where much of the property is owned by non-residents. By contrast, to account for the origins of high crime places, the theory I have proposed focuses attention on the owners of property—rather than local residents—in those neighborhoods where property values are low due to economics, discrimination, and politics.

Acknowledgments

I give special thanks to the following people (in alphabetical order) who provided me with assistance, of various types, in the preparation of this paper: Robert Brown, Francis Cullen, YongJei Lee, Shannon Linning, Tamara Madensen, David Weisburd, and the attendees at the 2016 Environmental Criminology and Crime Analysis meeting in Münster, Germany. I was also assisted by fate. While writing this chapter, three well written and insightful books were published—by Duneier, Desmond, and Moore—that helped me embed my ideas in a larger framework.

Notes

1. The empty regions within the city are separate municipalities for which we do not have crime data, and the University of Cincinnati campus, which has its own police service.
2. Although there are 52 officially recognized neighborhoods, the Cincinnati Area Geographic Information System, which provides the boundary files for the map, includes subneighborhood areas, resulting in the 75 areas examined here.
3. A comparison of the plots of standardized and unstandardized data shows that they are almost exactly the same, so neighborhood size is an unlikely confounder in this example.

References

Andresen, Martin A., and Nicolas Malleson. 2010. "Testing the Stability of Crime Patterns: Implications for Theory and Policy." *Journal of Research in Crime and Delinquency* 48: 58–82.

Apgar, William C., and Allegra Calder. 2005. "The Dual Mortgage Market: The Persistence of Discrimination in Mortgage Lending." Pp. 101–125 in Xavier de Souza Briggs (ed.), *Geography of Opportunity: Race and Housing Choice in Metropolitan America.* Washington, DC: The Brookings Institution.

BBC Newsbeat. 2016. "Fabric Agrees Strict New Licensing Deal with Islington Council to Reopen." November 21. www.bbc.co.uk/newsbeat/article/38054598/fabric-agrees-strict-new-licensing-deal-with-islington-council-to-reopen. Accessed 11–21–2016.

Bernard-Kuhn, Lisa. 2015. "Residents of Walnut Hills Apartment Building Live in Squalor, Landlord Gets $1.14M." March 16. www.wcpo.com/news/political/local-politics/residents-live-in-squalor-landlord-gets-114m. Accessed 6–9–2016.

Bichler, Gisela, Karin Schmerler, and Janet Enriquez. 2013. "Curbing Nuisance Motels: An Evaluation of Police as Place Regulators." *Policing: An International Journal of Police Strategies & Management* 36: 437–462.

Bonds, Michael. 2007. "Black Political Power Reassessed: Race, Politics and Federal Funds." *Journal of African American Studies* 11: 189–203.

Bowers, Kate, Shane Johnson, Rob T. Guerette, Lucia Summers, and Suzanne Poynton. 2011. "Spatial Displacement and Diffusion of Benefits among Geographically Focused Policing Interventions: A Meta Analytical Review." *Journal of Experimental Criminology* 7: 347–374.

Braga, Anthony A., David M. Hureau, and Andrew V. Papachristos. 2010. "The Relevance of Micro Places to Citywide Robbery Trends: A Longitudinal Analysis of Robbery Incidents at Street Corners and Block Faces in Boston." *Journal of Research in Crime and Delinquency* 48: 7–32.

Braga, Anthony A., Andrew V. Papachristos, and David M. Hureau. 2014. "The Effects of Hot Spots Policing on Crime: An Updated Systematic Review and Meta-Analysis." *Justice Quarterly* 31: 633–663.

Brantingham, Patricia L., and Paul J. Brantingham. 1981. "Notes on the Geometry of Crime." Pp. 27–54 in Paul J. Brantingham and Patricia L. Brantingham (eds.), *Environmental Criminology*. Prospect Heights, CA: Waveland.

Brantingham, Patricia L., and Paul J. Brantingham. 1993. "Environment, Routine, and Situation: Toward a Pattern Theory of Crime." Pp. 259–294 in Marcus Clarke and Ronald V. Felson (eds.), *Routine Activity and Rational Choice*. New Brunswick, NJ: Transaction.

Brantingham, Patricia L., and Paul J. Brantingham. 1995. "Criminality of Place: Crime Generators and Crime Attractors." *European Journal on Criminal Policy and Research* 3: 1–26.

Briggs, Xavier de Souza. 2005. "Introduction." Pp. 1–15 in Xavier de Souza Briggs (ed.), *Geography of Opportunity: Race and Housing Choice in Metropolitan America*. Washington, DC: The Brookings Institution.

Building Education Success Together. 2006. *Growth and Disparity: A Decade of U.S. Public School Construction*. Washington, DC: 21st Century Fund.

Burgess, Ernest. 1925. "The Growth of the City." Pp. 47–62 in Robert E. Park and Ernest Burgess (eds.), *The City*. Chicago, IL: University of Chicago Press.

Clarke, Ronald V., and Gisela Bichler-Robertson. 1998. "Place Managers, Slumlords and Crime in Low Rent Apartment Buildings." *Security Journal* 11: 11–19.

Clarke, Ronald V., and John E. Eck. 2003. *Becoming a Problem-Solving Crime Analyst: In 55 Small Steps*. London: Jill Dando Institute of Crime Science.

Clarke, Ronald V., and David Weisburd. 1994. "Diffusion of Crime Control Benefits: Observations on the Reverse of Displacement." Pp. 165–183 in Ronald V. Clarke (ed.), *Crime Prevention Studies*. Monsey, NY: Criminal Justice Press.

Cornish, Derek B., and Ronald V. Clarke. 2003. "Opportunities, Precipitators and Criminal Decisions: A Reply to Wortley's Critique of Situational Crime Prevention." Pp. 41–96 in Martha Smith and Derek Cornish (eds.), *Theory for Practice in Situational Crime Prevention*. Monsey, NY: Criminal Justice Press.

Desmond, Matthew. 2016. *Evicted: Poverty and Profit in the American City*. New York, NY: Crown.

Desmond, Matthew, and Nicol Valdez. 2012. "Unpolicing the Urban Poor: Consequences of Third-Party Policing for Inner-City Women." *American Sociological Review* 78: 117–141.

Drake, St. Clair, and Horace R. Cayton. 1945. *Black Metropolis: A Study of Negro Life in a Northern City.* New York, NY: Harcourt, Brace & Co.

Duneier, Mitchell. 2016. *Ghetto: The Invention of a Place, the History of an Idea.* New York, NY: Farrar, Straus, and Giroux.

Eck, John E. 1994. *Drug Markets and Drug Places: A Case-Control Study of the Spatial Structure of Illicit Drug Dealing.* Ph.D. Dissertation. College Park, MD: Department of Criminology and Criminal Justice, University of Maryland.

Eck, John E. 2002. "Preventing Crime at Places." Pp. 241–294 in Lawrence W. Sherman, David Farrington, Brandon Welsh, and Doris L. MacKenzie (eds.), *Evidence-Based Crime Prevention.* New York, NY: Routledge.

Eck, John E. 2015. "Who Should Prevent Crime at Places? The Advantages of Regulating Place Managers and Challenges to Police Services." *Policing* 9: 223–233.

Eck, John E., and Emily B. Eck. 2012. "Crime Place and Pollution: Expanding Crime Reduction Options through a Regulatory Approach." *Criminology & Public Policy* 11: 281–316.

Eck, John E., Jeffrey S. Gersh, and Charlene Taylor. 2000. "Finding Crime Hot Spots through Repeat Address Mapping." Pp. 49–64 in Victor Goldsmith, Philip G. McGuire, John H. Mollenkopf, and Timothy A. Ross (eds.), *Analyzing Crime Patterns: Frontiers of Practice.* Thousand Oaks, CA: Sage.

Eck, John E., and Rob T. Guerette. 2012. "Place-Based Crime Prevention: Theory, Evidence, and Policy." Pp. 354–383 in Brandon Welsh and David Farrington (eds.), *The Oxford Handbook of Crime Prevention.* New York, NY: Oxford University Press.

Eck, John E., and Julie Wartell. 1998. "Improving the Management of Rental Properties with Drug Problems: A Randomized Experiment." Pp. 161–185 in Lorraine Mazerolle and Janet Roehl (eds.), *Civil Remedies and Crime Prevention: Crime Prevention Studies.* Monsey, NY: Criminal Justice Press.

Economic Research Service. 2009. *Access to Affordable and Nutritious Food: Measuring and Understanding Food Deserts and Their Consequences: Report to Congress.* Washington, DC: U.S. Department of Agriculture.

Felson, Marcus. 1987. "Routine Activities and Crime Prevention in the Developing Metropolis." *Criminology* 25: 911–931.

Forsyth, Alasdair J. M., Martin Cloonan M., and Jean Barr. 2005. *Factors Associated with Alcohol-Related Problems within Licensed Premises.* Glasgow: Greater Glasgow NHS Board.

Galster, George. 1990. "Racial Steering in Urban Housing Markets: A Review of the Audit Evidence." *The Review of Black Political Economy* 19: 105–129.

Goldstein, Herman. 1979. "Improving Policing: A Problem Oriented Approach." *Crime & Delinquency* 25: 236–258.

Graham, Kathryn, and Ross Homel. 2008. *Raising the Bar: Preventing Aggression in and around Bars, Clubs and Pubs.* Cullompton, UK: Willan Publishing.

Green, Donald P., Dara Z. Strolovitch, and Janelle S. Wong. 1998. "Defended Neighborhoods, Integration, and Racially Motivated Crime." *American Journal of Sociology* 104: 372–403.

Groff, Elizabeth R., David Weisburd, and Sue-Ming Yang. 2010. "Is It Important to Examine Crime Trends at a Local 'Micro' Level? A Longitudinal Analysis of Street to Street Variability in Crime Trajectories." *Journal of Quantitative Criminology* 26: 7–32.

Guerette, Rob T., and Kate J. Bowers. 2009. "Assessing the Extent of Crime Displacement and Diffusion of Benefits: A Review of Situational Crime Prevention Evaluations." *Criminology* 47: 1331–1368.

Hammer, Matthew. 2011. "Crime Places of Comfort." Masters Demonstration Project. Cincinnati, OH: School of Criminal Justice, University of Cincinnati (May).

Hirsch, Arnold R. 1983. *Making the Second Ghetto: Race and Housing in Chicago, 1940–1960*. New York, NY: Cambridge University Press.

Hoyt, Homer. 1933. *One Hundred Years of Land Values in Chicago*. Chicago, IL: University of Chicago Press. Available from the Internet Archive, https://archive.org/details/onehundredyearso00hoytrich

James, Franklin J., and Eileen A. Tynan. 1986. "Segregation and Discrimination of Hispanic Americans: An Exploratory Analysis." Pp. 83–98 in John M. Goering (ed.), *Housing Desegregation and Federal Policy*. Chapel Hill, NC: The University of North Carolina Press.

Kraakman, Reiner H. 1986. "Gatekeepers: The Anatomy of a Third-Party Enforcement Strategy." *Journal of Law, Economics, & Organization* 2: 53–104.

Kusmer, Kenneth L. 1976. *A Ghetto Takes Shape: Black Cleveland, 1870–1930*. Carbondale, IL: University of Illinois Press.

Lee, YongJei. 2017. *Comparing Measures of Concentration of Crime at Places and Times*. Ph.D. Dissertation. School of Criminal Justice. Cincinnati, OH: University of Cincinnati.

Lee, YongJei, John E. Eck, Natalie Martinez, and SooHyun O. 2017. "The Concentration of Crime at Places: A Systematic Review and Meta-Analysis." *Crime Science* 6(6). DOI 10.1186/s40163-017-0069-x.

Lee, YongJei, John E. Eck, Murat Ozer, Rustu Deryol, and Robin Engle. 2014. "Inside High Crime Street Segments: Proprietary and Proximal Place Crime Concentration." Paper delivered at the American Society of Criminology Meeting, San Francisco. November, 19–22.

List, John A. 2004. "The Nature and Extent of Discrimination in the Marketplace: Evidence from the Field." *Quarterly Journal of Economics* 119: 49–89.

Madensen, Tamara D. 2007. *Bar Management and Crime: Toward a Dynamic Theory of Place Management and Crime Hotspots*. Ph.D. Dissertation. Division of Criminal Justice. Cincinnati, OH: University of Cincinnati.

Madensen, Tamara D., and John E. Eck. 2013. "Crime Place and Place Management." Pp. 554–578 in Pamela Wilcox and Francis Cullen (eds.), *The Oxford Handbook of Crime Theory*. New York, NY: Oxford University Press.

Massey, Douglas S., Jacob S. Rugh, Justin P. Steil, and Len Albright. 2016. "Riding the Stagecoach to Hell: A Qualitative Analysis of Racial Discrimination in Mortgage Lending." *City and Community* 15: 118–136.

Mazerolle, Lorraine Green, and Janet Ransley. 2005. *Third Party Policing*. New York, NY: University of Cambridge Press.

Mazerolle, Lorraine Green, Janet Roehl, and Colleen Kadleck. 1998. "Controlling Social Disorder Using Civil Remedies: Results for a Randomized Field Experiment in Oakland, California." Pp. 141–160 in Lorraine Mazerolle and Janet Roehl (eds.), *Civil Remedies and Crime Prevention, Crime*. Prevention Studies. Monsey, NY: Criminal Justice Press.

Meyer, Stephen Grant. 2000. *As Long as They Don't Move Next Door: Segregation and Racial Conflict in American Neighborhoods*. Lanham, MD: Roman Littlefield.

Miller, Zane L., and Bruce Tucker. 1998. *Changing Plans for America's Inner Cities: Cincinnati's Over-The-Rhine and Twentieth-Century Urbanism*. Columbus, OH: Ohio State University Press.

Mladenka, Kenneth R., and Kim Quaile Hill. 1978. "The Distribution of Urban Police Services." *The Journal of Politics* 40: 112–133.

Moore, Natalie Y. 2016. *The South Side: A Portrait of Chicago and American Segregation*. New York, NY: St. Martin's Press.

Nivola, Pietro S. 1978. "Distributing a Municipal Service: A Case Study of Housing Inspection." *The Journal of Politics* 40: 59–81.

Osofsky, Gilbert. 1971. *Harlem: The Making of a Ghetto: Negro New York, 1890–1930*. New York, NY: Harper Collins.

Payne, Troy C. 2015. "Reducing Excessive Police Incidents: Do Notices to Owners Work?" *Security Journal* 28: 1–18.

Payne, Troy C., and John E. Eck. 2007. "Who Owns Crime?" Paper resented at the Annual Meeting of the American Society of Criminology, November 14, Atlanta, GA.

Payne, Troy C., and Kathleen Gallagher. 2016. "The Importance of Small Units of Aggregation: Trajectories of Crime at Addresses in Cincinnati, Ohio, 1998–2012." *Criminology, Criminal Justice Law, & Society* 17: 20–36.

Payne, Troy C., Kathleen Gallagher, John E. Eck, and James Frank. 2013. "Problem Framing in Problem Solving: A Case Study." *Policing: An International Journal of Police Strategies & Management* 36: 670–682.

Pierce, Glenn, Susan Spaar, and LeBaron R. Briggs. 1988. *The Character of Police Work: Strategic and Tactical Implications*. Boston, MA: Center for Applied Social Research, Northeastern University.

Pritchett, Wendell E. 2003. "The 'Public Menace' of Blight: Urban Renewal and the Private Uses of Eminent Domain." *Yale Law & Policy Review* 21: 1–52.

Quirk, Hannah, Toby Seddon, and Graham Smith. 2014. *Regulation and Criminal Justice: Innovations in Policy and Research*. New York, NY: Cambridge University Press.

Rose, Carol M., and Richard R. W. Brooks. 2016. "Racial Covenants and Housing Segregation, Yesterday and Today." Pp. 161–176 in Adrienne Brown and Valerie Smith (eds.), *Race and Real Estate*. New York, NY: Oxford University Press.

Salins, Peter D. 1980. *The Ecology of Housing Destruction: Economic Effects of Public Intervention in the Housing Market*. New York, NY: New York University Press.

Sampson, Robert J., Stephen W. Raudenbush, and Felton Earls. 1997. "Neighborhoods and Violent Crime: A Multilevel Study of Collective Efficacy." *Science* 277: 918–924.

Sampson, Zachary T., Laura C. Morel, and Eli Murray. 2016. "Tampa Bay Walmarts Get Thousands of Police Calls: You Paid the Bill." *Tampa Bay Times*, May 11. Retrieved May 24, 2016 from www.tampabay.com/projects/2016/public-safety/walmart-police/

Scott, Michael S. 2004. "Shifting and Sharing Police Responsibility to Address Public Safety Problems." Pp. 385–409 in Nick Tilley (ed.), *Handbook of Crime Prevention and Community Safety*. Cullompton, UK: Willan.

Scott, Michael S., and Kelly Dedel. 2006. *Assaults in and Around Bars* (2nd ed.). Problem Specific Guide No. 1. Washington, DC: Office of Community Policing Services.

Shaw, Clifford. R., and Henry D. McKay. 1942. *Juvenile Delinquency and Urban Areas: A Study of Delinquents in Relation to Differential Characteristics of Local Communities in American Cities*. Chicago, IL: University of Chicago Press.

Sherman, Lawrence W., Patrick R. Gartin, and Michael E. Buerger. 1989. "Hot Spots of Predatory Crime: Routine Activities and the Criminology of Place." *Criminology* 27: 27–55.

Sherman, Lawrence W., and David Weisburd. 1995. "General Deterrent Effects of Police Patrol in Crime 'Hot Spots': A Randomized, Controlled Trial." *Justice Quarterly* 12: 625–648.

Snodgrass, Jon. 1976. "Clifford R. Shaw and Henry D. McKay: Chicago Criminologists." *British Journal of Criminology* 16: 1–19.

Spelman, William. 1995. "Once Bitten, Then What? Cross-Sectional and Time-Course Explanations of Repeat Victimization." *British Journal of Criminology* 35: 366–383.

Sternlieb, George. 1966. *The Tenement Landlord*. New Brunswick, NJ: Rutgers University Press.

Sugrue, Thomas J. 2005. *The Origins of the Urban Crisis: Race and Inequality in Postwar Detroit*. Princeton, NJ: Princeton University Press.

Sutton, Michael. 2010. *Stolen Goods Markets: Problem Specific Guide No. 57*. Washington, DC: Office of Community Policing Services.

Trickett, Alan, Dan Ellingworth, Tim Hope, and Ken Pease. 1995. "Crime Victimization in the Eighties: Changes in Area and Regional Inequality." *British Journal of Criminology* 35: 343–359.

Trickett, Alan, Denise R. Osborn, Julie Seymour, and Ken Pease. 1992. "What Is Different about High Crime Areas?" *British Journal of Criminology* 31: 81–89.

Weisburd, David. 2015. "The Law of Crime Concentration and the Criminology of Place." *Criminology* 53: 133–157.

Weisburd, David, Shawn Bushway, Cynthia Lum, and Sue-Ming Yang. 2004. "Trajectories of Crime at Places: A Longitudinal Study of Street Segments in the City of Seattle." *Criminology* 42: 283–321.

Weisburd, David, John E. Eck, Anthony Braga, Cody Telep, Breanne Cave, Kate Bowers, Gerben Bruinsma, Charlotte Gill, Elizabeth Groff, Joshua Hinkle, Julie Hibdon, Shane Johnson, Brian Lawton, Cynthia Lum, Jerry Ratcliffe, George Rengert, Travis Taniguchi, and Sue-Ming Yang. 2016. *Place Matters: Criminology for the 21st Century*. New York, NY: Cambridge University Press.

Weisburd, David, Elizabeth R. Groff, and Sue Ming Yang. 2013. *The Criminology of Place: Street Segments and Our Understanding of the Crime Problem*. New York, NY: Oxford University Press.

Weisburd, David, Laura A. Wyckoff, Justin Ready, John E. Eck, Joshua C. Hinkle, and Frank Gajewski. 2006. "Does Crime Just Move around the Corner? A Controlled Study of Spatial Displacement and Diffusion of Crime Control Benefits." *Criminology* 44: 549–592.

Wilcox, Pamela, and John E. Eck. 2011. "Criminology of the Unpopular: Implications for Policy Aimed at Payday Lending Facilities." *Criminology & Public Policy* 10: 473–482.

Wilson, James Q., and George L. Kelling. 1982. "Broken Windows: The Police and Neighborhood Safety." *The Atlantic Monthly* 249: 29–38.

Wolfe, Scott E., and David C. Pyrooz. 2014. "Rolling Back Prices and Raising Crime Rates? The Walmart Effect on Crime in the United States." *British Journal of Criminology* 54: 199–221.

Part IV

The Role of Place-Based Theory
in Criminal Justice

8

The Role of Place in Probation and Parole

Lacey Schaefer, Francis T. Cullen, and Sarah M. Manchak

A primary goal of corrections agencies is to reduce recidivism, which in turn improves offenders' lives and protects public safety. Most contemporary debate regarding correctional interventions has focused on the relative merits of rehabilitation as opposed to deterrence strategies. Research now is persuasive in showing the limited ability of punishment to specifically deter reoffending (Cullen, Jonson, and Nagin 2011; Cullen, Pratt, Micelli, and Moon 2002). By contrast, research reveals that corrections programs that adhere to the principles of effective treatment can be successful in diminishing recidivism (Andrews and Bonta 2010). Even here, however, interventions with offenders are limited by a near-exclusive focus on curing offenders of the propensity to offend—that is, of why they are motivated to break the law (Cullen, Eck, and Lowenkamp 2002; Schaefer 2013).

Yet, as studies in environmental criminology have shown, crime is caused not only by criminogenic propensity but also by access to place-based criminogenic opportunity (Clarke 2012). A large body of literature demonstrates that crime is reduced when opportunities for offending are minimized. Exercises in problem-oriented policing, for example, have amassed evidence that agencies can prevent offending when crime problems are well-understood and when interventions are developed that target the specific causes of these problems (Scott, Eck, Knutsson, and Goldstein 2008; Weisburd and Braga 2006). Since crime problems aggregate in certain places, crime reduction strategies must diagnose the facilitators of offending that are housed there. Accordingly, in order to prevent crime in these places, agencies must diagnose the crime-conducive features that are present in crime-prone places, developing interventions that eliminate or control these conditions. A growing number of case studies show that policing organizations in particular have grown quite adept at accomplishing these tasks (Clarke 1992; 1997; Clarke and Eck 2005).

Given these successes in crime prevention, it is a curious state of affairs that other agencies concerned with reducing offending have not mimicked this problem-oriented approach. Probation and parole authorities in particular have much to learn and gain from their policing counterparts. Community corrections officers, just like police officers, are interested in preventing crime, so it is logical for offender supervisors to consider an application of these problem-oriented strategies to probation and parole practices. In this chapter, we discuss what such an orientation might entail. Specifically, building on initial work on "environmental corrections," here we explore the insights of environmental criminology for limiting reoffending among correctional populations under supervision in the community (Cullen et al. 2002; Schaefer 2013; Schaefer, Cullen, and Eck 2016). In particular, we examine how these theories can guide offender community supervision strategies, with the goal of knifing off offender access to places that create the opportunity for crime and exacerbate criminal propensities. We also explore how probation and parole agents can teach offenders how to avoid and resist the enticements that are found in crime-inducing places. More generally, we argue that environmental criminology, with its focus on crime places, has the potential to contribute to corrective practice that is replacing "brute force" with smarter, more cost-effective approaches to pulling offenders out of a life of crime (see also Kleiman 2009).

Why Probation and Parole Fail

In order to reduce crime, we have to target the known causes of crime. Thus, if recidivism is to be lowered, probation and parole authorities must alter the things that lead their supervisees to reoffend. A central insight of environmental criminology is that criminal acts occur when an individual with the propensity to commit crime (a so-called motivated offender) encounters crime opportunities. Each of these components—a chance to commit crime and an offender willing to take advantage of such—is necessary for a crime to take place. Accordingly, smart probation and parole practices should thus focus on how to reduce both criminogenic propensities *and* access to criminogenic opportunities. On the positive side, important scientific advances have occurred that can guide such practice. Unfortunately, community supervision generally fails because these best practices in reducing propensity and opportunity are currently largely ignored.

In the first instance, probation and parole are often ineffective because they do not reduce propensity; specifically, they fail to adhere to the principles of effective correctional intervention (Andrews and Bonta 2010; Andrews et al. 1990; Gendreau, Cullen, and Bonta 1994; Gendreau, Little, and Goggin 1996). These principles indicate that when the dosage of intervention is commensurate with the offender's level of risk, when the intervention addresses the offender's criminogenic needs, and when the intervention is delivered in a way that the offender will be responsive to, recidivism is reduced (Andrews

1995; Cullen and Gendreau 2000; Cullen and Jonson 2011; Gendreau 1996). In spite of these best practices, a number of probation and parole agencies continue to emphasize deterrence and behavioral control, which are demonstrably unsuccessful in preventing reoffending (Cullen, Pratt, Miceli, et al. 2002; Cullen, Wright, and Applegate 1996; Gendreau et al. 1994; Petersilia and Turner 1993). Although we know how probation and parole authorities can reduce the propensity of offenders under community supervision (Gendreau, Goggin, Cullen, and Andrews 2000; Lowenkamp, Pealer, Smith, and Latessa 2006), unfortunately, the overwhelming majority of probation and parole programs fail to embody these principles (Bonta, Rugge, Scott, Bourgon, and Yessine 2008; Cullen and Jonson 2011; Listwan, Cullen, and Latessa 2006; Lowenkamp, Latessa, and Smith 2006). The regrettable reality is that community corrections interventions are routinely ignoring the evidence of how to diminish offender propensity (Matthews, Jones Hubbard, and Latessa 2001).

In the second instance, probation and parole often fail because they do not reduce opportunity; specifically, they ignore the fact that even the most highly motivated offender cannot commit a crime without the chance to do so (Clarke 2010). One way probation and parole agents can decrease crime is to limit offenders' access to chances to commit crime. If a crime occurs when a motivated offender converges in space and time with a suitable victim in the absence of a capable guardian (Clarke 2012; Cohen and Felson 1979), then probation and parole agencies should be able to prevent recidivism by eliminating offenders' access to attractive targets and enhancing guardianship (Clarke 2008; Clarke and Eck 2005; Cozens 2008). On the surface, it may seem as though probation and parole officers already engage in comparable practices; after all, offenders are subject to heightened surveillance, and their freedoms are restricted. Thus, the idea of opportunity reduction as a crime fighting tool is loosely implicit in existing supervision practices (Miller 2014). Yet this generic application of environmental criminology to probation and parole falls prey to three specific problems.

First, the notion of opportunity reduction is too vaguely applied, violating the "need principle" of effective correctional intervention. Quality crime reduction interventions are tailored to highly specific crime problems; the precise environmental crime inducement must be accurately identified if it is to be eliminated (Clarke and Eck 2005; Laycock 2005). However, probation and parole supervision case plans generally include nonspecific stipulations that are commonly thought to somehow indirectly reduce exposure to crime-conducive situations (such as instituting a curfew or not associating with other offenders). While these considerations may be pertinent toward the prevention of some offenders' relapse, blanket supervision conditions that are not based on the actual crime opportunities of each individual offender are misguided and will not work (Latessa, Cullen, and Gendreau 2002; Latessa and Holsinger 1998). To be effective, probation and parole agents must alter their clients' routine activities so that real crime opportunities are avoided altogether (Cullen et al. 2002; Taxman, Yancey, and Bilanin 2006).

Second, offenders often receive the same dosage of intervention irrespective of their probability of reoffending, which breaches the "risk principle" of effective supervision (Lowenkamp et al. 2006). Crime prevention strategies demonstrate that the developed solution must be commensurate to the crime problem (Laycock 2005). Moreover, the exact nature of the problem must be detailed through careful observation, measurement, and analysis. Reducing the crime opportunities present in a specific area requires that the dynamics of that area be understood. Unfortunately, probation and parole agencies often fail to assess the real risks of relapse for each offender, and do not tailor the intensity of the intervention to those risks (Latessa and Lowenkamp 2006; Lowenkamp and Latessa 2004, 2005).

Third, offenders are not taught to avoid high-crime environments and to resist available crime opportunities, thereby infringing the "responsivity principle" of effective intervention. Because offenders cannot be prevented from accessing all environments where chances to commit crime are available, behavioral change must be substituted for behavioral control for probation and parole to be effective (Taxman and Byrne 2001; Taxman, Young, and Byrne 2003). Probation and parole officers frequently rely on a fortress style of supervision, in which they meet with their clients behind a desk in their office and engage in a passive brand of service brokerage (Latessa 1999; Solomon et al. 2008). Officers often do not seek to identify and address offender needs proactively, but rather respond reactively when problems arise (e.g., supervision meeting is missed, a positive drug test is reported). Yet, in order to get offenders to avoid and resist crime opportunities, they must be trained in techniques that facilitate prosocial decision-making (Pearson, Lipton, Cleland, and Yee 2002; Smith, Schweitzer, Labrecque, and Latessa 2012).

Given these considerations, it is evident that current offender supervision practices fail to adhere to what works in preventing crime. Reducing the crime opportunities of probationers and parolees will require a reorientation of community corrections supervision, in which officers concern themselves less with behavior management and more with the actual crime-conducive environments to which their clients are exposed. This strategy is manifested in two specific ways, discussed in the proceeding sections. First, supervision case plans must include conditions that prevent offenders from encountering crime opportunities that are known to be tempting for each individual. Second, probation and parole officers must work with offenders to enhance decision-making processes that will allow them to avoid and resist remaining crime opportunities. These two methods will require that offender supervisors think about the environments in which their clients are embedded (Clear 1996; Clear and Corbett 1999). The extensive body of literature that outlines the association between place and crime has specific applications for probation and parole (Miller 2014; Schaefer et al. 2016), detailed in the discussion that follows.

Corrections of Place

Beyond general crime prevention practices, theories of opportunity reduction can greatly inform probation and parole supervision (Cullen et al. 2002; Schaefer et al. 2016). For instance, one relevant criminological truism is that offenses are not randomly distributed in space or time (Weisburd, Groff, and Yang 2012). This therefore indicates that crime *opportunities* are concentrated at certain places, such that discernible features of these hotspots are (comparatively more) likely to lead to crime. That is, because crimes are clustered spatiotemporally, so too must be attractive chances to commit crime. This is an important insight for probation and parole officers to consider, because it means that their supervisees may be more or less tempted to recidivate depending on the environments in which they find themselves. Some places may contain several factors that instigate or support the pathway that leads to an offense, while other situations may have few prompts for offending or may even present stimuli that disrupt the recidivism process. For these reasons, community corrections agencies would be well-advised to integrate the role of place in supervision.

Specifically, Madensen and Eck (2013) identify three types of places, each of which we see as having implications for an opportunity-reduction model of probation and parole. Proprietary places include owned locations at specific addresses, such as a house or a bar. Offender supervisors should be knowledgeable of the micro-settings that may prove to be problematic for their supervisees, and can develop specific case plan stipulations that eliminate access. Proximal places include clusters of proprietary places, such as a street segment. Probation and parole agencies should be aware of offenders' movements in and through these places, developing routines that help supervisees to avoid contact with criminogenic proximal places. Finally, pooled places include even larger aggregations of proprietary and proximal places, such as neighborhoods. Community corrections officers must be knowledgeable of the crime-conducive and -protective factors that are present in these areas, as offenders' routines must be redesigned with these realities in mind.

Probation and parole agents should be cognizant of the fact that places—whether an individual address, a small collection of these, or a larger neighborhood—are not themselves causes of crime. Rather, each of these physical places is host to social spaces; the place is a setting, containing activities, associates, antecedents, and antagonists that may encourage or facilitate crime (or, conversely, lack these criminogenic features or contain effective disruptions). Madensen and Eck (2013) describe several ways in which crime content is organized around places; again, we envision that these have implications for the ways in which probation and parole authorities should think about the environmental risks for recidivism that each offender has. Crime sites include places where offenses occur, and community corrections officers should consider the locations of their supervisees' past crimes. These places reveal a great deal of information about the stimuli that prompt offending and, as such, what factors should be addressed during supervision to avoid opportunities for recidivism. Convergent settings include places that bring together potential offenders, often with many non-offenders who are there for legitimate purposes (such as a transit hub). Probation and parole agents should recognize that their supervisees may not go out seeking to offend, but may routinely come into contact with these types of settings where the ingredients necessary for crime come together. Accordingly, offenders should be provided with supervision conditions that minimize access to these settings, or that provide explicit instructions for their prosocial use. Finally, comfort spaces include those places that offenders use to carry out their crimes, providing a space for meeting, supplying, and staging offenses. Again, community corrections officers can develop explicit directions that restrict their supervisees' access to these places.

In considering these ties between probation and parole and place, it is evident that offender supervision must be reoriented in several ways. In developing a community supervision paradigm that accounts for place-based criminogenic conditions, probation and parole authorities must be made aware of two key challenges. First, many agencies will have to modify how they conduct offender risk assessment. To prevent offenders from accessing crime opportunities, supervisors must first figure out not only what the relapse risks are for each offender but also *where they are located*. Second, community corrections officers must then develop strategies—which are reflected in case plans and supervision conditions—that implement these actuarial considerations. By addressing these challenges, probation and parole authorities will be able to steer their clients away from environments where crime opportunities abound and toward settings where prosocial influences are located. In short, assessing offenders' exposure and vulnerability to crime opportunities and then reducing those same opportunities with probation and parole supervision stipulations are integral to facilitating supervisees' lasting desistance from crime. These issues are examined in greater detail in the subsections that follow.

Rethinking Offender Risk Assessment

Designing probation and parole case plans that reduce offenders' *access to places* where the risks of reoffending are high requires that agencies first assess their clients' criminogenic risks and needs. Officers should ask themselves: What factors have triggered crime events for this offender in the past? Based on this offender's propensity, what situations might make this individual vulnerable to repeat offenses? Given this information, where are these crime opportunities located? How can we restructure this offender's routine activities so that these places are avoided? Finding valid and workable answers to these questions demands a reorientation to the intake, assessment, and case-planning processes that community corrections agencies administer. These updated considerations center around four themes: actuarialism, data collection and triangulation, crime opportunity identification, and geographic imagination.

Acutarialism. First, probation and parole authorities must participate in scientifically driven offender assessment, the merits of which have been thoroughly documented (Andrews and Bonta 2010; Bonta et al. 2008; Bonta, Wallace-Capretta, and Rooney 2000; Latessa and Holsinger 1998; Smith, Gendreau, and Swartz 2009). Rather than relying on subjective clinical judgments in determining offenders' risk of recidivism and the targets for change, supervisors must actuarially measure criminogenic needs. Existing risk-assessment instruments are used to identify the level and nature of supervisees' propensity to offend. Importantly, this same logic can be applied to community corrections supervision that emphasizes the importance of place. Thus, if we want to prevent probationers and parolees from committing additional crimes—such as preventing an offender's access to a crime-conducive place—then we must have a reliable estimate of what these specific risks are. Accordingly, probation and parole agencies should recognize that existing risk-assessment instruments need to be complemented by the use of empirically derived assessment instrumentation that is actuarial, measures place-based opportunities for offending, and is systematically administered.

Data Collection and Triangulation. That said, a second matter probation and parole officers should consider is new methods of collecting data in order to calculate these criminogenic risk factors. Corrections agencies should seek to triangulate traditional risk-assessment data, such as case file reviews and offender interviewing (which are undoubtedly helpful but also present limitations), with innovative methods and novel information (see Schaefer et al. 2016). For example, officers might consider shadowing their clients to observe their daily routines, taking note of any objectively risky situations that the offender encounters and what outlets for prosocial activities are available. Offender supervisors may also find it helpful to discuss the offender's past behaviors and future prospects with the individual's family members and friends, employers and work colleagues, or community mentors ("crime controllers") to help generate ideas about how to prevent recidivism. Actuarial assessment of criminogenic risks and needs is vital, and officers must be informed about the actual challenges their clients will face. Using different modes of data collection to gather variable kinds of information will help to ensure that the supervision case plan is tailored to the unique crime opportunities of each individual offender.

Crime Opportunity Identification. Building on this point, a third insight of environmental corrections is that offender supervisors must identify opportunities for relapse rather than measuring propensity alone (Cullen et al. 2002; Schaefer et al. 2016). When thinking about the development of events that lead to a crime, there are several distinguishable catalyzing factors. These "crime precipitators" (Schaefer 2013) can be addressed through conditions of supervision in order to reduce the opportunities for offending that probationers and parolees encounter (Taxman 2011). Although the external "causes" of crime are innumerable, it is instructive to think about three categories: associates, provocations, and time.

Having antisocial associates is one of the strongest predictors of offending (Andrews and Bonta 2010; Gendreau 1996). Whether through the learning and reinforcement of antisocial attitudes, the supply of the tools needed to commit crime, or actual co-offending, the peer systems of probationers and parolees can be highly instrumental in promoting recidivism. Using social network analyses, community corrections officers can evaluate the potential for crime opportunities when their clients interact with certain associates. Rather than simply stating that supervisees must stay away from all "known offenders" (a stipulation devoid of definitional specificity and difficult to monitor or enforce), offender supervisors should rather seek to identify those with whom the client is likely to get into trouble. A list of prohibited contacts may include past co-offenders, but might also incorporate associates that correspond with non-criminal activities that oftentimes lead to crime (such as heavy drinking with a friend or a hostile romantic relationship). The goal for probation and parole officers is to classify which of an offender's peers create or encourage the pursuit of opportunities for crime.

Additionally, community corrections agencies will want to identify the conditions that provoke clients to behave criminally. There are too many "crime-causing" variables to try and control each one; rather, probation and parole officers should design case plans that address the precise situational inducements that lead the offender to the offense (Cornish and Clarke 2003; Wortley 2001). Common prompts for crime include motivation/expected rewards, key emotions, types of social settings, intoxicants, or processual cues. Many of these prompts can be tied to specific activities. As opposed to prohibiting offenders from all activities believed to be indirectly related to recidivism (e.g., abstaining from all alcohol consumption), officers will be better served when they isolate the riskiest catalysts for crime for each individual offender.

Highly correlated with socializing and situations that contain prompts is time—both the day of the week (perhaps even the segment of the month or the season of the year) and the hour of the day. Criminal activities are often patterned and tend to concentrate in certain times, such as offending hotspots in liquor establishments at nighttime or spikes in theft in a city center during workdays (Ratcliffe 2010). There is clearly nothing criminogenic about times or days themselves (that is, 4:00 p.m. on a Monday or midnight on a Saturday cannot *cause* crime), yet who the offender is with and what they are doing at those times can lead to crime. Thus, the opportunities for recidivism can be observed in these temporal hotspots. This is important for probation and parole case planning, as these high-risk times can be addressed through supervision restrictions or the substitution of prosocial activities.

With these considerations in mind—the role of antisocial peers, prompts for crime events, and time in leading to reoffending—we can see that an organizing category for these crime opportunities can be identified: *place*. This insight is central to the development of a *corrections of place*. Certain places will contain co-offenders or wayward friends and provocations for criminal behavior; further, the merging of these people and events with places is often dependent on time. Thus, community corrections agents who want to prevent their clients from encountering risky people or crime-conducive activities must also consider the influence of place. Chances to commit crime are everywhere, but they are more or less present, obvious, and attractive in certain places, which probation and parole authorities must identify.

Geographic Imagination. As such, the fourth and final theme in rethinking offender assessment is the development of a geographic imagination. Crime analysts have long relied on spatial presentations of data, from isolating hotspots of arrests or locating concentrations of repeat civil calls for service, to evaluating the diffusion and displacement of crime following an intervention. Importantly, using general knowledge about the causes of crime, analysts can also map where opportunities for crime are likely to be concentrated. This capacity becomes even more useful for probation and parole officers who are able to incorporate specific information gained from the assessment processes completed with their clients (Schaefer 2013). Gathering information about the crime precipitators discussed earlier will reveal a great deal about places that may lead a supervisee to offend. Officers can likewise rely on past offending locales (proprietary places that operate as crime sites and comfort spaces) and neighborhood crime hotspots (proximal and pooled places that serve as convergent settings) to pinpoint risky places. With all of these data combined, probation and parole agencies can use mapping technologies that isolate the risks and resources in the offender's neighborhood, identifying potential safe zones or restricted areas as they relate to crime opportunities (Reentry Policy Council 2005; Solomon 2006; Solomon et al. 2008; Taxman 2006). The information gained from these assessments can then be applied to the development of an offender's case plan. Adjusting the goal of supervision to one of opportunity reduction (as opposed to control or deterrence) requires that community corrections agencies consider the role of place. Incorporating place-based supervision conditions will also mandate a new framework for probation and parole, discussed in the guiding principles that follow.

Rethinking Offender Supervision

It is evident that prevailing probation and parole practices are largely ineffective. Whether due to an overemphasis on control, a failure to reduce criminogenic risks, or an atheoretical reliance on generic service brokerage, community supervision is not working well; offenders are not regularly deterred, and public safety is not enhanced. What might be done differently then? As presented in this chapter, one possibility is to reorient offender supervision toward the reduction of criminal opportunity. For this transformation to occur, probation and parole officers must identify what makes a crime occur. More specifically, what are the precise reoffending risks unique to an individual offender?

The previous section highlighted the relevance of place in organizing information about an offender's opportunities to recidivate. Crimes are concentrated in space, so the opportunities that make those crimes possible are grouped, as well. Generally speaking, offenders do not randomly encounter or take advantage of chances to commit crime; rather, the precipitators to a crime event are clustered in certain crime-conductive places. As such, in looking at who the offender gets into trouble with and what kinds of activities precede offending (and then what times these associations and behaviors are taking place), probation and parole officers can determine *where* these risks are located. Community corrections agencies must start to map their clients' crime opportunities, whether literally (such as through spatial offense analyses) or conceptually (by drawing associations between specific risks and the environments where they are housed). With this information in hand, probation and parole officers can develop supervision case plans that emphasize place-based opportunity reduction.

Recalling the elements of a crime—a motivated offender, a suitable target, and the absence of capable guardianship—will help to inform effective opportunity-reduction supervision strategies. Probation and parole practices must be organized in a way that helps offenders to (1) prevent becoming motivated to commit crime, (2) avoid attractive targets, and (3) be surrounded by guardians who discourage crime. This framing is not merely ideological, but rather implicates techniques by which offender supervisors can reduce the crime opportunities of their clients. In this section, two outlets are presented that integrate these goals into opportunity-reduction case plans. First, offenders' daily routines can be structured through supervision stipulations so that crime opportunity hotspots are not only circumvented, but also replaced with hotbeds of prosocial influences. Second, people who help to prevent offenders from encountering and taking advantage of crime opportunities (such as relatives, mentors, and place managers) can be recruited to support the stipulations of the case plan and encourage prosocial change (Taxman, Young, and Byrne 2004). Taken together, these strategies can diminish the real chances to reoffend that probationers and parolees are likely to be exposed to and tempted by.

Redesigning Routine Activities. If crime occurs when a person with criminal propensity meets an opportunity to offend (Clarke 2012; Cohen and Felson 1979), then probation and parole supervision effectiveness can be enhanced by reducing motivation and controlling chances to commit crime (Cullen et al. 2002; Taxman et al. 2006). When offenders are assessed in order to design community corrections case plans, clear patterns often emerge. Supervision officers may note that their clients get into trouble when certain conditions are present—that is, when elements of a crime event converge. Likewise, offender evaluations may indicate when supervisees are *not* getting into trouble—other conditions may be present in those situations, or the "crime-causing" variables may simply be absent. Seen in this light, community-supervised offenders should not be seen as perpetually motivated criminals who go out looking for trouble (although these offenders do exist, the proportion is likely small compared to situationally motivated offenders). Instead, in the course of their daily activities, offenders may come into contact with the opportunity to commit crime (or have their motivation heightened) as a matter of routine (Felson and Clarke 1998). That is, although criminal propensity may be somewhat stable, the motivation to act can be suppressed or catalyzed depending on an offender's surroundings (Horney, Osgood, and Marshall 1995). For this reason, it is vital for probation and parole officers to develop supervision stipulations that redesign offenders' routine activities, steering them away from places that contain crime opportunities and toward places that contain desistance opportunities.

In the first instance, places that represent risks for relapse must be avoided. As discussed earlier, opportunity-reduction case plans must reflect the *actual* recidivism risks of each offender, based on information about past crime opportunities of which the offender took advantage. However, it may also be helpful for supervising officers to be knowledgeable about generally high-risk areas in the community that their clients may be susceptible to (Solomon et al. 2008; Taxman 2006). While there is nothing inherently criminogenic about a particular location, the situation that that place presents may be more likely to lead to crime than alternatives (Clarke 2008; Cornish and Clarke 2003). Places may be crime-conducive for a number of reasons (Madensen and Eck 2013). Thus, likely co-offenders, rivals, or victims may be present there (Farrell 1995; Felson 2003); the tools or facilitators needed to commit crime may be located there (Clarke and Eck 2005); the motivation to offend may be created by situations there (e.g., substance use or emotional volatility; Cornish and Clarke 2003); or the social environment there may condone offending (Anderson 1999; Cornish and Clarke 2008; Topalli 2005). Yet keeping offenders away from these risky places must extend beyond general supervision stipulations (e.g., "Probationer Smith is forbidden from socializing with known offenders.") that are unhelpfully vague and impossible to monitor. Rather, case plans must prohibit access to clearly identified places that contain specific inducements for crime that are known to be attractive opportunities for the given individual offender being supervised. In practice, this means that probation and parole officers must develop a new set of routine activities—a daily schedule of events including restrictions and obligations (see Schaefer 2013 for examples)—that navigates offenders away from crime opportunities not by mandate or force alone, but also by structure and prosocial reinforcement (Farrall 2002; National Research Council 2008).

In the second instance, then, places that represent chances to "go straight" must be integrated into offenders' daily routines. Behavior modification principles assert that activity patterns are not eliminated so much as they are replaced (Spiegler and Guevremont 2009); in community corrections, it is insufficient to prohibit a lifestyle alone, so agencies must provide alternatives (Maruna and Roy 2007). Indeed, avoiding crime opportunities altogether is a noble ideal and part of the solution, but compliance and desistance may be facilitated more effectively if prosocial substitutes are provided (Farrall 2002; Jannetta et al. 2009). By embedding offenders in prosocial routines, not only are they steering clear of temptations for relapse, but they are also developing anti-crime attitudes (Giordano, Cernkovich, and Rudolph 2002; LeBel, Burnett, Maruna, and Bushway 2008). Routine activities that substitute high-risk places with low-risk places not only diminish crime opportunities, but also expose offenders to prosocial role models, positive reinforcement for prosocial behavior, and chances to develop a prosocial identity (Kazemian 2007; Laub and Sampson 2001, 2003; Paternoster and Bushway 2009). The relationship between propensity and opportunity is reciprocal: prosocial activities can lead to prosocial thinking and vice versa, whereas antisocial attitudes can lead to antisocial behavior and vice versa (Bottoms, Shapland, Costello, Holmes, and Muir 2004; Schaefer 2013). Consequently, rather than trying to control access to crime-conducive places alone, probation and parole officers must work to enmesh their clients in daily routines that are anti-crime.

Recruiting Crime Controllers. Crime opportunities abound, and community corrections officers cannot constantly monitor high-risk places. Even when a thoughtfully produced opportunity-reduction case plan is in place, offender supervisors cannot guarantee that their clients will abide by the stipulations contained therein. Consequently, it is helpful for probation and parole authorities to incorporate the assistance of partners—people who can

(1) discourage offenders from attending crime-conducive places, (2) monitor offenders for compliance with supervision conditions and report violations, and (3) reduce the crime opportunities that exist in certain places. These people, collectively referred to as "crime controllers" (Eck 1994; Felson 1986, 1995), can not only prohibit access to situations where recidivism risks are high, but are also instrumental in promoting desistance. All three types of crime controllers can contribute to opportunity-reduction supervision, illustrated next.

First, offender handlers include people who can influence the behaviors of probationers and parolees. Formally, community corrections and police officers exert control over these offenders. Informally, supervisees' family, friends, colleagues, and community mentors can be recruited to participate in the supervision process. Research demonstrates that desistance is more likely for offenders with strong interpersonal relationships and community ties (National Research Council 2008; Warr 1998). This process is instrumental for probation and parole through three outlets. Foremost, an offender's social network can encourage offenders to "go straight," modeling anti-crime attitudes and enmeshing offenders into prosocial activities (Solomon et al. 2008; Taxman et al. 2004). Next, handlers are excellent agents of informal social control, and can actively discourage offenders from violating conditions of their supervision or attending risky places (Taxman 2006). Finally, those individuals in close contact with supervisees can monitor the offender for compliance with the case plan, notifying the community corrections officer of any problems (Reentry Policy Council 2005). Probation and parole authorities cannot watch all offenders at all times, so additional agents can be relied upon for surveillance. Not only will offenders be deterred from going to crime-conducive places if they know that many people are aware of their supervision conditions, but offenders may also be more inclined to heed the advice of an intimate other as opposed to the command of a corrections agent.

Second, target guardians include those individuals that can protect victims and help make targets less attractive. Many guardianship interventions can be incorporated into probation and parole supervision, such as through victim and neighborhood notifications about offenders returning to the area, or neighborhood watch, community safety, and target hardening initiatives (Reinventing Probation Council 2000). Additionally, community corrections partnerships with police are useful in implementing techniques of situational crime prevention (Clarke 1992; Ekblom 2011; Jannetta and Lachman 2011). The police are experts at crime prevention, and when provided with information about places that are risks for recidivism among probationers and parolees, officers can control access to those places and harden the targets that are tempting for offenders (Weisburd, Groff, and Yang 2014). Upon identification of problematic targets and places, police partnerships with probation and parole can deter offenders from encountering and pursuing crime opportunities (Parent and Snyder

1999); the police can help to inform community corrections authorities about crime-conducive places, and the police can monitor those places for restricted probationers and parolees.

Third, place managers include owners (and their representatives) of spaces, such as a supervisor at a business, a homeowner, or a bartender. Probation and parole authorities have information about the features of these spaces that lead to crime there. By working with place managers of high-risk spaces, crime opportunities can often be reduced (Cherney 2008). Community corrections officers know about the situations that lead to offending among their clients, but they may need help in eliminating those opportunities at their source. Particularly in partnership with police agencies and regulatory organizations, recidivism can be reduced by making changes to crime-conducive conditions in crime opportunity hotspots; whether through voluntary participation (place managers may heartily engage in crime prevention if given the knowledge and tools) or coerced through legal levers (such as through third party policing), probation and parole agencies can ensure fewer crimes among their clients by eliminating the opportunities for relapse.

Using the recommendations described here repositions probation and parole officers as "super controllers" (Sampson, Eck, and Dunham 2010). Super controllers are individuals and institutions that can develop incentives for the people who influence the actions of offenders, through both formal and informal social control; this can occur through encouragements or through deterrents, and can motivate prosocial behavior or limit criminal behavior. Aside from their roles as front-line offender handlers, offender supervisors also act as super controllers, soliciting and regulating the actions of other handlers, guardians, and managers in the reduction of opportunities for offending. Probation, parole, and police agencies are all formal authorities, and can compel compliance (such as through civic regulations) from contributors to crime problems when necessary (Mazerolle and Ransley 2005). Importantly, however, supervising officers can also solicit the involvement of people who can contribute to offenders' desistance by helping to establish cognitions and routines that avoid crime opportunities. In this way, chances for reoffending are controlled, but alternatives for prosociality are provided, as well.

Thinking About Place

Using insights from environmental criminology, this chapter has advanced tenets of an opportunity-reduction framework for probation and parole. We argue that the efficacy of corrections interventions might be enhanced by tailoring probation and parole conditions to the real crime opportunities of individual offenders. After an actuarial and triangulated offender assessment, supervision stipulations can be implemented that steer offenders away from places that are high-risk, and toward environments that are filled with prosocial influences. While this orientation to community corrections has the potential to significantly disrupt the process by which offenders encounter chances to commit crime, the other part of the crime event equation—propensity—incites two important issues.

First, no matter the strength of assessment or case plan design, some crime opportunities will remain unknown and unaccounted for. Perhaps the data collected are inaccurate or incomplete, new crime-conducive places emerge, or offenders are tempted by different things throughout their supervision term. No matter the case, corrections officials must acknowledge that their clients will occasionally find themselves in situations that may lead to crime. Second, no matter the degree of control exercised through supervision stipulations, some offenders will actively seek out environments that contain triggers for relapse. This is not to say that these offenders are intending to commit crime, but more that they have difficulty identifying risky situations and selecting appropriate responses. For these two reasons, reducing offenders' exposure to crime opportunities must also address the component of propensity.

It is important to note, however, that many offenders are not perpetually motivated to commit crime; many probationers and parolees do not go out looking for chances to recidivate. Offenders may become inclined to commit crime only when presented with the opportunity to do so. Far from the situation being accidental or serendipitous, offenders oftentimes lack the decision-making skills necessary to avoid high-risk environments. Consequently, here we draw an essential distinction, recognizing a difference between persistent propensity and situational propensity. In the former category, the motivation to offend is deep-seated and not easily adjusted by probation and parole authorities. In the latter category, criminal motivation is seen as circumstantially dependent and capable of being circumvented. To contribute toward relapse reduction, then, offender supervisors must provide offenders with the skillsets to avoid and resist available crime opportunities.

One method through which to accomplish this task is cognitive skills training. Correctional interventions that rely on cognitive-behavioral techniques are the most effective in reducing the propensity to offend (Gendreau, Smith, and French 2006; Landenberger and Lipsey 2005; Lipsey, Landenberger, and Wilson 2007; Pearson et al. 2002). These interventions help offenders to link thoughts with actions through mental restructuring, skill building, and reinforcement (Andrew and Bonta 2010; O'Donohue and Fisher 2012). Within the context of a "corrections of place," cognitive-behavioral methods can help to make offenders less likely to pursue crime opportunities and to remodel offenders' perceptions about crime and place (Schaefer et al. 2016). Because crime opportunities will invariably remain, probation and parole officers would be wise to teach their clients how to deal with those situations. This is achieved through two outlets. First, community corrections agents must teach *opportunity avoidance*, in which offenders are provided with the decision-making skills necessary to foresee and bypass crime-conducive situations. Second, supervisees must be trained in *opportunity resistance*, whereby offenders enhance their capacity to withstand chances to commit crime that they are presented with. Having fewer motivated offenders will translate into less crime. Reducing motivation, and therefore emboldening desistance, begins with altering the way offenders appraise situations and select behaviors—we want offenders to think about settings differently so that they behave differently.

Avoiding Crime Opportunities

One of the best ways for probationers and parolees to avoid crime-conducive places is to establish corrections case plans that outline low-risk routine activities. Opportunities to commit crime can be avoided with informed supervision stipulations, but the reality is that offenders will still have to make daily choices about how and where to spend their time. These remaining freedoms offer risks of relapse, but also allow community corrections clients to rehearse the skills needed to remain crime-free upon expiration of the supervision term. The process of evaluating situations for crime opportunities, and then identifying and acting upon the low-risk option, are specialized skills that must be learned, rehearsed, and reinforced. Effective cognitive-behavioral techniques exist that allow probation and parole agencies to provide their supervisees with these skills (such as skills training in consequential thinking). By helping offenders to (1) forecast the features of a place (such as who will be there and what kinds of activities will occur), (2) envision the likely outcomes of going there, and (3) make the prosocial choice, crime opportunities can be avoided.

Resisting Crime Opportunities

Chances to commit crime abound, and while opportunity avoidance skills and prosocial routine activity case plans can decrease access to these high-risk places, offenders will undoubtedly be confronted with tempting situations. In order to best prevent recidivism, then, probation and parole agents must teach offenders the skills needed to resist remaining crime opportunities. To do so, officers must alter the decision-making processes that their clients experience when faced with relapse risks. The overarching goal is to restructure the thought process of offenders so that the traditional linkages between environmental triggers and criminal behavior are broken, and replaced instead with resistance. Probation and parole staff can teach their supervisees (such as through cognitive skills trainings involving coping skills and problem-solving) how to assess their environment and resist opportunities to offend.

Involving Offenders

The central thesis of this chapter is that in order to prevent community-supervised offenders from recidivating, routine activities must be redesigned so that places containing risky crime opportunities are avoided and replaced with places that contain supports for desistance. To achieve this ideal, a case plan must be developed that strategically accounts for an offender's actual exposure and vulnerability to opportunities for relapse. Thus, supervision conditions must be customized to the risk level, criminogenic needs, and responsivity considerations of each probationer or parolee (Andrews and Bonta 2010; Taxman 2012). To steer offenders away from crime-conducive places and toward locales that contain prosocial influences, probation and parole agents must know where these places are, and what triggers these environments contain. How can this information be gained?

In addition to accessing an offender's records, conducting formal assessments, and learning about high-crime areas in an offender's community generally, one effective strategy is to involve offenders in the development of the community supervision case plan (Solomon et al. 2008). Offenders provide invaluable detail about the opportunities that they themselves are tempted by, and they may also be more likely to abide by supervision conditions that they help create (McMurran 2009). Probation and parole officers can communicate the rationale that guides the prescription of supervision goals and restrictions to their clients; this cooperative process often motivates offenders to actively participate toward desistance as opposed to complying due to threats of sanctions (Walters, Clark, Gingerich, and Meltzer 2007).

It is vital to offenders' lasting success—and thus toward the protection of public safety—that corrections interventions prompt behavioral *change* and not just behavioral *control* (Labrecque, Smith, Schweitzer, and Thompson 2013; Taxman et al. 2003). Accordingly, similar to efforts to treat propensity, efforts to reduce crime opportunities must be part of a general human services approach to offender rehabilitation (Andrews and Bonta 2010). Opportunity reduction is not intended to place offenders within an iron cage of control from which they cannot escape. Rather, opportunity reduction is to be pursued through an ethic of care in which diverting offenders from criminogenic places is seen as an integral part of correctional *rehabilitation*, not correctional control. The goal is to help offenders govern their lives more effectively and to avoid places that can lure them back into crime.

Toward the goal of change, soliciting the input of offenders is one method of customizing supervision case plans to the real crime opportunities that they will encounter. Moreover, the stipulations that offenders themselves help develop have incentives to "go straight" built-in. A similar mechanism to help offenders reintegrate is wraparound care, in which the family, friends, and community of the probationer or parolee take part in the supervision. Some offenders may be more greatly deterred by informal social control (such as pressure from a family member) than by formal punishment. Yet beyond deterrence and control, people with whom the offender interacts with frequently are in a prime position to encourage and support desistance and to provide opportunities for a prosocial lifestyle (National Research Council 2008; Taxman, Shepardson, and Byrne 2004; see also Laub and Sampson 2003).

Conclusion

In the United States, one in 48 adults is under community correctional supervision (Glaze and Bonczar 2011) at the cost of $12.9 billion annually (Kyckelhahn 2012). Freedoms are restricted and resources are expended because we believe that we are preventing crime, enhancing public safety, and bettering the lives of supervisees. Unfortunately, research demonstrates that standard models of probation and parole supervision are in many ways ineffective, leading criminologists to ask what might be done differently (Cullen et al. 2002). Drawing on an extensive body of research, evidence-based best practices are mounting that demonstrate how to reduce offending: address offender propensity (such as through the risk-need-responsivity model of effective correctional intervention; Andrews and Bonta 2010) and minimize crime opportunities (such as through problem-oriented crime prevention initiatives; Clarke 2010; Laycock 2005).

Sadly, the principles of effective correctional treatment and opportunity reduction are not regularly embodied in the standard delivery of offender supervision in the community. Rather, probation and parole officers too often adapt by falling into bureaucratic routines that emphasize case management and service brokerage above actual intervention (Schaefer et al. 2016). The assignment of high case loads, of course, contributes to such reactive supervision methods. But another contributing factor is the atheoretical nature of community corrections. By contrast, over the past two decades, policing has experienced a dramatic transformation guided by a new conceptual framework whose variants have adopted such labels as "broken-windows policing," "hotspots policing," and "problem-oriented policing" (Weisburd and Braga 2006). Even in the face of limited resources, police departments have focused attention on high-risk places based on a clear theory of proactive, innovative enforcement strategies. In the same way, offender supervision might be reinvented if it were guided by a new conceptual framework, rooted in the empirical research—opportunity-reduction supervision. As this chapter has detailed, the effectiveness of probation and parole depends on administrators understanding and implementing in their agencies a supervision model aimed at reducing opportunities for reoffending. This approach would involve (1) the creation of supervision case plans that establish new routine activities to guide offenders away from crime opportunities and toward prosocial influences, and (2) training offenders to think differently about crime opportunities so that they can make responsible choices.

The role of place is central to this model of opportunity-reduction supervision. Crime opportunities, and the temptations and facilitators for such, are concentrated in certain areas (Weisburd et al. 2012). Just as there are crime hotspots, so too are there clusters of chances to commit crime. Using specialized assessment technologies and case-planning processes (see Schaefer et al. 2016), supervision officers can steer offenders away from environments that contain relapse triggers and toward situations that are low-risk and contribute to desistance. By limiting access to places that are associated with temptations to commit crime (such as certain antisocial associates and activities), the process that leads offenders to take advantage of crime opportunities is disrupted. The logic that having fewer crime opportunities means less recidivism does not necessarily require that criminogenic places be altered. Rather, probation and parole supervision can be redesigned to structure offenders' lives in ways that routinely limit access to crime-conducive places (and the correlates housed therein), introduce new agents of crime control, and fill offenders' time with prosocial reinforcements (Cullen et al. 2002). Taken together, the tenets of opportunity-reduction supervision presented in this chapter rely on the knowledge of what works in preventing crime: by focusing on how community corrections clients interact with places and the crime opportunities located there, chances for recidivism are limited.

References

Anderson, Elijah. 1999. *Code of the Street: Decency, Violence, and the Moral Life of the Inner City*. New York, NY: W. W. Norton.

Andrews, D. A. 1995. "The Psychology of Criminal Conduct and Effective Treatment." Pp. 35–62 in James McGuire (ed.), *What Works: Reducing Reoffending: Guidelines from Research and Practice*. New York, NY: John Wiley.

Andrews, D.A., and James Bonta. 2010. *The Psychology of Criminal Conduct* (5th ed.). New Providence, NJ: Anderson/LexisNexis.

Andrews, .D, A., Ivan Zinger, Robert D. Hoge, James Bonta, Paul Gendreau, and Francis T. Cullen. 1990. "Does Correctional Treatment Work? A Clinically Relevant and Psychologically Informed Meta-Analysis." *Criminology* 28: 369–404.

Bonta, James, Tanya Rugge, Terri-Lynne Scott, Guy Bourgon, and Annie K. Yessine. 2008. "Exploring the Black Box of Community Supervision." *Journal of Offender Rehabilitation* 47: 248–270.

Bonta, James, Suzanne Wallace-Capretta, and Jennifer Rooney. 2000. "A Quasi-Experimental Evaluation of an Intensive Rehabilitation Supervision Program." *Criminal Justice and Behavior* 27: 312–329.

Bottoms, Anthony, Joanna Shapland, Andrew Costello, Deborah Holmes, and Grant Muir. 2004. "Towards Desistance: Theoretical Underpinnings for an Empirical Study." *The Howard Journal* 43: 368–389.

Cherney, Adrian. 2008. "Harnessing the Crime Control Capacities of Third Parties." *Policing: An International Journal of Police Strategies and Management* 31: 631–647.

Clarke, Ronald V. 1992. *Situational Crime Prevention: Successful Case Studies*. Albany, NY: Harrow and Heston.

Clarke, Ronald V. 1997. *Situational Crime Prevention: Successful Case Studies* (2nd ed.). Albany, NY: Harrow and Heston.

Clarke, Ronald V. 2008. "Situational Crime Prevention." Pp. 178–194 in Richard Wortley and Lorraine Mazerolle (eds.), *Environmental Criminology and Crime Analysis*. Cullumpton, UK: Willan.

Clarke, Ronald V. 2010. "Crime Science." Pp. 272–283 in Eugene McLaughlin and Tim Newburn (eds.), *The Sage Handbook of Criminological Theory*. Thousand Oaks, CA: Sage.

Clarke, Ronald V. 2012. "Opportunity Makes the Thief: Really? And So What?" *Crime Science* 1: 3.

Clarke, Ronald V., and John E. Eck. 2005. *Crime Analysis for Problem Solvers in 60 Small Steps*. Washington, DC: Office of Community Oriented Policing Services, U.S. Department of Justice.

Clear, Todd R. 1996. "Toward a Corrections of 'Place': The Challenge of 'Community' in Corrections." *National Institute of Justice Journal* 231: 52–56.

Clear, Todd R., and Ron P. Corbett. 1999. "Community Corrections of Place." *Perspectives* 23: 24–31.

Cohen, Lawrence E., and Marcus Felson. 1979. "Social Change and Crime Rate Trends: A Routine Activity Approach." *American Sociological Review* 44: 588–608.

Cornish, Derek B., and Ronald V. Clarke. 2003. "Opportunities, Precipitators and Criminal Decisions: A Reply to Wortley's Critique of Situational Crime Prevention." *Crime Prevention Studies* 16: 41–96.

Cornish, Derek B., and Ronald V. Clarke. 2008. "The Rational Choice Perspective." Pp. 21–47 in Richard Wortley and Lorraine Mazerolle (eds.), *Environmental Criminology and Crime Analysis*. Cullumpton, UK: Willan.

Cozens, Paul. 2008. "Crime Prevention through Environmental Design." Pp. 153–177 in Richard Wortley and Lorraine Mazerolle (eds.), *Environmental Criminology and Crime Analysis*. Cullumpton, UK: Willan.

Cullen, Francis T., John E. Eck, and Christopher E. Lowenkamp. 2002. "Environmental Corrections: A New Paradigm for Effective Probation and Parole Supervision." *Federal Probation* 66(2): 28–37.

Cullen, Francis T., and Paul Gendreau. 2000. "Assessing Correctional Rehabilitation: Policy, Practice, and Prospects." Pp. 109–175 in Julie Horney (ed.), *Criminal Justice 2000: Vol. 3. Policies, Processes, and Decisions of the Criminal Justice System*. Washington, DC: National Institute of Justice.

Cullen, Francis T., and Cheryl Lero Jonson. 2011. "Rehabilitation and Treatment Programs." Pp. 293–344 in James Q. Wilson and Joan Petersilia (eds.), *Crime and Public Policy*. New York, NY: Oxford University Press.

Cullen, Francis T., Cheryl Lero Jonson, and Daniel S. Nagin. 2011. "Prisons Do Not Reduce Recidivism: The High Cost of Ignoring Science." *The Prison Journal* 91: 48S–65S.

Cullen, Francis T., Travis C. Pratt, Sharon Levrant Miceli, and Melissa M. Moon. 2002. "Dangerous Liaison? Rational Choice Theory as the Basis for Correctional Intervention." Pp. 279–296 in Alex R. Piquero and Stephen G. Tibbetts (eds.), *Rational Choice and Criminal Behavior: Recent Research and Future Challenges*. New York, NY: Routledge.

Cullen, Francis T., John Paul Wright, and Brandon K. Applegate. 1996. "Control in the Community: The Limits of Reform?" Pp. 69–116 in Alan T. Harland (ed.), *Choosing Correctional Interventions That Work: Defining the Demand and Evaluating the Supply*. Newbury Park, CA: Sage.

Eck, John E. 1994. *Drug Markets and Drug Places: A Case-Control Study of the Spatial Structure of Illicit Drug Dealing*. Unpublished Doctoral Dissertation. University of Maryland, College Park.

Ekblom, Paul. 2011. "Deconstructing CPTED . . . and Reconstructing It for Practice, Knowledge Management and Research." *European Journal on Criminal Policy and Research* 17: 7–28.

Farrall, Stephen. 2002. *Rethinking What Works with Offenders: Probation, Social Context and Desistance from Crime.* Cullompton, UK: Willan.

Farrell, Graham. 1995. "Preventing Repeat Victimization." Pp. 469–534 in Michael Tonry and David Farrington (eds.), *Building a Safer Society: Strategic Approaches to Crime Prevention: Crime and Justice, Vol. 19.* Chicago, IL: University of Chicago Press.

Felson, Marcus. 1986. "Linking Criminal Choices, Routine Activities, Informal Control, and Criminal Outcomes." Pp. 119–128 in Derek B. Cornish and Ronald V. Clarke (eds.), *The Reasoning Criminal: Rational Choice Perspectives on Offending.* New York, NY: Springer-Verlag.

Felson, Marcus. 1995. "Those Who Discourage Crime." Pp. 53–66 in John E. Eck and David Weisburd (eds.), *Crime Places in Crime Theory.* Monsey, NY: Criminal Justice Press.

Felson, Marcus. 2003. "The Process of Co-Offending." Pp. 149–168 in Martha J. Smith and Derek B. Cornish (eds.), *Theory for Practice in Situational Crime Prevention.* Monsey, NY: Criminal Justice Press.

Felson, Marcus, and Ronald V. Clarke. 1998. *Opportunity Makes the Thief: Practical Theory for Crime Prevention.* London: Policing and Reducing Crime Unit, Home Office.

Gendreau, Paul. 1996. "The Principles of Effective Intervention with Offenders." Pp. 117–130 in Alan T. Harland (ed.), *Choosing Correctional Interventions That Work: Defining the Demand and Evaluating the Supply.* Newbury Park, CA: Sage.

Gendreau, Paul, Francis T. Cullen, and James Bonta. 1994. "Intensive Rehabilitation Supervision: The Next Generation in Community Corrections?" *Federal Probation* 58(1): 72–78.

Gendreau, Paul, Claire Goggin, Francis T. Cullen, and Donald A. Andrews. 2000. "The Effects of Community Sanctions and Incarceration on Recidivism." *Forum on Corrections Research* 12(May): 10–13.

Gendreau, Paul, Tracy Little, and Claire Goggin. 1996. "A Meta-Analysis of the Predictors of Adult Offender Recidivism: What Works!" *Criminology* 34: 575–607.

Gendreau, Paul, Paula Smith, and Sheila French. 2006. "The Theory of Effective Correctional Intervention: Empirical Status and Future Directions." Pp. 419–446 in Francis T. Cullen, John Paul Wright, and Kristie R. Blevins (eds.), *Taking Stock: The Status of Criminological Theory: Advances in Criminological Theory, Vol. 15.* New Brunswick, NJ: Transaction Publishers.

Giordano, Peggy C., Stephen A. Cernkovich, and Jennifer L. Rudolph. 2002. "Gender, Crime, and Desistance: Toward a Theory of Cognitive Transformation." *American Journal of Sociology* 107: 990–1064.

Glaze, Thomas P., and Lauren E. Bonczar. 2011. *Probation and Parole in the United States, 2010.* Washington, DC: Bureau of Justice Statistics, Office of Justice Programs, U.S. Department of Justice.

Horney, Julie, D. Wayne Osgood, and Ineke Haen Marshall. 1995. "Criminal Careers in the Short-Term: Intra-Individual Variabilty in Crime and Its Relation to Local Life Circumstances." *American Sociological Review* 60: 655–673.

Jannetta, Jesse, Brian Elderbroom, Amy L. Solomon, Meagan Cahill, Barbara Parthasarathy, and William D. Burrell. 2009. *An Evolving Field: Findings from the 2008 Parole Practices Survey.* Washington, DC: Urban Institute.

Jannetta, Jesse, and Pamela Lachman. 2011. *Promoting Partnerships between Police and Community Supervision Agencies.* Washington, DC: Office of Community Oriented Policing Services, U.S. Department of Justice.

Kazemian, Lila. 2007. "Desistance from Crime: Theoretical, Empirical, Methodological, and Policy Considerations." *Journal of Contemporary Criminal Justice* 23: 5–27.

Kleiman, Mark A. R. 2009. *When Brute Force Fails: How to Have Less Crime and Less Punishment*. Princeton, NJ: Princeton University Press.

Kyckelhahn., Tracey. 2012. *State Corrections Expenditures, FY 1982–2010*. Washington, DC: Bureau of Justice Statistics, Office of Justice Programs, U.S. Department of Justice.

Labrecque, Ryan M., Paula Smith, Myrinda Schweitzer, and Cara Thompson. 2013. "Targeting Antisocial Attitudes in Community Supervision Using the EPICS Model: An Examination of Change Scores on the Criminal Sentiment Scale." *Federal Probation* 16(3): 15–20.

Landenberger, Nana A., and Mark W. Lipsey. 2005. "The Positive Effects of Cognitive-Behavioral Programs for Offenders: A Meta-Analysis of Factors Associated with Effective Treatment." *Journal of Experimental Criminology* 1: 451–476.

Latessa, Edward J., ed. 1999. *Strategic Solutions: The International Community Corrections Association Examines Substance Abusers*. Lanham, MD: American Correctional Association.

Latessa, Edward J., Francis T. Cullen, and Paul Gendreau. 2002. "Beyond Correctional Quackery: Professionalism and the Possibility of Effective Treatment." *Federal Probation* 66(2): 43–49.

Latessa, Edward J., and Alexander M. Holsinger. 1998. "The Importance of Evaluating Correctional Programs: Assessing Outcome and Quality." *Corrections Management Quarterly* 2(4): 22–29.

Latessa, Edward J., and Christopher Lowenkamp. 2006. "What Works in Reducing Recidivism." *University of St. Thomas Law Journal* 3: 521–535.

Laub, John H., and Robert J. Sampson. 2001. "Understanding Desistance from Crime." Pp. 1–69 in Michael Tonry (ed.), *Crime and Justice: A Review of Research, Vol. 28*. Chicago, IL: University of Chicago Press.

Laub, John H., and Robert J. Sampson. 2003. *Shared Beginnings, Divergent Lives: Delinquent Boys to Age 70*. Cambridge, MA: Harvard University Press.

Laycock, Gloria. 2005. "Defining Crime Science." Pp. 3–24 in Melissa J. Smith and Nick Tilley (eds.), *Crime Science: New Approaches to Preventing and Detecting Crime*. Cullompton, UK: Willan.

LeBel, Thomas P., Ros Burnett, Shadd Maruna, and Shawn Bushway. 2008. "The 'Chicken and the Egg' of Subjective and Social Factors in Desistance from Crime." *European Journal of Criminology* 5: 131–159.

Lipsey, Mark W., Nana A. Landenberger, and Sandra Jo Wilson. 2007. "Effects of Cognitive-Behavioral Programs for Criminal Offenders." *Campbell Systematic Reviews* 6: 1–27.

Listwan, Shelley Johnson, Francis T. Cullen, and Edward J. Latessa. 2006. "How to Prevent Prisoner Re-Entry Programs from Failing: Insights from Evidence-Based Corrections." *Federal Probation* 70(3): 19–25.

Lowenkamp, Christopher T., and Edward J. Latessa. 2004. "Understanding the Risk Principle: How and Why Correctional Interventions Can Harm Low-Risk Offenders." Pp. 3–8 in *Topics in Community Corrections*. Washington, DC: National Institute of Corrections, U.S. Department of Justice.

Lowenkamp, Christopher T., and Edward J. Latessa. 2005. "Increasing the Effectiveness of Correctional Programming through the Risk Principle: Identifying Offenders for Residential Placement." *Criminology and Public Policy* 4: 263–290.

Lowenkamp, Christopher T., Edward J. Latessa, and Alexander Holsinger. 2006. "The Risk Principle in Action: What Have We Learned from 13,676 Offenders and 97 Correctional Programs?" *Crime and Delinquency* 51: 1–17.

Lowenkamp, Christopher T., Edward J. Latessa, and Paula Smith. 2006. "Does Correctional Program Quality Really Matter? The Impact of Adhering to the Principles of Effective Intervention." *Criminology & Public Policy* 5: 575–594.

Lowenkamp, Christopher T., Jennifer Pealer, Paula Smith, and Edward J. Latessa. 2006. "Adhering to the Risk and Need Principles: Does It Matter for Supervision-Based Programs?" *Federal Probation* 70(3): 3–8.

Madensen, Tamara D., and John E. Eck. 2013. "Crime Places and Crime Management." Pp. 557–578 in Francis T. Cullen and Pamela Wilcox (eds.), *The Oxford Handbook of Criminological Theory*. New York, NY: Oxford University Press.

Maruna, Shadd, and Kevin Roy. 2007. "Amputation or Reconstruction? Notes on the Concept of 'Knifing Off' and Desistance from Crime." *Journal of Contemporary Criminal Justice* 23: 104–124.

Matthews, Betsy, Dana Jones Hubbard, and Edward Latessa. 2001. "Making the Next Step: Using Evaluability Assessment to Improve Correctional Programming." *The Prison Journal* 81: 454–472.

Mazerolle, Lorraine, and Janet Ransley. 2005. *Third Party Policing*. New York, NY: Cambridge University Press.

McMurran, Mary. 2009. "Motivational Interviewing with Offenders: A Systematic Review." *Legal and Criminological Psychology* 14: 83–10000.

Miller, Joel. 2014. "Probation Supervision and the Control of Crime Opportunities: An Empirical Assessment." *Crime and Delinquency* 60: 1235–1257.

National Research Council. 2008. *Parole, Desistance from Crime, and Community Reintegration*. Washington, DC: National Academies Press.

O'Donohue, William T., and Jane E. Fisher. 2012. *Cognitive Behavior Therapy: Core Principles for Practice*. Hoboken, NJ: John Wiley.

Parent, Dale, and Brad Snyder. 1999. *Police-Corrections Partnerships*. Washington, DC: National Institute of Justice, Office of Justice Programs.

Paternoster, Ray, and Shawn Bushway. 2009. "Desistance and the 'Feared Self': Toward and Identity Theory of Criminal Desistance." *Journal of Law and Criminology* 99: 1103–1156.

Pearson, Frank S., Douglas S. Lipton, Charles M. Cleland, and Dorline S. Yee. 2002. "The Effects of Behavioral/Cognitive-Behavioral Programs on Recidivism." *Crime and Delinquency* 48: 476–496.

Petersilia, Joan, and Susan Turner. 1993. "Intensive Probation and Parole." Pp. 281–335 in Michael Tonry (ed.), *Crime and Justice: A Review of Research, Vol. 17*. Chicago, IL: University of Chicago Press.

Ratcliffe, Jerry H. 2010. "Crime Mapping: Spatial and Temporal Challenges." Pp. 5–24 in Alex R. Piquero and David Weisburd (eds.), *Handbook of Quantitative Criminology*. New York, NY: Springer.

Reentry Policy Council. 2005. *Report of the Re-Entry Policy Council: Charting the Safe and Successful Return of Prisoners to the Community*. New York, NY: Council of State Governments.

Reinventing Probation Council. 2000. *Transforming Probation through Leadership: The "Broken Windows" Model*. New York, NY: Center for Civic Innovation.

Sampson, Rana, John E. Eck, and Jessica Dunham. 2010. "Super Controllers and Crime Prevention: A Routine Activity Explanation of Crime Prevention Success and Failure." *Security Journal* 23: 37–51.

Schaefer, Lacey. 2013. *Environmental Corrections: Making Offender Supervision Work*. Unpublished Doctoral Dissertation, University of Cincinnati, Cincinnati, OH.

Schaefer, Lacey, Francis T. Cullen, and John E. Eck. 2016. *Environmental Corrections: A New Paradigm for Supervising Offenders in the Community*. Thousand Oaks, CA: Sage.

Scott, Michael, John Eck, Johannes Knutsson, and Herman Goldstein. 2008. "Problem-Oriented Policing and Environmental Criminology." Pp. 221–246 in Richard Wortley and Lorraine Mazerolle (eds.), *Environmental Criminology and Crime Analysis.* Cullumpton, UK: Willan.

Smith, Paula, Paul Gendreau, and Kristin Swartz. 2009. "Validating the Principles of Effective Intervention: A Systematic Review of the Contributions of Meta-Analysis in the Field of Corrections." *Victims & Offenders* 4: 148–169.

Smith, Paula, Myrinda Schweitzer, Ryan M. Labrecque, and Edward J. Latessa. 2012. "Improving Probation Officers' Supervision Skills: An Evaluation of the EPICS Model." *Journal of Crime and Justice* 35: 189–199.

Solomon, Amy L. 2006. "Does Parole Supervision Work? Research Findings and Policy Opportunities." *Perspectives* 30(2): 26–37.

Solomon, Amy, Jenny W. L. Osborne, Laura Winterfield, Brian Elderbroom, Peggy Burke, Richard P. Stroker, Edward E. Rhine, and William D. Burrell. 2008. *Putting Public Safety First: 13 Parole Supervision Strategies to Enhance Reentry Outcomes.* Washington, DC: Urban Institute.

Spiegler, Michael D., and David C. Guevremont. 2009. *Contemporary Behavior Therapy* (5th ed.). Belmont, CA: Wadsworth.

Taxman, Faye S. 2006. "What Should We Expect From Parole (And Probation) Under a Behavioral Management Approach?" *Perspectives* 30(2): 38–45.

Taxman, Faye S. 2011. "Parole: Moving the Field Forward through a New Model of Behavioral Management." Pp. 307–328 in Lior Gideon and Hung-En Sung (eds.), *Rethinking Corrections: Rehabilitation, Reentry, and Reintegration.* Thousand Oaks, CA: Sage.

Taxman, Faye S. 2012. "Crime Control in the Twenty-First Century: Science-Based Supervision (SBS)." *Journal of Crime and Justice* 35: 135–144.

Taxman, Faye, and James Byrne. 2001. "Fixing Broken Windows Probation." *Perspectives* 25: 22–30.

Taxman, Faye S., Eric S. Shepardson, and James M. Byrne. 2004. *Tools of the Trade: A Guide to Incorporating Science into Practice.* Washington, DC: National Institute of Corrections, U.S. Department of Justice.

Taxman, Faye, S., Christina Yancey, and Jeanne Bilanin. 2006. *Proactive Community Supervision in Maryland: Changing Offender Outcomes.* Baltimore, MD: Maryland Division of Parole and Probation.

Taxman, Faye S., Douglas Young, and James M. Byrne. 2003. "Transforming Offender Reentry into Public Safety: Lessons from OJP's Reentry Partnership Initiative." *Justice Research and Policy* 5: 101–128.

Taxman, Faye S., Douglas Young, and James M. Byrne. 2004. "With Eyes Wide Open: Formalizing Community and Social Control Intervention in Offender Reintegration Programmes." Pp. 233–260 in Shadd Maruna and Russ Immarigeon (eds.), *After Crime and Punishment: Pathways to Offender Reintegration.* Portland, OR: Willan.

Topalli, Volkan. 2005. "When Being Good Is Bad: An Expansion of Neutralization Theory." *Criminology* 43: 797–836.

Walters, Scott T., Michael D. Clark, Ray Gingerich, and Melissa L. Meltzer. 2007. *Motivating Offenders to Change: A Guide for Probation and Parole.* Washington, DC: National Institute of Corrections, U.S. Department of Justice.

Warr, Mark. 1998. "Life-Course Transitions and Desistance from Crime." *Criminology* 36: 183–216.

Weisburd, David, and Anthony A. Braga, eds. 2006. *Police Innovation: Contrasting Perspectives.* New York, NY: Cambridge University Press.

Weisburd, David, Elizabeth R. Groff, and Sue-Ming Yang. 2012. *The Criminology of Place: Street Segments and Our Understanding of the Crime Problem*. New York, NY: Oxford University Press.

Weisburd, David, Elizabeth R. Groff, and Sue-Ming Yang. 2014. "Understanding and Controlling Hot Spots of Crime: The Importance of Formal and Informal Social Controls." *Prevention Science* 15: 31–43.

Wortley, Richard. 2001. "A Classification of Techniques for Controlling Situational Precipitators of Crime." *Security Journal* 14(4): 63–82.

9

A Micro Place Perspective for Theory and Research on Police Behavior[1]

Breanne Cave

Overview

Anyone who has spent time working in urban communities develops a detailed understanding of just how much street blocks differ from one another. On one street, a long-time resident will happily spend hours talking about her experiences with the community, and will give intimate details about her relationships with her neighbors, past and present. On another street, no one will open the door to a person who they do not immediately recognize.

Researchers and community workers are not the only people who experience these block-by-block variations in the nature of urban spaces. The police often grapple with the problems of crime in small areas such as addresses and street segments—for instance, robberies centered around particular convenience stores, years-long conflicts between neighbors, and street blocks where residents have left public spaces to open air drug markets. This paper argues that current theories about how the environment impacts police activity can be enriched by attending to such place-based variations in the nature of crime problems and community life.

Lum (2011) argues for the importance of place in understanding police decision-making and activity. As Lum (2011) notes, insights from environmental criminology can be applied to the decisions that the police make in their patrol activities. The police, like everyone else, receive cues from the environment that impact their decisions about where to go and how to respond to the crime and disorder problems that they encounter. Lum's research on police decision-making in census block groups and street blocks illustrates the value of micro place units of analysis in police decision-making research (see, e.g., Lum 2011; Wu and Lum 2016).

Empirical evidence about the extent of variation of crime, disorder, and social life in places further supports Lum's contention that the cues to the police about the nature of the environment vary at the micro level. In a seminal article, Sherman, Gartin, and Buerger (1989) found that 3% of addresses in Minneapolis accounted for 50% of crime in the city. Other studies have found similar concentrations of crime among addresses and street segments in other cities, leading Weisburd (2015) to posit a law of crime concentration in place (see, e.g., Pierce, Spaar, and Briggs 1988; Weisburd and Amram 2014; Weisburd and Green 1995; Weisburd, Groff, and Yang 2012). Concentrations of crime are also stable in places over time, with most places showing very little change in crime, even over very long time periods (Andresen and Malleson 2011; Weisburd et al. 2012). Furthermore, some research has showed that other aspects of community life, including voting behavior and the prevalence of Section 8 vouchers, also vary significantly at the street level (Weisburd et al. 2012). Weisburd et al. (2012) argue that micro geographic units represent "small scale social systems" where residents develop common understandings, norms, and patterns of behavior (Taylor 1997; Wicker 1987).

One key aspect of studying police activity in places is examining which place characteristics are salient for understanding the behavior of the police. Existing neighborhood- and community-level theories of police decision-making may provide a useful framework for understanding police decision-making in places. However, the importance of these theories in predicting police activity in places has not been tested.

This study addresses this gap in research by examining how street segment context impacts police report writing during calls for service using data from a study of 449 street segments in Baltimore City, Maryland. Using neighborhood- and community-level theories of police decision-making as a framework, the study finds that crime, disorder, and segment sociodemographics have a significant impact on reports written for some types of calls for service, but not for others. Although neighborhood- and community-level theories provide a useful starting point for micro place studies of police behavior, the findings also suggest that alternative theories and perspectives should be developed to explain police activity in micro places. Micro place research on how the environment impacts police behavior may also require new theoretical perspectives and methodological approaches to be developed.

Community-Level Theory and Research About the Environment and Police Activity

Most research on police decision-making focuses on neighborhood and community units of analysis when explaining differences in police activity in different places. Existing theories use a number of different measures of neighborhood context and police decision-making, and make a variety of predictions about how the environment impacts different types of police activities. Four theories about how communities and neighborhoods impact the behavior of the police are described in Table 9.1.

This section briefly summarizes each theory, the measures of neighborhood context that are drawn from it, the type of police behavior that is theorized about, and the hypothesis drawn from the theory in this study. Because many of the following theories overlap conceptually, the hypotheses take the approach of testing one specific prediction that can be made on the basis of each theory, rather than testing the theory as a whole. The following section briefly discusses the benefits of this approach, as well as the challenges involved with drawing upon existing theory to explain police behavior at the street segment level.

Table 9.1
Summary of theories of the influence of the environment on police activity

Theory	Context	Police Behavior	Measure of Neighborhood Context	Hypothesis
Broken Windows theory (Wilson and Kelling 1982)	Neighborhood informal social order	Prevention of disorder, norm enforcement	Social cohesion, social control, residential tenure, racial heterogeneity, % in poverty	1. Less informal social order decreases the proportion of calls that result in a report.
Police-Community Relations theory (Sung 2002)	Neighborhood moral standing (race and ethnicity, age, socio-economic status, crime, and disorder)	Proactivity, coercion, and law enforcement	% African American, % Hispanic or Latino, respondent age, % without a high school degree, % working, % married	2. Lower neighborhood moral standing increases the proportion of calls that result in a report.
Negotiated Order theory (Klinger 1997)	Socio-economic status, crime, and disorder	Vigor (in terms of enforcement and patrol time)	Drug crime, violent crime, social disorder, physical disorder	3. More crime and disorder decreases the proportion of calls that result in a report.
Legal Cynicism theory (Sampson and Bartusch 1998; Kirk and Matsuda 2011)	Citizens' perceptions of legitimacy and effectiveness of police and law	Arrest	Police effectiveness, police legitimacy	4. Less perceived legitimacy and effectiveness decreases the proportion of calls that result in a report.

Broken Windows Theory

Broken Windows theory is described in a seminal article by Wilson and Kelling (1982). Wilson and Kelling (1982) note that the police play an important order maintenance role in the community through activities such as foot patrols, warning away rowdy teenagers, and asking strangers about their business in the area. But the police alone cannot maintain order and prevent crime. They rely on the community to act as partners in asserting neighborhood order and providing direct assistance to law enforcement. According to Wilson and Kelling (1982), when citizens withdraw from community life, police capacity to prevent and deter crime is reduced.

Evidence about the link between informal social control and police enforcement activity is mixed. Social disorganization and collective efficacy are often used to measure the extent of informal social order within a neighborhood (see e.g., Kirk and Matsuda 2011; Sun, Payne, and Wu 2008; Schulenberg, Jacob, and Carrington 2007; Cronin 2005). Several studies have found that the police are more likely to make arrests, make traffic stops, and charge youths with crime in neighborhoods with high levels of social disorganization (Schulenberg et al. 2007; Cronin 2005; Sun et al. 2008), but others have found that social disorganization is not a significant predictor of enforcement activity when crime and disorder are taken into account (Sung 2002; Johnson and Billings 2010). Additionally, Kirk and Matsuda (2011) found that higher neighborhood collective efficacy is linked to increased likelihood of arrest.

As Table 9.1 notes, this study follows Wilson and Kelling (1982) in predicting that having lower levels of neighborhood informal social order leads to fewer reports written during calls for service. Neighborhood informal social order is measured through social disorganization (including racial heterogeneity, residential tenure, and poverty) and collective efficacy (including social cohesion and social control). These measures, as well as all other measures used in this study, are described in more detail in Cave (2016).

Theory of Police-Community Relations

Much theory and research have noted that police enforcement activity disproportionately impacts members of racial and ethnic minority groups, including in terms of arrests (e.g., Kochel, Wilson, and Mastrofski 2011); stop, question, and frisks (Coviello and Persico 2015; Goel, Rao, and Shroff 2016); and traffic stops (Smith and Petrocelli 2001; Tillyer and Eck 2010). Sung's (2002) Police-Community Relations theory is not a new perspective in the sense that Sung predicts that police will be more enforcement-oriented when responding to crimes and calls for service that involve members of racial and ethnic minority communities. However, his theory does usefully elaborate on how socio-demographics impact police activity that focuses specifically on the community rather than individual citizen-officer interactions. Sung

(2002) notes that neighborhoods are stratified by race and class. Racial and class stratification acts as a marker of community moral standing, or worthiness for service or enforcement, to the police. When the police perceive that a neighborhood has lower moral standing, they behave in a more enforcement-oriented and less service-oriented way.

As noted, much of the research that focuses on the relationship between socio-demographics and policing focuses on interactions between individual citizens and officers rather than on officer behavior in neighborhoods and communities. Existing community-level research has had mixed findings. For instance, Smith and Klein (1984) found that police are less likely to make arrests during domestic violence calls when complainants are women, and when they live in impoverished communities. Varano, Schager, Cancino, and Swatt (2009) note that the police may be more likely to ignore crimes when victims are African Americans. Meehan and Ponder (2002) note that police are more likely to stop African Americans when driving through predominantly white neighborhoods than when they are driving through predominantly Black neighborhoods.

Table 9.1 notes that socio-demographic indicators of lower moral standing will predict more report writing by the police. In this study, street segment moral standing is measured by racial and ethnic composition, age, education, employment status, and marital status. Here, a segment with a higher proportion of racial and ethnic group residents, younger residents, less educated residents, more unemployed residents, and fewer married residents will experience more report writing per call for service.

Negotiated Order

In Negotiated Order theory, Klinger (1997) points to neighborhood disadvantage and police experience with crime and disorder as being important predictors of police activity. Police observations about the prevalence of crime and disorder, as well as their observations and experiences with neighborhood residents, determine their perceptions about the norms of social order in communities. These perceptions in turn shape the vigor with which police respond to crime and disorder problems. Police officers' assignment to districts and beats also influences their perceptions about the relative severity of crime in particular areas as well as the extent of their regular workload, so an officer who is assigned to a beat that has high levels of crime may respond differently to a crime problem than one who is assigned to a lower crime beat.

Research shows mixed support for the salience of crime and disorder in predicting police activity. For instance, some researchers have found that police are more active (in terms of arrests and vigor) when responding to neighborhoods with more crime (e.g., Johnson and Olschansky 2010; Sobol 2010). Terrill and Reisig (2003) found that police are more likely to use force during police-citizen encounters in neighborhoods with higher homicide rates. Sung

(2002) found that disorder is a significant predictor of arrest and physical coercion in neighborhoods, and Warner (1997) found that the nonrecording of crime is higher in neighborhoods with large numbers of calls for service, but that these effects are strongest in places with extremely high call volumes, which provides some support for Klinger's (1997) workload hypothesis.

On the basis of Negotiated Order theory and the workload hypothesis, Table 9.1 predicts that police will write fewer reports per call for service on high crime and disorder street segments. As the following section will discuss, this study was particularly well-suited for testing this hypothesis, as the sample includes streets with very high levels of crime. In this study, measures of crime and disorder include violent crime, drug crime, physical disorder, and social disorder. Violent and drug crime measures were used because a large proportion of the sample comprises drug and violent crime hotspots.

Legal Cynicism

Legal Cynicism theory emphasizes that police efforts to control crime rely on the presence of a community that is willing to reinforce informal controls and collaborate with the police to solve crime problems (see Kirk and Matsuda 2011; Sampson and Bartusch 1998). Citizens' attitudes toward the police and the law predict police response to crime and disorder problems, and police are less effective when citizens do not believe them to be legitimate and effective. Kirk and Matsuda note that "legal cynicism is a cultural frame in which the law and agents of its enforcement are viewed as illegitimate, unresponsive, and ill equipped to ensure public safety" (2011: 444).

When citizens do not believe that the police are legitimate authorities and that the law is relevant in their community, they are less likely to cooperate with the police to solve crime problems (Kochel, Parks, and Mastrofski 2013; Sunshine and Tyler 2003). Kirk and Matsuda found that citizens' perceptions about the legitimacy of the police and the law predict the frequency with which crime in Chicago communities leads to an arrest. Bennet (2004) similarly found that citizens who do not view the police as legitimate are less likely to call the police following non-serious crimes. Many researchers have also noted that citizens are less likely to cooperate with the police—for instance, talking to the police and assisting with finding suspected offenders—when they do not view the police to be legitimate (see, e.g., Anderson 2000; Sunshine and Tyler 2003; Tyler and Fagan 2006; Venkatesh 1997).

Hypothesis 4 in Table 9.1 predicts that the police will write fewer citations in response to calls for service on streets where citizens do not perceive police and the law to be legitimate and effective. It is worth noting that the relationship between citizens' perceptions of the police and police practices is likely to be complex, as citizens' indirect and direct experiences with police officers are likely to impact their perceptions of the police, which in turn informs their interactions with the police in their communities. This study focuses on understanding the strength and direction of the relationship between perceptions of the police and police behavior, rather than on disentangling the complex and recursive relationship between the two.

Complications for Applying Community-Level Theories to Predicting Police Behavior in Places

While the previous discussion has described each theory about the impact of the community and environment on police behavior as if they deal with distinct concepts and measures, it is worth noting that there is a great deal of overlap between these theories. For instance, both Broken Windows and Legal Cynicism theories emphasize the importance of citizens' willingness to cooperate and collaborate with the police in predicting the capacity of the police to prevent crime. Sung (2002) and Klinger (1997) both emphasize that police decision-making and actions are influenced in part by police officers' perceptions about whether citizens are deserving of police service—in Sung (2002), these perceptions are shaped by perceived moral standing, and in Klinger (1997), these perceptions are shaped by police knowledge of and perceptions about citizens' involvement in crime and disorder.

A second challenge is that not all theories agree about how specific features of the environment impact police behavior. For instance, Wilson and Kelling (1982) and Klinger (1997) predict that police activity—in terms of law enforcement and the maintenance of informal social norms—is reduced in communities with more crime, but Sung (2002) predicts that the police will be more active in enforcing laws in high crime communities. The focus of this paper is on using these theories to develop measures that can predict police behavior at the place level, but not necessarily in comparing the explanatory power of one theory as compared to another.

Lastly, the theories that this paper focuses on were selected because they examine how the environment impacts police activity, without examining in detail individual police-citizen interactions. There is a wide range of additional theoretical perspectives for understanding police-citizen interactions, but many of these focus on the characteristics of police organizations, officers, and citizens rather than on environmental factors for understanding and explaining police decision-making. Such theories are important to understanding the behavior of the police as a whole, but do not usually emphasize environmental context when explaining police behavior and decision-making.

Hypothesis Testing Baltimore, Maryland Crime Hotspots

Theories of how the environment impacts police behavior are primarily concerned with police decision-making in situations where the police could potentially respond to a crime or disorder scenario in different ways. This study focuses on several different types of calls for service, including drug offenses, traffic stops, field interviews, disorderly persons, as well as all crime and disorder calls for service. A series of regression models was developed to assess the salience of each set of measures summarized in Table 9.1 and more thoroughly described in Cave (2016) for predicting the proportion of calls for service that result in a written report.

The unit of analysis in this study is the street segment. A street segment is defined as the length of street from intersection to intersection including both sides of the road (see Weisburd et al. 2012). As noted earlier, many aspects of the urban environment, including crime, disorder, and socio-economic characteristics of communities, vary significantly at the street segment level. Theory and research suggest that such environmental characteristics predict police behavior at the community level. If the police are sensitive to cues in the environment to shape decision-making, as Lum (2011) suggests, then the cues that are relevant to explaining police behavior at the community level may also be relevant to understanding behavior at the street segment level.

Research Site and Sample

More than 3,700 surveys were carried out with residents of 449 street segments with different levels of crime and disorder in Baltimore City, Maryland. These surveys included a wide range of measures about the conditions of neighborhoods and communities. To test the salience of neighborhood-level theories about the impact of the environment on police behavior at the street segment level, survey responses were combined with in-person observations of street segments by trained researchers, as well as police calls for service data provided by the Baltimore Police Department.

Data were collected from the selected segments between August 15, 2013 and May 30, 2014. The streets were initially selected on the basis of the count of 2012 calls for service and the presence of a minimum of 20 inhabitable residential units. The research team selected four groups of street segments for inclusion in the study: (1) 126 violent crime hotspots; (2) 121 drug crime hotspots; (3) 55 combined spots; and (4) 147 comparison spots. Street segments had to be in the top 2.5% in the city overall to be included in one of the hotspots categories; combined streets were in the top 2.5% for both drug and violent crime. Comparison segments were drawn from all streets that met the residential unit criterion but did not have sufficient crime to be counted as a hotspot.

Generalized linear binomial logit models with robust standard errors were used to test the hypotheses. These models are used to analyze proportional outcome variables that have values that fall between 0 and 1; as noted previously, the outcome measure is the percentage of calls for service that result in a written report. Results are reported in terms of odds ratios and standard errors. Because a street segment had to have a minimum of one call for service of the

Table 9.2
Percentage of calls resulting in a report in the sampled segments

Variable	N	Mean	Std. Dev.
All crime and disorder	410	22.05	7.79
Car stops	338	6.37	15.76
Field interviews	346	22.47	25.32
Disorderly persons	389	6.09	10.84
Narcotics	329	21.92	28.58

type examined in order to be included in the regression models, the N of segments that could be analyzed varies in these models on the basis of how many segments had experienced the call type of interest during the study period.

Four types of calls for service are examined in this study: car stops, field interviews, disorderly persons, and narcotics. During the study period, these calls comprised about 31% of all calls for service in Baltimore City, and they were common in the selected street segments. These calls were also selected because the police have fairly broad discretion in whether to initiate a call, if the call was to be police-initiated, as well as how they respond to the call, if the call was citizen-initiated. A fifth category of calls for service, total crime and disorder calls, is also included in the analysis to provide an overall picture of how the police write citations in the selected street segments.

Table 9.2 shows the means and standard deviations of the percentage of calls for service that resulted in a citation in these segments for each call type. As the table shows, not all calls for service were equally likely to result in a report being written. While more than 20% of total calls for service, field interviews, and narcotics calls resulted in a report being written, fewer than 7% of calls for car stops and disorderly persons resulted in a report. Individual segments varied widely in terms of the number of reports that resulted from particular types of calls, with zero reports occurring in some segments for some categories of calls, and all calls resulting in reports in other segments.

Independent variables used in this study were drawn from calls for service data, in-person observations of street segment conditions, and resident surveys. Four groups of measures were developed during this study:

1. Segment informal social order: this group of measures was collected during household surveys and includes variables derived from collective efficacy and social disorganization research. Measures of social cohesion, social control, poverty, residential tenure, and racial heterogeneity are included in these models.
2. Segment socio-demographics: this group of measures includes the proportion of African American respondents, a dichotomous measure of Hispanic

or Latino composition, as well as measures of age, education, gender, and employment derived from resident surveys.

3. Crime and disorder: this group includes physical disorder recorded during in-person observations of street segment conditions, measures of social disorder collected during household surveys, and measures of crime derived from calls for service data provided by the Baltimore Police Department.

4. Police effectiveness and legitimacy: these measures are derived from household surveys. The measure of police effectiveness refers to the effectiveness of the police in preventing crime; the measure of police legitimacy refers to a combination of measures that assess residents' perceptions of the legitimacy of the police and the law.

Findings

Findings are summarized in Table 9.3, and are reported in terms of an odds ratio and standard error. On the whole, the models explained a modest amount of variance in the proportion of calls that resulted in a citation. Explained variance ranged between 0.044 and 0.187, and many of the measures examined were not significant predictors of police citation writing. The street segment environment explained more variance in citations written for narcotics calls and total calls for service than for car stops, field interviews, and disorderly person calls. This section describes the relationship between these models and each of the hypotheses listed in Table 9.1.

1. *Less informal social order reduces the chances of a report during a call for service (Broken Windows)*

    First, Wilson and Kelling (1982) suggest that the police are less active in communities with less informal social order. As Table 9.3 shows, most measures of community social order were not significant predictors of report writing during calls for services. As noted previously, measures of informal social control were drawn from collective efficacy and social disorganization theories, and include social control, social cohesion, poverty, residential tenure, and racial heterogeneity. The percentage of respondents living in poverty was the only significant predictor of report writing, and was a significant predictor only in the model for car stops. A 1% increase in the proportion of respondents living in poverty decreased the chance that a car stop call for service would result in a report by 95%. While this is consistent with Wilson and Kelling's (1982) theory, poverty was the only measure of informal community order that provided support for Broken Windows theory, and was only significant in a single model.

2. *Lower neighborhood moral standing increases the chances of a report during a call for service (Police-Community Relations)*

Next, Sung (2002) predicts that lower moral standing increases the chances of enforcement activity in neighborhoods, and conceptualizes moral standing as being related to poverty, race, and other socio-demographic measures. As Table 9.3 shows, most measures of segment socio-demographics—including respondent age, education, employment, and marital status—were not significant predictors of report writing in the sampled segments. However, measures of segment racial composition were significant predictors of the proportion of reports written during narcotics and car stop calls for service, and the proportion of people who were not working was also a significant predictor of the odds of a report being written during a field interview.

For instance, a 1% increase in the percentage of African Americans on a street increased the odds of a report being written during a narcotics call by 223%, and the odds of a report being written were 74% greater on streets with any Hispanic or Latino respondents as compared to streets with no Hispanic or Latino respondents. However, African American composition was not a significant predictor of car stop report writing, and the odds of a car stop call for service resulting in a report were 48% lower in street segments with any Hispanic or Latino respondents as compared to streets without Hispanic or Latino respondents. Lastly, a 1% increase in the proportion of people who are not working on a street segment reduced the odds of a report being written during a field interview call by 62%. Thus, the support for the hypothesis derived from Police-Community Relations theory is mixed, and most of the predictors were non-significant in these models.

3. *More crime and disorder decreases the chances of a report during a call for service (Negotiated Order)*

Based on Negotiated Order theory, the third hypothesis predicts that fewer calls for service will result in a written report on streets with higher levels of social disorder, physical disorder, drug calls for service, and violent calls for service. Table 9.3 shows that social disorder is a significant predictor of report writing for narcotics calls, with a one-unit change in social disorder predicting a 135% increase in the logged odds of a report being written. The logged count of narcotics calls for service is a significant predictor of the odds of a report being written during all calls for service, narcotics calls for service, and disorderly person calls for service. For instance, a one-unit increase in the logged count of narcotics calls predicted a 45% decrease in the odds of a report being written during a narcotics call, a 27% decrease in the odds of a report being written during all crime and disorder calls for service, and a 20% decrease in the odds of a report being written during disorderly person calls for service. Therefore, findings about the effects of social disorder seem to contradict Negotiated Order theory, but findings about the effects of narcotics calls for service seem to support the theory.

4. *Less perceived legitimacy and effectiveness decreases the chances of a report during a call for service (Legal Cynicism)*

Lastly, Legal Cynicism theory predicts that police will be less active in places where residents believe them to be ineffective and illegitimate. The findings summarized in Table 9.3 do not support the salience of citizens' perceptions of police effectiveness and legitimacy in predicting the odds of report writing at the street segment level, although it is worth noting that the single marginally significant effect (p = .096) for police effectiveness was not consistent with the predictions of Legal Cynicism. That is, a 1% increase in the proportion of respondents who believed that the police were effective decreased the odds of a report being written during a call for service by 22%. Aside from this single marginal effect, measures developed from Legal Cynicism theory were not significant predictors of the proportion of calls that resulted in a report being written in these models.

Implications

Crime pattern theory posits that a motivated offender rationally responds to cues about opportunities for crime encountered during their daily activities and routines (see, e.g., Brantingham and Brantingham 1993, 2008; Nasar and Fisher 1993; Taylor and Gottfredson 1986). Lum (2011) notes that police similarly respond to cues in the environment when they make decisions about how to respond to crime and disorder problems, arguing that environmental criminology perspectives are relevant to understanding police decisions. An environmental and pattern theory of policing extends the environmental criminology perspective and suggests that the police opportunistically seek out activities that will be most productive for achieving goals like maintaining order, preventing crime, and apprehending offenders.

Theories about police activity in neighborhoods, communities, and other spatial units imply that the nature of crime, disorder, and social life impacts police motivation and capacity to enforce laws and more informal social norms. In some places, crime is rare, the police enjoy broad support from citizens, and a strong community reinforces law enforcement efforts, while in other locations, the community is alienated from the police. This study, and other studies of police activity in places, show that police decision-making and activity vary throughout the environment, and that characteristics of smaller spatial units such as street segments and addresses have an impact on police officers' decisions to write reports during calls for service.

The street segments in Baltimore City analyzed during this study provide some initial insights about the relevance of place characteristics for

Table 9.3
Generalized linear models for report writing

Theory	Odds Ratio (Standard Error)	All Crime and Disorder	Field Interviews	Narcotics	Car Stops	Disorderly Persons
BW	Social control	1.04 (0.09)	0.98 (0.25)	0.91 (0.29)	0.56 (0.23)	1.03 (0.29)
	Social cohesion	0.96 (0.10)	0.95 (0.30)	1.10 (0.40)	0.72 (0.35)	1.13 (0.29)
	% in poverty	1.10 (0.22)	1.91 (0.92)	0.53 (0.33)	0.05** (0.05)	2.23 (1.24)
	Residential tenure	1.00 (0.00)	1.00 (0.00)	1.00 (0.00)	1.00 (0.00)	1.00 (0.00)
	Racial heterogeneity	0.98 (0.09)	1.17 (0.22)	1.07 (0.25)	1.64 (0.53)	0.97 (0.22)
PCR	% African American	1.11 (0.19)	1.55 (0.63)	3.23* (1.61)	1.01 (0.59)	1.74 (0.98)
	Hispanic/Latino composition	1.01 (0.08)	0.89 (0.17)	1.74* (0.38)	0.52* (0.16)	1.32 (0.31)
	Average age	0.99† (0.01)	1.01 (0.01)	1.00 (0.02)	0.99 (0.03)	1.00 (0.02)
	% without high school	0.91 (0.18)	0.67 (0.37)	1.94 (1.18)	3.77 (3.84)	1.48 (0.76)
	% not working	1.13 (0.22)	0.38* (0.19)	1.50 (0.81)	0.64 (0.51)	0.69 (0.37)
	% male	1.18 (0.18)	1.77 (0.81)	1.31 (0.74)	1.56 (1.30)	0.87 (0.47)
NO	Social disorder	0.88 (0.07)	0.84 (0.14)	2.35*** (0.49)	1.17 (0.35)	0.90 (0.19)
	Physical disorder	1.01 (0.04)	0.94 (0.10)	1.24† (0.16)	0.88 (0.17)	1.08 (0.12)
	Narcotics calls for service (logged)	0.83*** (0.02)	0.90 (0.07)	0.55*** (0.06)	1.05 (0.12)	0.80* (0.07)
	Violent crime calls for service	1.00 (0.00)	1.01 (0.00)	1.00 (0.01)	1.01 (0.01)	1.01 (0.01)
LC	Police effectiveness	0.78† (0.12)	0.74 (0.35)	1.72 (0.92)	0.61 (0.38)	2.27 (1.21)
	Police legitimacy	1.05 (0.11)	1.33 (0.38)	0.82 (0.30)	1.25 (0.51)	1.25 (0.40)
	N†	402	344	334	324	384
	r²	0.187	0.051	0.133	0.063	0.043

† p < 0.10; * p < 0.05; ** p < 0.01; *** p < 0.001

† Streets were excluded from the analysis if (1) no call of the type of interest occurred on the street, or (2) no report was written during the study period (August 15, 2013–June 30, 2014).

Theories: BW: Broken Windows; PCR: Police-Community Relations; NO: Negotiated Order; LC: Legal Cynicism understanding police decision-making in the context of writing reports as the result of a call for service. The presence of impoverished residents, segment racial and ethnic composition, social disorder, and crime in places were all significant predictors of report writing for different types of calls for service, though the overall amount of variance explained was modest. The first implication of these models is that it is useful to develop and elaborate on existing theory about how the environment impacts police decision-making to incorporate place-based effects. This kind of research offers challenges in both theory and methodology, as well as further research opportunities.

Using a Micro-Level Approach to Elaborate on
Neighborhood- and Community-Level Theory

An example of how place-based effects can be included in existing theory shows how multiple theoretical perspectives and units of analysis can be integrated to analyze and explain police decision-making. Klinger (1997) notes that the police make judgments about the norms of crime and disorder within a community and match the vigor of their enforcement activity to their perceptions about whether the observed activity is normal in a community. Police respond less vigorously to a crime that takes place in an already high crime community.

Findings about crime and disorder at the street segment level do not correspond to Klinger's (1997) theory, but might be explained by factors that operate at the street segment rather than community level. For instance, Rengert and Pelfrey (1997) used cognitive mapping to study the impact of the racial and ethnic composition of places on police cadets' perceptions of safety. They found that places with a high concentration of white residents were perceived to be safer, but that places that had a higher concentration of African Americans and Latinos were perceived to be more dangerous. These perceptions about the risk of places were more related to the race and ethnicity of residents than actual levels of violent crime. Newman (1972) also found that officers who felt that public housing complexes were disorderly take a more authoritative attitude when interacting with residents. The racial and ethnic backgrounds of residents and presence of disorder may therefore comprise cues that the police receive from the immediate micro environment, which lead them to form perceptions about risk in places.

In this study, the effect of narcotics crime on report writing in places conforms to Klinger's (1997) theory, but the effect of disorder does not. The place-based perspective would explain the effects of disorder as being caused by police response to immediately visible cues in the environment, which contributes to officers' perceptions of risk. But the amount and nature of crime that occurs at a particular street block are not physically obvious or may not be known to the individual officer, and therefore may not contribute to their perceptions of risk in the environment. Police responses to crime may, as Klinger (1997) suggests, be driven by factors such as individual officers' workload or their perceptions about the norms of crime in the broader community.

Many of the theories of police behavior developed on the neighborhood and community level take a general approach to conceptualizing police activities—using measures such as vigor, arrest, or the enforcement of norms. This study implies that the effects of the environment on the police may be specific to certain types of activities. For instance, the odds of a report being written on streets with a large Hispanic or Latino population were higher for narcotics calls for service, but lower for car stops. Sung (2002) provides a framework for distinguishing between different types of police behavior by characterizing police activity as being service- or enforcement-oriented. This study supports the idea of incorporating more detailed and nuanced measures of police behavior in theories about how the environment impacts the activities of the police.

Directions for Future Theory and Research

Studying police behavior in micro places can enhance existing theory and research in this area and offer a useful lens for understanding police behavior and decision-making. There are many important research gaps and challenges associated with studying police behavior in places that must be overcome in future research in this area.

One of the gaps in existing research about the police in places is a lack of observational or survey data about police activity at the street segment level. Research and the development of theory about police activity and decision-making have often relied on direct observations of the police, as well as interviews and conversations with officers (see, e.g., Muir 1979; Dejong, Mastrofski, and Parks 2001; Terrill and Mastrofski 2002). This develops richer understandings about the nature of crime problems, the details of police interventions, and the perceptions and intentions of the officers involved. Problem-oriented policing interventions, which are implemented in high crime places, often capture this type of information as a part of the initial problem-solving process or in implementation studies, and these types of studies can provide crucial insights about the nature of crime problems and police interventions that could not otherwise have been obtained (see, e.g., Eck 2015). A study by Weisburd, Telep, and Bueermann (2016) is currently underway and will collect systematic social observations of police officers working in high crime areas in four U.S. cities. Similar observational studies may shed light on the salience of the theories examined in this paper for explaining police behavior and decision-making in places.

Micro places offer unique challenges for studying police behavior. One of these is the relatively low base rate of arrests, calls, and encounters that occur between police and citizens on most street segments. The segments that were used in the Baltimore study of police reports were high crime streets selected from one of the highest crime cities in the United States. Nevertheless, many streets had no calls for service of one or more of the selected categories during the study period, and were therefore excluded from the regression models.

One method for dealing with this low base rate issue is to develop additional measures of police activity that have not traditionally been captured in studies of policing to date. For instance, body-worn and stationary cameras that observe crime hotspots can capture additional information about police-citizen interactions. Processing the volume of data involved is a daunting task, but machine learning and computing have rapidly advanced and can be used to create measures of police-citizen interactions from camera footage. Criminologists may be able to access detailed information about police-citizen interactions that extends well beyond traditional measures used for police activity—for instance, the length of conversations between police and citizens, facial expressions, and body posture. This provides more opportunities for understanding the nature of police-citizen encounters than has previously been possible in police research in this area and is a promising avenue for future research.

Finally, this study focused on a sample of high crime residential streets in Baltimore City. Future research should focus on whether place characteristics that were significant predictors of police activity in these settings are also important for predicting police activity in other settings. Police experience, exposure to streets with different population composition and levels of crime, and other factors may also mitigate or strengthen place effects on police behavior, and studies of these effects may also add much to research in this area.

Note

1. Data for this paper were obtained from a study by David Weisburd, Brian Lawton, Justin Ready, Amelia Haviland, Danielle Rudes, and Alese Wooditch. "Community Health, Anti-social Behavior and Safety at Street Segments: A Comparative Study." National Institute on Drug Abuse (5R01DA032639–03).

References

Anderson, Elijah. 2000. *Code of the Street: Decency, Violence, and Moral Life in the Inner City*. New York, NY: W.W. Norton & Company.

Andresen, Martin A., and Nicolas Malleson. 2011. "Testing the Stability of Crime Patterns: Implications for Theory and Practice." *Journal of Research in Crime and Delinquency* 48: 58–82

Bennett, Richard R. 2004. "Calling for Service: Mobilization of the Police across Sociocultural Environments." *Police Practice and Research* 5: 25–41.

Brantingham, Paul J., and Patricia L. Brantingham. 1993. "Environment, Routine and Situation: Towards a Pattern Theory of Crime." Pp. 259–288 in Ronald V. Clarke and Marcus Felson (eds.), *Routine Activities Theory and Rational Choice: Advances in Criminological Theory*, vol. 5. New Brunswick, NJ: Transaction Publishers.

Brantingham, Patricia L., and Paul J. Brantingham. 2008. "Crime Pattern Theory." Pp. 78–93 in Richard Wortley and Lorraine Mazerolle (eds.), *Environmental Criminology and Crime Analysis*. Collumpton, Devon: Willan Publishing.

Cave, Breanne. 2016. *Policing Places: The Influence of Street Segment Context on Police Activity*. Doctoral Dissertation. Fairfax, VA: George Mason University.

Coviello, Decio, and Nicola Persico. 2015. "An Economic Analysis of Black-White Disparities in the New York Police Department's Stop-and-Frisk Program." *The Journal of Legal Studies* 44: 315–360.

Cronin, Shea. 2005. "Contextual Determinants of Vehicle Searches By the Police." Conference Papers, The American Society of Criminology, Royal York, Ontario.

Dejong, Christina, Stephen D. Mastrofski, and Roger B. Parks. 2001. "Patrol Officers and Problem Solving: An Application of Expectancy Theory." *Justice Quarterly* 18: 31–61.

Eck, John E. 2015. "There Is Nothing So Theoretical as Good Practice: Police-Researcher Coproduction of Place Theory." Pp. 129–140 in Ella Cockbain and Johannes Knutsson (eds.), *Applied Police Research*. New York, NY: Routledge.

Goel, Sharad, Justin M. Rao, and Ravi Shroff. 2016. "Precinct or Prejudice? Understanding Racial Disparities in New York City's Stop-and-Frisk Policy." *The Annals of Applied Statistics* 10: 365–394.

Johnson, Richard R., and Ashley N. Billings. 2010. "Ecological Influence on State Police District Activity." *The Police Journal* 83: 305–323.

Johnson, Richard R., and Erica L. Olschansky. 2010. "The Ecological Theory of Police Response: A State Police Agency Test." *Criminal Justice Studies* 23: 119–131.

Kirk, David S., and Mauri Matsuda. 2011. "Legal Cynicism, Collective Efficacy, and the Ecology of Arrest." *Criminology* 49: 443–472.

Klinger, David A. 1997. "Negotiated Order in Patrol Work: An Ecological Theory of Police Response to Deviance." *Criminology* 35: 277–306.

Kochel, Tammy R., Roger Parks, and Stephen D. Mastrofski. 2013. "Examining Police Effectiveness as a Precursor to Legitimacy and Cooperation with the Police." *Justice Quarterly* 30: 895–925.

Kochel, Tammy R., David B. Wilson, and Stephen D. Mastrofski. 2011. "Effect of Suspect Race on Officers' Arrest Decisions." *Criminology* 49: 473–512.

Lum, Cynthia. 2011. "The Influence of Places on Police Decision Pathways: From Call for Service to Arrest." *Justice Quarterly* 28: 631–665.

Meehan, Albert J., and Michael C. Ponder. 2002. "Race and Place: The Ecology of Racial Profiling African American Motorists." *Justice Quarterly* 19: 399–430.

Muir, William K. 1979. *Police: Streeetcorner Politicians*. Chicago, IL: University of Chicago Press.

Nasar, Jack L., and Bonnie Fisher. 1993. "'Hot Spots' of Fear and Crime: A Multi-Method Investigation." *Journal of Environmental Psychology* 13: 187–206.

Newman, Oscar. 1972. *Defensible Space*. New York, NY: MacMillan.

Pierce, Glenn, Susan Spaar, and LeBaron Briggs. 1988. *The Character of Police Work: Strategic and Tactical Implications*. Boston, MA: Center for Applied Social Research, Northeastern University.

Rengert, George F., and William V. Pelfrey. 1997. "Cognitive Mapping of the City Center: Comparative Perceptions of Dangerous Places." *Crime Prevention* 8: 194–217.

Sampson, Robert J., and Dawn J. Bartusch. 1998. "Legal Cynicism and Subcultural (?) Tolerance of Deviance: The Neighborhood Context of Racial Differences." *Law and Society Review* 32: 777–804.

Schulenberg, Jennifer L., Joanna Jacob, and Peter Carrington. 2007. "Ecological Analysis of Crime Rates and Police Discretion with Young Persons: A Replication." *Canadian Journal of Criminology and Criminal Justice* 49: 261–277.

Sherman, Lawrence W., Patrick R. Gartin, and Michael E. Buerger. 1989. "Hot Spots of Predatory Crime: Routine Activities and the Criminology of Place." *Criminology* 27: 27–56.

Smith, Michael R., and Matthew Petrocelli. 2001. "Racial Profiling?: A Multivariate Analysis of Police Traffic Stop Data." *Police Quarterly* 4: 4–27.

Smith, Douglas A., and Jody R. Klein. 1984. "Police Control of Interpersonal Disputes." *Social Problems* 31: 468–481.

Sobol, James J. 2010. "The Social Ecology of Police Attitudes." *Policing: An International Journal of Police Strategies & Management* 33: 253–269.

Sun, Ivan Y., Brian K. Payne, and Yuning Wu. 2008. "The Impact of Situational Factors, Officer Characteristics, and Neighborhood Context on Police Behavior: A Multilevel Analysis." *Journal of Crime and Justice* 27: 33–60.

Sung, Hung-En. 2002. *The Fragmentation of Policing in American Cities*. Westpoint, CT: Greenwood Publishing.

Sunshine, Jason, and Tom R. Tyler. 2003. "The Role of Procedural Justice and Legitimacy in Shaping Public Support for Policing." *Law & Society Review* 37: 513–548.

Taylor, Ralph B. 1997. "Social Order and Disorder of Street Blocks and Neighborhoods: Ecology, Microecology, and the Systemic Model of Social Disorganization." *Journal of Research in Crime and Delinquency* 33: 113–155.

Taylor, Ralph B., and Stephen D. Gottfredson. 1986. "Environmental Design, Crime, and Prevention: An Examination of Community Dynamics." *Crime and Justice* 8: 387.

Terrill, William, and Stephen D. Mastrofski. 2002. "Situational and Officer-Based Determinants of Police Coercion." *Justice Quarterly* 19: 215–248.

Terrill, William, and Michael D. Reisig. 2003. "Neighborhood Context and Police Use of Force." *Journal of Research in Crime & Delinquency* 40: 291–321.

Tillyer, Marie S., and John E. Eck. 2010. "Getting a Handle on Crime: A Further Extension of Routine Activities Theory." *Security Journal* 24: 179–193.

Tyler, Tom R., and Jeffrey Fagan. 2006. "Legitimacy and Cooperation: Why Do People Help the Police Fight Crime in Their Communities?" SSRN Scholarly Paper No. ID 887737, 231–275.

Venkatesh, Sudhir A. 1997. "The Social Organization of Street Gang Activity in an Urban Ghetto." *American Journal of Sociology* 103: 82–111.

Varano, Sean P., Joseph A. Schager, Jeffrey M. Cancino, and Marc L. Swatt. 2009. "Constructing Crime: Neighborhood Characteristics and Police Recording Behavior." *Journal of Criminal Justice* 37: 553–563.

Warner, Barbara D. 1997. "Community Characteristics and the Recording of Crime: Police Recording of Citizens' Complaints of Burglary and Assault." *Justice Quarterly* 14: 631–650.

Weisburd, David L. 2015. "The Law of Crime Concentration and the Criminology of Place." *Criminology* 53: 133–157.

Weisburd, David L., and Shai Amram. 2014. "The Law of Concentrations of Crime at Place: The Case of Tel Aviv-Jaffa." *Police Practice and Research: An International Journal* 15: 101–114.

Weisburd, David L., and Lorraine Green. 1995. "Policing Drug Hot Spots: The Jersey City Drug Market Analysis Experiment." *Justice Quarterly* 12: 711–735.

Weisburd, David L., Elizabeth R. Groff, and Sue-Ming Yang. 2012. *The Criminology of Place: Street Segments and Our Understanding of the Crime Problem*. Oxford: Oxford University Press.

Weisburd, David, Cody W. Telep, and Jim Bueermann. 2016. "Enhancing Procedural Justice in Hot Spots Policing: A Multi-Site Randomized Trial." Proposal submitted to the Laura and John Arnold Foundation.

Wicker, Allan W. 1987. "Behavior Settings Reconsidered: Temporal Stages, Resources, Internal Dynamics, Context." Pp. 613–653 in Daniel Stokels and Irwin Altman (eds.), *Handbook of Environmental Psychology*. New York, NY: Wiley-Interscience.

Wilson, James Q., and George L. Kelling. 1982. "Broken Windows: The Police and Neighborhood Safety." *The Atlantic*, March: 29–38.

Wu, Xiaoyun, and Cynthia Lum. 2016. Online First. "Measuring the Spatial and Temporal Patterns of Police Proactivity." *Journal of Quantitative Criminology*.

10

Not Just What Works, But *How* It Works: Mechanisms and Context in the Effectiveness of Place-Based Policing

Cody W. Telep

Introduction

There is a strong and growing evidence base of rigorous studies demonstrating that police can effectively reduce crime when they focus on small places with high levels of criminal activity (see Braga, Papachristos, and Hureau 2014; Weisburd and Telep 2014). Place-based or hot spots policing, which entails police focusing greater resources on small units of geography with high levels of crime, has been associated with crime declines in a variety of contexts using a number of different strategies (Telep and Weisburd 2012). These strategies all share in common a focus on very small units of intervention and programs that provide extra attention to these small places. But less is known about how exactly hot spots policing works to reduce crime. Place-based policing has generally been guided by deterrence theory and environmental criminology theories focusing on crime and opportunity concentrations (see Braga and Schnell in this volume; Braga and Weisburd 2010; Nagin, Solow, and Lum 2015; Sherman et al. 2014). Less empirical attention, however, has been given to conceptualizing and measuring key propositions from these theories as part of hot spots evaluations (see Famega, Hinkle, and Weisburd 2017; Haberman 2016). Additionally, only limited attention has been given to assessing how particular police activities are linked to the effectiveness of place-based interventions. As a result, while the theories underlying place-based policing provide a plausible rationale and logic model for the strategy's effectiveness, there is still much to be learned about the mechanisms by which hot spots policing reduces crime.

I focus in this chapter on the importance of further exploring mechanisms and contextual issues to move hot spots policing work beyond the question of "does it work?" to "how does it work?" I focus here on increasing police patrols as a strategy in hot spots policing, recognizing that this is but one approach to addressing high crime areas (see Braga et al. 2014). The sections that follow include a discussion of the importance of mechanisms, particularly in experimental work. I explore theories underlying hot spots policing, work done on understanding the mechanisms explaining its effects, and key gaps in place-based policing research to date. Finally, I propose ways to begin to address these gaps and improve our understanding of how hot spots policing works to effectively reduce crime.

Why Mechanisms Matter

While there has been a recent emphasis across the social sciences in better specifying mechanisms, as Hedström and Ylikoski (2010) review there is not a consensus on how to define the concept of mechanisms or how best to identify them. I focus here on Hedström's (2005: 25) definition: "Mechanisms consist of entities (with their properties) and the activities that these entities engage in, either by themselves or in concert with other entities. These activities bring about change, and the type of change brought about depends on the properties of the entities and how the entities are organized spatially and temporally." While mechanisms play an important role in specifying causal processes, they have not always been well researched in criminal justice and related fields. As Granger (2011: 29) emphasizes in the context of research on schools, for example, "we need more attention paid to *why* and *under what conditions* things work as the ingredients in the 'what works' agenda."

The importance of specifying mechanisms in policing research has been raised by other scholars, perhaps most prominently by Pawson and Tilley (1997) in their call for "realist evaluation" (see Laycock 2001). They argue, in focusing on mechanisms and contextual effects, that the question should not be "what works?" but "what works for whom in what circumstances?" They point to studies of mandatory arrest for misdemeanor domestic violence as an example that is common in criminal justice and policing research: a series of studies suggested conflicting results and no simple answer to the question "does it work?" Arrests did not universally reduce recidivism, but did have a deterrent effect for particular types of offenders (e.g., those who were employed) and in particular cities. As Sherman (1992) alludes to, this was likely due to the differing contexts in which the policy was tested. Pawson and Tilley (1997) suggest this reinforces the need to look at mechanisms and how they operate across contexts. For realist evaluation to take place, careful attention must be given to theory at the outset in order to generate appropriate measures to evaluate different potential mechanisms.

And while theory plays an important role in identifying and examining mechanisms, this focus is not simply an exercise in theory development. A better understanding of mechanisms allows for greater attention to designing interventions most likely to be successful. As John Laub (2011: 17), then Director of the National Institute of Justice, argued in discussing translational criminology, "successful dissemination also requires that the evidence is implemented correctly. In other words, it is not just about finding evidence that something works; it is figuring out why it works and how to implement the evidence in real-world settings."

For purposes of this chapter, mechanisms get at the question of *how* hot spots policing reduces crime. The Hedström (2005) definition is especially useful, because it alludes to key concepts in the design and delivery of hot spots intervention. These include how police officers (the entities in this case) interact with criminal justice and non-criminal justice (e.g., citizen) actors to engage in particular activities designed to reduce crime. By definition these activities are organized spatially in hot spots, and as I discuss more later in the chapter, the temporal organization of these activities also plays a role in explaining effectiveness.

I organize the discussion of mechanisms and contextual issues using the three "pragmatic challenges" raised by Sampson, Winship, and Knight (2013: 593) in their article on translating research into useful policy guidance: mechanisms and pathways, heterogeneous effects, and contextualization. As they argue in making the case for the importance of considering these issues, "policy research requires more than the estimation of causal effects, even if precisely and well identified. Rather it requires system-level knowledge of how policy is expected to work within a larger social context. Methodological fine-tuning and even technical certainty, we argue, cannot substitute for theory, substantive knowledge, and attention to context" (Sampson et al. 2013: 588). I discuss each of these three challenges and their relevance to hot spots policing in more detail before turning to key areas for future research in place-based policing.

Mechanisms and Causal Pathways

The Need to Examine How Hot Spots Policing Works

While establishing the effectiveness of hot spots policing has been of great importance for improving policing policy and practice in efforts to make communities safer, further exploring the *"causes* of effectiveness" (Famega et al. 2017: 107) is essential both to maximize the chances of crime reduction and to provide proper guidance to police leaders on how to best implement place-based policing. The effectiveness of hot spots policing is now well established not only because of a large number of evaluations suggesting success, but also because so many of these studies were randomized experiments. The Braga et al. (2014) systematic review included ten randomized trials of the 19 eligible studies, and multiple additional experiments have been published since the completion of this review. Randomized experiments make it possible to causally link a particular intervention or program to a particular outcome and have higher levels of interval validity than other designs not relying on random assignment (see Weisburd 2010).

Thus, the large number of experimental trials makes it more reasonable to claim that hot spots policing *caused* a reduction in crime in a series of interventions. Critics, however, often point to shortcomings in experimental work. Two are especially relevant to this chapter. First, the causal statements in experiments are context-specific, an issue revisited later in the chapter.

Second, experiments do not inherently provide guidance on how a particular program was effective (or ineffective). Indeed, Pawson and Tilley's (1997) work on realist evaluation described earlier attacks experiments as generally too focused on the "does it work?" question at the expense of understanding how an intervention or treatment was effective (or ineffective). In the case of hot spots policing, the experimental design allows for an unbiased estimate of the average treatment effect across hot spots. This is typically measured with official data on crime calls or incidents. Explaining exactly how crime went down in a particular intervention often requires conjecture or post-hoc analyses, an issue discussed in more detail later in the chapter. Thus, more carefully examining mechanisms, while important for any research design, is especially important in experimental evaluation research. And as Sampson (2010: 498) points out, "Establishing causal mechanisms is as much about theory and observation as it is about estimating a single parameter in a statistical model *or* experiment."

Theory and observation during the intervention are required for better understanding the mechanisms at work. As Famega et al. (2017: 108) argue, "even randomized policing experiments with perfectly implemented interventions can only tell us *whether* the overall strategy had an impact on the outcome measures when the treatment is conceptualized as a black box in analyses . . . criminology is largely past only wanting to know *whether* a strategy works in reducing crime; the more functional focus is on *how* interventions do or do not work." Greene (2014: 197) makes a related argument in pointing to policing research's general emphasis on prediction or effectiveness, rather than the meaning of these findings; as he points out in reference to hot spots policing studies, "As the focus of much of this research is on 'outcomes' (e.g. reducing crime and disorder without displacement), how such accomplishments are achieved is largely understudied . . . Certainly, this does not invalidate this approach, but it does draw out possible concerns for linking the outcomes to the processes thought to produce them" (see also Haberman 2016).

Mechanisms in Hot Spots Policing

There are a host of different mechanisms that are potentially relevant to understanding the effectiveness of hot spots policing. As Sampson et al. (2013)

emphasize, policy makers are typically interested in achieving outcomes via particular processes and not others. I focus first on less preferred causal processes, displacement and incapacitation, before turning to an extended discussion of deterrence and police patrols in hot spots policing. I then briefly discuss other possible mechanisms, including opportunity blocking and building informal social control, and the need to potentially explore multiple causal pathways.

Displacement and Incapacitation. If crime was reduced in hot spots policing simply through the mechanism of displacement (which evidence suggests it is not), then it likely would not be viewed as a useful policy despite its effectiveness in crime reduction. Similarly, hot spots policing may not be viewed as an efficient policy if the main mechanism underlying its effectiveness was incapacitation through arresting high rate offenders and removing them from hot spots. While research more conclusively suggests immediate spatial displacement is not the primary mechanism at work in hot spots policing (see the discussion later in this chapter; Bowers, Johnson, Guerette, Summers, and Poynton 2011; Braga et al. 2014; Weisburd et al. 2006), less empirical attention has been paid to incapacitation. While hot spots interventions do not typically focus solely or even primarily on increasing arrests, aggressive order maintenance is a commonly used strategy (e.g., Braga et al. 1999; Braga and Bond 2008). This raises largely unanswered questions about the efficiency and cost-effectiveness of the approach and the balance between effectiveness and the criminal justice costs of arrest and incarceration (see Durlauf and Nagin 2011).

Deterrence. The issue of how policing strategies work more generally was recently raised by Nagin et al. (2015: 74); as they argue, "The policing literature as it relates to crime control is largely evaluative—by how much, if at all, do police numbers and deployment strategies affect crime rates? The mechanism by which any effect is achieved is left in the background." Nagin et al. (2015) propose a deterrence model of police effects in which the effectiveness of police is determined by the number of officers, how they are deployed, and how successful they are in blocking criminal opportunities.

Deterrence is the most common mechanism used to explain the success of hot spots policing. Indeed the article detailing the first hot spots experiment was titled "General deterrent effects of police patrol in crime 'hot spots'" (Sherman and Weisburd 1995). Simply arguing for the importance of deterrence, however, still leaves many questions unanswered. Using deterrence as a guide, hot spots policing would be expected to reduce crime by increasing the certainty of punishment for potential offenders, which should reduce the likelihood of offending. This highlights the role of police as sentinels or capable guardians (Nagin 2013) in increasing the risk for potential offenders of being caught. While it is unlikely that police can affect individual levels of criminal propensity (Cullen and Pratt 2016), their efforts can still potentially alter how offenders view a particular situation, which may in turn make a criminal event less likely (Eck and Madensen 2017). But the identification of deterrence as a mechanism still leaves open a number of questions and measurement challenges. Two are especially relevant to consider.

First, how can deterrence be measured in the field? This is quite clearly a challenge to testing deterrence as a mechanism. While crime declines in a hot spots intervention are congruent with a deterrent effect, they also do not rule out other possible explanations. Official police data alone do not provide insight into whether potential offenders operating in hot spots altered their cost-benefit calculation and avoided committing a crime because of the intervention. This issue was raised by Nagin et al. (2015: 95), who highlighted "the importance of gaining a better understanding of offenders' perceptions of the linkage between apprehension risk and target and situational characteristics. Although a large ethnographic literature exists on this topic, adding a quantitative dimension based on survey data to existing qualitative research would be highly valuable." This creates logistical difficulties, but is an important area for future research to consider in surveys and interviews with offenders and potential offenders.

Second, if deterrence is the primary mechanism at work in hot spots interventions, how can the deterrent impacts of the police be best maximized? In other words, as Weisburd and Telep (2014: 203) argue, "While the evidence on the effectiveness of hot spots policing is persuasive, there still remains the question of what specifically police officers should be doing at hot spots to most effectively reduce crime. The literature thus far has not provided the same level of guidance."

I briefly discuss different strategies to tackle hot spots later in the chapter, but note here that the focus in this chapter is on increasing presence through police patrol. But even with a focus on something seemingly as simple as increasing presence, there are still a host of questions to answer. As Sherman and colleagues (2014) describe, adding extra patrol presence requires decisions about the total dosage in terms of manpower hours added to hot spots, the number of visits per day or frequency of presence, the intermittency or time between visits, and the level of uncertainty or the extent to which intermittency varies by day (see also Famega et al. 2017). These are all crucial questions for the temporal organization of hot spots policing. Questions are also raised about how deterrence operates as a mechanism when police are present vs. not. Deterrence operates more clearly when citizens can see an officer and avoid offending in his or her presence. But, what about instances when officers are not there, but potential offenders perceive an officer *may* be nearby or likely to be present at any moment? And what about the time period after hot spots interventions end? Work by Sorg, Haberman, Ratcliffe, and Groff

(2013) suggests post-intervention treatment decay occurs fairly quickly, particularly in an intervention focused on increasing presence. Further unraveling how deterrence operates under these different circumstances is important for future research.

Deterrence and Uncertainty. A hot spots randomized trial in Sacramento, California helps illustrate some of these issues in testing deterrence as a mechanism. Telep, Mitchell, and Weisburd (2014) found that having officers visit hot spots for about 15 minutes at a time in a random order during their downtime between responding to calls was associated with a significant decline in overall calls for service and serious incidents in the treatment hot spots relative to the control street segments. The intervention was guided by Koper's (1995) work suggesting the benefits of medium-length stops in an unpredictable order.

But how did the intervention effectively reduce crime? Drawing upon research by Sherman (1990) on police crackdowns, Telep and colleagues (2014) point to the potential for brief, intermittent increases in police presence to reduce crime by deterring potential offenders both when police are present and when they are not, because of the unpredictability of increased police presence. These 15 minute stops could have maximized the deterrent ability of the police by creating uncertainty in perceptions of potential offenders about the risk of being apprehended.

The concepts of risk and uncertainty have a long tradition in economics, dating to the work of Knight (1921), who differentiated risk from uncertainty based on whether the probability of an event occurring could be estimated. The risk of an event occurring has a probability that can be calculated, while the likelihood of an uncertain event cannot be. Knight's (1921) work and later expansion of his work by Meltzer (1982) focused on markets and the use of firms to reduce uncertainty, but the ideas can be applied to hot spots policing as well. While potential offenders may not be able to estimate the risk of apprehension with total certainty, they likely have some hypothesis about the likelihood of being apprehended. A potential offender could be deterred by increasing the probability of apprehension to a level so high that the crime is too risky to commit. But if the police intervention is, for example, increased presence on Friday nights, then the risk level is increased, but also very predictable, and thus is unlikely to deter offending at other times. The potential advantage of increased presence for about 15 minutes at a time at randomly dispersed times of day is the increase in not only risk, but also uncertainty, because the probability of apprehension at any particular time becomes more difficult for the potential offender to estimate.

The usefulness of increasing uncertainty or ambiguity is at least partially supported by recent survey-based deterrence research in criminology. In a sample of young adults, Loughran, Paternoster, Piquero, and Pogarsky (2011) found some support for the idea that increasing levels of uncertainty in punishment can increase deterrence because individuals tend to be "ambiguity averse." However, in a sample of juvenile offenders, increasing uncertainty was only effective for increasing deterrence in non-contact (e.g., property) crimes, but in the case of contact (e.g., violent) crimes, ambiguity actually increased the likelihood of offending when the perceived risk of detection was low. Despite these mixed findings, Loughran et al. (2011: 1056) emphasize the potential benefits of a "Koper curve" hot spots policing approach, noting, "With the same amount of resources, an alteration of police policy by manipulating the ambiguity of the certainty of arrest would enable them to enhance the deterrent effect they have. Our finding with respect to ambiguity suggests it would be worthwhile for law enforcement to exploit any vagueness in perceptions of the risk of punishment."

While this is a plausible pathway to explain the Sacramento results, no part of the intervention tested the reasonableness of this explanation. While recognizing the challenge in doing so, a study with a larger budget (this study was carried out without research funding) could have incorporated interviews that measured perceptions of the risk of punishment for known offenders operating in hot spots areas. Surveys could also have been used to examine whether perceptions of the likelihood of punishment changed among residents and visitors to the hot spots before vs. during the intervention. It is also important to note that the Sacramento experiment tested 15 minute stops compared to a control group that did not receive any extra patrol, so the study does not provide experimental evidence on whether 15 minutes is the ideal stop length. Future studies should experiment with police patrols of varying lengths.

Reducing Opportunities for Crime. Making matters even more complex, deterrence is but one of the possible pathways by which hot spots policing could impact crime. Eck and Madensen (2017) discuss a number of other plausible pathways by which police can affect offender decision making, suggesting the need to consider ways to measure a host of mechanisms. While police may have direct impacts on offenders as described earlier, they can also indirectly impact offenders, through, for example, working with place managers to implement situational crime prevention efforts or building informal social control in handlers who can control the behavior of offenders. Such efforts may go beyond the scope of patrol-based hot spots strategies, but suggest the complexity of examining how hot spots policing works, especially when police use more problem-oriented approaches (see later in the chapter).

The five overarching methods for addressing crime opportunities in situations described by Clarke and Eck (2005)—increasing the risk, increasing the effort, reducing rewards, reducing provocations, and removing excuses—highlight the multiple possible mechanisms at work in situational prevention efforts. Increasing police patrols in hot spots largely fits in with deterring offenders through increasing the risk and increasing the effort of committing crime. Most patrol-based interventions will stop here. But as Eck and Madensen (2017) describe, police interventions could also impact situations through altering reward structures, depending on the activities officers engage in while present in hot spots. Blocked opportunities, of course, are not a focus of only hot spots efforts, but also represent a primary mechanism underlying routine activity theory and non-police-based situational crime prevention efforts (Clarke 1995; Cohen and Felson 1979; Eck and Weisburd 1995). If police remove or reduce the attractiveness of opportunities for crime, then crime may be reduced regardless of offender perceptions of punishment risk.

This creates yet another measurement challenge. In examining changes in opportunity structures, one would ideally measure both offenders' subjective perceptions of the likelihood of rewards or benefits from crime and the objective ability of offenders to find an opportunity to commit a crime. Work by Weisburd, Groff, and Yang (2012) offers some insight into measuring opportunities at micro units of geography in Seattle, but these are generally static measures (e.g., number of parks, street type) or dynamic measures that are generally unresponsive to police actions (e.g., number of employees, number of residents). Measuring opportunities (and opportunities blocked) in the context of a hot spots policing evaluation would require a more precise measure of suitable targets that police could reasonably alter through their presence or actions.

Building on the potential importance of police efforts focused on building informal social control, a current program in Brooklyn Park, MN examines community engagement as a mechanism by which focused policing could reduce crime (Weisburd, Davis, and Gill 2015). The program trains officers to focus on partnerships that can "build residents' willingness to take ownership of local crime issues" (Weisburd et al. 2015: 5). Such efforts to build collective efficacy in high crime locations (see Sampson et al. 1997) suggest another pathway for hot spots policing that focuses on the police working not as sentinels or opportunity blockers, but as motivators and educators. In a related way, hot spots policing could affect crime through how officers treat citizens in encounters occurring within hot spots. I revisit this later in the chapter with a discussion of the relationship between hot spots policing and police legitimacy.

The extent to which police can successfully build trust and informal social control within hot spots, however, is essentially unknown. Indeed, this was a main conclusion of Weisburd, Hinkle, Braga, and Wooditch's (2015) review of what we know about the mechanisms underlying broken windows policing. While broken windows policing does not require hot spots as the unit of analysis, the theory suggests a sequential process where police efforts to deal with disorder will reduce fear and help increase community informal social control (Wilson and Kelling 1982). But Weisburd and colleagues (2015) found just one study that measured the impact of disorder policing on informal social control. Not all hot spots studies are designed to reduce crime through building informal control, but those that do incorporate community building or resident outreach efforts must consider the best ways to assess this causal pathway. At the very least, more research is needed on whether police working in crime hot spots can change resident perceptions of informal social control and, if so, to understand how those changes in perceptions are related to crime outcomes.

Effect Heterogeneity

A second issue raised by Sampson and colleagues (2013) is the importance of considering effect heterogeneity. That is, particular interventions may only be effective for particular subgroups or kinds of individuals. As noted earlier, this is a common outcome in criminal justice and policing research (e.g., Sherman 1992). In the case of hot spots policing, the treatment is delivered to places not people, but effect heterogeneity is still relevant. Indeed, a consideration of mechanisms and contextual effects might be less relevant if effects were universally positive. If hot spots policing *always* was effective, understanding *how* it was effective would be of less importance, at least from a policy perspective, than ensuring it was successfully implemented. But while the bulk of the evidence suggests hot spots policing works, the Braga et al. (2014) review found great variability in effect size. Some of this variation was attributable to intervention type (problem-oriented studies tended to have larger effects) or methodology (quasi-experiments tended to have larger effects), but other factors related to the particular hot spots targeted or officer activities engaged in could also play a role.

Effect heterogeneity is not only relevant across studies, but also within them. Sherman (2002: 235) notes this is especially relevant in experiments: "The strength of that research design is its ability to reduce uncertainty about the average effects of a policy on vast numbers of people. The limitation of the research design is that it cannot escape variability in treatments, responses and implementation." In other words, experiments provide a clear answer on the question of "on average, does this treatment work?" but a less clear answer in terms of "will this treatment work in this particular case?"

Returning to the hot spots randomized trial in Sacramento (Telep et al. 2014) helps illustrate this issue. As described earlier, research on deterrence suggests increasing uncertainty in the minds of potential offenders may only be an effective deterrent for particular crime types. This suggests the model in Sacramento may have varying effects depending on both crime type and type of offender. These issues were not examined, but are worthy of future research. When examining hot spot pairs individually, Telep et al. (2014) did find variability across pairs. Indeed, despite the overall effect favoring the treatment group, in four of the 21 pairs, calls went up in the treatment hot spot relative to the control hot spots. Without further data collection, though, it was not possible to state with any confidence why this variability occurred. Was it a result of the types of crimes or offenders operating in those hot spots? Or did it have to do with particular officer activities and citizen interactions? Or was it some combination of all these factors?

Comparing Multiple Treatments

A number of recent hot spots policing evaluations have begun to deal with issues related to effect heterogeneity through more carefully comparing the impact of different hot spots treatments. I review these studies briefly here, although I recognize this discussion would have also been appropriate earlier in considering the mechanisms by which hot spots policing operates. Comparing multiple interventions in a single study helps to address the question "what type of hot spots policing strategy works best?" It does not fully address the questions raised by Sampson et al. (2013) about subgroups. For example, no studies I am aware of have explored how the effectiveness of place-based policing is impacted by the types of individuals living, working, and offending in a particular hot spot. But a number of recent studies have begun to further explore how particular officer actions and activities might impact the effectiveness of place-based efforts.

Cataloguing what officers spend their time doing is one important step in better understanding what hot spots policing looks like. Officer logs were used to document problem solving responses in hot spots studies in Jersey City, NJ (Braga et al. 1999) and Boston (Braga et al. 2011). Braga and Bond (2008) took this a step further, using mediation analysis to examine the relative effectiveness of situational prevention strategies, misdemeanor arrests, and social service strategies implemented as part of a problem-oriented hot spots policing strategy in Lowell, MA, and finding the strongest evidence for situational efforts.

More recently, four experiments compared the effects of multiple hot spots policing treatments simultaneously. Taylor, Koper, and Woods (2011) compared directed patrol to problem-oriented policing in Jacksonville, FL, finding evidence of a longer-term impact of problem solving in hot spots. Rosenfeld, Deckard, and Blackburn (2014) compared directed patrol to directed patrol along with self-initiated activities in St. Louis, MO, finding self-initiated activities, particularly arrest and occupied vehicle checks, drove effectiveness in reducing gun assaults. Groff et al. (2015) compared three treatments in hot spots in Philadelphia, finding evidence of effectiveness for an intelligence-led focus on high rate offenders, but not for problem-oriented policing or foot patrol. In St. Louis County, Kochel, Burruss, and Weisburd (2015) found crime declines in both directed patrol and problem solving hot spots compared to control sites.

This review of recent studies suggests a great deal of progress in unpacking what "hot spots policing" is and how different approaches vary in terms of effectiveness. It also highlights the effect heterogeneity inherent in evaluation work. Even within this small group of studies, the effectiveness of problem-oriented policing and the use of arrest as a tool were inconsistent across studies. Much work remains to better understand what types of strategies are most appropriate for particular types of hot spots and in particular contexts, an issue I discuss next.

Contextual Effects and Feedback Loops

Context

Finally, Sampson et al. (2013) raise the issue of contextual effects. Understanding effectiveness requires understanding how the impact of hot spots policing varies across different types of jurisdictions with different types of crime problems. The experimental evidence about hot spots policing is persuasive, but statistically generalizable only to the contexts where it has been evaluated. In other words, "hot spots policing caused a reduction in crime" should really be replaced with causal statements applicable to particular studies. For example, hot spots policing caused a reduction in crime in treatment group violent crime hot spots in Jersey City, NJ relative to control hot spots during the six month period following a problem-oriented policing intervention (Braga et al. 1999).

The Braga et al. (2014) review did find positive results from 19 of the 25 tests of hot spots policing, suggesting its effectiveness in a number of contexts, but these contexts do not represent a random or even representative sample of jurisdictions nationally. In other words, while internal validity levels are high, external validity levels may not be (see Clarke and Cornish 1972). Indeed, while hot spots interventions have shown success in multiple medium and large cities, most studies, as is common in policing research, have focused on large urban areas (Cave, Telep, and Grieco 2015). We still know little about the prospects for hot spots policing in more rural or suburban environments (Weisburd and Telep 2014).

Feedback Loops

Sampson and colleagues (2013: 601) discuss context not only in terms of environmental differences, but also in considering interdependencies and the fact that "a policy intervention in one part of the criminal justice system will have reverberations, quite possibly changing the intended outcome of the intervention." I explore here two areas where critics of hot spots policing have suggested potential "reverberations" as a result of feedback loops, lower level of police legitimacy and spatial displacement.

Police Legitimacy. Critics of hot spots policing, while not arguing against its crime control effectiveness, have questioned whether the decrease in crime might come at the expense of citizen perceptions of police legitimacy (see Rosenbaum 2006). If hot spots policing is implemented in an intensive way that is viewed by citizens as unfair, then it has the potential to reduce crime in the short term while increasing crime in the long term by damaging citizen perceptions of police legitimacy (see Tyler 1990, 2004). Such an impact requires both that citizens perceive hot spots policing as unfair and that those perceptions of unfairness then translate to a reduced likelihood of obeying the law. Research to date has not found evidence that intensive policing in hot spots leads to reduced perceptions of police legitimacy (Ratcliffe, Groff, Sorg, and Haberman 2015; Weisburd, Hinkle, Famega, and Ready 2011), especially in the long term (Kochel et al. 2015). Nonetheless, this research has only surveyed residents living in hot spots, who may or may not be the individuals police working in hot spots have the most contact with.

Stressing the need for more research, the President's Task Force on 21st Century Policing (2015) argued that "research conducted to evaluate the effectiveness of crime fighting strategies should specifically look at the potential for collateral damage of any given strategy on community trust and legitimacy." While research suggests that lower levels of perceived police legitimacy in general tend to be associated with higher levels of offending (Tyler, Goff, and MacCoun 2015), no research to date has specifically determined whether hot spots policing interventions in particular affect compliance with the law through changing legitimacy perceptions.

While research has generally focused on the potential negative consequences of hot spots policing for police legitimacy, it is also possible hot spots policing could be implemented in ways that enhance procedural justice. Infusing hot spots policing with procedural justice in an effort to both reduce crime and improve perceptions of police legitimacy is the focus of a current multisite randomized trial funded by the Laura and John Arnold Foundation and led by Jim Bueermann, David Weisburd, Breanne Cave, and me. In four sites, 40 or more hot spots will be identified for the study. Half the hot spots in each site will be assigned to a standard hot spots policing condition with increased presence and attention by an assigned officer team. The other half of the hot spots will also receive extra attention by an officer team, but this team will receive intensive training on incorporating procedural justice into police-citizen interactions. Importantly, this study will measure perceptions of not only residents, but also those who have contact with the police. Additionally, the study will use systematic social observation (SSO) to carefully monitor officer behavior in both groups (see more on SSO later in the chapter). The results of this study will provide much needed empirical data on whether it is possible to disrupt and indeed reverse the negative feedback loop that some critics argue occurs as a result of hot spots policing.

Crime Displacement. The second area where critics have pointed to potential negative reverberations of hot spots policing is spatial displacement. As alluded to earlier, if hot spots policing reduces crime by creating new hot spots in nearby locations where offenders are pushed, then the intervention cannot be viewed as a net positive. Research generally suggests that spatial displacement is not common in hot spots policing interventions (Braga et al. 2014; Bowers et al. 2011), and, indeed, a spatial diffusion of benefits (Clarke and Weisburd 1994) where crime also decreases in areas surrounding targeted hot spots is more likely to occur.

As Johnson, Guerette, and Bowers (2014) argue, however, less is known about exactly why crime is not displaced in focused police interventions (see Weisburd and Telep 2012). Weisburd and colleagues' (2006) multi-method data collection efforts offered important insights through a combination of crime data, systematic social observation, offender interviews, and ethnographic work with offenders. Their findings suggested displacement was uncommon because nearby areas may not offer the same opportunities and because of the dangers and difficulties of relocating criminal activity. The qualitative work was especially useful for understanding why there was not displacement. Indeed, based on interviews with arrested drug dealers, Weisburd et al. (2006: 578) point to "dealers' intimacy with the area in which they work" as "one of the primary mechanisms preventing spatial displacement."

Most commonly, though, research simply examines crime counts in areas surrounding targeted hot spots for evidence of displacement or diffusion. Thus, even though displacement is an individual-level phenomenon, it is typically only measured as a geographic process. Thus, and in line with the earlier discussion about deterrence, more research is needed that considers how individuals react to hot spots interventions and how that affects their propensity to offend in areas nearby. Additionally, focusing on displacement exclusively in the few blocks surrounding hot spots has limited the ability of most hot spots interventions to examine spatial displacement to areas further away. Mazeika's (2014) examination of whether offenders are displaced to other parts of Washington, DC as a result of police crackdowns similarly suggests limited spatial displacement, even when examining an entire jurisdiction, but more research incorporating individual-level data is needed on different types of hot spots interventions. This is in line with earlier work on displacement by Reppetto (1976) and Bennett and Wright (1984), which emphasized the importance of considering the impact of police activities on individual offenders, and not just using aggregate crime data to assess displacement.

What Can Be Done Moving Forward?

My examination of mechanisms and context suggests a number of areas for future work on place-based policing to address. I discuss three areas where more could be done to better understand *how* hot spots policing works. While recognizing that some of these solutions are time- and resource-intensive (Weisburd, Hinkle et al. 2015), I also think it well worth the investment to provide better guidance to agencies interested in implementing evidence-based approaches to reducing crime.

Specifying a Theory of Action

First, greater attention should be paid to specifying a theory of action for hot spots interventions at the outset. This is commonly ignored in hot spots policing interventions for a number of reasons. As reviewed earlier, many hot spots interventions are multi-faceted in an effort to throw everything possible at the problem, without necessarily including a careful consideration of how each intervention component is expected to affect outcomes of interest. Additionally, researchers are frequently brought in after planning for an intervention has occurred (or sometimes after the intervention itself has already occurred). Post-hoc evaluations make it impossible to consider mechanisms and how to best measure them at the outset. This is a challenge not just in hot spots policing, but policing (and criminal justice) interventions more generally. Indeed, Zimring (2012: 204) notes that is a primary challenge in assessing how crime declined in New York City in the 1990s and early 2000s: "The practical problem is that many of the specific mechanisms at work in New York City in the 1990s and since are unknown." Most policing evaluations would benefit from pre-intervention discussions between agencies and researchers to create a logic model for the intervention and develop appropriate measures to test the theory of action (see Gill, Weisburd, Telep, Vitter, and Bennett 2014).

Collecting Additional Data

Second and related to the first point, whenever possible, additional data collection efforts should be used to better understand the processes underlying the hot spots intervention. As Nagin and Weisburd (2013: 673) emphasize, "criminologists must begin the process of identifying what data are needed early on. They must make the scene and encourage policy makers and practitioners to collect information that will aid the evaluation later." The specific data needed will depend in part on the theoretical propositions hypothesized to be relevant. But it is clear that the question of "how is hot spots policing effective?" will be better answered with more data on officer actions and how citizens respond to these actions. It is likely that mixed method approaches combining multiple forms of quantitative data with qualitative data collection efforts will be most productive in fully understanding mechanisms at work (Greene 2014). Here I discuss three forms of data collection, two quantitative and one qualitative, that could be more frequently incorporated into hot spots policing evaluations.

To further address the question of where officers are spending their time, technology is making it increasingly possible to precisely track dosage levels in hot spots interventions. Automatic vehicle location (AVL) technology tracks the exact location of a patrol car repeatedly. This has obvious benefits for officer safety in terms of monitoring patrol cars, but it also has benefits for assessing where officers are going during their shift. In hot spots policing studies, saturation patrol is often an important component of the intervention, and so AVL technology could allow the department to assess how often officers are visiting hot spots and whether treatment is being delivered as intended (see Weisburd, Groff et al. 2015). While police unions are reluctant to allow departments to closely monitor AVL data, there is potential here to better identify officers' spatial location during their shift.

Revisiting the Sacramento hot spots study described earlier, Telep et al. (2014) reported on treatment dosage using the number of visits per hot spot and total hour spent in each spot using dispatch data because officers used a special call code when responding to treatment group hot spots. While this gives a general measure of dosage, AVL data provides a more precise measure less subject to undercounting (e.g., when officers forget to use the call code while present) or overcounting (e.g., when officers remain in the hot spot call code even after leaving the hot spot). Additionally, work by Sorg and colleagues (2014) suggested officers may patrol outside of their assigned hot spots, especially if the intervention requires presence for long periods of time. This is especially problematic if officers are also patrolling in control sites or displacement catchment areas. Thus, AVL data would be useful in tracking not only treatment dosage, but also misapplied dosage to non-treatment areas.

While AVL technology allows for more accurate measures of dosage and the temporal scope of hot spots policing, additional data collection efforts should also focus on what activities officers engage in while present in hot spots. Official data sources, such as citations, investigative reports, and arrest reports, provide some insight into the enforcement activities of officers. Particularly for interventions that involve more than simply increasing presence, additional tracking mechanisms are essential. Official data sources alone will provide entirely inadequate data on problem solving in hot spots, for example. As noted earlier, some attempts have been made to better track officer behavior through activity forms. And while these forms rely on officers to accurately document their activities in hot spots, they are a useful supplement to official data sources, particularly for activities related to community outreach or situational crime prevention that are unlikely to show up in departmental records (Alpert and Moore 1993).

Systematic social observation (SSO) offers an even better way to assess what activities officers are engaged in and provides a more objective measure of police-citizen interactions. SSO makes use of protocols in field observations of the police to ensure that data collection is standardized within and across observers. As Mastrofski, Parks, and McCluskey (2010: 243–244) note, "it offers enhanced prospects of validity, and in many situations it provides for increased confidence in reliability, because of the researcher's direct access to the phenomenon of interest and greater control and transparency of data encoding. Further, it affords greater precision in capturing details of the phenomenon and its context."

SSO is not without potential threats to validity. A primary one is the possibility of observer error in recalling events. While multiple observers of the same scene would be ideal to avoid this, it becomes difficult in terms of both cost and logistics to use more than one observer per officer. Another concern is reactivity effects. Are officers responding differently when observers are watching their actions? Research on this topic is limited, but in a long-term project where officers are being observed repeatedly, it seems less likely that reactivity would be a major problem. SSO has been an important component of a small but growing number of research studies on police behavior. Famega and colleagues (2005), for example, used SSO in Baltimore to assess both how officer time was allocated and the reason for officer actions over the course of 163 shifts. Their finding that 75 percent of officer time is unassigned suggests that simply examining calls for service data is insufficient for understanding what officers are doing during their shifts.

To date, SSO has generally been used as a tool to examine police behavior in general, not as part of an evaluation. The study I described earlier on procedural justice in hot spots policing is the first I am aware of to incorporate SSO into a hot spots evaluation. Telep and colleagues (2014) note the lack of SSO or other observational data as a limitation in understanding how the hot spots treatment in Sacramento was effective. They were "unable to use ride alongs or systematic social observation to assess what officers were actually doing when they patrolled in crime hot spots. . . . In a related way, we cannot be sure of how officer activities in the hot spots affected our overall findings" (Telep et al. 2014: 929).

The proliferation of body cameras may also allow for systematic coding of officer behavior at a lower cost than systematic social observation. To date, body camera footage has not been integrated into hot spots policing interventions, but research in this area is expanding rapidly (see Lum, Koper, Merola, Scherer, and Reioux 2015), and the use of camera data to code officer activities seems like a promising avenue for future studies. As with AVL data, concerns about officer and citizen privacy and police union reluctance to have body camera data shared create challenges, but this could be an important source of information on what officers are doing in the field moving forward. Worden and McLean (2014) successfully used officer dashboard camera footage to code police-citizen interactions during stops for indicators of procedural justice. Similarly coding body camera data (which should provide clearer footage than dash cams) for indicators of hot spots policing (e.g., problem solving, enforcement, community engagement, or presence, depending on the intervention) would be valuable in future studies.

Qualitative data collection efforts could take a number of forms depending on the particular hot spots policing strategy. Building on the work of Weisburd and colleagues (2006) in their mixed methods evaluation of why crime is not easily displaced, these efforts could include interviewing offenders arrested as part of the intervention to understand how their perceptions of risk were affected by police efforts and using an ethnographer to more closely examine how offender behavior is affected by hot spots interventions. Hot spots studies to date have generally not included contact with offenders because of funding constraints, which has limited the ability to understand if and how offenders respond to increased police activity in targeted locations.

Conducting Multi-Site Studies

And third, multi-site studies are an especially useful way to make clearer statements about how context impacts the effects of hot spots policing. I recognize that these studies are more complicated and costly, but prior studies in criminal justice (Weisburd and Taxman 2000) and hot spots policing specifically (Weisburd et al. 2011) suggest their feasibility. The use of multiple sites is beneficial not only for assessing context, but also for increasing statistical power, which can be an issue when a single agency may only be able to provide treatment to a small number of hot spots. Multi-site studies require a great deal of coordination with police agencies, funders, and research partners, but would greatly enhance the external validity of research findings. The Metaketa Initiative through Evidence in Governance and Politics,[1] which is focusing on funding cross-national, comparable interventions to allow for generalizable knowledge, is one potential model for doing this. To date, the Metaketa Initiative has focused on public information, with plans to expand to policing projects in 2017.

Conclusion

This chapter has focused on the importance of mechanisms and contextual factors in further explaining the effectiveness of hot spots policing. While there is strong empirical support for the success of place-based policing in reducing crime, less is known about exactly how hot spots policing works (see Haberman 2016). I have reviewed recent work addressing the "how?" question through a more careful focus on treatment dosage and content, but more work is needed to further explore these issues. The questions I have raised are important to address in order to design and implement effective hot spots policing programs. Without greater attention to mechanisms, police leaders have little guidance on what specifically they should replicate and incorporate in creating hot spots policing programs.

These are challenging issues, even with this chapter's focus primarily on increasing police patrols in hot spots. Integrating other types of interventions into micro geographies will require even greater attention to clearly specifying mechanisms and theories of action. What is important to emphasize in closing is that a reliance on official crime data alone will rarely be sufficient in understanding *how* a police strategy worked (or did not work) to reduce crime. There is no doubt that up-to-date data and rigorous crime analysis should be used to guide the development and evaluation of place-based interventions. But evaluations should rely on more than just official data to assess process and impacts.

A recent *Los Angeles Times* article on officers pushing back against predictive models (see Ridgeway 2013) in Burbank, CA suggests the limits of a data-driven approach that is overly reliant on data alone (Tchekmedyian 2016). As an example, officers were sometimes sent to patrol at police stations, presumably because these locations typically have high crime volume as a reporting location. That particular error could be fixed rather simply in the computer model, but suggests the need to be thoughtful in the design, implementation, and evaluation of place-based policing efforts. More careful attention to these issues can help move policing research forward to better understand not just whether hot spots policing works, but how to make it work best in a particular context.

Note

1. See more on the Metaketa Initiative at http://egap.org/metaketa.

References

Alpert, Geoffrey, and Mark Moore. 1993. "Measuring Police Performance in the New Paradigm of Policing." Pp. 109–142 in John J. DiIulio, Geoffrey P. Alpert, Mark H. Moore, George F. Cole, Joan Petersilia, Charles H. Logan, and James Q. Wilson (eds.), *Performance Measurement for the Criminal Justice System*. Washington, DC: Bureau of Justice Statistics, U.S. Department of Justice.

Bennett, Trevor, and Richard Wright. 1984. *Burglars on Burglary: Prevention and the Offender*. Brookfield, VT: Gower Publishing.

Bowers, Kate J., Shane D. Johnson, Rob T. Guerette, Lucia Summers, and Suzanne Poynton. 2011. "Spatial Displacement and Diffusion of Benefits among Geographically Focused Policing Interventions: A Meta Analytical Review." *Journal of Experimental Criminology* 7: 347–374.

Braga, Anthony A., and Brenda J. Bond. 2008. "Policing Crime and Disorder Hot Spots: A Randomized Controlled Trial." *Criminology* 46: 577–608.

Braga, Anthony A., David M. Hureau, and Andrew V. Papachristos. 2011. "An Ex Post Facto Evaluation Framework for Place-Based Police Interventions." *Evaluation Review* 35: 592–626.

Braga, Anthony A., Andrew V. Papachristos, and David M. Hureau. 2014. "The Effects of Hot Spots Policing on Crime: An Updated Systematic Review and Meta-Analysis." *Justice Quarterly* 31: 633–663.

Braga, Anthony A., and Cory Schnell. This Volume. "Beyond Putting 'Cops on Dots': Applying Theory to Advance Policy Responses to Crime Places."

Braga, Anthony A., and David L. Weisburd. 2010. *Policing Problem Places: Crime Hot Spots and Effective Prevention*. New York, NY: Oxford University Press.

Braga, Anthony A., David L. Weisburd, Elin J. Waring, Lorraine G. Mazerolle, William Spelman, and Frank Gajewski. 1999. "Problem-Oriented Policing in Violent Crime Places: A Randomized Controlled Experiment." *Criminology* 37: 541–580.

Cave, Breanne, Cody W. Telep, and Julie Grieco. 2015. "Rigorous Evaluation Research among U.S. Police Departments: Special Cases or a Representative Sample?" *Police Practice and Research: An International Journal* 16: 254–268.

Clarke, Ronald V. G. 1995. "Situational Crime Prevention." Pp. 91–150 in Michael Tonry and David Farrington (eds.), *Building a Safer Society: Strategic Approaches to Crime Prevention: Crime and Justice: A Review of Research*, vol. 19. Chicago, IL: University of Chicago Press.

Clarke, Ronald V. G., and Derek B. Cornish. 1972. *The Controlled Trial in Institutional Research: Paradigm or Pitfall for Penal Evaluators?* London: Her Majesty's Stationary Office.

Clarke, Ronald V. G., and John E. Eck. 2005. *Crime Analysis for Problem Solvers in 60 Small Steps*. Washington, DC: Office of Community Oriented Policing Services, U.S. Department of Justice.

Clarke, Ronald V. G., and David Weisburd. 1994. "Diffusion of Crime Control Benefits: Observations on the Reverse of Displacement." Pp. 165–184 in Ronald V. Clarke (ed.), *Crime Prevention Studies*, vol. 2. Monsey, NY: Criminal Justice Press.

Cohen, Lawrence E., and Marcus Felson. 1979. "Social Change and Crime Rate Trends: A Routine Activity Approach." *American Sociological Review* 44: 588–608.

Cullen, Francis T., and Travis C. Pratt. 2016. "Toward a Theory of Police Effects." *Criminology and Public Policy* 15: 799–811.

Durlauf, Steven N., and Daniel S. Nagin. 2011. "Imprisonment and Crime: Can Both Be Reduced?" *Criminology and Public Policy* 10: 13–54.

Eck, John E., and Tamera D. Madensen. 2017. "Police and Offender Choices: A Framework." Pp. 374–397 in Wim Bernasco, Henk Elffers, and Jean-Louis van Gelder (eds.), *The Oxford Handbook of Offender Decision Making*. New York, NY: Oxford University Press.

Eck, John E., and David Weisburd. 1995. "Crime Places in Crime Theory." Pp. 1–33 in John E. Eck and David Weisburd (eds.), *Crime and Place: Crime Prevention Studies*, vol. 4. Monsey, NY: Willow Tree Press.

Famega, Christine N., James Frank, and Lorarine Mazerolle. 2005. "Managing Police Patrol Time: The Role of Supervisor Directives." *Justice Quarterly* 22: 540–559.

Famega, Christine, Joshua C. Hinkle, and David Weisburd. 2017. "Why Getting Inside the 'Black Box' Is Important: Examining Treatment Implementation and Outputs in Policing Experiments." *Police Quarterly* 20: 106–132.

Gill, Charlotte, David Weisburd, Cody W. Telep, Zoe Vitter, and Trevor Bennett. 2014. "Community-Oriented Policing to Reduce Crime, Disorder and Fear and Increase Satisfaction and Legitimacy Among Citizens: A Systematic Review." *Journal of Experimental Criminology* 10: 399–428.

Granger, Robert C. 2011. "The Big Why: A Learning Agenda for the Scale-Up Movement." Pp. 28–32 in *Pathways: A Magazine on Poverty, Inequality, and Social Policy* Winter 2011.

Greene, Jack R. 2014. "New Directions in Policing: Balancing Prediction and Meaning in Police Research." *Justice Quarterly* 31: 193–228.

Groff, Elizabeth R., Jerry H. Ratcliffe, Cory P. Haberman, Evan T. Sorg, Nola M. Joyce, and Ralph B. Taylor. 2015. "Does What Police Do at Hot Spots Matter? The Philadelphia Policing Tactics Experiment." *Criminology* 53: 23–53.

Haberman, Cory P. 2016. "A View Inside the 'Black Box' of Hot Spots Policing from a Sample of Police Commanders." *Police Quarterly* 19: 488–517.

Hedström, Peter. 2005. *Dissecting the Social: On the Principles of Analytical Sociology*. Cambridge, UK: Cambridge University Press.

Hedström, Peter, and Petri Ylikoski. 2010. "Causal Mechanisms in the Social Sciences." *Annual Review of Sociology* 36: 49–67.

Johnson, Shane D., Rob T. Guerette, and Kate Bowers. 2014. "Crime Displacement: What We Know, What We Don't Know, and What It Means for Crime Reduction." *Journal of Experimental Criminology* 10: 549–571.

Knight, Frank H. 1921. *Risk, Uncertainty and Profit*. Boston, MA: Houghton-Mifflin.

Kochel, Tammy R., George Burruss, and David Weisburd. 2015. *St. Louis Hot Spots in Residential Areas (SCHIRA) Final Report: Assessing the Effects of Hot Spots Policing Strategies on Police Legitimacy, Crime, and Collective Efficacy*. Carbondale, IL: Department of Criminology and Criminal Justice, Southern Illinois University Carbondale.

Koper, Christopher S. 1995. "Just Enough Police Presence: Reducing Crime and Disorderly Behavior By Optimizing Patrol Time in Crime Hot Spots." *Justice Quarterly* 12: 649–672.

Laub, John H. 2011. "Strengthening NIJ: Mission, Science and Process." *NIJ Journal* 268: 16–21.

Laycock, Gloria. 2001. "Research for Police: Who Needs It?" In *Trends and Issues in Crime and Criminal Justice*. Canberra: Australian Institute of Criminology.

Loughran, Thomas A., Raymond Paternoster, Alex R. Piquero, and Greg Pogarsky. 2011. "On Ambiguity in Perceptions of Risk: Implications for Criminal Decision Making and Deterrence." *Criminology* 49: 1029–1061.

Lum, Cynthia, Christopher S. Koper, Linda M. Merola, Amber Scherer, and Amanda Reioux. 2015. *Existing and Ongoing Body Camera Research: Knowledge Gaps and Opportunities: A Research Agenda for the Laura and John Arnold Foundation*. Fairfax, VA: Center for Evidence-Based Crime Policy, George Mason University.

Mastrofski, Stephen D., Roger B. Parks, and John D. McCluskey. 2010. "Systematic Social Observation in Criminology." Pp. 225–247 in Alex R. Piquero and David Weisburd (eds.), *Handbook of Quantitative Criminology*. New York, NY: Springer.

Mazeika, David M. 2014. *General and Specific Displacement Effects of Police Crackdowns: Criminal Events and "Local Criminals"*. Ph.D. dissertation. College Park, MD: University of Maryland.

Meltzer, Allan H. 1982. "Rational Expectations, Risk, Uncertainty, and Market Responses." Pp. 3–22 in Paul Wachtel (ed.), *Crises in the Economic and Financial Structure*. New York, NY: Lexington Books.

Nagin, Daniel S. 2013. "Deterrence in the Twenty-First Century." Pp. 199–263 in Michael Tonry (ed.), *Crime and Justice: A Review of Research*, vol. 42. Chicago, IL: University of Chicago Press.

Nagin, Daniel S., and David Weisburd. 2013. "Evidence and Public Policy: The Example of Evaluation Research in Policing." *Criminology and Public Policy* 12: 651–679.

Nagin, Daniel S., Robert M. Solow, and Cynthia Lum. 2015. "Deterrence, Criminal Opportunities, and Police." *Criminology* 53: 74–100.

Pawson, Ray, and Nick Tilley. 1997. *Realistic Evaluation*. London: Sage.

President's Task Force on 21st Century Policing. 2015. *Final Report of the President's Task Force on 21st Century Policing*. Washington, DC: Office of Community Oriented Policing Services, U.S. Department of Justice.

Ratcliffe, Jerry H., Elizabeth R. Groff, Evan T. Sorg, and Cory P. Haberman. 2015. "Citizens' Reactions to Hot Spots Policing: Impacts on Perceptions of Crime, Disorder, Safety and Police." *Journal of Experimental Criminology* 11: 393–417.

Reppetto, Thomas A. 1976. "Crime Prevention and the Displacement Phenomenon." *Crime & Delinquency* 22: 166–177.

Ridgeway, Greg. 2013. "The Pitfalls of Prediction." *NIJ Journal* 271: 34–40.

Rosenbaum, Dennis P. 2006. "The Limits of Hot Spots Policing." Pp. 245–263 in David Weisburd and Anthony A. Braga (eds.), *Police Innovation: Contrasting Perspectives*. New York, NY: Cambridge University Press.

Rosenfeld, Richard, Michael J. Deckard, and Emily Blackburn. 2014. "The Effects of Directed Patrol and Self-Initiated Enforcement on Firearm Violence: A Randomized Controlled Study of Hot Spot Policing." *Criminology* 52: 428–449.

Sampson, Robert J. 2010. "Gold Standard Myths: Observations on the Experimental Turn in Quantitative Criminology." *Journal of Quantitative Criminology* 26: 489–500.

Sampson, Robert J., Stephen W. Raudenbush, and Felton Earls. 1997. "Neighborhoods and Violent Crime: A Multilevel Study of Collective Efficacy." *Science* 277: 918–924.

Sampson, Robert J., Christopher Winship, and Carly Knight. 2013. "Translating Causal Claims: Principles and Strategies for Policy-Relevant Criminology." *Criminology and Public Policy* 12: 587–616.

Sherman, Lawrence W. 1990. "Police Crackdowns: Initial and Residual Deterrence." Pp. 1–48 in Michael Tonry and Norval Morris (eds.), *Crime and Justice: A Review of Research*, vol. 12. Chicago, IL: University of Chicago Press.

Sherman, Lawrence W. 1992. *Policing Domestic Violence: Experiments and Dilemmas*. New York, NY: Free Press.

Sherman, Lawrence W. 2002. "Evidence-Based Policing: Social Organization of Information for Social Control." Pp. 217–248 in Elin Waring and David Weisburd (eds.), *Crime & Social Organization: Advances in Criminological Theory*, vol. 10. New Brunswick, NJ: Transaction Publishers.

Sherman, Lawrence W., Patrick R. Gartin, and Michael E. Buerger. 1989. "Hot Spots of Predatory Crime: Routine Activities and the Criminology of Place." *Criminology* 27: 27–56.

Sherman, Lawrence W., Stephen Williams, Barak Ariel, Lucinda R. Strang, Neil Wain, Molly Slothower, and Andre Norton. 2014. "An Integrated Theory of Hot Spots Patrol Strategy: Implementing Prevention by Scaling Up and Feeding Back." *Journal of Contemporary Criminal Justice* 30: 95–122.

Sherman, Lawrence W., and David Weisburd. 1995. "General Deterrent Effects of Police Patrol in Crime Hot Spots: A Randomized Controlled Trial." *Justice Quarterly* 12: 625–648.

Sorg, Evan T., Cory P. Haberman, Jerry H. Ratcliffe, and Elizabeth R. Groff. 2013. "Foot Patrol in Violent Crime Hot Spots: The Longitudinal Impact of Deterrence and Posttreatment Effects of Displacement." *Criminology* 51: 65–102.

Sorg, Evan T., Jennifer D. Wood, Elizabeth R. Groff, and Jerry H. Ratcliffe. 2014. "Boundary Adherence during Place-Based Policing Evaluations: A Research Note." *Journal of Research in Crime and Delinquency* 51: 377–393.

Taylor, Bruce, Christopher S. Koper, and Daniel J. Woods. 2011. "A Randomized Controlled Trial of Different Policing Strategies at Hot Spots of Violent Crime." *Journal of Experimental Criminology* 7: 149–181.

Tchekmedyian, Alene. 2016. "Police Push Back against Using Crime-Prediction Technology to Deploy Officers." *Los Angeles Times*, October 4.

Telep, Cody W., Renée J. Mitchell, and David Weisburd. 2014. "How Much Time Should the Police Spend at Crime Hot Spots?: Answers from a Police Agency Directed Randomized Field Trial in Sacramento, California." *Justice Quarterly* 31: 905–933.

Telep, Cody W., and David Weisburd. 2012. "What Is Known about the Effectiveness of Police Practices in Reducing Crime and Disorder?" *Police Quarterly* 15: 331–357.

Tyler, Tom R. 1990. *Why People Obey the Law: Procedural Justice, Legitimacy, and Compliance*. New Haven, CT: Yale University Press.

Tyler, Tom R. 2004. "Enhancing Police Legitimacy." *Annals of the American Academy of Political and Social Science* 593: 84–99.

Tyler, Tom R., Phillip Atiba Goff, and Robert J. MacCoun. 2015. "The Impact of Psychological Science on Policing in the United States: Procedural Justice, Legitimacy, and Effective Law Enforcement." *Psychological Science in the Public Interest* 16: 75–109.

Weisburd, David. 2010. "Justifying the Use of Non-Experimental Methods and Disqualifying the Use of Randomized Controlled Trials: Challenging Folklore in Evaluation Research in Crime and Justice." *Journal of Experimental Criminology* 6: 209–227.

Weisburd, David, Michael Davis, and Charlotte Gill. 2015. "Increasing Collective Efficacy and Social Capital at Crime Hot Spots: New Crime Control Tools for Police." *Policing: A Journal of Policy and Practice* 9: 265–274.

Weisburd, David, Elizabeth R. Groff, and Sue-Ming Yang. 2012. *The Criminology of Place: Street Segments and Our Understanding of the Crime Problem*. New York, NY: Oxford University Press.

Weisburd, David, Elizabeth R. Groff, Greg Jones, Breanne Cave, Karen L. Amendola, Sue-Ming Yang, and Rupert F. Emison. 2015. "The Dallas Patrol Management Experiment: Can AVL Technologies Be Used to Harness Unallocated Patrol Time for Crime Prevention." *Journal of Experimental Criminology* 11: 367–391.

Weisburd, David, Joshua C. Hinkle, Anthony A. Braga, and Alese Wooditch. 2015. "Understanding the Mechanisms Underlying Broken Windows Policing: The Need for Evaluation Evidence." *Journal of Research in Crime and Delinquency* 52: 589–608.

Weisburd, David, Joshua C. Hinkle, Christine Famega, and Justin Ready. 2011. "The Possible 'Backfire' Effects of Hot Spots Policing: An Experimental Assessment of Impacts on Legitimacy, Fear and Collective Efficacy." *Journal of Experimental Criminology* 7: 297–320.

Weisburd, David, and Faye S. Taxman. 2000. "Developing a Multicenter Randomized Trial in Criminology: The Case of HIDTA." *Journal of Quantitative Criminology* 16: 315–340.

Weisburd, David, and Cody W. Telep. 2012. "Spatial Displacement and Diffusion of Crime Control Benefits Revisited: New Evidence on Why Crime Doesn't Just Move Around the Corner." Pp. 142–159 in Nick Tilley and Graham Farrell (eds.), *The Reasoning Criminologist: Essays in Honour of Ronald V. Clarke*. New York, NY: Routledge.

Weisburd, David, and Cody W. Telep. 2014. "Hot Spots Policing: What We Know and What We Need to Know." *Journal of Contemporary Criminal Justice* 30: 200–220.

Weisburd, David, Laura A. Wyckoff, Justin Ready, John E. Eck, Joshua C. Hinkle, and Frank Gajewski. 2006. "Does Crime Just Move Around the Corner? A Controlled Study of Spatial Displacement and Diffusion of Crime Control Benefits." *Criminology* 44: 549–592.

Wilson, James Q., and George L. Kelling. 1982. "Broken Windows: The Police and Neighborhood Safety." *Atlantic Monthly* 211: 29–38.

Worden Robert E., and Sarah J. McLean. 2014. *Assessing Police Performance in Citizen Encounters: Police Legitimacy and Management Accountability*. Washington, DC: National Institute of Justice, U.S. Department of Justice.

Zimring, Franklin E. 2012. *The City That Became Safe: New York's Lessons for Urban Crime and its Control*. New York, NY: Oxford University Press.

11

Beyond Putting "Cops on Dots": Applying Theory to Advance Police Responses to Crime Places

Anthony A. Braga and Cory Schnell

Hot spots policing is generally recognized as an effective approach to crime prevention that should be engaged by police departments in the United States and other countries. There is a strong and growing body of rigorous scientific evidence that the police can control crime hot spots without simply displacing crime problems to other places. Putting police officers in high crime locations may be an old and well-established idea. The availability of powerful crime mapping software packages has allowed police departments to identify and address problem places more easily than was possible in the days when pin maps were necessary to examine crime concentrations (Weisburd and Lum 2005). Many police departments now report having the capability to manage and analyze crime data in sophisticated ways and, through management innovations such as Compstat, hold officers accountable for controlling hot spot locations (Weisburd, Mastrofski, McNally, Greenspan, and Willis 2003). In the words of then-New York Police Department Deputy Commissioner Jack Maple, "the main principle of deployment can be expressed in one sentence: 'map the crime and put the cops where the dots are.' Or, more succinctly: 'Put cops on dots.'" (1999: 128).

The age and popularity of an idea, however, do not necessarily mean that it is being done optimally. The police have well understood the part of the place-based policing revolution that recognizes the efficiency of scale in focusing their resources on crime hot spots. However, there is mounting scientific evidence that suggests *how* police address crime hot spots matters. Police officers should strive to use problem-oriented policing and situational crime prevention techniques to address the place dynamics, situations, and characteristics that cause a "spot" to be "hot." Increased traditional policing strategies, such as patrol- and arrest-based interventions, do not deal with the underlying conditions that cause crime places to persist over time. While evaluations show that traditional tactics do generate crime control gains when applied to crime hot spots, a larger body of theoretical and empirical evidence suggests alternative responses that address underlying criminogenic conditions at places produce stronger crime control impacts that are likely to be more durable over time.

In addition to crime prevention effectiveness concerns, how police address crime hot spots matters to the people who reside in, work at, and use these places. If the police response is limited to increasing traditional enforcement in these small areas, the crime control benefits generated by hot spots policing programs could be undermined by overly aggressive and indiscriminate police enforcement efforts at hot spots. This orientation to putting cops on dots could result in negative consequences for police-community relationships and undue burdens on minority citizens (Rosenbaum 2006; Tonry 2011). Changing crime opportunities at places through problem-oriented policing and situational crime prevention strategies could reduce arrests and imprisonment as well as crime (Durlauf and Nagin 2011). Blending community policing activities into applications of hot spots policing also seems well positioned to improve police-community relations in targeted locations (Braga 2016).

We begin this essay by briefly describing problem-oriented policing and situational crime prevention. The available program evaluation evidence that suggests problem-oriented policing as a more potent response to crime places is then reviewed. Subsequent sections apply criminological theory to understand why the type of police work at crime places matters and depict how the complexity of problems at crime places requires more nuanced police responses than traditional police tactics provide. We then consider community policing as an important complement to problem-oriented and situational crime prevention responses in the implementation of hot spots policing programs. The concluding section summarizes the main arguments made in the essay.

Problem-Oriented Policing and Situational Crime Prevention

The reactive methods of the "traditional" or standard model of policing (Skogan and Frydl 2004; Weisburd and Eck 2004) are often described as "incident-driven policing." Under this model, departments are aimed at resolving individual incidents instead of solving recurring crime problems (Eck and Spelman 1987). Officers respond to repeated calls and never look for the underlying conditions that may be causing like groups of incidents. Officers become frustrated because they answer similar calls and seemingly make no real progress. Citizens become dissatisfied because the problems that generate their repeated calls still exist (Eck and Spelman 1987). In 1979, Herman Goldstein proposed an alternative; he felt that police should go further than answering call after call, that they should search for solutions to recurring problems that generate the repeated calls. Goldstein (1979, 1990) described this strategy as the "problem-oriented approach" and envisioned it as a department-wide activity.

Problem-oriented policing seeks to identify the underlying causes of crime problems and to frame appropriate responses using a wide variety of innovative approaches (Goldstein 1979). Using a basic iterative approach of problem identification, analysis, response, assessment, and adjustment of the response, this adaptable and dynamic analytic approach provides an appropriate framework to uncover the complex mechanisms at play in crime problems and to develop tailor-made interventions to address the underlying conditions that cause crime problems (Eck and Spelman 1987; Goldstein 1990). After a problem has been clearly defined and analyzed, police officers confront the challenge of developing a plausibly effective response. The development of appropriate responses is closely linked with the analysis that is performed. The analysis reveals the potential targets for an intervention, and it is at least partly the idea about what form the intervention might take that suggests important lines of analysis. Effective responses often depend on getting other people to take actions that reduce the opportunities for criminal offending, or to mobilize informal social control to drive offenders away from certain locations.

The developing field of situational crime prevention has also supported the problem-oriented policing movement since its genesis in the British Government's Home Office Research Unit in the early 1980s (Clarke 1997). Instead of preventing crime by altering broad social conditions such as poverty and inequality, situational crime prevention advocates changes in local environments to decrease opportunities for crimes to be committed. Situational crime prevention techniques comprise "opportunity-reducing measures that are, (1) directed at highly specific forms of crime (2) that involve the management, design, or manipulation of the immediate environment in as systematic and permanent way as possible (3) so as to increase the effort and risks of crime and reduce the rewards as perceived by a wide range of offenders" (Clarke 1997: 4). The situational analysis of crime problems follows an action-research model that systematically identifies and examines problems, develops solutions, and evaluates results. This simple but powerful perspective is applicable to crime problems facing the police, security personnel, business owners, local government officials, and private citizens. Indeed, Goldstein's (1990) formulation of problem-oriented policing shares many similarities to the action-research underpinnings of situational prevention (Clarke 1997).

It is worth noting here that, while the identification and analysis of crime problems may lead to a place-based response, problem-oriented policing and situational crime prevention are not synonymous with places. The analytical frameworks common to both crime prevention perspectives strive to describe the shape of the problem itself, and the dimensions that best show how it is concentrated. The crime prevention power of problem-oriented policing and situational crime prevention is rooted in the development of appropriate responses tailored to the underlying conditions that cause crime problems to persist. Dealing with crime hot spots is one possible avenue for intervention. However, depending on the nature of the problem to be addressed, appropriate crime reduction interventions could be focused on chronic offenders, repeat victims, social networks, patterns of criminal behavior, and crime facilitators such as weapons.

The Empirical Evidence on Hot Spots Policing and Crime Control

The empirical observation that a small number of places generate the bulk of urban crime problems suggested to scholars and crime policy analysts that the police could be more effective in controlling crime if they concentrated their resources in these hot spot locations (Braga and Weisburd 2010; Sherman, Gartin, and Buerger 1989; Weisburd 2008). The first formal evaluation of hot spots policing, a test of concentrated police patrol in crime hot spots in Minneapolis during the early to mid 1990s (Sherman and Weisburd 1995), spawned a series of rigorous hot spots policing studies. A string of careful academic reviews of hot spots policing evaluations consistently documented that these programs reduced crime in hot spot areas without simply displacing crime problems elsewhere; in fact, many evaluations revealed a diffusion of crime control benefits from targeted areas to the proximate areas (see Clarke and Weisburd 1994; Eck 2002; Sherman and Eck 2002; Weisburd and Eck 2004). The U.S. National Research Council's Committee to Review Research on Police Policy and Practices was not ambiguous in its conclusions regarding the effectiveness and importance of hot spots policing. The committee concluded:

> There has been increasing interest over the past two decades in police practices that target very specific types of criminals, and crime places. In particular, policing crime hot spots has become a common police strategy for addressing public safety problems. While there is only weak evidence suggesting the effectiveness of targeting specific types of offenders, a strong body of evidence suggests that taking a focused geographic approach to crime problems can increase policing effectiveness in reducing crime and disorder.
>
> (Skogan and Frydl 2004: 246–247)

Campbell Systematic Review of the Effects of Hot Spots Policing and Crime

The most detailed examination of the impact of hot spots policing on crime is an ongoing systematic review conducted for the Campbell Collaboration. There is consensus among those who advocate for evidence-based crime policy that systematic reviews are an important tool in analyzing evidence for effective crime prevention strategies. Formed in 2000, the Campbell Collaboration Crime and Justice Group aims to prepare and maintain systematic reviews of criminological interventions and to make them electronically accessible to scholars, practitioners, policy makers, and the general public (Farrington and Petrosino 2001; see also www.campbellcollaboration.org). In systematic reviews, researchers attempt to gather relevant evaluative studies in a specific area (e.g., the impact of correctional boot camps on offending), critically appraise them, and come to judgments about what works "using explicit, transparent, state-of-the-art methods" (Petrosino, Boruch, Soydan, Duggan, and Sanchez-Meca 2001: 21). Rigorous methods are used to summarize, analyze, and combine study findings.

As part of the Campbell Collaboration Crime and Justice Group's efforts to build a scientific knowledge base on effective crime prevention practices, a systematic review has been conducted on an ongoing basis on the crime prevention effects of hot spots policing programs (Braga 2001, 2005). The most recent iteration of the Campbell hot spots policing review identified 19 rigorous evaluations involving 25 tests of hot spots policing programs (Braga, Papachristos, and Hureau 2014). Ten eligible studies used quasi-experimental research designs (52.6%) and nine eligible studies used randomized controlled trials (47.4%) to evaluate the effects of hot spots policing on crime. The 19 eligible studies were:

1. Minneapolis Repeat Call Address Policing (RECAP) Program (Sherman, Buerger, and Gartin 1989)*
2. New York Tactical Narcotics Teams (Sviridoff, Sadd, Curtis, and Grinc 1992)
3. St. Louis Problem-Oriented Policing in 3 Drug Market Locations Study (Hope 1994)
4. Minneapolis Hot Spots Patrol Program (Sherman and Weisburd 1995)*
5. Jersey City Drug Markets Analysis Program (DMAP) (Weisburd and Green 1995)*
6. Kansas City Gun Project (Sherman and Rogan 1995a)
7. Kansas City Crack House Police Raids Program (Sherman and Rogan 1995b)*
8. Beenleigh Calls for Service Project (Criminal Justice Commission 1998)
9. Jersey City Problem-Oriented Policing at Violent Places Project (Braga et al. 1999)*
10. Houston Targeted Beat Program (Caeti 1999)
11. Oakland Beat Health Program (Mazerolle, Price, and Roehl 2000)*
12. Pittsburgh Police Raids at Nuisance Bars Program (Cohen, Gorr, and Singh 2003)
13. Buenos Aires Police Presence after Terror Attack Study (DiTella and Schargrodsky 2004)

14. Philadelphia Drug Corners Crackdowns Program (Lawton, Taylor, and Luongo 2005)
15. Jersey City Displacement and Diffusion Study (Weisburd et al. 2006)
16. Lowell Policing Crime and Disorder Hot Spots Project (Braga and Bond 2008)*
17. Jacksonville Policing Violent Crime Hot Spots Project (Taylor, Koper, and Woods 2011)*
18. Philadelphia Foot Patrol Program (Ratcliffe, Taniguchi, Groff, and Wood 2011)*
19. Boston Safe Street Teams Program (Braga, Hureau, and Papachristos 2011)

* = Randomized Controlled Trial

A noteworthy majority of the hot spots policing evaluations concluded that hot spots policing programs generated significant crime control benefits in the treatment areas relative to the control areas. Twenty of the 25 tests (80%) of hot spots policing interventions reported noteworthy crime control gains associated with the approach. The five tests that did not report crime control benefits were the Minneapolis RECAP treatment at commercial addresses, the New York Tactical Narcotics Team in the 70th Precinct, the Beenleigh Calls for Service Project, the Houston Targeted Beat Program's problem-oriented policing intervention, and the Jacksonville direct-saturation patrol intervention.

Meta-analysis is a method of systematic reviewing designed to synthesize empirical outcomes of studies, such as the effects of a specific crime prevention intervention on criminal offending behavior (Wilson 2001). Meta-analysis uses specialized statistical methods to analyze the relationships between findings and study features (Lipsey and Wilson 2001). The "effect size statistic" is the index used to represent the findings of each study in the overall meta-analysis of study findings and represents the strength and direction (positive or negative) of the relationship observed in a particular study (e.g., the size of the treatment effect found) (Lipsey and Wilson 2001). The "mean effect size" represents the average effect of treatment on the outcome of interest across all eligible studies in a particular area, and is estimated by calculating a mean that is weighted by the precision of the effect size for each individual study. Due to limited information in the original evaluation reports, the Campbell Collaboration review meta-analysis only included effect sizes for 20 main effects tests and 13 displacement and diffusion tests in 16 eligible studies. All 13 displacement and diffusion tests were limited to examining immediate spatial displacement and diffusion effects, that is, whether focused police efforts in targeted areas resulted in crime "moving around the corner" or whether these proximate areas experienced unintended crime control benefits.

The forest plots in Figure 11.1 show the standardized difference in means between the treatment and control or comparison conditions (effect size) with

Combined Effect Sizes for Study Outcomes

Study name	Outcome	Statistics for each study			Std diff in means and 95% CI
		Std diff in means	Standard error	p-Value	
KC Gun	Gun crimes	0.866	0.275	0.002	
Phila. Drug Corners	Combined	0.855	0.258	0.001	
Buenos Aires Police	Motor vehicle theft incidents	0.617	0.169	0.000	
JC Disp. Prost.	Prostitution events	0.525	0.149	0.000	
JC Disp. Drug	Drug events	0.441	0.131	0.001	
Minn. RECAP Resid.	Total calls	0.369	0.132	0.005	
Boston SST	Total violent incidents	0.341	0.020	0.000	
Oakland Beat Health	Drug calls	0.279	0.056	0.000	
JC DMAP	Combined	0.147	0.270	0.585	
Lowell POP	Total calls	0.145	0.034	0.000	
JC POP	Combined	0.143	0.043	0.001	
Phila. Foot Patrol	Violent incidents	0.143	0.021	0.000	
Pittsburgh Bar Raids	Drug calls	0.125	0.038	0.001	
NYC TNT 67	Combined	0.087	0.077	0.257	
Minn. Patrol	Total calls	0.061	0.015	0.000	
KC Crack	Total calls	0.051	0.039	0.188	
Minn. RECAP Comm.	Total calls	0.015	0.137	0.913	
Jacksonville POP	Combined	-0.005	0.092	0.959	
NYC TNT 70	Combined	-0.027	0.080	0.739	
Jacksonville Patrol	Combined	-0.055	0.096	0.568	
		0.184	0.035	0.000	

-2.00 -1.00 0.00 1.00 2.00
Favors Control   Favors Treatment

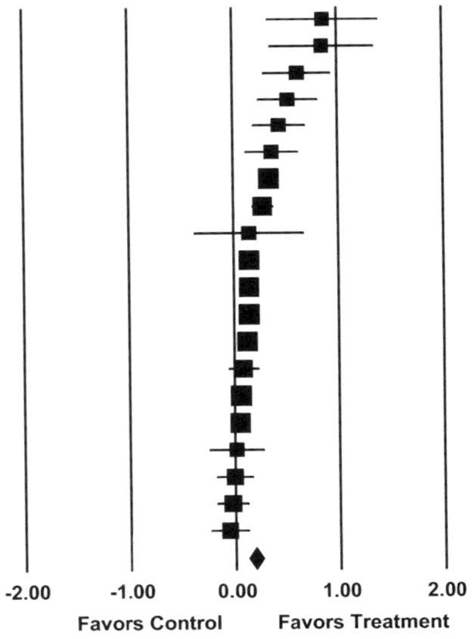

Meta-Analysis Random Effects Model, Q = 184.021, df = 10, p<0.000

Figure 11.1 Meta-analysis of effects of hot spots policing programs on crime.

Source: Braga, Papachristos, and Hureau (2012), p. 58.

a 95% confidence interval plotted around them for all tests. Points plotted to the right of 0.00 indicate a treatment effect; in this case, the test showed a reduction in crime or disorder. Points to the left of 0.00 indicate a backfire effect where control conditions improved relative to treatment conditions. The meta-analysis of main effect sizes found a statistically significant overall mean effect in favor of hot spots policing strategies (.184). Nine of the 13 displacement/diffusion tests reported effect sizes that favored diffusion effects over displacement effects. Only the Philadelphia Foot Patrol experiment reported a statistically significant displacement effect. The displacement/diffusion meta-analysis suggests a small but statistically significant overall diffusion of crime control benefits effect (.104) generated by the hot spots policing strategies.

The Campbell systematic review documented that hot spots policing programs have adopted problem-oriented policing, focused drug enforcement, increased patrol, increased gun searches and seizures, and zero-tolerance policing to control high-activity crime places. Braga et al. (2012) characterized these varied programs as two fundamentally different types of approaches to control problem places. Problem-oriented policing programs represent police-led efforts to change the underlying conditions at hot spots that cause them to generate recurring crime problems (Goldstein 1990). The other hot spots policing interventions represent increased traditional policing activities concentrated at specific places to prevent crime through general deterrence and increased risk of apprehension. Of the 20 main effects hot spots policing tests, ten (50%) evaluated the impacts of problem-oriented policing on crime and ten (50%) evaluated the impacts of increased traditional policing tactics on crime.

The Braga et al. (2012) meta-analysis used program type as an effect size moderator to compare these two different police approaches to controlling crime at hot spots (see Figure 11.2).

The analysis revealed that problem-oriented policing programs produced a larger overall mean effect size (.232) that was twice the size of the increased traditional policing overall mean effect size (.113). As Table 11.1 reveals, the 95% confidence intervals overlap for these two distinct types of police interventions in the violent crime, property crime, and drug offense categories. This suggests that the mean effect sizes for the subcategories may not be dissimilar. Nevertheless, problem-oriented policing interventions generated larger mean effect size point estimates relative to increased policing interventions for all crime outcome categories. The most noteworthy differences were in the property crime category (increased policing did not generate a statistically significant mean effect size, while problem-oriented policing did) and the disorder offense category (95% confidence intervals do not overlap).

Finally, Braga et al. (2012) also examined the crime displacement and diffusion of crime control benefits effects reported in evaluations of these two general types of hot spots policing programs. Problem-oriented policing programs produced a small but statistically significant overall diffusion of benefits effect

Hot Spots Program Type as Moderator of Study Outcomes

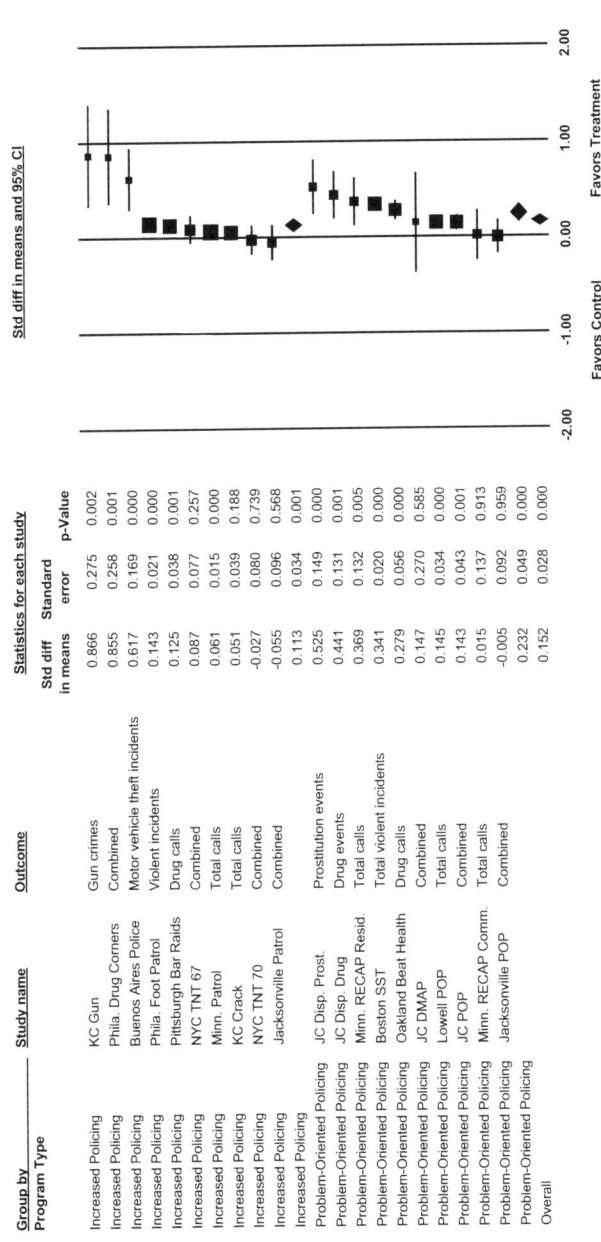

Group by Program Type	Study name	Outcome	Std diff in means	Standard error	p-Value
Increased Policing	KC Gun	Gun crimes	0.866	0.275	0.002
Increased Policing	Phila. Drug Corners	Combined	0.855	0.258	0.001
Increased Policing	Buenos Aires Police	Motor vehicle theft incidents	0.617	0.169	0.000
Increased Policing	Phila. Foot Patrol	Violent incidents	0.143	0.021	0.000
Increased Policing	Pittsburgh Bar Raids	Drug calls	0.125	0.038	0.001
Increased Policing	NYC TNT 67	Combined	0.087	0.077	0.257
Increased Policing	Minn. Patrol	Total calls	0.061	0.015	0.000
Increased Policing	KC Crack	Total calls	0.051	0.039	0.188
Increased Policing	NYC TNT 70	Combined	-0.027	0.080	0.739
Increased Policing	Jacksonville Patrol	Combined	-0.055	0.096	0.568
Increased Policing			0.113	0.034	0.001
Problem-Oriented Policing	JC Disp. Prost.	Prostitution events	0.525	0.149	0.000
Problem-Oriented Policing	JC Disp. Drug	Drug events	0.441	0.131	0.001
Problem-Oriented Policing	Minn. RECAP Resid.	Total calls	0.369	0.132	0.005
Problem-Oriented Policing	Boston SST	Total violent incidents	0.341	0.020	0.000
Problem-Oriented Policing	Oakland Beat Health	Drug calls	0.279	0.056	0.000
Problem-Oriented Policing	JC DMAP	Combined	0.147	0.270	0.585
Problem-Oriented Policing	Lowell POP	Total calls	0.145	0.034	0.000
Problem-Oriented Policing	JC POP	Combined	0.143	0.043	0.001
Problem-Oriented Policing	Minn. RECAP Comm.	Total calls	0.015	0.137	0.913
Problem-Oriented Policing	Jacksonville POP	Combined	-0.005	0.092	0.959
Problem-Oriented Policing			0.232	0.049	0.000
Overall			0.152	0.028	0.000

Meta-Analysis Random Effects Model

Increased Policing Q = 42.615, df = 9, p<0.000
Problem-Oriented Policing Q = 51.718, df = 9, p<0.000
Between Group Q = 89.688, df = 1, p<0.000

Figure 11.2 Moderator analysis of the impact of program type on the effects of hot spots policing programs on crime.

Source: Braga et al. (2012), p. 65.

Table 11.1
Moderator analyses of study outcome types and
hot spots policing program types

Crime Category	N Studies	Effect Size	95% C.I.
Violent crimes	12	.175*	.061, .289
Problem-oriented policing	7	.190*	.016, .396
Increased traditional policing	5	.157*	.014, .300
Property crimes	9	.084+	−.010, .178
Problem-oriented policing	4	.101*	.021, .181
Increased traditional policing	5	.087	−.067, .241
Drug offenses	5	.249*	.103, .395
Problem-oriented policing	3	.261*	.170, .352
Increased traditional policing	2	.139*	.065, .212
Disorder offenses	6	.151*	.052, .251
Problem-oriented policing	4	.331*	.101, .562
Increased traditional policing	2	.063*	.031, .096
Displacement/diffusion effects	13	.104*	.073, .136
Problem-oriented policing	8	.093*	.073, .113
Increased traditional policing	5	.106	−.210, .418

Note: Random effects meta-analysis models used in all reported effect sizes.

$+ = p < .10$

$* = p < .05$

Source: Braga et al. (2012), p. 57.

(.093, $p < .05$) in areas immediately surrounding the treatment hot spots relative to areas immediately surrounding the control hot spots. While increased policing programs also produced a small diffusion of benefits effect, it was not statistically significant.

Applying Theory to Understand Why the Type of Police Work at Crime Places Matters

In a recent article, Steven Durlauf and Daniel Nagin (2011) suggest that crime and incarceration in the United States would both be reduced if resources were shifted from imprisonment to policing. Among other focused police interventions, they specifically point to evaluations of hot spots policing deployment strategies as evidence that the police, when properly oriented, can prevent crime. For instance, in the Minneapolis hot spots patrol experiment, Sherman and Weisburd (1995) claimed evidence of place-specific "micro-deterrence" associated with increased police presence in hot spot areas (p. 646). Reflecting on the theoretical and policy lessons learned from hot spots policing evaluations, Durlauf and Nagin (2011) argue that increasing police visibility in small places will heighten potential offenders' perceived risk of apprehension and, as a result, generate substantial marginal deterrent effects.

When the police are not spatially concentrated in crime hot spots, it is well known that traditional policing tactics, such as preventive patrol, rapid response, and ad-hoc investigations, are not effective in controlling crime (Greenwood, Chaiken, and Petersilia 1977; Kelling, Pate, Dieckman, and Brown 1974; Spelman and Brown 1984). In contrast, problem-oriented policing has been found to be an effective crime reduction strategy for a wide range of crime problems in a variety of settings (Braga 2008; Weisburd and Eck 2004; Weisburd, Telep, Hinkle, and Eck 2008). Importantly, as with problem-oriented policing, a rigorous review of the available evaluation evidence found that situational crime prevention programs were associated with noteworthy reductions in targeted crime problems (Guerette 2009). As such, it may not be very surprising that problem-oriented strategies and situational crime prevention measures outperform traditional policing tactics when used to control crime hot spots.

Requiring officers to employ problem-oriented policing and situational crime prevention strategies at hot spots seems well positioned to generate crime control impacts in at least two ways. First, analyzing the underlying problems that give rise to crime hot spots, implementing tailored responses, and monitoring whether these responses generated the desired crime control impacts will require officers to be present in hot spots areas. Depending on the nature of the problems at the place, certain responses may also include enforcement strategies. As such, problem-oriented officers will necessarily be increasing their visibility in crime places in ways that seem likely to impact offenders' perceptions of the risk of apprehension. Second, problem-oriented responses, if implemented properly, will modify the criminal opportunity structure in these places that generate persistent crime problems. Changes in place characteristics, dynamics, and situations can make these locations much less attractive to criminals. On the other hand, perhaps problem-oriented policing and situational crime prevention approaches may be better suited for chronic hot spots relative to short-term hot spots, which may only require a more traditional response such as simply increasing police presence for a limited time period.

Researchers have demonstrated that the concentration of crime at particular places is generally stable over time. Weisburd, Bushway, Lum, and Yang (2004) analyzed crime incidents at the level of street segments in Seattle over a 14 year period and found that, year to year, about 50% of the crime was concentrated in approximately 4.5% of street segments. Importantly, these analyses revealed that there was a high degree of stability of crime at micro places over time. In other words, crime remained concentrated in a small number of micro places in Seattle rather than spread across the city over time. In a similar longitudinal analysis, Braga, Papachristos, and Hureau (2010) found that 75% of gun assault incidents remained concentrated in only 5% of street segments and intersections in Boston between 1980 and 2008. These findings suggest that police interventions that do not address the underlying conditions that cause crime to be strongly coupled to specific places over time will not have lasting crime control impacts. In other words, traditional policing tactics concentrated in chronic crime hot spots seem doomed to produce short-term crime control gains only.

A number of criminological theories strongly support the notion that problem-oriented policing, and the complementary situational crime prevention approach, can be effective in controlling high-activity crime places. Criminal opportunity theories, such as rational choice, routine activities, and environmental criminology, have influenced and supported the study of crime places. The importance of focusing police resources on crime hot spots is also informed by the "broken windows" thesis on the relationship between disorder and more serious crimes. Finally, whether through social disorganization or crime opportunity theories, many criminologists have noted that areas characterized by low levels of informal social control tend to have higher levels of crime. These criminological theories and their relevance to policing crime places are briefly reviewed here.

Rational Choice

The rational choice perspective assumes that "crime is purposive behavior designed to meet the offender's commonplace needs for such things as money, status, sex, and excitement, and that meeting these needs involves the making of (sometimes quite rudimentary) decisions and choices, constrained as these are by limits of time and ability and the availability of relevant information" (Clarke 1995: 98; see also Cornish and Clarke 1986). Rational choice makes distinctions between the decisions to initially become involved in crime, to continue criminal involvement, and to desist from criminal offending, as well as the decisions made to complete a particular criminal act. This separation of the decision-making processes in the criminal event from the stages of criminal involvement allows the modeling of the commission of crime events in a way that yields potentially valuable insights for crime prevention. Of particular importance to effective crime prevention practice, the decision processes and information utilized in committing criminal acts can vary greatly across offenses; ignoring these differences and the situational contingencies associated with making choices may reduce the ability to effectively intervene (Clarke 1995).

The emphasis of the rational choice perspective on concepts of risk, reward, and effort in criminal decision-making has been used to inform the development of situational crime prevention strategies that seek to change offender appraisals of criminal opportunities (Clarke 1997). In the case of high-activity crime places, modeling an offender's choice of committing crimes at one place over another may provide avenues for intervention. For example, a robber may choose a "favorite" spot because of certain desirable attributes that facilitate an ambush, such as an unsecured abandoned building, poor lighting, and untrimmed bushes. One obvious response to this situation would be to raze the derelict property, improve the lighting, and trim the bushes. Changes in the physical environment may discourage potential offenders from frequenting an area by altering criminal opportunities at a place. Strategies to ameliorate physical incivilities (thereby changing site features and facilities) may diminish the number of easy opportunities at the place and, thus, discourage offenders from frequenting targeted places.

Routine Activity

Rational choice is often combined with routine activity theory to explain criminal behavior during the crime event (Clarke and Felson 1993). Rational offenders come across criminal opportunities as they go about their daily routine activities and make decisions on whether to take action. The source of the offender's motivation to commit a crime is not addressed (it is assumed that offenders commit crimes for any number of reasons); rather, the basic ingredients for a criminal act to be completed are closely examined. Routine activity theory posits that a criminal act occurs when a likely offender converges in space and time with a suitable target (e.g., victim or property) in the absence of a capable guardian (e.g., property owner or security guard) (Cohen and Felson 1979).

Routine activity theory provides the theoretical underpinnings for the well-known problem analysis "crime triangle" that breaks crime down into the features of places, features of offenders, and features of victims (see, e.g., Hough and Tilley 1998). This analytic device was intended to help crime analysts and police officers visualize crime problems and understand relationships between the three elements. The crime triangle has been reformulated to help police think about the response as well as the analysis.

Figure 11.3 Crime analysis triangle.

Source: Clarke and Eck (2007), section 8.

The latest formulation of the crime triangle adds an outer level of "controller" for each of the original three elements; problems are created when offenders and targets come together and controllers fail to act (Eck 2003):

- For the target/victim, the *guardian* is usually someone who protects their own belongings or those of family members, friends, neighbors, and co-workers.
- For the offender, this is the *handler*, someone who knows the offender well and who is in a position to exert some control over his or her actions. Handlers include parents, siblings, teachers, friends, and spouses.
- For the place, the controller is the *place manager*, a person who has some responsibility for controlling behavior in the specific location such as a bus conductor or teacher in school.

(adapted from Clarke and Eck 2003: 9)

When searching for appropriate responses to problem places, the revised crime triangle can help police think about what might be done to prevent offenders from re-offending by making better use of handlers, what victims can do to reduce the probability of being targets, and what changes could be made to the places where crimes occur (Clarke and Eck 2003).

In many cases, place managers will be proactive in dealing with crime and disorder problems and willing to work with the police to create safe environments. Sometimes, unfortunately, police officers need to force irresponsible or negligent parties to take action. Third-party policing is defined as "police efforts to persuade or coerce organizations or non-offending persons, such as public housing agencies, property owners, parents, health and building inspectors, and business owners to take some responsibility for preventing crime or reducing crime problems" (Buerger and Mazerolle 1998: 301). The police use a range of civil, criminal, and regulatory rules and laws to engage or force third parties into taking some crime control responsibility. The ultimate targets of third-party policing efforts are the people engaged in deviant and criminal behavior at the place, typically drug dealers, gang members, vandals, and petty criminals. The engagement of place managers and the use of civil remedies can be important situational strategies used by police officers seeking to control crime hot spots. Research has revealed that third-party policing is an effective mechanism to control drug problems and is promising in controlling violent crime, disorderly youth, and property crime problems (Mazerolle and Ransley 2006).

Environmental Criminology

Environmental criminology, also known as crime pattern theory, explores the distribution and interaction of targets, offenders, and opportunities across time and space (Brantingham and Brantingham 1991). According to Eck and

Weisburd (1995), this occurs because offenders engage in routine activities. Environmental criminology is important in understanding the nature of crime at places because it combines rational choice and routine activity theory to explain the distribution of crime across places. Understanding the characteristics of places, such as facilities, is important as these attributes give rise to the opportunities that rational offenders will encounter during their routine activities. Environmental criminologists unravel crime problems through studying offender decision-making processes and small (e.g., shopping mall or housing project) and intermediate-level (e.g., neighborhood or city) analyses of very specific types of crimes occurring at very particular locations in these areas (Brantingham and Brantingham 1991).

Studies of environmental factors of crime have shown that commercial properties located near main roads have an increased risk of robbery, and affluent homes located adjacent to poorer areas are more likely to be burglarized. In both cases, the offenders' "journey to work" was greatly reduced by the proximity of the targeted places to the offenders' homes or to a major thoroughfare. A key insight from these studies was that the offender's target search time, the amount of effort expended by the offender to locate a suitable target, was related to risk of victimization at that place (as described by Clarke 1995). According to Marcus Felson (2006), offenders find suitable targets through *personal knowledge* of the victim (your neighbor's son might know when you are away from your house), *work* (a burglar working as a telephone engineer might overhear that you will be taking vacation next week), and overlapping *activity spaces* (where people live, work, shop, or seek entertainment).

The concept of place is essential to crime pattern theory (Eck and Weisburd 1995). Not only are places logically required (an offender must be in a place when an offense is committed), their characteristics influence the likelihood of a crime and the likelihood that particular places become crime hot spots. Place characteristics highlighted by routine activity theory include the presence and effectiveness of managers and the presence of capable guardians. Crime pattern theory links places with desirable targets and the context within which they are found by focusing on how places come to the attention of potential offenders. Environmental criminology inquiries can yield powerful insights on the nature of crime problems recurring at hot spot locations that can greatly enhance the potency of crime prevention strategies.

"Broken Windows" Thesis and Collective Efficacy

In their seminal "broken windows" article, Wilson and Kelling (1982) argue that social incivilities (e.g., loitering, public drinking, and prostitution) and physical incivilities (e.g., vacant lots, trash, and abandoned buildings) cause residents and workers in a neighborhood to be fearful. Fear causes many stable families to move out of the neighborhood, and the remaining residents isolate themselves and avoid others. Anonymity increases, and the level of informal social control decreases. The lack of control and escalating disorder attract more potential offenders to the area, and this increases serious criminal behavior (see also Kelling and Coles 1996). Wilson and Kelling (1982) argued that serious crime developed because the police and citizens did not work together to prevent urban decay and social disorder. The key policy implication for the police is more serious crime can be reduced by dealing with underlying disorderly conditions.

Research on crime hot spots suggests that disorder clusters in space and time with more serious crimes. In their closer look at crime in Minneapolis hot spots, Weisburd, Maher, and Sherman (1992) found that assault calls for service and robbery of person calls for service were significantly correlated with "drunken person" calls for service. In her longitudinal analysis of small places in Seattle, Yang (2010) found strong correlations between levels of violence and levels of disorder that persisted over a 16 year time period. At the neighborhood level, however, the available research evidence on the connections between disorder and more serious crime is mixed (see, e.g., Skogan 1990; Taylor 2001). To some observers, the impact of disorder on crime is mediated through the ability of neighborhood residents to exert informal social control over public spaces. For instance, using systematic social observation data to capture social and physical incivilities on the streets of Chicago, Sampson and Raudenbush (1999) found that, with the exception of robbery, public disorder was not significantly related to most forms of serious crime when neighborhood characteristics such as poverty, stability, race, and "collective efficacy" were considered. Collective efficacy is a measure of informal social control that is generally defined as "social cohesion among neighbors combined with their willingness to intervene on behalf of the common good" (Sampson, Raudenbush, and Earls 1997: 918).

A more recent study of crime hot spot areas in Chicago found some support for both broken windows and collective efficacy theories in explaining the concentration of specific crime types at places (St. Jean 2007). However, this research also found that different kinds of crime occur most often in locations that offer perpetrators specific "ecological advantages." For instance, drug dealers and robbers were primarily attracted to locations with businesses like liquor stores, fast-food restaurants, and check-cashing outlets (St. Jean 2007). In St. Jean's research, interviews with offenders revealed that criminals found certain facilities and site features at specific places provided compelling opportunities to commit crimes.

In an extension of their seminal longitudinal analysis of crime at street segments, Weisburd, Groff, and Yang (2012) found that variables supporting both opportunity and social disorganization theories of crime were associated with persistent high crime streets in Seattle. While crime opportunity theory measures generated the strongest effects, collective efficacy, property values, and housing assistance variables were also found to be associated with the persistence of high levels of crime at street segments. Weisburd et al. (2012) argue that social and health interventions designed to address economic deprivation, unsupervised teens, and low collective efficacy may be more effective and less costly if concentrated at crime hot spots rather than spread across broader communities or neighborhoods. They further speculate that formal social control programs, like hot spots policing and particular types of situational measures, may not be enough to alter the long-term trajectories of chronic crime hot spots. Rather, complementary programs to address the underlying social and structural characteristics of small crime places may be necessary.

The potential crime control payoff of "lowering the scale" of social and health interventions to chronic hot streets remains unproven, however. Informal social controls, whether via situational prevention or collective efficacy mechanisms, matter in crime control and prevention. Situational prevention provides clear guidance to police on how to achieve reductions in crime through the application of 25 techniques designed to increase the difficulties of crime, increase its risks, reduce its rewards, remove excuses for crime, and reduce temptations and provocations (Cornish and Clarke 2003). Familiar concepts, such as improving guardianship and promoting more effective place management, are suggested by situational crime prevention advocates. By contrast, the game plan for stimulating collective efficacy in neighborhoods is not nearly as clear or as direct at crime places. Indeed, Sampson's (2011) ideas for promoting stable and long-lasting community-based organizations are very broad, principle-based recommendations that provide little advice on the actual work of initiating or enhancing community-based groups in identifiable hot spot locations. Altogether, there is little tangible evidence on proven methods to stimulate collective efficacy in socially disorganized areas whether these locations are large neighborhoods or small street segments.

The Complexity of Crime Places Requires More Nuanced Police Responses

High-activity crime places tend to have multiple problems, and the problems at crime places can be quite complex and involved (Braga and Weisburd 2010; Weisburd et al. 1992). Figure 11.4 shows the crime problems of one violent crime hot spot included in the Jersey City Problem-Oriented Policing at Violent Places randomized experiments (Braga 1997; Braga et al. 1999).

The violence at the place was driven by a disorderly drug market situated in a vacant lot, shoplifting problems that led to strong-arm robberies in a retail shopping mall, and a poorly managed bar that over-served alcohol to customers who became involved in fistfights to settle drunken disputes. The location also suffered from high levels of burglaries emanating from a dilapidated apartment building. One-dimensional traditional enforcement strategies that attempt to control crime by increasing police visibility or improving the likelihood that

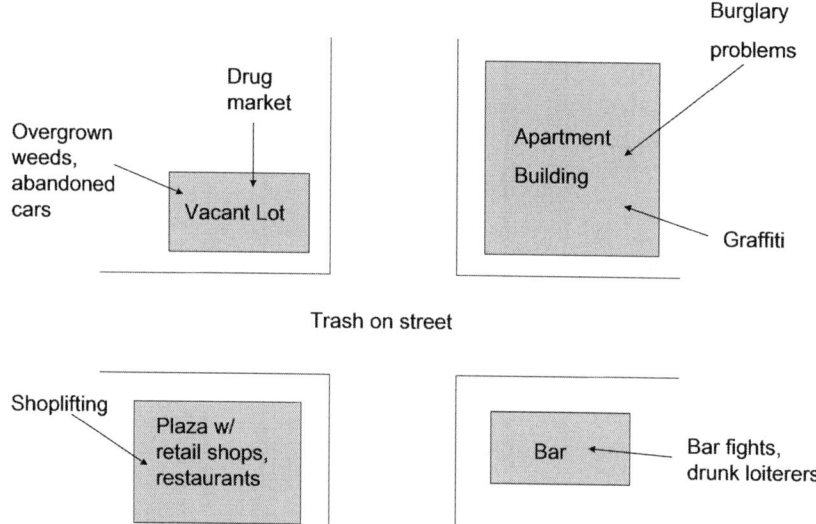

Figure 11.4 Characteristics of a Jersey City violent crime hot spot location.

Source: Braga (1997), p. 59.

offenders who commit crimes in hot spots are apprehended and prosecuted are clearly limited in changing the underlying conditions that cause violence to persist at this hot spot location. Without addressing the proximal causes of ongoing violence, increased traditional policing at this place would generate short-term violence reductions that would dissipate after the police moved on to other crime concerns.

Problem-oriented policing and situational crime prevention provide police officers with an analytical framework to diagnose the underlying conditions and develop tailored strategies that can change the longer-term crime trajectories of highly active crime places. In response to an increase in violent crime during the mid 2000s, the Boston Police Department (BPD) implemented the Safe Street Team (SST) program to control hot spots that generated a disproportionate amount of violence in Boston through the use of problem-oriented policing interventions (Braga et al. 2011; Braga and Schnell 2013). A team of one sergeant and six patrol officers was assigned to implement the program in the targeted 13 violent crime hot spots. A rigorous quasi-experimental evaluation revealed that violent crime in treated hot spots decreased by 17% relative to comparison hot spots without causing any immediate spatial displacement. Importantly, the evaluation examined the impact of the problem-oriented policing intervention over a ten year study time period, suggesting that the observed reductions represented longer-term changes in the criminal opportunity structures in the targeted violent crime places.

Similar to experiences in other jurisdictions (e.g., Braga and Bond 2008), the number and complexity of problems at the Boston violent crime places required responses that went far beyond traditional policing activities. The identified problems and their underlying causes were highly varied across the 13 SST violent crime hot spot locations (Braga et al. 2011). The number of problems identified and analyzed ranged from three to seven, with an average of 4.5 violent crime problems tackled per SST hot spot area. For instance, the Downtown Crossing and Tremont/Stuart SST officers faced street violence problems tied to three very different disorder-based problems. First, both of these teams bordered the Boston Common area, which suffers from a large and transient homeless population. While many homeless individuals did not cause violence in the area, a small number of mentally disordered and criminally active individuals engaged in street fights to settle disputes and committed robberies of other homeless people, shoppers, and workers in the area. Second, large groups of high school students congregate around Boston Common during the afternoons after school release. Most of the students did not cause problems; however, gang members blended into this crowd, sold drugs to homeless individuals and others, and sometimes fired guns when in dispute with rival gang members. Third, during the late night hours, the many clubs and pubs in the Common area attracted young adults who tended to drink too much alcohol and get into fights inside the bars and out on the streets. Other SST areas, such as Codman Square (C-11), faced street robbery problems generated by local hoodlums preying on commuters, gang violence between rival factions of local youth, disorderly bars over-serving clients, and drug market violence.

The quality of problem-oriented policing varied across the SST places. The available literature on problem-oriented policing consistently documents that implementing the approach can be quite challenging for many officers (Clarke 1998; Read and Tilley 2000). Some sergeants and officers were quite adept at using available BPD computer mapping and software programs to analyze data in their hot spot areas and produced more sophisticated analyses. Several officers received support from BPD crime analysts to unravel the nature of violence in their places. Other officers tended to rely more on their informal assessments based on experiences in the area and produced less nuanced analytical products. Nevertheless, the process of identifying discrete problems that cause violent crime to concentrate at specific places and unraveling the underlying conditions that gave rise to those problems was a highly productive exercise across most SST areas. The place-level analyses of problems advanced a set of problem-oriented responses that were far more nuanced when compared to standard policing actions taken by BPD officers in other parts of the city.

The 13 teams implemented, on average, 30.5 problem-oriented policing interventions per place, comprising 15 situational/environmental interventions, 6.1 enforcement interventions, and 9.4 community outreach/social service interventions. For instance, in the Orchard Park SST area, high school youth using public transportation were repeatedly robbed and often assaulted by other local youth when commuting between the train station and their high school. The offenders usually robbed the students of their Apple iPods, Apple iPhones, and other technology when they walked in secluded areas and were not paying attention to their surroundings. In addition to increasing their presence and making robbery arrests in the area, SST officers made the place less attractive to youth robbers by collaborating with public works to fence a vacant lot and trim overgrown bushes and other vegetation that helped conceal robbers from their victims. The officers then collaborated with the local high school to raise awareness among the students that they should be aware of their surroundings and refrain from using smart phones and other items that were attractive to robbers when commuting in the risky area. The officers also sponsored a contest for students to design robbery awareness fliers and posters that used slogans and lingo that would appeal to youth. The fliers were distributed to all high school students, and posters were displayed on school grounds, in the train station, and in the windows of stores on the route between the train station and the school.

Community Policing and Hot Spots Policing Programs

Community policing should be the foundation of any focused crime prevention approach. While community policing programs have not been found to be effective in reducing crime, they have been found to generate positive effects on citizen satisfaction, perceptions of disorder, and perceptions of police legitimacy (Gill, Weisburd, Telep, Vitter, and Bennett 2014). Moreover, community engagement strategies can provide important input to help focus police on underlying problems at high crime places. Developing close relationships with community members could help the police gather information about crime and disorder problems and understand the dynamics and situations that cause these problems to recur. Community members can also help with key components of strategies tailored to specific problems by making improvements to the physical environment and through informal social control of high-risk people at places. In this way, police strategies focusing on particular places, and the people who live in and use these spaces, would cease to be regarded as a form of profiling and become a generator of community engagement projects. Indeed, a central idea in community policing is to engage residents so they can exert more control over situations and dynamics that contribute to their own potential for victimization and, by doing so, influence area crime levels.

Preventing crime by addressing underlying crime-producing situations and dynamics reduces harm to potential victims as well as harm to would-be offenders by not relying solely on arrest and prosecution actions. Community engagement in developing appropriately focused strategies would help to safeguard against indiscriminate and overly aggressive enforcement tactics and other inappropriate policing activities, which erode the community's trust and confidence in the police and inhibit cooperation. Collaborative partnerships between police and community members improve the transparency of law enforcement actions and provide residents with a much-needed voice in crime prevention work. Ongoing conversations with the community can ensure that day-to-day police-citizen interactions are conducted in a procedurally just manner that enhances community trust and compliance with the law (Tyler 2006).

Communities expect the police to control crime. Ineffective strategies will undoubtedly undermine police legitimacy. As described earlier, effective place-based crime prevention efforts are characterized by increasing potential offenders' risk of apprehension and by reducing their opportunities to commit crimes. While arrests are inevitable, police should be oriented toward preventing crimes from happening in the first place. Police presence in crime hot spots can change offender perceptions of risk without generating mass arrests or subjecting large numbers of people to investigative stops. While in these places, police can change the physical and spatial characteristics, such as poor lighting, abandoned buildings, disorderly bars, and the like, that attract potential offenders. These kinds of preventive strategies can reduce the number of young minority men caught up in the criminal justice system and, in turn, could diminish the harms associated with mass incarceration in these vulnerable communities (Braga 2016).

The ideals of community policing have been around for a long time. Unfortunately, many police departments do not seem to be embracing these approaches with fidelity to the original principles (Braga 2015; Braga and Brunson 2015). The available research evidence "suggests that community policing has been unevenly implemented within police departments, with responsibility for community-based initiatives sometimes relegated to specialized units composed of a small number of officers rather than spread across police departments" (Skogan and Frydl 2004: 105–106). Further, the vitality of existing hot spots policing efforts has been threatened by the use of crime control management strategies that privilege numerical targets for increased arrests, summonses, and stops over problem-solving work (Braga 2016).

It is perhaps not surprising that even though community policing has been widely adopted at least in principle, substantial conflict continues to occur between police and the communities they serve. It is high time that police departments reinvest in implementing community policing with a much more meaningful commitment to problem-solving and prevention-oriented approaches that emphasize the role of the public in helping to set police priorities. The ubiquity of hot spots policing in most urban police departments seems like an opportunity to regain some much-needed traction in a more robust implementation of community and problem-oriented policing. The Boston SST experience, described earlier, provides one example of what these kinds of programs could look like in practice. However, other jurisdictions have also tested these approaches. For instance, the Cincinnati Collaborative Agreement, which arose from a court suit and mediated negotiation stemming from community concern over police-involved shootings of African-American men, specifies the use of problem-oriented and community policing strategies to guide the Cincinnati Police Department's hot spots policing efforts. A recent evaluation suggests that the Cincinnati reforms can be credited with decreasing arrests and jail entries while reducing crime (Engel, Corsaro, and Ozer 2017).

Conclusion

Putting cops on dots clearly matters to control crime. However, what the cops do on those dots also matters greatly. The theoretical and empirical criminological evidence reviewed here suggests that criminogenic dynamics, situations, and attributes of particular places cause them to become crime hot spot locations. The obvious policy implication is that the police need to address the underlying conditions at chronic hot spot locations that cause these places to be attractive to criminals. As such, we suggest police should be moving away from simply increasing traditional police enforcement activities and toward implementing community problem-solving strategies in crime hot spots. The available research evidence suggests that the payoffs in terms of crime prevention benefits and community reaction outcomes could be substantial.

Robust hot spots policing efforts would then require the expansion of the toolbox of policing far beyond traditional law enforcement responses to crime such as heightened presence and increased arrests. Alternative prevention strategies, such as razing abandoned buildings, controlling access to venues, target hardening, and protecting repeat victims, require activities that are very different from traditional law enforcement actions and the development of partnerships with a wider range of individuals and organizations. From this perspective, hot spots policing requires that police be concerned not only about places, offenders, and victims but also about potential non-police guardians. If the goal of the police is to improve safety at places, then it is natural in hot spots policing to be concerned with place managers, guardians, and handlers of offenders who frequent the area. More generally, dealing with crime hot spots brings the attention of the police to the full range of people and contexts that are part of the crime problem.

Only a handful of research studies have considered the impacts of hot spots policing programs on community perceptions. The Campbell review identified three program evaluations that considered community outcomes (Braga et al. 2012). In contrast to concerns that hot spots policing can easily become zero-tolerance, and indiscriminate, aggressive tactics can drive a wedge between the police and communities (Rosenbaum 2006; Tonry 2011), these three evaluations revealed the community members had positive opinions and experiences when subjected to hot spots policing initiatives. In a randomized controlled trial explicitly designed to test the impacts of hot spots enforcement on community perceptions in three mid-sized California cities that was completed after the Campbell review, Weisburd, Hinkle, Famega, and Ready (2011) did not find any evidence of "backfire effects" associated with a policing disorder intervention: the hot spots policing program delivered in this study had no significant impacts on fear of crime, police legitimacy, collective efficacy, or perceptions of crime or social disorder.

It is important to note that these four evaluations interviewed or surveyed residents and business owners in hot spot areas and did not interview individuals arrested, detained, and/or interrogated as a result of these focused police actions. It is possible these individuals may have very different opinions and experiences when compared to those of community members who do not experience direct law enforcement actions. A recent evaluation of the adverse system side effects of drug hot spot crackdowns in Philadelphia found that initiative strained the local judicial system by generating a high volume of arrests that resulted in a significant increase in fugitive defendants (Goldkamp and Vilcica 2008). Short-term crime gains produced by particular types of hot spots policing initiatives could undermine the long-term stability of specific neighborhoods through the increased involvement of mostly low-income minority men in the criminal justice system. Implementing situational prevention strategies that reduce police reliance on aggressive enforcement strategies at crime hot spots seems well positioned to yield positive benefits for police-community relations. More explicit tests of this proposition are clearly needed.

In closing, it is important to note that the existing literature suggests that problem-oriented policing as practiced in the field is characterized by weak problem analysis and a preponderance of traditional policing tactics implemented to address targeted crime problems (see, e.g., Scott 2000). Police executives interested in experimenting with this approach should be mindful of these limitations. Nevertheless, while it is difficult for police agencies to implement the "ideal" version of problem-oriented policing, some scholars suggest that even "shallow" problem-solving better focuses police crime prevention efforts at crime hot spots (Braga and Weisburd 2006). As practical experience and knowledge of effective problem-solving work accumulates in police departments, it seems likely that the capacity of police officers to implement more robust problem-oriented policing at places will improve in tandem. Therefore, police departments should make the necessary administrative arrangements and organizational investments to support problem-oriented policing at crime hot spots. These investments seem likely to improve public safety and police-community relations.

References

Braga, Anthony A. 1997. *Solving Violent Crime Problems: An Evaluation of the Jersey City Police Department's Pilot Program to Control Violent Places.* Ph.D. Dissertation, Rutgers University. Ann Arbor, MI: University Microfilms International.

Braga, Anthony A. 2001. "The Effects of Hot Spots Policing on Crime." *Annals of the American Academy of Political and Social Science* 455: 104–125.

Braga, Anthony A. 2005. "Hot Spots Policing and Crime Prevention: A Systematic Review of Randomized Controlled Trials." *Journal of Experimental Criminology* 1: 317–342.

Braga, Anthony A. 2008. *Problem-Oriented Policing and Crime Prevention* (2nd ed.). Monsey, NY: Criminal Justice Press.

Braga, Anthony A. 2015. *Crime and Policing Revisited*. New Perspectives on Policing Series. Washington, DC: U.S. Department of Justice, National Institute of Justice.

Braga, Anthony A. 2016. "Better Policing Can Improve Legitimacy and Reduce Mass Incarceration." *Harvard Law Review Forum* 129: 233–241.

Braga, Anthony A., and Brenda J. Bond. 2008. "Policing Crime and Disorder Hot Spots: A Randomized Controlled Trial." *Criminology* 46: 577–608.

Braga, Anthony A., and Rod K. Brunson. 2015. *The Police and Public Discourse on 'Black on Black' Violence*. New Perspectives on Policing Series. Washington, DC: U.S. Department of Justice, National Institute of Justice.

Braga, Anthony A., David M. Hureau, and Andrew V. Papachristos. 2011. "An Ex-Post-Facto Evaluation Framework for Place-Based Police Interventions." *Evaluation Review* 35: 592–626.

Braga, Anthony A., Andrew V. Papachristos, and David M. Hureau. 2010. "The Concentration and Stability of Gun Violence at Micro Places in Boston, 1980–2008." *Journal of Quantitative Criminology* 26: 33–53.

Braga, Anthony A., Andrew V. Papachristos, and David M. Hureau. 2012. "Hot Spots Policing Effects on Crime." *Campbell Systematic Reviews* 2012: 8. DOI: 10.4073/csr.2012.8

Braga, Anthony A., Andrew V. Papachristos, and David M. Hureau. 2014. "The Effects of Hot Spots Policing on Crime: An Updated Systematic Review and Meta-Analysis." *Justice Quarterly* 31: 633–663.

Braga, Anthony A., and Cory Schnell. 2013. "Evaluating Place-Based Policing Strategies: Lessons Learned from the Smart Policing Initiative in Boston." *Police Quarterly* 16: 338–356.

Braga, Anthony A., and David L. Weisburd. 2006. "Problem-Oriented Policing: The Disconnect Between Principles and Practice." Pp. 133–154 in David L. Weisburd and Anthony A. Braga (eds.), *Police Innovation: Contrasting Perspectives*. New York, NY: Cambridge University Press.

Braga, Anthony A., and David L. Weisburd. 2010. *Policing Problem Places: Crime Hot Spots and Effective Prevention*. New York, NY: Oxford University Press.

Braga, Anthony A., David L. Weisburd, Elin J. Waring, Lorraine Green Mazerolle, William Spelman, and Frank Gajewski. 1999. "Problem-Oriented Policing in Violent CrimePlaces: A Randomized Controlled Experiment." *Criminology* 37: 541–580.

Brantingham, Patricia J., and Paul L. Brantingham, eds. 1991. *Environmental Criminology* (2nd ed.). Prospect Heights, IL: Waveland Press.

Buerger, Michael, and Lorraine Green Mazerolle. 1998. "Third-Party Policing: A Theoretical Analysis of an Emerging Trend." *Justice Quarterly* 15: 301–328.

Caeti, Tory J. 1999. *Houston's Targeted Beat Program: A Quasi-Experimental Test of Patrol Strategies*. Ph.D. Dissertation. Sam Houston State University. Ann Arbor, MI: University Microfilms International.

Clarke, Ronald V. 1995. "Situational Crime Prevention." Pp. 91–150 in Michael Tonry and David Farrington (eds.), *Building a Safer Society: Strategic Approaches to Crime Prevention—Crime and Justice*, vol. 19. Chicago, IL: University of Chicago Press.

Clarke, Ronald V., ed. 1997. *Situational Crime Prevention: Successful Case Studies* (2nd ed.). Albany, NY: Harrow and Heston.

Clarke, Ronald V. 1998. "Defining Police Strategies: Problem Solving, Problem-Oriented Policing and Community-Oriented Policing." Pp. 315–329 in Tara O'Connor Shelley and Anne C. Grant (eds.), *Problem-Oriented Policing: Crime-Specific Problems, Critical Issues, and Making POP Work*. Washington, DC: Police Executive Research Forum.

Clarke, Ronald V., and John E. Eck. 2003. *Become a Problem-Solving Crime Analyst in 55 Small Steps*. London: Jill Dando Institute of Crime Science.

Clarke, Ronald V., and John E. Eck. 2007. *Understanding Risky Facilities*. Problem-Oriented Guides for Police, Problem Solving Tools Series, No. 6. Washington, DC: U.S. Department of Justice, Office of Community Oriented Policing Services.

Clarke, Ronald V., and Marcus Felson. 1993. "Introduction: Criminology, Routine Activity, and Rational Choice." Pp. 1–14 in Ronald V. Clarke and Marcus Felson (eds.), *Routine Activity and Rational Choice, Advances in Criminological Theory*, vol. 5. New Brunswick, NJ: Transaction Press.

Clarke, Ronald V., and David L. Weisburd. 1994. "Diffusion of Crime Control Benefits: Observations on the Reverse of Displacement." Pp. 165–184 in Ronald V. Clarke (ed.), *Crime Prevention Studies*, vol. 2. Monsey, NY: Criminal Justice Press.

Cohen, Jacqueline, Wilpen Gorr, and Piyusha Singh. 2003. "Estimating Intervention Effects in Varying Risk Settings: Do Police Raids Reduce Illegal Drug Dealing at Nuisance Bars?" *Criminology* 41: 257–292.

Cohen, Lawrence E., and Marcus Felson. 1979. "Social Change and Crime Rate Trends: A Routine Activity Approach." *American Sociological Review* 44: 588–605.

Cornish, Derek B., and Ronald V. Clarke, eds. 1986. *The Reasoning Criminal: Rational Choice Perspectives on Offending*. New York, NY: Springer-Verlag.

Cornish, Derek B., and Ronald V. Clarke. 2003. "Opportunities, Precipitators and Criminal Decisions: A Reply to Wortley's Critique of Situational Crime Prevention." Pp. 41–96 in Martha J. Smith and Derek B. Cornish (eds.), *Theory for Practice in Situational Crime Prevention, Crime Prevention Studies*, vol. 16. Monsey, NY: Criminal Justice Press.

Criminal Justice Commission. 1998. *Beenleigh Calls for Service Project: Evaluation Report*. Brisbane, Queensland: Criminal Justice Commission.

DiTella, Rafael, and Ernesto Schargrodsky. 2004. "Do Police Reduce Crime? Estimates Using the Allocation of Police Forces after a Terrorist Attack." *American Economic Review* 94: 115–133.

Durlauf, Steven, and Daniel Nagin. 2011. "Imprisonment and Crime: Can Both Be Reduced?" *Criminology & Public Policy* 10: 13–54.

Eck, John E. 2002. "Preventing Crime at Places." Pp. 241–294 in Lawrence Sherman, David Farrington, Brandon Welsh, and Doris L. MacKenzie (eds.), *Evidence-Based Crime Prevention*. New York, NY: Routledge.

Eck, John E. 2003. "Police Problems: The Complexity of Problem Theory, Research and Evaluation." Pp. 79–114 in Johannes Knutsson (ed.), *Problem-Oriented Policing: From Innovation to Mainstream, Crime Prevention Studies*, vol. 15. Monsey, NY: Criminal Justice Press.

Eck, John E., and William Spelman. 1987. *Problem-Solving: Problem-Oriented Policing in Newport News*. Washington, DC: National Institute of Justice.

Eck, John E., and David L. Weisburd. 1995. "Crime Places in Crime Theory." Pp. 1–34 in John E. Eck and David L. Weisburd (eds.), *Crime and Place, Crime Prevention Studies*, vol. 4. Monsey, NY: Criminal Justice Press.

Engel, Robin, Nicholas Corsaro, and M. Murat Ozer. 2017. "Changing How Police View Arrest: The Critical Role of Police in Criminal Justice Reform." *Criminology & Public Policy* 16.

Farrington, David P., and Anthony Petrosino. 2001. "The Campbell Collaboration Crime and Justice Group." *The ANNALS of the American Academy of Political and Social Science* 578: 35–49.

Felson, Marcus. 2006. *Crime and Nature*. Thousand Oaks, CA: Sage Publications.

Gill, Charlotte, David L. Weisburd, Cody Telep, Zoe Vitter, and Trevor Bennett. 2014. "Community-Oriented Policing to Reduce Crime, Disorder and Fear and Increase Satisfaction and Legitimacy Among Citizens: A Systematic Review." *Journal of Experimental Criminology* 10: 399–428.

Goldkamp, John, and E. Rely Vilcica. 2008. "Targeted Enforcement and Adverse System Side Effects: The Generation of Fugitives in Philadelphia." *Criminology* 46: 371–410.

Goldstein, Herman. 1979. "Improving Policing: A Problem-Oriented Approach." *Crime & Delinquency* 25: 236–258.

Goldstein, Herman. 1990. *Problem-Oriented Policing*. Philadelphia, PA: Temple University Press.

Greenwood, Peter, Jan Chaiken, and Joan Petersilia. 1977. *The Investigation Process*. Lexington, MA: Lexington Books.

Guerette, Robert. 2009. "The Push, Pull, and Expansion of Situational Crime Prevention Evaluation: An Appraisal of Thirty-Seven Years of Research." Pp. 29–58 in Johannes Knutsson (ed.), *Evaluating Crime Reduction Initiatives, Crime Prevention Studies*, vol. 24. Monsey, NY: Criminal Justice Press.

Hope, Timothy. 1994. "Problem-Oriented Policing and Drug Market Locations: Three Case Studies." Pp. 5–32 in Ronald V. Clarke (ed.), *Crime Prevention Studies*, vol. 2. Monsey, NY: Criminal Justice Press.

Hough, Michael, and Nick Tilley. 1998. *Getting the Grease to Squeak: Research Lessons for Crime Prevention*. Crime Detection and Prevention Series Paper 85. London, UK: Home Office.

Kelling, George, and Catherine Coles. 1996. *Fixing Broken Windows: Restoring Order and Reducing Crime in Our Communities*. New York, NY: Free Press.

Kelling, George, Tony Pate, Duane Dieckman, and Charles Brown. 1974. *The Kansas City Preventive Patrol Experiment: A Technical Report*. Washington, DC: Police Foundation.

Lawton, Brian, Ralph Taylor, and Anthony Luongo. 2005. "Police Officers on Drug Corners in Philadelphia, Drug Crime, and Violent Crime: Intended, Diffusion, and Displacement Impacts." *Justice Quarterly* 22: 427–451.

Lipsey, Mark, and David B. Wilson. 2001. *Practical Meta-Analysis*. Applied Social Research Methods Series, vol. 49. Thousand Oaks, CA: Sage Publications.

Maple, Jack. 1999. *The Crime Fighter: How You Can Make Your Community Crime Free*. New York, NY: Broadway.

Mazerolle, Lorraine, James F. Price, and Jan Roehl. 2000. "Civil Remedies and Drug Control: A Randomized Field Trial in Oakland, California." *Evaluation Review* 24: 212–241.

Mazerolle, Lorraine, and Janet Ransley. 2006. "The Case for Third-Party Policing." Pp. 191–206 in David L. Weisburd and Anthony A. Braga (eds.), *Police Innovation: Contrasting Perspectives*. New York, NY: Cambridge University Press.

Petrosino, Anthony, Robert Boruch, Haluk Soydan, Lorna Duggan, and Julio Sanchez-Meca. 2001. "Meeting the Challenges of Evidence-Based Policy: The Campbell Collaboration." *The ANNALS of the American Academy of Political and Social Science* 578: 14–34.

Ratcliffe, Jerry, Travis Taniguchi, Elizabeth Groff, and Jennifer Wood. 2011. "The Philadelphia Foot Patrol Experiment: A Randomized Controlled Trial of Police Patrol Effectiveness in Violent Crime Hot Spots." *Criminology* 49: 795–831.

Read, Timothy, and Nick Tilley. 2000. *Not Rocket Science? Problem-Solving and Crime Reduction.* Crime Reduction Series Paper 6. London, UK: Policing and Crime Reduction Unit, Home Office.

Rosenbaum, Dennis. 2006. "The Limits of Hot Spots Policing." Pp. 245–266 in David L. Weisburd and Anthony A. Braga (eds.), *Police Innovation: Contrasting Perspectives.* New York, NY: Cambridge University Press.

Sampson, Robert J. 2011. "The Community." Pp. 210–236 in James Q. Wilson and Joan Petersilia (eds.), *Crime and Public Policy.* New York, NY: Oxford University Press.

Sampson, Robert, and Stephen Raudenbush. 1999. "Systematic Social Observation of Public Spaces: A New Look at Disorder in Urban Neighborhoods." *American Journal of Sociology* 105: 603–651.

Sampson, Robert, Stephen Raudenbush, and Felton Earls. 1997. "Neighborhoods and Violent Crime." *Science* 277: 918–924.

Scott, Michael. 2000. *Problem-Oriented Policing: Reflections on the First 20 Years.* Washington, DC: U.S. Department of Justice, Office of Community Oriented Policing Services.

Sherman, Lawrence, Michael Buerger, and Patrick Gartin. 1989. "Repeat Call Address Policing: The Minneapolis RECAP Experiment." Final Report to the U.S. Department of Justice, National Institute of Justice. Washington, DC: Crime Control Institute.

Sherman, Lawrence, and John E. Eck. 2002. "Policing for Crime Prevention." Pp. 295–329 in Lawrence Sherman, David P. Farrington, Brandon Welsh, and Doris L. MacKenzie (eds.), *Evidence-Based Crime Prevention.* New York, NY: Routledge.

Sherman, Lawrence, Patrick Gartin, and Michael Buerger. 1989. "Hot Spots of Predatory Crime: Routine Activities and the Criminology of Place." *Criminology* 27: 27–56.

Sherman, Lawrence, and Dennis Rogan. 1995a. "Effects of Gun Seizures on Gun Violence: 'Hot Spots' Patrol in Kansas City." *Justice Quarterly* 12: 673–694.

Sherman, Lawrence, and Dennis Rogan. 1995b. "Deterrent Effects of Police Raids on Crack Houses: A Randomized Controlled Experiment." *Justice Quarterly* 12: 755–782.

Sherman, Lawrence, and David L. Weisburd. 1995. "General Deterrent Effects of Police Patrol in Crime Hot Spots: A Randomized Controlled Trial." *Justice Quarterly* 12: 625–648.

Skogan, Wesley. 1990. *Disorder and Decline: Crime and the Spiral of Decay in American Neighborhoods.* New York, NY: Free Press.

Skogan, Wesley, and Kathleen Frydl, eds. 2004. *Fairness and Effectiveness in Policing: The Evidence.* Committee to Review Research on Police Policy and Practices. Committee on Law and Justice, Division of Behavioral and Social Sciences and Education. Washington, DC: The National Academies Press.

Spelman, William, and Dale Brown. 1984. *Calling the Police: Citizen Reporting of Serious Crime.* Washington, DC: U.S. Government Printing Office.

St. Jean, Peter K. B. 2007. *Pockets of Crime: Broken Windows, Collective Efficacy, and the Criminal Point of View.* Chicago: University of Chicago Press.

Sviridoff, Michelle, Susan Sadd, Richard Curtis, and Ralph Grinc. 1992. *The Neighborhood Effects of Street-Level Drug Enforcement: Tactical Narcotics Teams in New York.* New York, NY: Vera Institute of Justice.

Taylor, Bruce, Christopher Koper, and Daniel Woods. 2011. "A Randomized Controlled Trial of Different Policing Strategies at Hot Spots of Violent Crime." *Journal of Experimental Criminology* 7: 149–181.

Taylor, Ralph. 2001. *Breaking Away from Broken Windows: Baltimore Neighborhoods and the Nationwide Fight against Crime, Grime, Fear, and Decline.* Boulder, CO: Westview Press.

Tonry, Michael. 2011. "Less Imprisonment Is No Doubt a Good Thing: More Policing Is Not." *Criminology & Public Policy* 10: 137–152.

Tyler, Tom R. 2006. *Why People Obey the Law* (2nd ed.). Princeton, NJ: Princeton University Press.

Weisburd, David L. 2008. *Place Based Policing*. Ideas in American Policing Series, No. 9. Washington, DC: Police Foundation.

Weisburd, David L., Shawn Bushway, Cynthia Lum, and Sue-Ming Yang. 2004. "Trajectories of Crime at Places: A Longitudinal Study of Street Segments in the City of Seattle." *Criminology* 42: 283–322.

Weisburd, David L., and John E. Eck. 2004. "What Can Police Do to Reduce Crime, Disorder, and Fear?" *The ANNALS of the American Academy of Political and Social Science* 593: 42–65.

Weisburd, David L., and Lorraine Green. 1995. "Policing Drug Hot Spots: The Jersey City DMA Experiment." *Justice Quarterly* 12: 711–736.

Weisburd, David L., Elizabeth Groff, and Sue-Ming Yang. 2012. *The Criminology of Place: Street Segments and Our Understanding of the Crime Problem*. New York, NY: Oxford University Press.

Weisburd, David L., and Cynthia Lum. 2005. "The Diffusion of Computerized Crime Mapping Policing: Linking Research and Practice." *Police Practice and Research* 6: 433–448.

Weisburd, David L., Joshua Hinkle, Christine Famega, and Justin Ready. 2011. "The Possible 'Backfire' Effects of Broken Windows Policing at Crime Hot Spots: An Experimental Assessment of Impacts on Legitimacy, Fear and Collective Efficacy." *Journal of Experimental Criminology* 7: 297–320.

Weisburd, David L., Lisa Maher, and Lawrence Sherman. 1992. "Contrasting Crime General and Crime Specific Theory: The Case of Hot Spots of Crime." Pp. 45–69 in Freda Adler and William S. Laufer (eds.), *New Directions in Criminological Theory, Advances in Criminological Theory*, vol. 4. New Brunswick, NJ: Transaction Press.

Weisburd, David L., Stephen Mastrofski, Ann Marie McNally, Rosann Greenspan, and James Willis. 2003. "Reforming to Preserve: Compstat and Strategic Problem Solving in American Policing." *Criminology and Public Policy* 2: 421–457.

Weisburd, David L., Cody Telep, Joshua Hinkle, and John E. Eck. 2008. "The Effects of Problem-Oriented Policing on Crime and Disorder." *Campbell Systematic Reviews*. DOI: 10.4073/csr.2008.14

Weisburd, David L., Laura Wyckoff, Justin Ready, John E. Eck, Joshua Hinkle, and Francis Gajewski. 2006. "Does Crime Just Move around the Corner? A Controlled Study of Spatial Displacement and Diffusion of Crime Control Benefits." *Criminology* 44: 549–592.

Wilson, David B. 2001. "Meta-Analytical Methods for Criminology." *The ANNALS of the American Academy of Political and Social Science* 578: 71–89.

Wilson, James Q., and George L. Kelling. 1982. "Broken Windows: The Police and Neighborhood Safety." *Atlantic Monthly* (March): 29–38.

Yang, Sue-Ming. 2010. "Assessing the Spatial-Temporal Relationship between Disorder and Violence." *Journal of Quantitative Criminology* 26: 139–163.

Contributors

Shai Amram is a PhD student at the Institute of Criminology at the Hebrew University of Jerusalem and works as an analysis researcher in the Ministry of Public Security—Israel.

Anthony A. Braga is a Distinguished Professor in and Director of the School of Criminology and Criminal Justice at Northeastern University.

P. Jeffrey Brantingham is Professor of Anthropology at University of California, Los Angeles.

Gerben J.N. Bruinsma is Senior Researcher of the Netherlands Institute for the Study of Crime and Law Enforcement (NSCR), Amsterdam and Professor Emeritus of Environmental Criminology of the Vrije Universiteit of Amsterdam.

Breanne Cave is a Senior Research Associate at the Police Foundation.

Francis T. Cullen is a Distinguished Research Professor Emeritus and Senior Research Associate in the School of Criminal Justice at the University of Cincinnati.

John E. Eck is Professor of Criminal Justice at the University of Cincinnati.

Wilpen Gorr is Professor Emeritus of Public Policy and Management Information Systems, H. John Heinz III College, Carnegie Mellon University.

YongJei Lee is Assistant Professor in the School of Public Affairs at University of Colorado, Colorado Springs.

Sarah M. Manchak is an Assistant Professor in the School of Criminal Justice at the University of Cincinnati.

George O. Mohler is Associate Professor of Computer and Information Science at Indiana University—Purdue University Indianapolis.

Lieven J.R. Pauwels is Professor of Criminology at Ghent University (Belgium) and Director of the Institute of International Research on Criminal Policy (IRCP).

Troy C. Payne is Associate Professor of Justice in the College of Health at the University of Alaska Anchorage.

Lacey Schaefer is Lecturer in the School of Criminology and Criminal Justice and a Research Associate with the Griffith Criminology Institute at Griffith University.

Cory Schnell is a postdoctoral research associate at the University of Cincinnati.

Maor Shay is a PhD student at the Institute of Criminology at the Hebrew University of Jerusalem.

Martin B. Short is Assistant Professor of Mathematics at Georgia Institute of Technology.

Marie Skubak Tillyer is Associate Professor in the Department of Criminal Justice at the University of Texas at San Antonio.

Cody W. Telep is Assistant Professor of Criminology and Criminal Justice at Arizona State University.

David Weisburd is a Distinguished Professor of Criminology, Law and Society at George Mason University, and Walter E. Meyer Professor of Law and Criminal Justice at the Hebrew University.

Pamela Wilcox is Professor in the School of Criminal Justice at the University of Cincinnati.

Roie Zamir is a PhD student at the Institute of Criminology at the Hebrew University of Jerusalem.

Index

Note: Page numbers in *italic* indicate a figure and page numbers in **bold** indicate a table on the corresponding page.